Globalizing the US Presidency

New Approaches to International History

Series Editor
Thomas Zeiler, Professor of American Diplomatic History,
University of Colorado Boulder, USA

New Approaches to International History covers international history during the modern period and across the globe. The series incorporates new developments in the field, such as the cultural turn and transnationalism, as well as the classical high politics of state-centric policymaking and diplomatic relations. Written with upper level undergraduate and postgraduate students in mind, texts in the series provide an accessible overview of international, global, and transnational issues, events and actors.

Published
Decolonization and the Cold War, edited by Leslie James and Elisabeth Leake (2015)
Cold War Summits, Chris Tudda (2015)
The United Nations in International History, Amy Sayward (2017)
Latin American Nationalism, James F. Siekmeier (2017)
The History of United States Cultural Diplomacy, Michael L. Krenn (2017)
International Cooperation in the Early Twentieth Century, Daniel Gorman (2017)
Women and Gender in International History, Karen Garner (2018)
International Development, Corinna Unger (2018)
The Environment and International History, Scott Kaufman (2018)
United States Relations with China and Iran, Edited by Osamah H. Khalil (2019)

Forthcoming
The International LGBT Rights Movement, Laura Belmonte
Canada and the World since 1867, Asa McKercher
Reconstructing the Postwar World, Francine McKenzie
The First Age of Industrial Globalization, Maartje Abbenhuis and Gordon Morrell
Global War, Global Catastrophe, Maartje Abbenhuis and Ismee Tames
Public Opinion and Twentieth-Century Diplomacy, Daniel Hucker

Globalizing the US Presidency

Postcolonial Views of John F. Kennedy

Edited by
Cyrus Schayegh

BLOOMSBURY ACADEMIC
LONDON • NEW YORK • OXFORD • NEW DELHI • SYDNEY

BLOOMSBURY ACADEMIC
Bloomsbury Publishing Plc
50 Bedford Square, London, WC1B 3DP, UK
1385 Broadway, New York, NY 10018, USA
29 Earlsfort Terrace, Dublin 2, Ireland

BLOOMSBURY, BLOOMSBURY ACADEMIC and the Diana logo are trademarks of Bloomsbury Publishing Plc

First published in Great Britain 2020
Paperback edition published 2021

Copyright © Cyrus Schayegh, 2020

Cyrus Schayegh has asserted his right under the Copyright, Designs and Patents Act, 1988, to be identified as Editor of this work.

For legal purposes the Acknowledgments on p. xi constitute an extension of this copyright page.

Series design by Catherine Wood
Cover image: "Kenedi-ye chini!" [The Chinese Kennedy], Courtesy of Ettela'at Newspaper, Tehran

All rights reserved. No part of this publication may be reproduced or transmitted in any form or by any means, electronic or mechanical, including photocopying, recording, or any information storage or retrieval system, without prior permission in writing from the publishers.

Bloomsbury Publishing Plc does not have any control over, or responsibility for, any third-party websites referred to or in this book. All internet addresses given in this book were correct at the time of going to press. The author and publisher regret any inconvenience caused if addresses have changed or sites have ceased to exist, but can accept no responsibility for any such changes.

A catalogue record for this book is available from the British Library.

A catalog record for this book is available from the Library of Congress.

ISBN: HB: 978-1-3501-1850-8
PB: 978-1-3502-4046-9
ePDF: 978-1-3501-1851-5
eBook: 978-1-3501-1852-2

Series: New Approaches to International History

Typeset by Deanta Global Publishing Services, Chennai, India

To find out more about our authors and books visit www.bloomsbury.com and sign up for our newsletters.

*For Fakhri Garakani and the many other extraordinary "ordinary" women
and men who people the pages of this book*

Contents

List of Illustrations — ix
Acknowledgments — xi
List of Abbreviations — xii

Introduction and a Note on the US Imperial-Postcolonial Field
    Cyrus Schayegh — 1

Part I Actors

1   First New Nation or Internal Colony? Modernization Theorists, Black Intellectuals, and the Politics of Colonial Comparison in the Kennedy Years *Sam Klug* — 19
2   John F. Kennedy as Viewed by Africans *Philip E. Muehlenbeck* — 34
3   "I Named My Son Kennedy": Rural Kenyan Perceptions of John F. Kennedy during Decolonization *Kara Moskowitz* — 48
4   Brazilian Public Opinion of John F. Kennedy and the Alliance for Progress in Cold War Brazil (1961–63) *Felipe Loureiro* — 64

Part II Appropriation: Domestic Contexts

5   "An Example for Other Small Nations to Follow": John F. Kennedy, Ireland, and Decolonization *David P. Kilroy* — 85
6   Global Media, Emotions, and the "Kennedy Narrative": Kennedy as Seen from the "Global South" *Sönke Kunkel* — 100
7   From Hope to Disillusionment: Moroccan Perceptions of the Kennedy Presidency *David Stenner* — 115
8   Foreign Gifts and US Imperial Ambiguities: The Kennedy Years *Cyrus Schayegh* — 130

Part III Appropriation, Cont'd: Antagonisms and Contestations

9   Watching, Countering, and Emulating Peaceful Evolution: PRC Responses to Kennedy Administration Cultural Diplomacy and Global Strategy *Matthew D. Johnson* — 151

10 Whose Revolution? López Mateos, Kennedy's Mexican Visit, and the Alliance for Progress *Vanni Pettinà* 169

11 Camelot in Korea: The Paradox of John F. Kennedy in Authoritarian South Korea, 1961–63 *Inga Kim Diederich* 183

12 John F. Kennedy through the Lens of a Divided Vietnam *Aaron Lillie and Diu-Huong Nguyen* 201

Part IV Intermediaries and Afterlives

13 The President's Messenger: American Visions, Indian Citizens, and National Development in the Kennedy Years *Benjamin Siegel* 221

14 Mediating the Kennedy Presidency: James Baldwin's Decade in Turkey *Begüm Adalet* 235

15 "The Kennedys Know Something about That, Too": Law, Lineage, and Martyrdom in US-South Africa Relations *Myra Ann Houser* 250

Conclusion: "Someone Talking the Same Language with All of Us" *Robert B. Rakove* 264

List of Contributors 275
Bibliography 277
Index 280

Illustrations

Figures

0.1	Castro, Chou en-Lai, Kennedy, and Nehru side by side in the Moroccan paper *al-Istiqlal*	7
4.1	Brazilian and Latin American public opinion on the United States, urban areas, November–December 1962 (percent)	73
4.2	Confidence of Brazilian and Latin American public opinion on the US ability to provide wise leadership for other countries, urban areas, November–December 1962 (percent)	74
4.3	Awareness of Brazilian and Latin American public opinion on Kennedy's Alliance for Progress, urban centers, November–December 1962 (percent)	76
4.4	Level of approval of Kennedy's Alliance for Progress by Brazilian and Latin American public opinion, urban centers, November–December 1962 (percent)	77
6.1	Peruvian Sculptor Carlos Pazos presents his Kennedy bust to US chief of protocol Angier Biddle Duke in the Cabinet Room, White House, March 29, 1962	102
6.2	An example of a typical cartoon on the Alliance for Progress as USIA disseminated them by the millions in Latin America	106
6.3	Another example of a typical cartoon on the Alliance for Progress as USIA disseminated them by the millions in Latin America	107
8.1	Fakhri Garakani, portrait of Jesus	131
8.2	The Shah gifting land deeds to peasants	136
8.3	Caroline Kennedy with her father at church	140
8.4	"Kenedi-ye chini!" (The Chinese Kennedy!)	141
9.1	A recently elected Kennedy listens intently to CIA director Allen Dulles' "Cold War" instructions	156
9.2	Kennedy serving fragrant "peace strategy" buns from a grisly kitchen. The ingredients are "invasion of Vietnam," "invasion of Congo," "interference in Laos," and "A"(-bomb) seasoning	157
9.3	Kennedy binds the wrists of a kneeling African American (rendered, by contrast, in heroic socialist realist style) with restraints of "civil rights" and "legal acts," aided by a ferocious police dog	158

9.4 Kennedy, as a perfected bodhisattva-like figure, is shown surrounded by symbols of coercive and noncoercive power 158

10.1 Kennedy, at the microphones, delivers remarks during his visit to the Unidad Independencia (Independencia Housing Project) in Mexico City, 30 June 1962 177

11.1 Advertisement for the Korean edition of *John Kennedy: A Political Profile* 187

11.2 President Kennedy and General Park Chung Hee 189

11.3 "A Real Hi Man: Hi Man Park [sic], 3, goes western in the Far East as he draws his shooting iron in front of his home in Seoul, South Korea. The youngster is the son of Sen. Chung Hee Park, chairman of South Korea's supreme council. The cowboy outfit was a gift from Mrs. Jacqueline Kennedy during the general's recent visit to President Kennedy in Washington"—AP Wirephoto 190

11.4 Park Chung Hee and John and Jacqueline Kennedy with children's *hanbok* gifted to the Kennedys by Park 191

11.5 Park Chung Hee's wife, Mrs. Yuk Young-soo, visiting a city orphanage 192

11.6 "Yet Another GI Lynching Incident" 194

11.7 "Kennedy's sudden death—the tragedy of our generation" 195

16.1 "The Bullet Is Stronger than the Ballot" 272

Tables

4.1 Awareness of Brazil's Public Opinion as to Who the US President Was, São Paulo and Rio de Janeiro, September 1961 69

4.2 Brazil's Public Opinion on John F. Kennedy, São Paulo and Rio de Janeiro, September 1961 70

4.3 Brazil's Public Opinion on Whether John F. Kennedy Was Sincere in His Declaration about the Brazilian August 1961 Political Crisis, São Paulo and Rio de Janeiro, September 1961 71

4.4 Reasons Expressed by Brazil's Public Opinion to Believe that John F. Kennedy Was Sincere in His Declaration about the Brazilian August 1961 Political Crisis, São Paulo and Rio de Janeiro, September 1961 (percent) 72

4.5 Reasons for the Lack of Confidence in the US Leadership by Brazilian and Latin American Public Opinion, Urban Centers, November–December 1962 (percent) 75

4.6 Reasons Stated by Brazil's and Latin America's Public Opinion for Not Fully Approving the Alliance for Progress, Urban Centers, November–December 1962 (percent) 77

Acknowledgments

This volume began in 2017 as a conference at Princeton University. It was generously funded by the Princeton Institute for International and Regional Studies, the David A. Gardner '69 *Magic* Project Grants, and the departments of Near Eastern Studies and History. Erez Manela's and Kiran Patel's comments at the conference helped shape it; so did two anonymous reviewers. Tom Zeiler, the editor of the Bloomsbury New Approaches to International History series, editor Maddie Holder, and editorial assistant Dan Hutchins all were a true pleasure to work with.

Abbreviations

AHR	American Historical Review
APP	American Presidency Project
CSSH	Comparative Studies in Society and History
CWH	Cold War History
DH	Diplomatic History
FRUS	Foreign Relations of the United States
IHR	International History Review
IJAHS	International Journal of African Historical Studies
JAfH	Journal of African History
JAmH	Journal of American History
JAS	Journal of American Studies
JICH	Journal of Imperial and Commonwealth History
JLAS	Journal of Latin American Studies
LAT	Los Angeles Times
MAS	Modern Asian Studies
NYT	New York Times
PP	Past and Present

Introduction and a Note on the US Imperial-Postcolonial Field

Cyrus Schayegh

John F. Kennedy is the most lastingly iconic twentieth-century US president.[1] Films about him and his administration and family abound.[2] Scholarship persists, even as its tenor has shifted twice, from reverence, in the 1960s and 1970s, to critique, in the 1970s to 1990s, to an uneasy balance since.[3] And historians continue to stress Kennedy's enduring attention to foreign affairs in general and postcolonial conditions in particular.[4] A journey across Asia in 1951 and a Mexican honeymoon in 1953; a high-profile senatorial speech supporting Algeria in 1957; frequent references to Africa on the campaign trail in 1960: this and much more culminated in President Kennedy becoming "in effect, Secretary of State for the third world."[5]

This volume's gist differs somewhat from those oft-cited—and exaggerating—words by Arthur Schlesinger Jr., though. While taking note of Kennedy's policies, we do not concentrate on them; or on the fact that his "vision remained trapped between the imperatives of security and the ambitions of idealism" and that his "foreign policy whipsawed between the extremes of confrontation and reconciliation"; or, again, on how Kennedy and his administration "engaged" postcolonial countries.[6] Rather, we explore how he was pulled in by postcolonial women and men: how they viewed and appropriated him. We look at the relationship between Kennedy and postcolonial people principally through their eyes, not his. Our stories play in postcolonial places more than in America. And most of our characters are postcolonial.

Further, this volume shows that many postcolonial men and women took to Kennedy not simply in reaction to his actions. They showed a keen interest in him because his public persona, rhetoric, symbolic politics, and some of his policies picked up their very own demand: for a better life, and to count and be heard in the world after a good century of European imperialism. Yes, Kennedy mastered "what marketers would call a 'brand'"[7] and skillfully crafted a political narrative[8] also regarding postcolonial countries. But his "powerful story" worked only because it "responded to the aspirations and political expectations of populations across the 'Global South,'" as Sönke Kunkel states in his chapter.

In this volume, then, Kennedy is a *Projektionsfläche*: a screen onto which postcolonial people projected their wishes and hopes. In effect, this book seeks simultaneously to provincialize and to de-provincialize—de-Americanize and globalize—Kennedy. In the final analysis it in fact is not strictly speaking about him. Rather, it asks what the postcolonial Kennedy can tell us about the changing shape of the globe's hierarchical interconnectedness at a time when decolonization peaked, fully globalizing the Cold War, when old media grew and new media burst forth, and when the world was captivated by new frontiers and young explorers.

Here, one may take a leaf out of New Imperial History, which "treat[s] [European] metropole and colony in a single analytic field."[9] Domestic/foreign, inside/outside, postcolonial/American were more symbiotic than we tend to think. They formed a joint US imperial-postcolonial field. This view, I'd argue, is this volume's cumulative added value, the whole that is more than the sum of its parts. Hence, I will end on it, discussing it in this chapter's concluding section.

Historiography

This volume stands on broad shoulders. First and generally, historians have since the early 1990s recognized that in the Cold War postcolonial people were actors, not only acted upon.[10] And when one "tak[es] off the Cold War lenses," one sees decolonization as a process older than, and autonomous from, the Cold War, though intertwined with it.[11] Secondly and more specifically, recent multi-archival monographs have detailed postcolonial citizens' interest in Kennedy, and show that even while the United States under Kennedy mattered greatly—and often did harm[12]—postcolonial citizens' own agency and pasts crucially shaped their country's development, too.[13] In parallel, scholars of postwar US-postcolonial relations and, more generally, of the Cold War in the Third World have for a good decade now examined "interdependent domestic and international fields of political and social power," in Gilbert Joseph's words.[14] Thirdly, this volume is part of a movement to inter- and trans-nationalize US history, including diplomatic history. Born decades back, that movement crystallized in the 1990s and came of age the following decade.[15] A known practitioner, Matthew Connelly, described its agenda as follows: "Rather than continue to see diplomatic history as a subfield of U.S. history or any national history, I think we need to recognize that diplomatic history is instead a subfield of the larger and still expanding fields of international and transnational history." Not everybody signed off on this maximalist definition, though. In a response, Thomas Borstelmann described US diplomatic history as "the hinge between domestic U.S. history and world history: we function like a traditional Western barroom door, swinging both ways, and doing so easily, readily, continuously."[16] I will revisit this discussion at the very end of this chapter.

How does this volume contribute to these intersecting literatures? First, as outlined earlier, it suggests that Kennedy functioned as a *Projektionsfläche*; provincializes *and* de-provincializes him; and underwrites the idea of a joint US-postcolonial field. Secondly, its cast of actors is extensive, including elites as well as regular people, intellectuals and peasants, students and journalists and lawyers, to mention just some. And thirdly, even if the monographs in the second afore-noted scholarly field highlight postcolonial agency, they ultimately turn around issues to which Washington—under Kennedy and other postwar US presidents—was central, like the Alliance for Progress. In contrast, this volume demonstrates that many issues discussed by postcolonial actors using Kennedy as a reference point were domestic in nature, and that their interest in the US president refracted postcolonial situations, hopes, and mindsets.

The chapters

Situation*s*; hope*s*; mindset*s*: this plural form is not accidental. While this edited volume pursues cohesion, focusing on one reference point—Kennedy—and a delimited timespan—the 1960s—its authors study various postcolonial appropriations of the US president. "Their" postcolonial world is not homogeneous. (Related, some parts and groups are more accessible to researchers than others, an epistemological issue noted for instance by Aaron Lillie and Diu-Huong Nguyen.) The authors also showcase numerous archives, employing a range of languages and embracing more than a dozen countries from the Americas to Europe, Africa, and Asia. And they deploy multiple methods: often textual study of archival documents and printed matter, but oral history and some quantitative analysis, too.

I have sorted the volume's chapters into three main themes. The four chapters of Part I, "Actors," study how Kennedy's America was seen as a colony by a critical African American intellectual elite (Sam Klug); how not only elites but also masses shaped perceptions of Kennedy in Africa (Philip E. Muehlenbeck); how in Kenya this held true "even" for peasants and what role media and Kennedy's policies played (Kara Moskowitz); and, in contrast, how few Brazilian peasants knew Kennedy and how urbanites who did were focused on his persona (Felipe Loureiro). Part II is titled "Appropriation: Domestic Contexts." Kennedy's acceptance of Irish self-views as a model for decolonization helped spark his ancestral homeland's enthusiasm for him (David P. Kilroy). Postcolonial media outlets helped diffuse Kennedy's charismatic persona for domestic commercial reasons, rather than simply following a politically driven US lead (Sönke Kunkel). In Morocco, domestic politics, not just regional and global affairs, explains why Kennedy's popularity waned in 1960–63 (David Stenner). And an Iranian's unrequited gift to Kennedy and other foreigners' gifts reveal ambiguities abroad about Washington's and its president's imperial nature (Cyrus Schayegh).

Part III is called "Appropriation, Cont'd: Antagonisms and Contestations." The PRC, while lambasting Kennedy, emulated his stepped-up cultural diplomacy (Matthew D. Johnson). During Kennedy's visit to Mexico, President Adolfo López Mateos and key officials framed his Alliance for Progress as merely a mirror of their long-ruling Partido Revolucionario Institucional's supposed progressiveness (Vanni Pettinà). In South Korea, paradoxically, both the authoritarian Park Chung Hee and his critics used Kennedy's rhetoric; interpretations clashed (Inga Kim Diederich). And in South Vietnam, counterintuitively, most Catholics came to loath Kennedy while some Communists liked him; and the communist North's critique was not entirely uniform (Aaron Lillie and Diu-Huong Nguyen). Finally, Part IV, "Intermediaries and Afterlives," contains three chapters. In India, US ambassador Kenneth Galbraith's familiarity with the subcontinent, economic expertise, and can-do attitude helped shape views of "his" president, too (Benjamin Siegel). In Turkey, African American intellectual James Baldwin, a frequent visitor, helped shape critiques of John, and Robert, Kennedy's domestic and foreign policies during the 1960s (Begüm Adalet). And Robert Kennedy's and some US lawyers' concern about apartheid helped to keep the Kennedy name alive in black South Africa after 1963/1968 (Myra Ann Houser). Finally, Robert B. Rakove's conclusion provides a thoughtful analysis of these chapters.

Media

A number of themes cut across many chapters in these four parts. I'd like to pick out two. One is media. The appropriation of Kennedy bandwagoned on the expansion of older and newer media forms in the late colonial and postcolonial countries from the 1940s. From the Second World War if not because of it, Moskowitz notes, media expanded in Kenya. Founded in 1946, *al-'Alam* was consumed across Morocco (Stenner). More Africans bought a radio after the invention, in 1948, of the transistor (Moskowitz). And, a last example, in 1951, Vietnam's communists launched an organ, *Nhan Dan*, and other newspapers and radio stations were launched, too (Lillie and Nguyen).[17] By the late 1950s, then, "global mass communication" was in full transformation, as Kunkel argues. In consequence, the First Lady's 1962 White House tour film swept cinemas globally (Kunkel), not only US television.[18] The Mexican government printed an English-language newspaper just to advance its own interpretation of Kennedy's state visit, in 1962 (Pettinà). Korean newspaper articles on Kennedy, but not on domestic politicians, habitually featured a photograph (Diederich). Following Kennedy's election, an Iranian newspaper translated and serialized his *Profiles in Courage* (Schayegh) and a Korean press speed-translated James Burns's biography of him (Diederich). In India sales of biographies skyrocketed after the president's assassination (Siegel). Many an African villager owned a Kennedy picture, clipped from papers (Muehlenbeck). And Egyptian television aired Kennedy's funeral four times (Muehlenbeck). A contrast is illuminating: PRC newspapers rarely published pictures of Kennedy, caricaturing him instead (Johnson).

Media consumption was not passive. Postcolonial women and men interpreted Kennedy through images and texts that, while created by him, *they* found relevant and asked for. (Kennedy, US television, and the US audience were similarly symbiotic.[19]) Moreover, media was not vaguely "somewhere." Rather, media actors followed distinct directions. Kennedy reinforced the US Information Agency, placing texts and images about US policy and the president in postcolonial, and other, media outlets, and tracking "world public opinion";[20] and US officials gathered translations of postcolonial media, as Adalet shows for J. Edgar Hoover. In the reverse direction flowed postcolonial demands for US material on Kennedy. Sometimes, third places and actors mediated. Thus, the BBC broadcasted Kennedy's funeral, "birth[ing] . . . global television news."[21] (Circulation between postcolonial countries existed, too.[22]) As Loureiro notes for Brazil and Lillie and Nguyen for Vietnam, there were areas, often rural, where Kennedy remained barely known. Then again, views and images of him could circulate widely within a given country, sometimes involving diverse languages, like in Siegel's India. Moreover, newspapers could play an important role as translators, literally and figuratively, as when Adalet's Turkish journalists interviewed James Baldwin also on the subject of Kennedy. Similarly, a Korean women's magazine "translated" Jacqueline for its readers as a wife who uses her skills for her husband's sake, Diederich shows. And Schayegh's study of gifts to Kennedy shows that postcolonial women and men translated Kennedy's persona and policies into a language meaningful to themselves.

Emotions and symbolic politics

A second theme is emotions and symbolic politics, also concerning race. Emotions are omnipresent in this volume. Take Kunkel's statement that postcolonial citizens "openly expressed their emotions for Kennedy"; the "awe" and "envy" in Lillie's and Nguyen's opening vignette; or Winnie Madikizela-Mandela's approach to Edward Kennedy, related by Houser. Think of views of Kennedy's "absolute honesty of purpose" (Kunkel) and "sincere" leadership (Loureiro). Or consider expressions of loss following the president's assassination (Muehlenbeck).[23] All this was not starry-eyed naivety: emotions were complex; feelings of loss co-existed with disappointment about policies, as Stenner shows. The mid-1950s to 1960s were a spell in which many dreamed of another world, lighter, more just, less violent. This juncture can be seen as an emotional disposition[24] of vigilant optimism, peaking in the early 1960s interlude between late European colonialism and the twin disappointment of postcolonial state authoritarianism and Western neocolonialism.[25] Kennedy registered this early postcolonial climate, whose relative lack of cynicism mirrored many contemporary Americans' mood; understood that Washington cannot only coerce but must convince; and reacted accordingly. He expanded "hearts and minds" institutions like the US Information Agency.[26] He had his way with words, as Lillie and Nguyen show when quoting a Vietnamese citizen who felt that Kennedy's inauguration "reinforced hopes of what might be."[27] And he and Jacqueline engaged in stage craft and symbolic politics.

They did so abroad: in Jacqueline's publicized boat ride on the Ganges River (Siegel); in their famed first visit to Paris, where she shone; during Kennedy's address to the Irish parliament (Kilroy); or during his "Ich bin ein Berliner" visit to Germany, a model of "politics as theater."[28] And they did so at home, too. They redesigned the White House as the policy and representational center of an empire-*cum*-democracy, combining imperial French aesthetics with clean lines and a certain "cool."[29] They projected impressions of their vibrant epicenter for world and worldly affairs abroad, for instance, facilitating the dissemination of Jacqueline's 1962 televised guided tour of the White House (Kunkel).

And much more than his predecessor, Dwight D. Eisenhower, Kennedy brought foreign dignitaries to the White House: not only Europeans but also Latin Americans (Kunkel), Asians (Diederich), and Africans (Muehlenbeck). Postcolonial media coverage followed suit, commenting also on visits by third countries' leaders (Stenner). This interest was not the least due to the Kennedys receiving some nonwhite guests not only downstairs but in the upstairs living quarters, too. This fact fascinatingly confirms that "while [Kennedy] scholars may bemoan the confusion of style and substance, oratory and action, it is often difficult to distinguish between them."[30] It stretches the argument, generally, that *"le spectacle est essentiel au pouvoir"* ("spectacle is essential for power") and, specifically, that the president and his wife mastered public political theater.[31] Inviting nonwhite men who are not servants into the living quarters of the world's foremost white—if non-WASP, Irish Catholic—family, that is, into the sanctum also of the family's white woman, was a tremendously symbolic act regarding race. Kennedy saw himself as a human being, equal to people of color.[32]

In return, to many people of color, Kennedy was on an existential level on their side—was theirs, even. Libapu, a Kenyan farmer-carpenter who never saw a picture of him, told Moskowitz he had thought Kennedy is black, and one Frederick Kemboi mentioned that "we were thinking that Kennedy had some relationship with Africa." No surprise, then, that Kennedy was pictured not only with whites but nonwhites, too. African leaders used photos of themselves with Kennedy domestically, and Africans owned Kennedy pictures cut from newspapers (Muehlenbeck). In Alexandria, shop owners displayed portraits of their Egyptian and the US president. Iranians produced and bought tea sets bearing his portrait together with the habitual Safavid Shah Abbas sets.[33] And a 1962 front page of the Moroccan paper *Istiqlal* featured a fascinating multiple portrait (Figure 0.1).[34]

Moreover, if in the United States, "shortly after Kennedy died, it was common for [Kennedy] to be associated to the slaughtered heroes of myth: to Adonis, Baldr, Dionysus, Osiris, Tammuz, and even to Jesus himself,"[35] in postcolonial countries he was seen to have shared the fate of martyred heroes of decolonization like Patrice Lumumba (Muehlenbeck), and in Kenya, many named their children Kennedy (Moskowitz): very much "theirs," indeed.

This brings me to a note on the significance of Kennedy versus other US presidents for colonial subjects and postcolonial citizens. Three names that stand out are Abraham Lincoln, Woodrow Wilson, and Franklin D. Roosevelt. All have been studied through non-American lenses.[36] Global interactions with them differed, for their times and fields of action—racial emancipation, national self-determination, and Great-Depression-era economics, respectively—differed, too. But all three also share something that separates them from Kennedy. They interested non-Americans principally for their policies, while Kennedy did so also for his persona. Who he was and projected to be—one's identification with him, put crudely—counted as much if not much more (Loureiro) than what he did.

If one explanation was Kennedy's approach to race, another was his age. The youngest US president ever elected and the first born in the twentieth century, in 1917, he presented himself as a genuinely new, forward-looking force. Many, though far from all, postcolonial men and women answered positively. This generational trait also situated Kennedy within a cast of young leaders and heroes of decolonization, while distancing him from his direct peers. Men like Anthony Eden, born in 1897, Nikita Khrushchev (1894), Eisenhower and Charles de Gaulle (1890), and Konrad Adenauer (1876) were, to paraphrase Thomas Borstelmann's description of Eisenhower, "children of the nineteenth century" and its racial hierarchies.[37] By contrast, Morocco's Hassan II was born in 1929, Che Guevara in 1928, Fidel Castro in 1926, Norodom Sihanouk in 1922, Nasser in 1918, Ahmed Ben Bella in 1916, Kwame Nkrumah in 1909, and Sukarno in 1901.[38]

Figure 0.1 Castro, Chou en-Lai, Kennedy, and Nehru side by side in the Moroccan paper *al-Istiqlal*.

This generational reality mattered to Kennedy. Here he is, addressing the Democratic National Convention in July 1960 to accept his nomination as presidential candidate in his famous "New Frontier" speech.

> All over the world, particularly in the newer nations, young men are coming to power—men who are not bound by the traditions of the past—men who are not blinded by the old fears and hates and rivalries—young men who can cast off the old slogans and delusions and suspicions. The Republican nominee-to-be [Richard Nixon], of course, is also a young man. But his approach is as old as McKinley. His party is the party of the past. . . . Their pledge is a pledge to the status quo—and today there can be no status quo. For I stand tonight facing west on what was once the last frontier . . . on the edge of a New Frontier—the frontier of the 1960's—a frontier of unknown opportunities and perils—a frontier of unfulfilled hopes and threats.[39]

Analyzing the US empire and postcolonial countries as a joint field

This passage was about more than generational politics, though. Kennedy put himself and an intrepid United States he hoped to lead in the same category as postcolonial countries and their young male leaders. More precisely, the resolve of "newer nations" to break through the status quo was an example Americans should follow (by electing Kennedy). No leader of the modern global North having accepted, however rhetorically, nonwhites as national role models, this view was unprecedented.[40]

It did have a context, however. In the 1950s, US sociologists had posited the emergence of "mass man" and "organization man," subservient to large corporations and emptied of authentic feelings and purpose.[41] Machinist cogs were replacing pioneering Frontier Man. This danger showed abroad, too. In Asia, wiry communist aid agents, living with the locals, were out-toughing and outsmarting flabby US counterparts. This, at least, was the indictment of "the most popular, influential, and controversial novel written in the 1950s about America's relations with Asia," *The Ugly American*, which sold six million copies. The book had a US hero, too, though: Homer Atkins. Can-do and salt of the earth, he showed how one could defeat communists abroad.[42] His story also suggested how and where Americans might best undo Organization Man and become their pioneering selves again: by ruggedly spreading wholesome US modernity, in the Third World. Through institutions like Kennedy's Peace Corps, in other words, which *The Ugly American* helped inspire, and about which pundit Norman Cousins remarked in 1961: "Idealism is back in style. The reason for it goes by the name of the American Peace Corps. Instead of dreary conversation about the meaninglessness of existence, students are now earnestly exchanging ideas about the different needs of communities in Asia and Africa."[43]

Read together, the afore-referenced texts point to an interesting possibility: that of analyzing the postwar US empire—a term from which we should not shy away—and postcolonial countries as one joint field.

This approach can build on Ann Stoler and Frederick Cooper's by now classic call to "treat [European] metropole and colony in a single analytic field." Especially in Britain, that call undergirded New Imperial History.[44] Seeing metropoles and colonies as mutually constitutive rather than categorically different, scholars have focused on connecting and overlapping places and biographies, bodies of knowledge, and political and cultural organizations and practices. And they have abandoned hub-and-spokes views of empire for less centrist terms like the "imperial web," which integrated presumably distinct quasi-national frontier settler stories within a broader imperial framework,[45] and "imperial formation."[46] Some also have pushed beyond Stoler's and Cooper's focus on empire, "extending [the] analytical focus to the multiple networks of exchange that arose from the imperial experience."[47]

But did not European and US empires differ, one formal and territorial, the other not, and hence, is not the European metropolitan-colonial field model useless for us? Not quite. Comparing London and Washington, Julian Go has argued that "formal and informal empire might be better thought of as two ends of a blurry continuum."[48]

Covering much bandwidth, each is heterogeneous, a patchwork; on top, the mixture of imperial practices—their distribution along the continuum—shifts over time.[49] While different, London's empire thus was less unlike Washington's than meets the eye, and vice versa. They interplayed, too, and Washington learned much from British (and other European) imperial practices. Moreover, consider the following six aspects. Not only postwar Washington but already the nineteenth-century British Empire facilitated globalization, if involuntarily, and was shaped by it.[50] Washington's fin-de-siècle Caribbean-central American-Pacific "insular and isthmian imperialism [formed] a formal infrastructure or ground floor on which later, less formal expansion could be built"; the United States could do so because Britain reduced its Latin American presence to focus on Germany.[51] Relations with nation-states were central to postwar Washington's exercise of power, for the US international empire was "an imperial project . . . which achieve[d] imperial ends" importantly "by working through the states of others";[52] however, respective issues were not entirely alien to London, which for instance granted far-reaching autonomy to interwar white settler colonies.[53] Postwar Washington's empire started with its crucial role, at London's and Moscow's sides, in defeating and occupying Germany and Japan, whose attempted imperial conquest of Eurasia had transformed (dare we say imperialized?) US national security doctrine,[54] and in whose affairs Washington remained involved. Postwar Washington has had more, and more far-flung, military bases than any other state, most governed by its own laws and manned overwhelmingly by its own citizens.[55] And last but not least, until the 1960s Cold War Washington relied on European empires.[56]

This analytical "joint US imperial-postcolonial field" needs to be handled with caution, however. It does not imply uniformity. First, as the international element—"achiev[ing] imperial ends by working through the states of others"[57]—was the key for imperial Washington, postcolonial countries are much more sovereign, and hence somewhat more distinct, than European colonies. Secondly, Washington has entertained widely different relationship to different countries; besides, its relationship to a given country often has changed over time. Thirdly, the postwar US empire faced a powerful state-based ideological counterforce, Soviet- and Chinese-led communism, which interfered with the US-postcolonial field: something unknown to nineteenth-century European empires. Fourthly, relations between postcolonial countries and Western postimperial entities like Britain, France, Germany, and the European Economic Community interfered with the field, too.[58] So did, fifthly, South-South relations, which principally after 1945 came to encompass a (politically crucial) interstate dimension. And sixthly, we need to ask how the postwar US empire's unprecedented global scope sits with a model focusing "only" on the postcolonial-US field. After all, Washington dominated the Western Hemisphere from around 1900; replaced imperial German and Japanese hegemony over West and East Eurasia in 1945; since then, has dominated the world's sea, air, and space commons, Soviet challenges notwithstanding; gradually replaced Britain in the Middle East after 1945; and pushed into decolonizing Africa from the late 1950s.

The pluriformity of the US imperial-postcolonial field is not exceptional, though. It characterized the afore-mentioned nineteenth- to mid-twentieth-century webs, formations, and exchange networks, too. But their postwar successor was more pluriform. Discourses and practices constitutive of European metropolitan-colonial fields, though waning, had postwar echoes. Also, colonies of half a dozen European empires became dozens of postcolonial nation-states. And last, the US-postcolonial field intersected with three substantial postwar developments noted above: decolonization increased South-South inter*state* relations; state-based communism expanded and grew bolder; and Washington's posture and interests became truly world-embracing.

This last point means that the postwar US imperial-postcolonial field was not categorically separate in space, actors, and content. Conceptualizing its complex intersections with other developments is beyond this text, however. Having acknowledged the issue, I will outline the US imperial-postcolonial field as if it were separate, while occasionally referencing intersections.

Earlier, I suggested that from the later 1950s to the 1960s Americans saw postcolonial contemporaries not simply as underdeveloped Oriental Others in need of guidance but as optimist activists who were taking the world by the horns, daring to shape their future, and become history's spearhead (and this at a time when Sputnik scared Americans). Americans certainly believed that their own modernizational, economic, and political model was supreme, and would beat the Soviets. Still, the collective postcolonial emotional disposition impressed them, doubly because to them the Third World was perhaps *the* place where American individuals could become their pioneering selves again. In this sense, the US empire, more than leading, followed, and Kennedy, more than shaping his postcolonial contemporaries, reacted to their hopes and demands.[59]

Postcolonial actors helped constitute the joint US imperial-postcolonial field, too. In this volume, the primary example concerns some—but most decidedly not all—such actors voicing their struggles for existential freedom, sovereignty, and racial equality not only—though mainly—in a direct way but also by refracting it through the mirror of Kennedy.[60] To be crystal clear: they *most certainly* did not need Kennedy to know their struggle was legitimate. At the same time, he, who evinced interest in them, in a sense provided an ultimate legitimation. This was ironic, for it signaled an implicit recognition of being within the field of power of a new, international empire just when decolonization was about not being bound to foreign powers anymore.

Examples abound in this volume. Kunkel notes that Latin Americans took to calling Jacqueline Kennedy *la reina* (the queen). Muehlenbeck shows how African leaders used photographs with Kennedy to "boost their legitimacy at home. . . . Pictures of a 1959 meeting between Guinean President Sékou Touré and Kennedy, at Disneyland, when Kennedy was still a senator, were 'displayed even in the smallest villages,' and were highly prized by Guineans." Zebedeo Omwando, a farmer whose letter to Kennedy opens Moskowitz's chapter, treated the president as if he'd indeed be "*His* Highness," which is how he addressed him.[61] "The perception of a friendly, intimate relationship with a US president, who also offered material aid, appealed to rural Kenyans and blended readily into established patron-client relationships," Moskowitz concludes. At the core of my chapter stands the story of how an Iranian woman, Fakhri Garakani, wagered the US president would exchange gifts with her, a non-US citizen, following an Iranian pattern of gifts traded between unequals—as if he were her own leader. And I point out that ironically, foreigners whose political gifts explicitly rejected inequality between people and nations hoped that in exchange for their gift they might be heard by a most powerful man.

Let me sum up. Firstly, the US imperial-postcolonial field was symbiotic yet heterogeneous and unequal. It was not all-encompassing, though, that is, does not explain everything in the United States and postcolonial countries. It's a way to tackle a question occupying also other imperial historians: "how to write about such vastly different places, processes, and people as those contained within the nineteenth-century British Empire *at the same time*."[62] Secondly, its content as covered here—others may see things differently—was an emotional disposition that ranged from the mid-1950s to the 1960s, peaking early that decade, and which was underwritten by specific culturo-political practices. Its focal point was an existential optimism in the feasibility and likelihood of a better future. That is, it included, but was about much more than, the parallels and links between African American and Third World liberation struggles, discussed here (Adalet, Houser, Klug, Kunkel, Moskowitz, Mühlenbeck, Stenner) and elsewhere.[63] Thirdly, the field's genesis was more complex, and its nature hence more ambiguous, than prewar European metropolitan-colonial fields. It emerged at the intersection of two equally historic postwar developments, the crystallization of anti-imperial liberation and the rise of a truly worldwide US empire; on top, that empire's modus operandi was international. Fourthly, the field was doubly unequal. Liberation struggles shaped it more than the US empire in terms of their historic, existential force.[64] But in terms of raw power it was the US empire that shaped it more, and by looking for it to legitimize their struggle, some postcolonial citizens recognized it implicitly if not explicitly. And fifth, the postwar US imperial-postcolonial field overlapped with other simultaneous developments, most importantly strengthening South-South interstate relations, the Cold War, and the persistence of minor power centers in the global North other than Moscow and Washington. Hence, it could be broadened and seen as forming part of wider fields.

Conclusion

Let me end on a historiographic note. A symbiotic view of "the postcolonial/American" and "the domestic/foreign," through the concept of "the joint field," makes a cautious step beyond certain conceptualizations current in three intersecting bodies of literature. It backs critiques of postwar US transnational history as a field that, while fruitfully undermining US exceptionalism, too often eschews empire.[65] Moreover, it goes one step further than concepts like "circuits" or "two-way street" that historians use to finesse our understanding of the United States' postwar nature as a great power that, however, was influenced by others, too. It does so by blurring, though not negating, distinctions between "outside" and "domestic."[66] And last, "the joint field," and more broadly speaking this volume as a whole, point to the possibility of supplementing certain depictions of the scholarly literature on US diplomatic history. Earlier, I cited Borstelmann's poetic image of that literature as "the hinge between domestic U.S. history and world history: we function like a traditional Western barroom door, swinging both ways, and doing so easily, readily, continuously."[67] This image is not wrong. And yet, if this volume demonstrates anything, it is the need to pay closer attention to when, how, and why that metaphorical door starts disappearing from view.

Notes

1. John Hellman, *The Kennedy Obsession: The American Myth of JFK* (New York: Columbia University Press, 1997); Mark White, *Kennedy: A Cultural History of an American Icon* (London: Bloomsbury, 2013); Michael Hogan, *The Afterlife of John F. Kennedy* (New York: Cambridge University Press, 2017); Lee Konstantinou, "The Camelot Presidency," in *Cambridge Companion to John F. Kennedy*, ed. Andrew Hoberek (Cambridge: Cambridge University Press, 2015), 149–63.
2. David Lubin, *Shooting Kennedy: JFK and the Culture of Images* (Berkeley: University of California Press, 2003); Gregory Frame, "The Myth of John F. Kennedy in Film and Television," *Film & History* 46, no. 2 (2016): 21–34.
3. James Giglio, "Writing Kennedy," in *A Companion to John F. Kennedy*, ed. Marc Selverstone (Chichester: Wiley Blackwell, 2014), 7–30; Burton Kaufman, "John F. Kennedy as World Leader: A Perspective on the Literature," *DH* 17, no. 3 (1993): 447–69; Andrew Preston, "Kennedy, the Cold War, and the National Security State," in *Cambridge Companion*, 99.
4. Stephen Rabe, *John F. Kennedy: World Leader* (Washington: Potomac, 2010).
5. Arthur Schlesinger, *A Thousand Days* (Boston: Mariner, 1965), 509.
6. Quotes: Preston, "Kennedy," 90, and Robert Rakove, *Kennedy, Johnson, and the Nonaligned World* (Cambridge: Cambridge University Press, 2013), xxi. Key texts include Rabe, *Kennedy*; Vaughn Rasberry, "JFK and the Global Anticolonial Movement," in *Cambridge Companion*, 118–33; Frank Costigliola, "US Foreign Policy from Kennedy to Johnson," in *The Cambridge History of the Cold War*, ed. Melvyn Leffler and Odd Arne Westad (Cambridge: Cambridge University Press, 2010), 112–33.
7. Hogan, *Afterlife*, 17.
8. Hellman, *Kennedy*, 99.
9. Ann Stoler and Frederick Cooper, "Between Metropole and Colony," in *Tensions of Empire*, ed. Ann Stoler and Frederick Cooper (Berkeley: University of California Press, 1997), 4.
10. Odd Arne Westad, *The Global Cold War* (Cambridge: Cambridge University Press, 2005); Christopher Goscha and Christian Ostermann, ed., *Connecting Histories: Decolonization and the Cold War in Southeast Asia, 1945-1962* (Washington: Woodrow Wilson Center Press, 2009); Greg Brazinsky, *Winning the Third World: Sino-American Rivalry during the Cold War* (Chapel Hill: The University of North Carolina Press, 2017); Samantha Christiansen and Zachary Scarlett, "Introduction," in *The Third World in the Global 1960s*, ed. Samantha Christiansen and Zachary Scarlett (New York: Berghahn, 2013), 1; Mark Bradley, "Decolonization, the Global South, and the Cold War, 1919-1962," in *Cambridge History of the Cold War*, 464–85; Robert McMahon, ed., *The Cold War in the Third World* (New York: Oxford University Press, 2013).
11. Matthew Connelly, "Taking off the Cold War Lenses," *AHR* 105, no. 3 (2000): 739–69. See also Prasenjit Duara, "The Cold War as a Historical Period," *JGH* 6 (2011): 457–80.
12. Stephen Rabe, *The Killing Zone: The United States Wages Cold War in Latin America* (Oxford: Oxford University Press, 2012), 86–118; Greg Grandin, *The Last Colonial Massacre: Latin America in the Cold War* (Chicago: University of Chicago Press, 2004).

13 Thomas Field, *From Development to Dictatorship: Bolivia and the Alliance for Progress in the Kennedy Era* (Ithaca: Cornell University Press, 2014); Gregg Brazinsky, *Nation Building in South Korea: Koreans, Americans, and the Making of a Democracy* (Chapel Hill: University of North Carolina Press, 2007).
14 Gilbert Joseph, "What We Now Know and Should Know," in *In from the Cold: Latin America's New Encounter with the Cold War*, ed. Joseph and Daniela Spenser (Durham: Duke University Press, 2008), 4. See also Piero Gleijeses, *Conflicting Missions: Havana, Washington, and Africa, 1959-1976* (Chapel Hill: University of North Carolina Press, 2002); Tanya Harmer, *Allende's Chile and the Inter-American Cold War* (Chapel Hill: University of North Carolina Press, 2011); Edward Miller, *Misalliance: Ngo Dinh Diem, the United States, and the Fate of South Vietnam* (Cambridge: Harvard University Press, 2013); Jonathan Brown, *Cuba's Revolutionary World* (Cambridge: Harvard University Press, 2017).
15 Akira Iriye, "Culture and Power: International Relations as Intercultural Relations," *DH* 3 (1979): 115-28. Michael Hunt, "Internationalizing U.S. Diplomatic History," *DH* 15, no. 1 (1991): 1-11.
16 Matthew Connelly et al., "SHAFR in the World," *Passport* 42, no. 2 (2011): 5, 11. Other key texts include Akira Iriye, "Internationalizing International History," in *Rethinking American History in a Global Age*, ed. Thomas Bender (Berkeley: University of California Press, 2002), 47-62; Michael Hogan, "The 'Next Big Thing': The Future of Diplomatic History in a Global Age," *DH* 28, no. 1 (2004): 1-22; Robert McMahon, "Toward a Pluralist Vision," in *Explaining the History of American Foreign Relations*, ed. Michael Hogan and Thomas Paterson (New York: Cambridge University Press, 2004), 35-50; Thomas Zeiler et al., "Diplomatic History Today," *JAmH* 95, no. 4 (2009): 1053-91; Erez Manela, "The United States in the World," in *American History Now*, ed. Eric Foner and Lisa McGirr (Philadelphia: Temple University Press, 2011), 201-20; Andrew Preston and Doug Rossinow, "Introduction: America within the World," in *Outside In*, ed. Preston and Rossinow (Oxford: Oxford University Press, 2016), 1-18.
17 See also James Brennan, "Radio Cairo and the Decolonization of East Africa," in *Making a World after Empire*, ed. Christopher Lee (Athens: Ohio University Press, 2010), 173-95.
18 Hogan, *Afterlife*; Mary Watson, "A Tour of the White House," *Presidential Studies Quarterly* 18, no. 1 (1998): 91-99.
19 Lubin, *Kennedy*; David Halberstam, "Introduction," in *The Kennedy Presidential Press Conferences*, ed. George Johnson (New York: Earl Coleman, 1978), i-iv.
20 Mark Haefele, "Kennedy, the USIA, and World Public Opinion," *DH* 25, no. 1 (2001): 63-84.
21 Aniko Bodroghkozy, "The BBC and the Black Weekend: Broadcasting the Kennedy Assassination and the Birth of Global Television News," *The Sixties* 9, no. 2 (2016): 242-60.
22 Christopher Lee, "Introduction," in *World after Empire*, 1-42; Nataša Mišković, "Introduction," in *The Non-Aligned Movement and the Cold War*, ed. Nataša Mišković et al. (London: Routledge, 2014), 1-18; Jürgen Dinkel, *The Non-Aligned Movement* (Leiden: Brill, 2018).
23 More broadly, see Philip Muehlenbeck, *Betting on the Africans: Kennedy's Courting of African Nationalist Leaders* (New York: Oxford University Press, 2012).
24 Introductions to the history of emotions include Ute Frevert, *Emotions in History* (Budapest: Central European University Press, 2011); Piroska Nagy and Ute Frevert (comment), "History of Emotions," in *Debating New Approaches to History*, ed.

Marek Tamm and Peter Burke (London: Bloomsbury, 2019), 189–216. See also William Reddy, *The Navigation of Feeling: A Framework for the History of Emotions* (Cambridge: Cambridge University Press, 2001), 124–26, on "emotional regime."

25 This may be connected to the literature on the long / global 1960s: Christiansen and Scarlett, *Third World*; "The Sixties and the World Event," special issue of *boundary 2* 36, no. 1 (2009): 1–210; Chen Jian et al., eds., *The Routledge Handbook of the Global 1960s* (London: Routledge, 2018). A classic is Fredric Jameson, "Periodizing the 60s," in *The 60s without Apology*, ed. Sohnya Sayres et al. (Minneapolis: University of Minnesota Press, 1984), 178–209.

26 Haefele, "Kennedy"; Gregory Tomlin, *Murrow's Cold War: Public Diplomacy for the Kennedy Administration* (Nebraska: Potomac, 2016); Jason Parker, *Hearts, Minds, Voices: U.S. Cold War Public Diplomacy and the Formation of the Third World* (New York: Oxford University Press, 2016); Frank Ninkovich, "U.S. Information Policy and Cultural Diplomacy," *Foreign Policy Association Headline Series* 308 (1996): 3–63.

27 Bui Diem, *In the Jaws of History* (Bloomington: Indiana University Press, 1999), 117, quoted in Lillie and Nguyen's chapter.

28 Andreas Daum, *Kennedy in Berlin* (Cambridge: Cambridge University Press, 2008), 4.

29 Hogan, *Afterlife*.

30 Rasberry, "JFK," 120, citing Thomas Noer, *Cold War and Black Liberation* (1985), 34.

31 Julien Bonhomme and Nicolas Jaoul, "Grands hommes vus d'en bas," *Gradhiva* 11 (2010): 7.

32 Related, Anders Stephanson, "Senator John F. Kennedy: Anti-Imperialism and Utopian Deficit," *JAS* 48, no. 1 (2014): 1–24, argued that Kennedy saw decolonization not only as a function of the Cold War. For colonial backgrounds, see Ann Stoler, *Carnal Knowledge and Imperial Power* (Berkeley: University of California Press, 2010).

33 Rami Khouri and Nazanin Shahrokni, information to author, March 17, 2015, Beirut.

34 "Peace," *al-Istiqlal*, October 27, 1962, 1. I thank David Stenner for the image.

35 Godfrey Hodgson, "JFK and the 1960s," *The Sixties* 8, no. 2 (2015): 214.

36 Richard Carwardine and Jay Sexton, eds., *The Global Lincoln* (New York: Oxford University Press, 2011); Erez Manela, *The Wilsonian Moment* (Oxford: Oxford University Press, 2007); Kiran Patel, *The New Deal* (Princeton: Princeton University Press, 2015).

37 Thomas Borstelmann, *The Cold War and the Color Line* (Cambridge: Harvard University Press, 2001), 86.

38 Older were Mao Tsedong, Ho Chi Minh, and Jawaharlal Nehru, born in 1893, 1890, and 1889, respectively.

39 Available online: https://www.jfklibrary.org/Asset-Viewer/AS08q5oYz0SFUZg9uOi4iw.aspx (accessed January 4, 2019).

40 This did not contradict Kennedy's belief that America was the world's modernizer: Michael Latham, *Modernization as Ideology* (Chapel Hill: University of North Carolina Press, 2000).

41 William Whyte, *The Organization Man* (New York: Simon and Schuster, 1956); Paul Goodman, *Growing Up Absurd* (New York: Random House, 1960); David Riesman, *The Lonely Crowd* (New Haven: Yale University Press, 1950).

42 Christina Klein, *Cold War Orientalism: Asia in the Middlebrow Imagination, 1945-1961* (Berkeley: University of California Press, 2003), 58. William Lederer and Eugene Burdick, *The Ugly American* (New York: Norton, 1958).

43 Quoted in Elizabeth Cobbs Hoffman, *All You Need Is Love: The Peace Corps and the Spirit of the 1960s* (Cambridge: Harvard University Press, 2000), 33.

44 Stoler and Cooper, "Between Metropole and Colony," 4.

45 Tony Ballantyne, *Orientalism and Race* (Basingstoke: Palgrave, 2001).
46 Ann Stoler et al., eds., *Imperial Formations* (Santa Fe: SARP, 2007); Paul Kramer, "Power and Connection: Imperial Histories of the United States in the World," *AHR* 116, no. 5 (2011): 1349.
47 Durba Ghosh and Dane Kennedy, "Introduction," in *Decentring Empire*, ed. Durba Ghosh and Dane Kennedy (Hyderabad: Orient Longman, 2006), 2. An excellent overview is Alan Lester, "Imperial Circuits and Networks: Geographies of the British Empire," *History Compass* 4, no. 1 (2006): 124–41.
48 Julian Go, *Patterns of Empire* (Cambridge: Cambridge University Press, 2011), 11. Similarly: Stephen Howe, *Empire* (Oxford: Oxford University Press, 2002), 15.
49 For Britain, see John Darwin, *The Empire Project* (Cambridge: Cambridge University Press, 2009).
50 Gary Magee and Andrew Thompson, *Empire and Globalisation* (Cambridge: Cambridge University Press, 2010); Martin Thomas and Andrew Thompson, "Empire and Globalisation," *IHR* 36, no. 1 (2014): 142–70.
51 Thomas McCormick, "From Old Empire to New," in *Colonial Crucible*, ed. Alfred McCoy and Francisco Scarano (Madison: University of Wisconsin Press, 2009), 73.
52 Kramer, "Power," 1366.
53 A. G. Hopkins, "Rethinking Decolonization," *PP* 200 (2008): 211–47; Duncan Bell, *The Idea of Greater Britain* (Princeton: Princeton University Press, 2007). See also Antoinette Burton, ed., *After the Imperial Turn* (Durham: Duke University Press, 2003), 5.
54 Andrew Preston, "Monsters Everywhere: A Genealogy of National Security," *DH* 38, no. 3 (2014): 477–500; Robert McMahon, "How the Periphery Became the Center," in *Foreign Policy at the Periphery*, ed. Bevan Sewell et al. (Lexington: University Press of Kentucky, 2017), 19–35.
55 David Vine, *Base Nation* (New York: Metropolitan, 2015).
56 William Louis and Ronald Robinson, "The Imperialism of Decolonization," *JICH* 22 (1994): 462–511.
57 Kramer, "Power," 1366.
58 For the last, see Véronique Dimier, *The Invention of a European Development Aid Bureaucracy: Recycling Empire* (London: Palgrave, 2014). For the non-uniformity of the First and Second World cores, see Andrew Rotter, "Narratives of Core and Periphery," in *Foreign Policy at the Periphery*, 60.
59 The emotional-historical aspect here can be associated to the argument that the postwar United States developed a "sentimental discourse of integration that imagined the forging of bonds between Asians and Americans," positing a *certain* "racial equality" between the two: Klein, *Cold War Orientalism*, 17, 15.
60 For decolonization's existential dimension, touching the soul, as it were, see Yoav Di-Capua, *No Exit* (Chicago: University of Chicago Press, 2018).
61 My italics.
62 Lester, "Geographies," 127 (my italics).
63 Penny Von Eschen, *Race against Empire: Black Americans and Anticolonialism, 1937–1957* (Ithaca: Cornell University Press, 1997); Mary Dudziak, *Cold War Civil Rights: Race and the Image of American Democracy* (Princeton: Princeton University Press, 2000); Borstelmann, *Cold War*; Cynthia Young, *Soul Power: Culture, Radicalism, and the Making of a Third World Left* (Durham: Duke University Press, 2006); Nico Slate, *Colored Cosmopolitanism: The Shared Struggle for Freedom in the United States and India* (Cambridge: Harvard University Press, 2012); Brenda Plummer, *In Search*

of Power: African Americans in the Era of Decolonization, 1956–1974 (New York: Cambridge University Press, 2013); John Munro, *The Anticolonial Front: The African American Freedom Struggle and Global Decolonization, 1945–1960* (Cambridge: Cambridge University Press, 2017).

64 Christiansen and Scarlett, "Introduction," 1; Young, *Soul Power*.
65 Kramer, "Power," 1380; Andrew Rotter, "Chaps Having Flaps: The Historiography of U.S. Foreign Relations, 1980-1995," in *America in the World*, ed. Frank Costigliola and Michael Hogan (Cambridge: Cambridge University Press, 2014), 51–52. See also Jürgen Osterhammel, "Imperien," in *Transnationale Geschichte*, ed. Gunilla Budde et al. (Göttingen: Vandenhoeck & Ruprecht, 2006), 58. For the field, see Ian Tyrrell, "Reflections on the Transnational Turn in United States History," *JGH* 4 (2009): 453–74.
66 All quotes: Carl Guarneri, *Locating the United States in Twentieth-Century World History* (Washington: AHA, 2011), 23. There is a massive literature on "the United States in the World"; see, for example, Manela, "United States."
67 Related, see Andrew Johns and Mitchell Lerner, eds., The *Cold War at Home and Abroad: Domestic Politics and US Foreign Policy since 1945* (Lexington: University of Kentucky Press, 2018).

Part I

Actors

1

First New Nation or Internal Colony? Modernization Theorists, Black Intellectuals, and the Politics of Colonial Comparison in the Kennedy Years

Sam Klug

In June 1959, in the Grand Ballroom of the Waldorf-Astoria Hotel in New York, Senator John F. Kennedy gave the keynote address at the Second Annual Meeting of the American Society for African Culture (AMSAC). Kennedy, recently appointed chair of the Subcommittee on African Affairs in the Senate Foreign Relations Committee, spent much of his speech highlighting the potential of US development aid to contribute to economic growth in Africa. At several moments, he referred to the American Revolution as a precursor to the ongoing process of decolonization in Africa. Quoting Thomas Paine's view of liberty radiating outward from the Thirteen Colonies—"From a small spark kindled in America, a flame has arisen not to be extinguished"—Kennedy insisted "that very flame is today lighting what was once called 'the Dark Continent.'"[1]

The day before, in a panel session at the same conference, two African American writers, J. Saunders Redding and Harold Cruse, also debated how to understand the relationship between the history of the United States and African decolonization.[2] They came to sharply different conclusions. Whereas Cruse saw in African independence movements a sign that African Americans should shift their goals from integration to cultural "rebirth," Redding countered that African Americans, unlike the "new nations" on the continent, "are not a *people* in Cruse's sense of the word" and that seeing their situations as analogous would only "cut American Negroes off" from their American heritage.[3] Redding and Cruse debated the status of African American culture and politics in terms not only of diasporic connections across the Atlantic but of a shared history of colonial oppression in Africa and North America.

Kennedy's speech and the debate between Cruse and Redding illuminate a crucial feature of the political culture of the postwar United States, one that is obscured when their ideas are segregated in our historical imagination.[4] Kennedy's invocation of Thomas Paine in a speech primarily dedicated to American foreign aid policy in Africa reflected a widely held view of the United States as the "first new nation"—the first national community to win its independence from European colonial rule.

This idea, articulated by social scientists, policymakers, and politicians, has long been acknowledged as an important element of modernization theory and the period in American foreign policy it helped to define.[5] The debate between Cruse and Redding, meanwhile, marked a flashpoint in a decades-long debate over how African Americans should understand the relationship between their own intellectual production and political activism and that of the decolonizing world. Seen together, these two moments at the 1959 AMSAC Conference highlight the increasing relevance of debates about the nature and meaning of colonialism to American politics and intellectual life in the Kennedy era. By tracing these debates across the realms of the social sciences, the US foreign policy apparatus, and black political thought, we can better appreciate the role decolonization played in the ideological development of both American liberalism and the black freedom movement in the 1960s.

The depiction of the United States as the first new nation coincided with and was reinforced by Kennedy's rise through American politics. Although John Foster Dulles, the secretary of state of Kennedy's predecessor, Dwight D. Eisenhower, had claimed that the United States held "natural sympathy" for the decolonizing world because of its own experience as "the first colony in modern times to have won independence," the image of the United States as a political model for the decolonizing world resonated particularly strongly with Kennedy's Washington.[6] Sociologist Seymour Martin Lipset, author of an influential work of social science titled *The First New Nation*, later described his work as the product of "those bygone almost bucolic days of the New Frontier."[7] Lipset's association between the image of the first new nation and that of the new frontier suggests a close relationship between the imperial nostalgia of Kennedy's slogan and the portrayal of the United States as a natural ally of the decolonizing world. The discourse of the first new nation served important purposes in Cold War liberalism, as policymakers sought to portray the United States as preternaturally aligned with anti-colonialism—regardless of actual US policy—while seeking to steer anti-colonial movements away from an alignment with the Soviet Union.[8]

Yet this political language did more than simply seek to win friends in the Cold War. It contained a distinctive historical imagination of the American Revolution, portraying this conflict as an uprising against a foreign power, but, importantly, not as a social revolution dedicated to overturning economic hierarchies within the colony.[9] While other scholars have explored this portrayal of the American Revolution as a model for anti-colonial revolts, this chapter emphasizes, first, the ways that the first new nation discourse sought to influence postcolonial politics.[10] American elites promoted the federal system of the United States as a promising model for decolonizing states. In contrast to postcolonial leaders themselves, who looked to early America as an exemplar for decolonizing nations who sought to form federations to build greater power in the international political economy, leading American social scientists and state officials argued that federalism offered a means to manage internal pluralism rather than to project strength externally.[11]

Secondly, this chapter explores how the first new nation discourse intervened in a fervently contested global conversation about the definition of colonialism. American liberal intellectuals and Kennedy administration policymakers put forth a narrow definition of colonialism as a system of political rule by a foreign power. They defined colonialism more narrowly than did the new states themselves, which succeeded in passing a resolution in the UN General Assembly in 1960 denouncing "colonialism in all its manifestations" and asserting their right to "freely dispose of their natural wealth without prejudice to any obligations arising out of international economic co-operation."[12] The question of just what "colonialism in all its manifestations" meant was of substantial importance for American policymakers in the Cold War, who insisted on a stark distinction between formal political rule and continuing relations of economic dependence, while simultaneously portraying Soviet control in Eastern Europe as a form of colonialism worthy of condemnation from the Third World.

Finally, this chapter will show how the debate over the definition of colonialism took on a new importance among African Americans in the early 1960s and stimulated an important turn in black politics. Harold Cruse was the most influential among a number of black intellectuals in the United States who developed a new vocabulary of "internal colonialism" to describe American racial hierarchy in this period. Although this concept took on greater political importance in the late 1960s and early 1970s, accompanying the rise to prominence of the Black Power movement on a national stage, its proximate sources were located in the early 1960s. In contrast to the policymakers and social scientists who promoted the image of the United States as the first new nation, those who imagined African Americans as an internal colony embraced a broad definition of colonialism that included cultural domination, spatial segregation, and racialized economic inequality, rejecting a definition that focused solely on political sovereignty.

Two political languages, then, arose during the Kennedy era as competing ways of reckoning with the relationship of the United States to global decolonization: one depicted the United States as the first new nation; the other portrayed it as a site of internal colonialism. For many Americans, from white social scientists and Kennedy administration officials to black activists and intellectuals, the relationship between American history and governance and the global system of colonialism became central to the political culture of the Kennedy era. The development of a vocabulary of internal colonialism in the early 1960s further reflected the beginnings of a shift in black political thought and helped set the stage for the much more contentious politics of colonial comparison in the Black Power era.[13]

Federalism and pluralism in the new nations

Ideas about constitutional design, national sovereignty, and civic values pervaded the first new nation discourse. Leading modernization theorists were divided on the relative primacy of economic growth, political structures, and cultural values in the transition to what they saw as modern society, and American elites both inside and outside government saw the relationship between formal institutions and cultural values as the key to the establishment of stable polities in postcolonial societies. The relationship was particularly important to Lipset, whose 1963 book *The First New Nation: The United States in Historical and Comparative Perspective* was the most sustained and prominent attempt to elaborate the relevance of the political structure of the early United States to the decolonizing world.

In the world of modernization and development theory, Lipset was a joiner, not a pioneer. Although his early scholarship focused on the internal democracy of trade unions and the comparative development of socialism in the United States and Canada, as a member of the program committee for the 1962 World Congress of Sociology, Lipset contributed to the decision to make "development" the focus of the conference, following Kennedy's efforts to brand the 1960s the "decade of development."[14] Lipset realized that his expertise in the history of political parties and trade unions in the United States could be reframed in the new terms of development that were sweeping his fields of sociology and political science. As he reflected at the 1962 conference, "Perhaps the first new nation can contribute more than money to the latter-day ones; perhaps its development can show how revolutionary, equalitarian and populist values become incorporated into a stable nonauthoritarian polity."[15] Lipset argued that postcolonial states faced similar problems as the early United States, from economic weakness to the absence of a unifying central authority to the divisions of a pluralistic society, all of which the United States had purportedly overcome only through a slow process of institutional development.

While Lipset claimed that the political institutions of the United States could serve as a model for the decolonizing world, he also suggested reasons why the new nations of the twentieth century might have difficulty living up to the American example. These reasons, according to Lipset, were rooted less in an unequal international political economy than in cultural values. Like many modernization theorists, Lipset was influenced by Talcott Parsons's emphasis on "value-orientations" as causal forces in social change.[16] Expanding his account from the congress in his book *The First New Nation*, he argued that the "key values" of the United States, which "stem from our revolutionary origins," are the values of "equality and achievement."[17] The cultural emphasis in Lipset's approach left little that appeared directly transferable from the experience of the early United States to the decolonizing world.

Lipset was not entirely pessimistic, however. If he perceived the "value-orientations" of postcolonial societies as incompatible with the full complement of American institutions, he envisioned federalism as a potentially transferable political form. He shared this belief with elements of the state policymaking apparatus, notably with the State Department's Benjamin Gerig. Gerig insisted not only that the revolutionary birth of the United States was a "natural" source of the nation's contemporary policy, but that its civil war further offered a lesson for "new states" about the dangers of secession and fragmentation.[18] A "federal system which balances a large degree of autonomy with effective centralized government," Gerig claimed, could offer regions that might otherwise seek their own states a degree of self-determination short of national independence.[19] While Gerig saw federalism as a way to provide autonomy short of national self-determination to groups that challenged a new state's authority, Lipset imagined other advantages. Federalism, to him, offered a way of managing racial and ethnic pluralism by creating a cross-cutting source of division. Democracy was only sustainable, in Lipset's mind, if social differences of class, race, religion, and language were not the primary sources of citizens' allegiances and political mobilizations: "Democracy needs cleavage within linguistic or religious groups, not between them. But where such divisions do not exist, federalism seems to serve democracy well."[20] Federalism was a means of producing difference along a new axis, in order to ensure that other social differences did not determine the political alignments in a new polity.

"In all its manifestations": Defining colonialism amid the end of empires

Debates about the applicability of American political institutions to newly independent states were intertwined with contestations over the meaning of colonialism at the height of decolonization. The scope of what should and should not be labeled "colonial" was a matter of intense political concern in the late 1950s and early 1960s.[21] At the Bandung conference in 1955, twenty-nine Asian and African states declared themselves against "colonialism in all its manifestations," a phrase that was repeated in the UN General Assembly's Declaration on the Granting of Independence to Colonial Countries and Peoples in December 1960.[22] The phrase captured several ambiguities of the moment, as "all its manifestations" could include both Soviet dominance in Eastern Europe and Central Asia and continuing forms of political and economic influence short of formal rule by the United States and its Cold War allies in newly independent states.[23] In this context, American diplomats identified the lexicon of empire as an arena where foreign policy goals were at stake. State Department official Francis T. Williamson noted that decolonization presented a "semantic" problem for the United States and sought a new language that might "avoid . . . the emotionalism and partisanship surrounding the word 'anti-colonial.'"[24] While some figures joined Williamson in objecting to the term "colonialism" altogether, more common among liberals, including Kennedy administration policymakers, was to define colonialism narrowly—as a strictly political system, which had the unfortunate but unintended effects of producing racial and cultural hierarchies. The image of the United States as the first new nation was useful in this ideological project.

The writings of Rupert Emerson, the foremost expert on decolonization among US political scientists, were representative of American elites' understanding of colonialism as defined fundamentally by alien political rule and only incidentally by international hierarchy or racial domination. Emerson had studied with British socialist Harold Laski at the London School of Economics in the interwar period and served in both the Foreign Economic Administration and the Department of State in the 1940s. Up until the late 1950s, his area of scholarly focus was Southeast Asia.[25] He combined sympathy for independence movements in Asia and Africa with an admiration for nineteenth-century European nationalists, for whom "the virtue of nationalism lay at least as much in the belief that it would be a bridge to the brotherhood of man as in the calculation of the benefits it would bring to the particular nation concerned."[26] Influenced by Laski, he hoped that anti-colonial nationalism would ultimately be tempered into a liberal internationalism and a plural world government.[27]

To make such a transition possible, Emerson sought to decouple the problem of colonialism as alien rule from the problem of racial hierarchy. Recognizing that contests over the meaning of colonialism would become increasingly salient as newly independent nations gained a greater voice on the world stage, he sought to defend a narrow definition: "It is idle to think that the well-established category of colonies . . . can be merged with the other comparable evils of mankind."[28] Colonialism, to him, was "the establishment and maintenance for an extended time of rule over an alien people which is separate from and subordinate to the ruling power."[29] Postcolonial rulers and citizens were more likely to be seduced by the dangerous elements of nationalism when they identified their former rulers with ideologies of racial superiority and practices of racial discrimination, and they were more likely to overreach in their criticisms of capitalism and "the West" when they identified both with a project of protecting a global system of white supremacy.[30] For this reason, Emerson was sharply critical of the white minority regimes in the settler colonies of Kenya, Algeria, the Rhodesias, and South Africa, which lent credence to these dangerous linkages. Although he emphasized that "an African nationalism which seeks to get its own back through an expropriation and expulsion of Europeans . . . would lead to painful consequences for all concerned," Emerson eagerly anticipated the end of the political domination of white minorities in those states.[31] However, he rendered the problem of white settlers as the leading edge of the problem of racial and ethnic pluralism in postcolonial states—arguing that "the white settlers raise peculiarly acutely the problem of the lack of that national homogeneity which any simple version of self-determination presupposes"—rather than as an extreme manifestation of the racial logic of the broader colonial system.[32]

Many African American writers agreed that European settler colonies in Africa were particularly volatile examples of colonialism's potential for racial violence, but they interpreted the relationship between the settler colonies and other forms of colonial rule differently. Several events in 1960—particularly the Sharpeville Massacre in South Africa and Charles de Gaulle's rejection of a ceasefire in Algeria—brought this issue to the forefront of black internationalist concerns in the United States. The scholar-activist St. Clair Drake identified the settler colonies as crucial test cases for the United States in the Cold War struggle for Third World loyalties: "If South Africa and the other settler areas are sought after to join into military bastions for the West, all the African people will be turning away from the West in revulsion."[33] Horace Cayton, the sociologist and foreign affairs correspondent for the *Pittsburgh Courier*, turned the attention of his weekly column to Algeria for months on end in 1960, highlighting the potential danger *pied noir* "extremists" posed to the possibility of a peace settlement centered around Algerian independence.[34] To these figures, the settler colonies were instructive as acute demonstrations of the potential for racial violence embedded in the colonial project writ large. Settler colonies in Africa further exemplified the continuities between the colonial system now deemed anachronistic in world governance and the racial order of the United States. This connection posed a challenge to the language of the first new nation, which presented an image of the country as structurally and ideologically aligned with the decolonizing world.

Although Emerson's *From Empire to Nation* was written for academic audiences, some readers saw in it an approach to the decolonizing world that policymakers should follow. Modernization theorist David Apter pronounced that "it ought to be a guidebook for a new frontiersman."[35] While Emerson's channels of policy influence were never quite so direct as Apter hoped, his analytical treatment of colonialism and racism as only incidentally linked supported the public relations efforts of the Kennedy administration. Kennedy acknowledged links between domestic racial inequality and global imperialism when seeking to win African American votes, regularly bringing up his interest in African affairs and his sympathy for anti-colonial movements during the 1960 campaign.[36] In the sphere of foreign policy, on the other hand, he and his advisers often sought to disavow the connection between European colonial rule and the US racial order. In his speech about the Algerian war on the Senate floor in 1957, which helped him build a reputation as a friend to the decolonizing world, he expressed concern that "Western imperialism" was viewed as a more significant problem than "Soviet imperialism" in the eyes of much of the world.[37]

Once Kennedy took office, the notion that colonialism and racism were inextricably linked posed a problem for the administration's Cold War strategy. G. Mennen Williams, Kennedy's assistant secretary of state for African affairs, noted the same issue after making three trips to the African continent in 1961. He had been chosen for his position in part because of his support for civil rights and his popularity among black voters in his home state of Michigan, and he worked to make the administration take Jim Crow more seriously as a problem for foreign policy.[38] At the same time, he sought to convince African Americans that they must separate the issues of colonialism and racism in order to see the Soviet threat more clearly. "Colonialism, for many Africans, doesn't mean domination of one people by another, but the domination of black men by white men," he claimed in a speech at the Episcopal Society for Cultural and Racial Unity in Chicago. "Such definitions distort and obscure our whole fight for freedom and our struggle against communism."[39] Williams's appeal to African Americans to view colonialism in a narrowly political light, later published in the popular periodical *Negro Digest*, was framed as an effort to secure their loyalty to American foreign policy. As it came in the midst of a speech calling for "racial peace" at home, however, it betrayed a deeper anxiety about the separability of the domestic and foreign spheres of racial governance. Indeed, Williams delivered his speech at a moment when African Americans were rethinking the nature and meaning of colonialism themselves and developing a new language of politics based on an understanding of American racial hierarchy as a form of colonialism.

Black intellectuals and colonial comparison in the Kennedy era

Reflections on the relationship between American racial hierarchy and colonial rule, and between anti-colonial movements and the black freedom struggle in the United States, have a long history in African American thought. Contests over the appropriate language of comparison across these different racial regimes have been recurrent features of African American internationalism. Transnational analogies between race and caste, on the one hand, and racial oppression and imperialism, on the other, framed attempts to forge solidarities among African Americans and South Asians and shaped the development of American social-scientific scholarship on race from the late nineteenth century through the 1960s.[40] During the Second World War, the shared features of European fascism and the Jim Crow system in the United States caused the *Pittsburgh Courier* to call for a "double victory" over both, a call which many African Americans extended to include victory over imperial rule by the Allied powers as well.[41] In the 1950s, the question of the relationship between American racial hierarchy and European colonial rule in Africa was a central concern of the multilingual group of scholars, politicians, and activists centered around the Société Africaine de Culture in Paris and its American counterpart, the American Society for African Culture.[42]

Between the late 1950s and the middle of the 1960s, many black intellectuals began envisioning the relationship between decolonization and the black freedom struggle in a new way. In the late 1950s, the relationship was primarily debated in terms of exemplarity and inspiration. Martin Luther King, Jr., in a sermon delivered after his return from the independence ceremonies in Ghana in 1957, discussed anti-colonial movements as an example from which black Americans might draw inspiration, strategic lessons, and philosophical reinforcement in their parallel struggle for freedom.[43] By the middle of the 1960s, an increasing number of African Americans—including, occasionally, King—began to describe American racism as a form of colonialism. This shift had several crucial effects. First, it provided a new way for black thinkers and activists to call into question the self-image of the United States as a liberal democracy by associating it not with the vanguard of newly independent nation-states—as the first new nation discourse sought to do—but with the recently discredited form of rule these states had thrown off. Secondly, it portrayed the struggles of African Americans in the United States and colonized peoples in Africa and Asia as part of the same global movement, offering civil rights and Black Power groups who sought to build material connections across borders a new language of transnational solidarity not reliant on older notions of the "darker world." Thirdly, it presented a novel social theory of the origins and operation of racial hierarchy in the United States. The remainder of this chapter explores the beginnings of the shift by African American intellectuals and activists toward an understanding of American racism as a form of colonialism and illuminates how this shift operated in part as a response to the first new nation discourse. These debates in the Kennedy era conditioned the much more contentious politics of colonial comparison that accompanied the rise of the Black Power movement in the latter half of the decade.

The emergence of civil rights as a problem for Cold War foreign policy and the recognition that decolonization would transform American racial politics were not simultaneous events. Harold Isaacs, a white scholar at the Massachusetts Institute of Technology Center for International Studies, a leading center for modernization theory, noted in his influential book *The New World of Negro Americans* that, when he began his research in 1957, "it had become common . . . to hear about the effect of American race problems on American standing in the world, but much less common to give heed to the reverse effect, that is, the way in which changes in the world were forcing changes in the American society."[44] By the time of the book's publication in

1963, the "reverse effect" had become equally important. The Pan-Africanist scholar John Henrik Clarke located the moment of transition precisely, at least for his own experience. The protests by African Americans at the UN in New York in February 1961, after the assassination of Patrice Lumumba, marked the moment when "the plight of the Africans still fighting to throw off the yoke of colonialism and the plight of the Afro-Americans, still waiting for a rich, strong and boastful nation to redeem the promise of freedom and citizenship became one and the same."[45] The precepts of modernization theory filtered into Clarke's understanding of the relationship between African Americans and Africans, as both groups, in his mind, faced the dual challenge of restoring their cultures to a place of respect after centuries of Euro-American cultural hegemony while simultaneously adjusting these cultures to the industrialized world. Africans are "looking back and reevaluating the worth of old African ways of life, while concurrently looking forward to the building of modern and industrialized African states," a dualism that was "basically the same" for African Americans.[46] The "new Afro-American nationalists" in organizations like the Nation of Islam and the New Alajo Party in Harlem "feel that the Afro-American constitutes what is tantamount to an exploited colony within a sovereign nation."[47] Clarke's argument and phraseology reflected a growing sense that decolonization offered not only an inspiring example but a new framework for understanding American society.

Although the phrases "domestic colonialism" and "internal colonialism" had been used before, they became keywords of black political thought only in the 1960s, thanks largely to the writings of Harold Cruse. Cruse developed his understanding of the concept of "domestic colonialism" in conversation with leading figures in AMSAC. A former member of the Communist Party, he "transferred [his] cultural loyalties in th[e] direction" of AMSAC in the late 1950s.[48] His relationship with AMSAC's leadership soured quickly. In his debate with J. Saunders Redding at the AMSAC conference in 1959, the latter attacked him for a recently published article. Entitled "An Afro-American's Cultural Views," it argued that African Americans, thanks to the emphasis civil rights leaders placed on "integration," were "out of step with the rest of the colonial world."[49] Redding's critique, published in full a year after the conference in *The New Leader*, insisted that Cruse's attempt "not only to link but to equate the American Negro's struggle for full citizenship with the African Negro's struggle for political independence as the ultimate goal of race nationalism" was a sign of his "total blindness to the truth."[50] Although this conflict with Redding influenced Cruse's break with AMSAC, it only inspired him further to pursue his attempt to envision black American culture in a colonial frame.

The image of the United States as the first new nation featured in Cruse's work as a foil for his developing understanding of African Americans as subjects of a regime of domestic colonialism. In the midst of decolonization, "the Americanism of 1776 becomes an expression of a frightening reactionary military might in 1960," while "the symbol of French liberty of 1789 becomes the barrier to national independence in the hills of Algeria."[51] Far from serving as an inspiration to the decolonizing world, the early history of the United States was a symbol of the exhaustion of the revolutionary traditions of the West as a whole. Beyond his rejection of the anti-colonial self-image of the United States, which was widespread among African Americans of many political persuasions as well as many white Americans on the left, Cruse elaborated an understanding of American racial hierarchy as parallel to the colonial system. While he claimed that the United States was "never a 'colonial' power . . . in the strictest sense of the word"—ignoring both the nation's status as a settler empire and its territorial holdings in the Caribbean, Pacific, and elsewhere—Cruse suggested that "the nature of economic, cultural and political exploitation common to the Negro experience in the United States differs from pure colonialism only in that the Negro maintains a formal kind of halfway citizenship within the nation's geographical boundaries."[52] Cruse went further in his 1962 essay, "Revolutionary Nationalism and the Afro-American," which he published in the New Left journal *Studies on the Left*. Cruse contended that decolonization demanded a complete realignment in the way that African Americans should conceive of their status within the United States. He rejected the frameworks of analysis promoted by both the Communist left and the civil rights leadership. "The Negro," Cruse wrote, was not simply an exploited worker or a second-class citizen of American democracy but rather "the subject of domestic colonialism."[53] This position reflected the shared history of the slave trade and European colonial expansion, which meant that "from the beginning, the American Negro has existed as a colonial being."[54] Even after emancipation, in Cruse's narrative, African Americans only attained the status of "semi-dependent[s]," not recognized as "an integral part of the American nation."[55]

Cruse's argument relied on a broad conception of colonialism. Although he framed his own concept as opposed to the analyses offered by the Marxist left, Cruse's formulation was influenced by the endorsement of "self-determination in the black belt" by the Communist Party of his youth.[56] Detached from the question of territory and looking beyond political sovereignty and alien rule, Cruse's conception of "domestic colonialism" defined colonial status as one of cultural degradation and racialized forms of economic exploitation. Cruse's language both reflected and contributed to the ongoing, international debate over the semantics of colonialism during a period of decolonization. At the same time that Kennedy administration officials were invested in narrowing the term's meaning in order to gain African American support for the Cold War efforts of the United States, Cruse sought to widen it. Though inflected by his experiences in Cuba, which he visited in 1960, and his interpretations of nationalist movements in Africa, Cruse's embrace of the language of colonialism had more to do with his dissatisfaction with prevailing African American political strategies than with a deep engagement with anti-colonial struggles. It reflected his hopes to reorient black politics away from what he saw as a narrow goal of desegregation.

Cruse's writings were, of course, not the only efforts by African Americans in the early 1960s to reframe the black freedom struggle in the terms of decolonization.[57] Even so, his "Revolutionary Nationalism and the Afro-American" wielded considerable influence. The San Francisco-based Afro-American Association, a study group that included Black Panther Party founders Huey P. Newton and Bobby Seale, read and debated Cruse's work. Max Stanford (later Muhammad Ahmad) of the Revolutionary Action Movement cited it as a significant influence on his politics.[58] Most strikingly, Malcolm X was so taken with the article that he carried *Studies on the Left* in the bookstore of his Harlem mosque.[59] Both Cruse's particular writings and the broader intellectual milieu of which they were a part turned the idea of internal colonialism into a touchstone of black politics in the years to come.[60]

Indeed, by the time Stokely Carmichael issued his famous call for "Black Power" in 1966, the language of internal colonialism had gained much more widespread popularity. It became a defining element of black political thought in the Black Power era. Many thinkers and organizations, including those critical of the Black Power movement as well as those associated with it, embraced the language of internal colonialism as a way to understand American racial oppression in terms that departed from the framing of the "Negro problem" that had predominated in American social science and political debate since the early twentieth century.[61] Moreover, Black Power organizations employed the language of internal colonialism in their programs of action for a wide range of political purposes, from local efforts by War on Poverty-funded initiatives to reduce black unemployment to the Black Panther Party's sweeping call for "a United Nations-supervised plebiscite to be held throughout the black colony."[62] If the semantics of colonialism were largely the concern of State Department officials like Francis T. Williamson at the start of the 1960s, black politics brought them to the center of national debate by the latter half of the decade.

* * *

Kennedy's time at the center of national politics, from his 1957 speech on Algeria as a senator to his support for proxy wars in Vietnam and Laos as president, made the decolonizing world a more visible concern in US foreign policy, even if it had already emerged as the central object of strategic interest by the mid-1950s.[63] But foreign policy was not the only sphere in which questions raised by the accelerating pace of decolonization interceded on American public life in the Kennedy era. From modernization theorists to black intellectuals to Kennedy himself, Americans in the late 1950s and early 1960s were deeply concerned with the relationships among global colonial rule, American history, and contemporary American society. Charting the paths of the political languages they developed to understand these relationships, from the image of the United States as the first new nation to analyses of American regimes of internal colonialism, helps to illuminate the transformation decolonization wrought, not only in international society but in the political culture of the United States.

Notes

1 John F. Kennedy, "The United States and Africa: A New Policy for a New Era," in *Summary Report: Second Annual Conference* (New York: American Society of African Culture, 1959), 8.
2 Lawrence Jackson, *The Indignant Generation: A Narrative History of African American Writers and Critics, 1934–1960* (Princeton: Princeton University Press, 2011), 467–69.
3 J. Saunders Redding, "Negro Writing in America," *The New Leader*, May 1960, 8.

4 A brief but compelling attempt to link policy discourse on the decolonizing world with the ideas of anti-colonial thinkers in this period can be found in Vaughn Rasberry, "JFK and the Global Anticolonial Movement," in *The Cambridge Companion to John F. Kennedy*, ed. Andrew Hoberek (Cambridge: Cambridge University Press, 2015), 118–33.
5 The historical literature on modernization is large and growing. For US-focused works, see especially Daniel Immerwahr, *Thinking Small: The United States and the Lure of Community Development* (Cambridge: Harvard University Press, 2015); Nick Cullather, *The Hungry World: America's Cold War Battle against Poverty in Asia* (Cambridge: Harvard University Press, 2010); Nils Gilman, *Mandarins of the Future: Modernization Theory in Cold War America* (Baltimore: The Johns Hopkins University Press, 2003); and Michael Latham, *Modernization as Ideology: American Social Science and "Nation Building" in the Kennedy Era* (Chapel Hill: University of North Carolina Press, 2000).
6 John Foster Dulles, "International Unity," *The Department of State Bulletin* 30, no. 782 (1954): 936.
7 Seymour Martin Lipset, *The First New Nation: The United States in Historical and Comparative Perspective* (New York: W. W. Norton & Company, 1979 [1963]), v.
8 Robert Rakove, *Kennedy, Johnson, and the Nonaligned World* (Cambridge: Cambridge University Press, 2013); Thomas Paterson, ed., *Kennedy's Quest for Victory: American Foreign Policy, 1961–1963* (New York: Oxford University Press, 1989).
9 This vision systematically marginalized indigenous peoples' experiences and relationship to the American state. See David Myer Temin, "Custer's Sins: Vine Deloria Jr. and the Settler-Colonial Politics of Civic Inclusion," *Political Theory* 46, no. 3 (2018): 357–79.
10 Michael Latham, *The Right Kind of Revolution* (Ithaca: Cornell University Press, 2011).
11 An account of postcolonial federations that thoughtfully examines the rhetorical uses of the first new nation analogy is found in Adom Getachew, *Worldmaking after Empire: The Rise and Fall of Self-Determination* (Princeton: Princeton University Press, 2019).
12 UN General Assembly, Resolution 1514, Declaration on the Granting of Independence to Colonial Countries and Peoples, A/RES/1514, December 14, 1960. Available online: http://www.un.org/en/decolonization/declaration.shtml.
13 Ann Stoler urges scholars to treat comparison "not as a methodological problem, but as a historical object" and to attend to how actors have developed regimes of comparison to serve particular political purposes. See Ann Stoler, "Tense and Tender Ties: The Politics of Comparison in North American History and (Post) Colonial Studies," *JAmH* 88, no. 3 (2001): 829–65.
14 Seymour Martin Lipset, "Steady Work: An Academic Memoir," *Annual Review of Sociology* 22 (1996): 15.
15 Seymour Martin Lipset, "The United States—The First New Nation," *Transactions of the Fifth World Congress of Sociology, Washington, D.C., 2–8 September, 1962 Volume 3*, (Louvain: International Sociological Association, 1964), 308.
16 Gilman, *Mandarins*, 72–112.
17 Lipset, *First New Nation*, 2.
18 Benjamin Gerig, "United States Attitude on the Colonial Question," Folder 25, Box 1, Benjamin Gerig Papers, Library of Congress.
19 Ibid.

20 Seymour Martin Lipset, *Political Man: The Social Bases of Politics* (New York: Doubleday, 1960), 92.
21 Conflicts over the meaning of colonialism in this period were paralleled by the rising popularity and shifting meanings of the term "decolonization": Todd Shepard, *The Invention of Decolonization: The Algerian War and the Remaking of France* (Ithaca: Cornell University Press, 2006), 55–81; Stuart Ward, "The European Provenance of Decolonization," *PP* 230 (2016): 227–60.
22 "Final Communique of the Asian-African Conference," in George McTurnan Kahin, *The Asian-African Conference, Bandung* (Ithaca: Cornell University Press, 1956), 82.
23 On the US diplomatic effort to influence the Third World to see Soviet expansion as a form of colonialism, see Jason Parker, "Cold War II: The Eisenhower Administration, the Bandung Conference, and the Reperiodization of the Postwar Era," *DH* 30, no. 5 (2006): 867–92.
24 Francis Williamson, review of *The Idea of Colonialism*, *AHR* 64, no. 2 (1959): 336.
25 Many thanks to Thomas Meaney for sharing an unpublished paper on Emerson, which provided essential information about his early career and political influences.
26 Rupert Emerson, *From Empire to Nation: The Rise to Self-Assertion of Asian and African Peoples* (Boston: Beacon Press, 1960), 387.
27 For more on Laski's influence on transatlantic debates about international institutions, see Or Rosenboim, *The Emergence of Globalism: Visions of World Order in Britain and the United States, 1939–1950* (Princeton: Princeton University Press, 2017), 252–58.
28 Emerson, *Empire to Nation*, 310.
29 Rupert Emerson, "Colonialism," Box 1, Rupert Emerson Papers, Harvard University Archives.
30 Emerson, *Empire to Nation*, 370, 382.
31 Rupert Emerson, "The Character of American Interests in Africa," in *The United States and Africa*, ed. Walter Goldschmidt (New York: The American Assembly, 1958).
32 Emerson, *Empire to Nation*, 341. Lorenzo Veracini, "'Settler Colonialism': Career of a Concept," *JICH* 41, no. 2 (2013): 313–33, emphasizes the ambiguity in how settler colonies were imagined in relation to other forms of colonial rule amid the anti-colonial uprisings of the 1960s.
33 St. Clair Drake, "Why Ghana's Nkrumah Supports Lumumba in Congo," *New Journal and Guide*, October 15, 1960.
34 Horace Cayton, World At Large, *Pittsburgh Courier*, February 13, March 5, and March 26, 1960.
35 David Apter, review of Rupert Emerson, *Empire to Nation*, in *The Journal of Politics* 23, no. 3 (1961): 590–91.
36 James Meriwether, "'Worth a Lot of Negro Votes': Black Voters, Africa, and the 1960 Presidential Campaign," *JAmH* 95, no. 3 (2008): 737–63.
37 Kennedy, "The Challenge of Imperialism: Algeria, July 2, 1957," in *"Let the Word Go Forth": The Speeches, Statements, and Writings of John F. Kennedy*, ed. Theodore Sorensen (New York: Laurel, 1991), 331–37. I largely agree with Anders Stephanson's argument that Kennedy saw the Cold War as "an aspect of the more fundamental conflict in world history between 'imperialism' and 'freedom.'" Stephanson, "Senator John F. Kennedy: Anti-Imperialism and Utopian Deficit," *JAS* 48, no. 1 (2014): 1–24.
38 Thomas Noer, *Soapy: A Biography of G. Mennen Williams* (Ann Arbor: The University of Michigan Press, 2005), 247.
39 G. Mennen Williams, "Why Racial Peace is Imperative," *Negro Digest* 11, no. 12 (1962): 30.

40 Nico Slate, *Colored Cosmopolitanism: The Shared Struggle for Freedom in the United States and India* (Cambridge: Harvard University Press, 2012).
41 Penny Von Eschen, *Race against Empire: Black Americans and Anticolonialism, 1937–1957* (Ithaca: Cornell University Press, 1997); and Brenda Plummer, *Rising Wind: Black Americans and U.S. Foreign Affairs, 1935–1960* (Chapel Hill: University of North Carolina Press, 1996).
42 John Munro, *The Anticolonial Front: The African American Freedom Struggle and Global Decolonization, 1945–1960* (Cambridge: Cambridge University Press, 2017), 239–45.
43 Martin Luther King, Jr., "'The Birth of a New Nation,' Sermon Delivered at Dexter Avenue Baptist Church, April 7, 1957," in *The Papers of Martin Luther King, Jr., Volume IV*, ed. Clayborne Carson et al. (Berkeley: University of California Press, 2000), 155–67.
44 Harold Isaacs, *The New World of Negro Americans* (New York: Viking Press, 1963), x.
45 John Henrik Clarke, "The New Afro-American Nationalism," *Freedomways* 1, no. 3 (1961): 285.
46 Ibid., 291.
47 Ibid., 293, 295.
48 Cruse to James Harris, January 20, 1959, Folder 6, Box 2, Harold Cruse Papers, Tamiment Library and Robert F. Wagner Labor Archives, New York. On the place of AMSAC in the broader universe of black internationalism in this period, see Merve Fejzula, "Black Cultural Citizenship between State and Nation, 1947–66" (PhD diss., University of Cambridge, forthcoming).
49 Harold Cruse, "An Afro-American's Cultural Views," in *Rebellion or Revolution?* (New York: William Morrow, 1968), 40. For an account of Redding's critique, see Jackson, *Indignant Generation*, 468.
50 Redding, "Negro Writing in America," 8.
51 Harold Cruse, "Cuba and the North American Negro," Folder 1, Box 4, Harold Cruse Papers.
52 Cruse, "Negro Nationalism's New Wave," in *Rebellion or Revolution?*, 69.
53 Cruse, "Revolutionary Nationalism and the Afro-American," in *Rebellion or Revolution?*, 74.
54 Ibid., 76.
55 Ibid., 76, 77.
56 Harvey Klehr and William Tompson, "Self-Determination in the Black Belt: Origins of a Communist Policy," *Labor History* 30, no. 3 (1989): 354–66.
57 See, especially, Cynthia Young, *Soul Power: Culture, Radicalism, and the Making of a U.S. Third World Left* (Durham: Duke University Press, 2006).
58 Donna Jean Murch, *Living for the City: Migration, Education, and the Rise of the Black Panther Party in Oakland, California* (Chapel Hill: The University of North Carolina Press, 2010), 71–96; Muhammad Ahmad, *We Will Return in the Whirlwind: Black Radical Organizations, 1960–1975* (Chicago: Charles H. Kerr Publishing, 2008).
59 Cedric Johnson, "Between Revolution and the Racial Ghetto: Harold Cruse and Harry Haywood Debate Class Struggle and the 'Negro Question,' 1962–8," *Historical Materialism* 24, no. 1 (2016): 12–13; Van Gosse, "More than Just a Politician: Notes on the Life and Times of Harold Cruse," in *Harold Cruse's The Crisis of the Negro Intellectual Reconsidered*, ed. Jerry Watts (New York: Routledge, 2004), 26–27.
60 On the rise of the "anti-colonial vernacular" in the Black Power movement, see Sean Malloy, *Out of Oakland: Black Panther Party Internationalism during the Cold War* (Ithaca: Cornell University Press, 2017).

61 As Brandon Terry notes, the semantic shift toward the colonial analogy in the Black Power era reflected the "felt need for more adequate metaphors to characterize those *structural* and *cultural* dimensions of the racial order," dimensions that were not captured in the vocabularies of "prejudice," "discrimination," or "second-class citizenship." See Brandon Terry, "Requiem for a Dream: The Problem-Space of Black Power," in *To Shape a New World: Essays on the Political Philosophy of Martin Luther King, Jr.*, ed. Tommie Shelby and Brandon Terry (Cambridge: Harvard University Press, 2018), 313–14.

62 "Ten-Point Program: What We Want, What We Believe," in Curtis Austin, *Up Against the Wall: Violence in the Making and Unmaking of the Black Panther Party* (Fayetteville: University of Arkansas Press, 2008), 355.

63 Robert McMahon, "How the Periphery Became the Center: The Cold War, the Third World, and the Transformation in US Strategic Thinking," in *Foreign Policy at the Periphery*, ed. Bevan Sewell et al. (Lexington: The University Press of Kentucky, 2017), 19–35.

2

John F. Kennedy as Viewed by Africans

Philip E. Muehlenbeck

In a recent essay comparing the African policies of US presidents ranging from Theodore Roosevelt through Barack Obama, Annar Cassam, a Tanzanian who was the former personal assistant to Julius Nyerere and later a high-ranking official at UNESCO, derided the United States for its actions toward Africa. He criticized Roosevelt for leading a hunting expedition that killed nearly 12,000 animals after he left the Oval Office. She labeled Richard Nixon as racist and claimed that he cared even less for Africans than Roosevelt cared about the continent's animals. Ronald Reagan and George H. W. Bush came under fire, too, for helping to cause "mass poverty and serious damage to health and education services." He categorized Bill Clinton's and Barack Obama's administrations as having "benign neglect" for Africa. Cassam writes that John F. Kennedy was the "one, remarkable exception" to this string of American ambivalence (or worse) toward Africa. According to Cassam, Kennedy took great interest in the continent when the "rest of the elite, in government or academia, had very little interest" and became the only US president who was "a friend of Africa."[1]

Kennedy became the thirty-fifth president of the United States of America during an exciting and optimistic time in Africa. The first wave of African independence had begun on March 6, 1957, when Kwame Nkrumah led Ghana to independence. By the time of Kennedy's inauguration in January 1961, eighteen more African states had left French, British, and Belgian colonial control. Kennedy's sympathy for African nationalism, as a senator and on the presidential campaign trail, had helped swell the African continent with hope that under his leadership Washington would be more responsive to its needs. Once in office, Kennedy devoted more time and effort toward relations with Africa than any other American president. For him, courting African nationalism was essential for competing against the Soviet Union. He saw the developing world as the decisive battlefield of the Cold War, and criticized his predecessor, Dwight D. Eisenhower, for having ignored the "sleeping giant" of African nationalism.[2]

Kennedy opened up the executive mansion to receive eleven African heads of state in 1961, ten in 1962, and another seven in 1963.[3] He averaged meeting nearly one African head of state per month—Eisenhower one African leader per year. As of 2019, Kennedy had met more African leaders per month than any other US president.[4]

The purpose of this chapter is twofold. First, it briefly outlines how Kennedy invested heavily in new policies as well as symbolics in his relations with African leaders, and how this could strengthen the latter's domestic legitimacy. Secondly, it examines and explains how Kennedy was viewed by a wide range of Africans, from the first generation of postcolonial leaders to the leaders of white minority ruled countries, and to the "man on the street" in rural African villages.

Kennedy's "courting of African nationalism"

When Kennedy took office, the UN General Assembly was in plenary session. Leaders from across the world were in New York City, and virtually all wanted to visit the new president. Kennedy, though, had a focus: Africans. "If African leaders want to meet me, good. Invite them down here."[5] Africans would continue to visit the White House at an unprecedented pace throughout Kennedy's term, oftentimes at Kennedy's own initiative. It was with purposeful symbolic significance that Nkrumah made the first official visit by a foreign head of state to the Kennedy White House, and that Tunisia's Habib Bourguiba was accorded the first state visit.

With his natural charm, grace, and informality, Kennedy was able to put his African guests at ease and convey his profound sympathy for African nationalism. Eisenhower rarely took the time to meet with African leaders, and when he did, African leaders often complained that they were not shown the same level of respect and pomp and circumstance as leaders from other parts of the world. Kennedy was a study in contrast.[6] After each White House meeting, he brought the visiting African dignitary upstairs to his family's private quarters and introduced them to his wife and children, a gesture that deeply touched his visitors.

Kennedy also encouraged African leaders to correspond with him personally, and engaged in extensive personal correspondence with dozens of African heads of state. This, too, stood in stark contrast to the Eisenhower administration. And Kennedy won the admiration of African leaders for attempting to see African problems as they themselves did. Cassam writes that he "was never arrogant or patronising [toward African leaders] but always generous in his acknowledgement of their struggles for freedom. . . . Above all, he treated them as equals."[7]

Kennedy's eagerness to meet with African leaders differed so much from his predecessors that this in itself made for front-page news throughout Africa. Even Africans critical of his policies were impressed with his commitment to meeting with visiting African dignitaries.[8] As a result, during the Kennedy administration, the United States was for the first time viewed as sympathetic to the aspirations of African nationalism. In Africa, Kennedy became well respected for his aggressive efforts to find common ground with popular Pan-Africanist leaders like Sékou Touré, Gamal Abdul Nasser, and Nkrumah, all of whom had been shunned by the Eisenhower administration.

African leaders used their relationship with Kennedy to boost their legitimacy at home. The Guinean government wanted to affiliate itself with the ideas and image of the young American president. Pictures of a 1959 meeting between Guinean president Sékou Touré and Kennedy, at Disneyland, when Kennedy was still a senator, were "displayed even in the smallest villages" and were highly prized by Guineans. Stationed as an Operation Crossroads volunteer in the small town of Mamou, about 100 miles northeast of the capital Conakry, in 1961, American college student Vince Farley recalls pictures of Kennedy in the most surprising places. "We'd be walking five miles on bruce trails and we'd go into a little hut and there was a picture of Kennedy and Touré." Farley saw no pictures of other foreign leaders, like Nikita Khrushchev, Fidel Castro, or even Touré's friend Nkrumah. Yet, "You'd go into a little village and there would be a mud hut. Inside there would be a calendar on the wall with a picture of Kennedy."[9]

African reaction to Kennedy's civil rights bill

In June 1963 Kennedy addressed the American people asking for a civil rights bill. As he had hoped, his proposed civil rights bill was widely applauded in the developing world, especially Africa. Many of Africa's first-generation leaders such as Nkrumah and Nnamdi Azikiwe, Nigeria's first president, had been educated in the United States and experienced firsthand the pervasiveness of American racism—perhaps giving them extra appreciation for Kennedy's pro-active proposal of the bill. Nkrumah "was overcome with emotion and sent Kennedy his sincere and profound thanks."[10] Ghana's press, previously critical of US racial policies, began to acknowledge that Kennedy's leadership was moving in the right direction and that his efforts were sincere.[11] Nkrumah authorized the United States Information Agency (USIA) to build exhibits titled, "President Kennedy Calls for Equal Rights for US Negro Citizens" for display in the central libraries of Accra and Kumasi; the municipal libraries of Sekondi, Cape Coast, Koforidua, Ito, and Tale; and other locations in Accra, including the YMCA center, the Boy Scout and Girl Scout centers, and the USIA library.[12]

Kenyan students studying in the United States sent letters home filled with excitement over Kennedy's civil rights address. "In practically every letter, reference was not only to the administrative policies of the Kennedy Administration, but also to Kennedy himself as a person, and the impact that he was making as a President on the American population, and on American policy" remembered nationalist Tom Mboya.[13] Assistant Secretary of State for African Affairs G. Mennen Williams later remembered, "Africans saw that [Kennedy] was determined to have the federal government assure equal rights for all its citizens."[14]

A State Department report on African reactions to the status of civil rights in the United States found that "the President's words and the President's actions were clearly understood and appreciated."[15] Ambassador Philip Kaiser reported from Dakar that Senegalese president Lépold Sédar Senghor was warmly praising Kennedy. He "understands 'revolutionary' significance of what [the] President is trying to accomplish. He was following developments closely and was confident that thanks to President's leadership cause of morality and justice would win out."[16] Sudan's foreign minister said that he was "greatly impressed by [the] drive of President Kennedy and [his] administration and [the] scope of [their] program."[17] Similarly, Nyasaland's President Hastings Banda was pleased with Kennedy's handling of America's racial problems and considered the American president "courageous in sticking his political neck out in contrast to previous Presidents who hid behind state's rights."[18]

Similar reactions were recorded across the African continent. Some African leaders went as far as comparing Kennedy to Abraham Lincoln. Presidents Gregoire Kayibanda of Rwanda, Mobito Keita of Mali, David Dacko of the Central African Republic, Amadou Ahidjo of Cameroon, and Moktar Ould Daddah of Mauritania were among those who praised Kennedy's "courageous policies" and supported them "without reservations."[19] From Monrovia, Liberian president William Tubman congratulated Kennedy for "the bold and courageous action you have taken at this time to insure to all of your fellow citizens equality of rights, privileges, and opportunities."[20] After returning from a trip to Africa, Williams reported that the nation's position in Africa remained "strong because of our past policy and President Kennedy's image."[21] Most of Africa's leaders appreciated the Kennedy administration's efforts to end racial discrimination and attributed these efforts in large part to the president himself.

The view of Kennedy in white minority southern Africa

Kennedy was viewed quite differently by the white minority regimes of apartheid South Africa, Rhodesia, and Portuguese Africa: as nothing less than a threat to their way of life. When Williams visited Northern Rhodesia, he was punched in the jaw upon arrival by a white Rhodesian upset with the Kennedy administration policy.[22] Likewise, the South African government viewed Kennedy's efforts to court African nationalism, criticize minority rule in southern Africa, and advocate for civil rights at home with great trepidation. It felt that Kennedy's administration was "blinded by hatred for South Africa," and that by courting the nationalist leaders of sub-Saharan Africa, the United States was siding with radical anti-American governments that were unwilling or unable to stand up against international communism. This came at the expense of what South Africa perceived as its own, and Rhodesia's and Portuguese Africa's stable, Christian, pro-American, and fiercely anti-communist regimes.[23] After the Bay of Pigs invasion in April 1961, some South African government officials even feared that the US military might invade southern Africa and overthrow the apartheid regime.[24]

Even in the wake of Kennedy's assassination, the South African press ran stories critical of his African policies. South African Foreign Minster Eric Louw reportedly labeled the slain president "an unremitting enemy of South Africa and an opponent of her race policies."[25] Pretoria's hatred for Kennedy, however, was not so much a result of unsatisfactory bilateral relations, but rather a byproduct of growing ties between Washington and black Africa and his administration's advancement of civil rights within the United States.

The Portuguese government, irked that the Kennedy administration had become the first US administration to vote against Lisbon's continued colonial presence in Africa at the UN, had even more animosity toward Kennedy than the South Africans or Rhodesians. After Kennedy's assassination, Portugal was one of only two nations in the world (communist China being the other) which did not send its condolences to Washington.²⁶ Six years later, Richard Nixon, upon becoming president, told Portuguese foreign minister Franco Nogueira, "Just remember, I'll never do to you what Kennedy did."²⁷ While revisionist historians may not view Kennedy's handling of white minority rule in southern Africa as much of a departure in US foreign policy, Africans (both black and white), Lisbon, and Richard Nixon all surely did.

African reactions to Kennedy's assassination

The response of the majority of black Africans to Kennedy's death was quite different. When the news broke during a diplomatic reception in Abidjan, President Felix Houphouët-Boigny "sat plunged in gloom throughout." The British ambassador reported that he was "struck by the genuine, and really personal sense of grief, that seemed to be felt by all the Africans present."²⁸ Houphouët-Boigny was so moved by Kennedy's assassination that he declared a two-day national holiday of mourning in the Ivory Coast.

In Guinea, a country with which Washington had poor relations before Kennedy took office, Sékou Touré said, "I have lost my only true friend in the outside world."²⁹ Guinea's ambassador to the United States sent a telegram to Secretary of State Dean Rusk expressing his country's "heartfelt condolences," adding "our sorrow is tremendous over the loss of this hero of whose courage and wisdom the world stood in such great need."³⁰ In Ghana, Nkrumah telephoned Ambassador William Mahoney to verify whether the news of Kennedy's assassination was true and to ask if he could do anything. Mahoney had been a close personal friend to Kennedy and was "beside himself with grief." He asked the Ghanaian president to "Say a Hail Mary" to which Nkrumah, his voice breaking, whispered, "I am already on my knees."³¹ Later Nkrumah's eyes swelled with tears as he talked with Williams about what had happened in Dallas.³² In a moving fifteen-minute eulogy, he told his countrymen:

> In spite of his brief term of office, President Kennedy had made an indelible mark on the history of our time. He will be remembered as a distinguished champion for peace and the rights of man. His inspiration, his tremendous courage, his integrity and the warmth of his feeling for his fellow men will be a beacon to those who share his convictions and aspirations. John Kennedy's achievements in international affairs have been remarkable. We in Africa will remember him above all for his uncompromising stand against racial and religious bigotry, intolerance, and injustice. . . . His presence, his sense of understanding and appreciation of the grave issues confronting our world, and his genuine interest in the solution of the problems confronting developing countries made me regard him . . . as a man whom the world could expect great things, as a man who could become one of the most important leaders of our time.³³

Two weeks after Kennedy's death, British economist Barbara Ward visited Nkrumah in his office. On his desk was a picture of the Kennedy family that he had received as a present from Jacqueline Kennedy. With tears in his eyes he said, "I have written her, and I have prayed for them both. Nothing shocked me so deeply as this." The Ghanaian president "had always felt that if there were misunderstandings between Ghana and the United States, they would be resolved if only he could get through to Kennedy, whom he saw as his friend, the friend of Africa."[34]

Similarly, Algerian Premier Ben Bella phoned the American ambassador in Algiers. In tears and "obviously shaken," he said "I can't believe it. Believe me, I'd rather it happen to me than him."[35] Without Kennedy, Ben Bella saw little hope for friendly relations between Washington and Algiers. According to US ambassador William Porter, the Algerian premier "ascribed to Kennedy everything he thought good in the United States: the fight against the big trusts, against the segregationists."[36] Years later Ben Bella recalled: "Kennedy seemed to represent the moderate element, in opposition to the bellicose policy of his country . . . . I remember that when the telegram came with the news . . . I leapt to my feet, staggered by the news. Without waiting to summon my cabinet, I telephoned at once to the radio station. I dictated a statement in which I immediately denounced the racialist and police-organized machinations of which Kennedy had been the victim."[37] A few days later, in the presence of his entire cabinet, diplomatic corps, an honor guard, and thousands of the general public, Ben Bella named a large square in the Algiers suburb of El-Bier in the memory of Kennedy, the first time such an honor had been bestowed upon a non-African.[38]

Delegations from twenty-seven African nation-states would attend Kennedy's state funeral. Among the attendees was Haile Selassie, emperor of Ethiopia, nine African foreign ministers, sixteen African ambassadors, the president of Algeria, the prime minister of Tunisia, prince of Morocco, and vice president of Liberia.[39] This was an impressive showing of high-level African representatives given the short turn around between Kennedy's death and funeral as well as the relative difficulty of travel between Africa and the United States in 1963.

Many of Africa's leaders suspected that US racism was behind Kennedy's death. David Dacko, president of the Central African Republic, described Kennedy's death as "an affliction which strikes the whole black race."[40] The president of Gabon's Supreme Court called the American president "a martyr of the blacks."[41] Similarly, the Nigerian president Azikiwe called Kennedy's assassination "a setback for those who believe in fair play and social justice for the black race all over the world."[42] Many other African leaders, Ben Bella, Nkrumah, and Nasser included, saw Kennedy as a man who strove for the liberty and dignity of all human beings without distinction of race or color. Following his assassination it was widely believed throughout the continent that Kennedy's death was perpetrated in response to his support for African nationalism and/or domestic civil rights.[43]

The feeling of loss was not limited to Africa's leaders but felt by common people as well. The news of Kennedy's assassination spread rapidly. From Algiers to Dar es Salaam, from Cairo to Accra, and even in the most distant and isolated villages, Africans mourned. In Nairobi, 6,000 people packed into a cathedral for Kennedy's memorial service.[44] Mboya reported:

> The shock that was registered in this country was particularly noticeable because it was the first time that the death of a foreigner, and a foreign head of State, had registered so sharply. It was as though someone very close at home had died and

people reacted spontaneously in practically every little town and village in this country... I saw very clearly that President Kennedy's personality had penetrated deep in the villages quite remote from the normal political atmosphere of the country.... [In Africa] President Kennedy offered much excitement and hope in the future. [Kenyans] saw in him a young man who understood the modern world and the problems of the younger generation.... Another thing is that people saw in President Kennedy, in Africa at any rate, a very enlightened approach insofar as the Cold War was concerned... [Kennedy] gave the world that much more hope.[45]

In Cairo, among the messages left by thousands of mourners visiting the US embassy was that "Kennedy was the first American President who really understood the Afro-Asian world."[46] The film of Kennedy's funeral was shown four times on Cairo television.[47] In Conakry, the US embassy reported: "People expressed their grief without restraint, and just about everybody in Guinea seemed to have fallen under the spell of the courageous young hero of far away, the slayer of the dragons of discrimination, poverty, ignorance, and war."[48] In the Ivory Coast, a national state mass was held at the same time as the funeral in Washington. James Wine, the American ambassador in Abidjan, "didn't realize the depth of the penetration of the Kennedy personality into the darkest corners of the earth" until the assassination. When he arrived at the embassy, there was an Ivorian standing and waiting to see him. The visitor said, "Well, I have no business coming here. I run a little store up in a place called Bouke (a city about 40 km from Abidjan). I came here his morning simply to say that I never knew President Kennedy, I never saw President Kennedy, but he was my friend."[49]

At the time of Kennedy's assassination, Holden Roberto, the Angolan rebel and nationalist leader, was lobbying the UN to take a firmer stand against Portuguese colonialism. It was the fourth consecutive year in which he had traveled to New York to argue his case, and it also became his last. After Kennedy's death he returned to Africa "broken hearted," realizing that without Kennedy's leadership the Western powers would no longer pressure Lisbon.[50]

"Not even the death of Dag Hammarskjold dismayed Africans as much as did the death of John Kennedy" editorialized *West Africa*. "It was not the late President's efforts to integrate America's Negro citizens into the nation which made Africa's leaders feel his death to be such a terrible loss," the journal continued:

Those efforts, brave though they were, have still not achieved their object, which, indeed, is still far off. It was, instead, Mr. Kennedy's work in reducing world tension, and his deep interest in Africa—which many African leaders, including Dr. Nkrumah, Sir Abubakar, and President Sekou Toure, knew at first hand from conversations with him—which made Africans feel that he was a sincere friend.[51]

Pictures of the slain American president were quickly displayed in both African public buildings and private homes. *West Africa* printed a few of the "many long letters" it received.[52] "Oh! What a blow to world peace," began one lament. "Now that the youthful, ever-cheerful, smiling President has fallen at the hands of the assassin, the best the world, and especially the youth of the world, can do is to struggle to uphold the ideals for which the President stood."⁵³ Another writer remembered Kennedy as "an unflinching supporter of the developing nations, ready and willing to help them to develop educationally and economically. His speeches at the United Nations and elsewhere were always sincere, fluent and rich in literary culture." The writer continued by comparing Kennedy to two of history's most respected men, "It would not be out of place to describe him as an amalgam of Abraham Lincoln and Mahatma Gandhi, a devoted apostle of social reform and a dedicated man of peace. We shall never see his like again."⁵⁴

Africans sensed that Kennedy's sympathy for their cause was sincere, and appreciated that he viewed their continent as something more than just a pawn in the Cold War chess match. He was "held in high esteem by almost everybody in black Africa. They thought he cared. They had access to him," remembered a former State Department Africanist.⁵⁵ Similarly, USIA officer Stephen Paterson Belcher writes that many Africans he met considered Kennedy a "godparent . . . Kennedy had successfully changed our foreign policy alignment from an East-West rivalry to a North-South struggle for mutual understanding and cooperation. The Africans appreciated this. Every country in Africa looked upon Kennedy as their particular friend and supporter."⁵⁶

Days after the tragic events in Dallas, the British ambassador to the Ivory Coast telegraphed London that Kennedy would soon join Patrice Lumumba as an African martyr. The American president had "captured the imagination of the Africans both because of his youth and 'dynamism' and because they regarded him as responsible for the policy of standing up to the (racism in the American) South." He concluded by predicting that if Lyndon B. Johnson continued Kennedy's Africa policies, "the President's death may be found to have given quite a boost to the American effort in this part of the world."⁵⁷

Unfortunately, this prediction would not prove to be true. American policy makers generally neglected Africa following Kennedy's death. Nonetheless, many Africans still fondly remember Kennedy's legacy. Sargent Shriver wrote how common it was for him to walk into an African village hut, years after his brother-in-law's death, and find a picture of Kennedy—torn from a newspaper and placed beside the family album or mementos.⁵⁸ Visiting Ethiopia, Kenya, and Ghana in the late 1980s, Harris Wofford found "that in the homes of ordinary people no other American president or world leader had joined the faded photographs of John Kennedy."⁵⁹ Even Cameroonian president Ahidjo kept a picture of Kennedy in the reception area of his residential compound decades after Kennedy's death which he would point out to his guests by explaining, "Well, there's my hero."⁶⁰

Streets, schools, and parks all across Africa were renamed in honor of the slain American president, his likeness soon graced African currency and stamps, and his gravesite at Arlington National Cemetery became a site of pilgrimage for African leaders visiting Washington. Vince Farley, the aforementioned Operation Crossroads volunteer, subsequently had a distinguished career in the State Department, serving in the Bureau of African Affairs and in US embassies in Niger, Mauritania, and the Ivory Coast. He remembers that whenever the US government gave grants to build schools in Africa,

> You'd go to the village and there would be a flag covering the plaque on the wall. I never knew what name they were going to name the school, but I could tell you

that there were only three possibilities: John F. Kennedy, Martin Luther King, or maybe Jimmy Carter—but probably John F. Kennedy . . . . This was the village elders saying: "We have received this grant from the US government and we're going to name the school after Kennedy, not after an African leader."[61]

William Attwood wrote after leaving his post:

A lot of the good will for our policies is still due to what he said and did in those two-and-a-half years . . . . For example, there are many people in Kenya named after him. Even though he was never in Kenya, many people felt that he was the first American leader who ever really understood Africa.[62]

Similarly, Phillip Pillsbury Jr. wrote about his time serving at the American embassy in Bamako, Mali:

I remember that I was in the interior, or the bush as they call it there in January '64, and I spoke Bambala at the time. I'd learned the local language, and I was talking with a man in a village and he started to talk about Kennedy, and I was astonished. He actually started to cry because he had associated himself with Kennedy, not from hearing the news directly on the Voice [of America], but rather from what he heard from the village wise man, the Marabou . . . . This villager was to me an extraordinary indication of the appeal of John F. Kennedy.[63]

Conclusion

On November 22, 1963, the mutual understanding that had developed between the United States and many of the leaders of Africa died at Parkland Memorial Hospital in Dallas, Texas. During Johnson's presidency, the level of American aid to Africa quickly dropped as the new president had little personal interest in the continent and quickly became preoccupied with the Vietnam War. The Johnson administration effectively ended the era of major American funding for African development, as the new president, in the words of Harris Wofford, radically "converted American policies in Africa."[64] Johnson's attitude toward, and knowledge of, Africa can be summed up by the question he asked Averell Harriman about Ghana, "Tell me, Av, what's the goddam name of that place?"[65]

Sékou Touré spoke for many African nationalists when he informed Williams that he was skeptical whether Johnson would continue Kennedy's policy of pressuring the remaining white governments of Africa to accept majority rule. "The only people I have ever trusted were you and Kennedy," he told Williams.[66] Furthermore, he, as for example Nkrumah and Nyerere, was demoralized by Johnson's role in ensuring that former Katangan separatist, Moise Tshombe, became Congolese prime minister. The Johnson administration's hiring of white mercenaries to aid Tshombe prompted Nyerere to fume, "There are three dead men who, if they should come to life today, would ask, *What* is happening? They are President Kennedy, Dag Hammarskjold and

Patrice Lumumba."⁶⁷ Adlai Stevenson, US ambassador to the UN, lamented that under Kennedy, Washington was thought of as a champion of Africa, but under Johnson it had become as despised as the Belgians.⁶⁸

Africans across the continent bewailed the fact that the new president had reestablished the old Eisenhower policy of supporting Portugal and South Africa in staving off African nationalism.⁶⁹ The Africanists that Kennedy had brought into his administration no longer had a voice in Washington. The continent was once again relegated to the background of American foreign policy, and the "boost" that the British ambassador predicted for the American image in Africa soon fizzled out.

Still, Johnson proved more sympathetic to Africa's needs than many of the American policymakers who followed him. By the late 1960s both Congress and the Nixon administration had revolted against what it perceived as Kennedy's excessive commitment to Africa, cutting economic assistance to the continent to 29 percent of its 1962 level and concentrating aid on only ten countries.⁷⁰ Zambian president Kenneth Kaunda lashed out against Washington's neglect during a 1975 White House state dinner in his honor. He lamented the direction that America's policy toward Africa had veered off on since Kennedy's death. He was nostalgic for the days when

> an America whose Assistant Secretary for African Affairs, "Soapy" Williams, could be slapped in the face by a white reactionary on our soil and yet, undaunted, still smile, still stand by American principles of freedom, justice and national independence based on majority rule.
>
> Yes, the reactionaries hated Americans for spoiling the natives, as they would say, for helping dismantle colonialism.
>
> We ask and wonder what has happened to America. Have the principles changed? The aspirations of the oppressed have not changed at all. In desperation their anger has exploded their patience. Their resolve to fight, if peaceful negotiations are impossible, is born by our history.⁷¹

This abandonment of Kennedy's African policies significantly contributed to the deteriorating image of the United States in the developing world. After Kennedy's death Washington became increasingly obsessed over the Cold War, turning its back on nationalist movements in the developing world and instead choosing to support autocratic dictators and fund destructive proxy wars. This caused many of the same people who had once held Kennedy, and by extension the United States, in such high esteem to begin to chafe at Washington's neglect for their plight.

Kennedy supported African nationalism before 1960 and before virtually any other American in public office. His support for African nationalism stemmed from a combination of strategic long-term considerations regarding the necessity of promoting a positive image of the United States in the developing regions of the world and a moral conviction that as a great power the United States should aid the fledgling states of the world. In doing so he cemented his place in the history, hearts, and minds of Africa and fulfilled the prophecy made by the editors of *West Africa* only a week after this death, "no American can again win in Africa the status of the President who understood so well, and who shared, the African attitude to the world."[72]

Africans revered Kennedy for his sympathy for their causes—support for African nationalism, advocacy of a civil rights bill within the United States, and opposition to white minority rule in Africa—even more than was warranted. The Camelot mystique was strongly felt in Africa, probably even more so than in the United States. As one US foreign service who served on the continent later observed, "Africans were revolutionaries overthrowing colonial powers—and that is what Kennedy was in their mind, he was a revolutionary leader—young and overthrowing the colonial powers. That was their image of him."[73] This is not to say that Kennedy did not merit the admiration that Africans gave him, but rather that his legacy on the continent was aided by both his magnetic public persona and tragic death. While the differences in his policies toward Africa were recognized, for Africans it was Kennedy's *words* and *style* that spoke louder than his *actions*. The main factor in Kennedy's success over the continent was the fact that through his personal diplomacy and use of political symbolism he was able to convince Africans that he was genuinely interested in their continent.

Notes

1 Annar Cassam, "JFK: Dreams for Africa" (2013) (unpublished essay in the possession of the author).
2 For an in-depth study, see Philip Muehlenbeck, *Betting on the Africans: John F. Kennedy's Courting of African Nationalist Leaders* (New York: Oxford University Press, 2012).
3 Arthur Schlesinger Jr., *A Thousand Days: John F. Kennedy in the White House* (Boston: Houghton Mifflin, 1965), 558.
4 *Visits to the U.S. by Foreign Heads of State and Government,* The United States State Department's Office of the Historian. Available online: https://history.state.gov/departmenthistory/visits (accessed March 23, 2017). Analysis by author using data found on aforementioned site. Data was computed by adding number of visits from African Heads of State during a president's term, minus brief meetings at the UN General Assembly. The number of visits was then divided by the number of months each president served in office to reach a composite average of the number of African heads of state each president received per month. The results were as follows: Kennedy 0.823 per month, George W. Bush 0.6354, Carter 0.583, George H. W. Bush 0.563, Reagan 0.427, Ford 0.345, Nixon 0.343, Clinton 0.292, Johnson 0.230, Obama 0.202, Eisenhower 0.083.
5 Kennedy, quoted in G. Mennen Williams, *Africa for the Africans* (Grand Rapids: William Eerdmans Publishing, 1969), 161. See also Letter, Assistant Secretary of State for African Affairs Williams to Secretary of State Dean Rusk, April 13, 1961, Folder "Trips-Status Report-Africa, 1961-1962," Box 24, Records of G. Mennen Williams (RGMW), General Records of the Department of State (GRDS), Record Group (RG) 59, National Archives, College Park (NARA).
6 Muehlenbeck, *Africans*, especially chapters 1–2.

7   Cassam, "JFK," 5.
8   Thomas Noer, *Soapy: A Biography of G. Mennen Williams* (Ann Arbor: University of Michigan Press, 2005), 232.
9   Vince Farley, interview with author, December 10, 2003, via telephone.
10 David Rooney, *Kwame Nkrumah: The Political Kingdom in the Third World* (New York: St. Martin's Press, 1988), 229.
11 "Status Report of African Reactions to Civil Rights in the United States" Memorandum from National Security Council Member William H. Brubeck to National Security Advisor McGeorge Bundy, July 12, 1963, Folder "Civil Rights, 7/12/63-7/19/63," Box 295: "Subjects Series," National Security Files (NSF), John F. Kennedy Presidential Library, Boston (JFKL).
12 Telegram, USIA Accra to USIA Washington, August 7, 1963, Folder "Ghana," Box "Record Relating to Exhibits in Foreign Countries," Records of the US Information Agency, RG 306, NARA.
13 Tom Mboya, recorded interview by Gordon P. Hagberg, March 10, 1965, John F. Kennedy Oral History Program (JFKOHP), JFKL.
14 Williams, *Africa*, 175.
15 "Status Report of African Reactions to Civil Rights in the United States," July 6, 1963, Folder "Civil Rights," Box 16, "Subject File, 1961-1966," RGMW, 1961-1966, GRDS, NARA.
16 Telegram, Philip Kaiser, US ambassador to Senegal, to Rusk, June 21, 1963, RGMW, GRDS, NARA.
17 Telegram, William Rountree, US ambassador to Sudan, to Rusk, June 27, 1963, RGMW, GRDS, NARA.
18 Telegram, US embassy in Nyasaland, to Rusk, June 27, 1963, RGMW, GRDS, NARA.
19 Telegram, US embassy in Mauritania, to Rusk, June 24, 1963, Telegram, US embassy in the Central African Republic to Rusk, June 18, 1963, Telegram, William Handley, US ambassador to Mali to Rusk, July 3, 1963, Telegram, US embassy in Yaounde, Cameroon, to Department of State, July 8, 1963, and Telegram, Charles Withers, Ambassador to Rwanda, to Rusk, July 8, 1963, all in RGMW, GRDS, NARA.
20 "Status Report of African Reactions to Civil Rights in the United States" Memorandum from National Security Council Member William H. Brubeck to Bundy, July 12, 1963, Folder "Civil Rights, 7/12/63-7/19/63," Box 295: "Subjects Series," NSF, JFKL.
21 Williams, quoted in Mary Dudziak, "Birmingham, Addis Ababa, and the Image of America," in *Window on Freedom*, ed. Brenda Plummer (Chapel Hill: University of North Carolina Press, 2003), 194.
22 *Time*, September 8, 1961.
23 South African foreign minister Eric Louw, quoted in Thomas Noer, *Cold War and Black Liberation* (Columbia: University of Missouri Press, 1985), 149.
24 Letter, South African ambassador to Washington W.C. Naudé to Louw, April 27, 1961, folder "United States of America: Policy in Africa, volume 6," BTS 1/33/8/3, National Archives of South Africa, Pretoria.
25 Telegram, John Dunrossil, British Embassy in Pretoria, to P. M. Foster, British Foreign Office, West and Central African Department, December 7, 1963, FO 371/167503, National Archives of the United Kingdom, Kew (TNA).
26 Reports on the "International Reaction to Death of President Kennedy, 1963," FO 371/168407, TNA. See also Luis Nuno Rodrigues, "To the 'Top of the Mountain'

and 'Down to the Valley': The United States and Portugal During the Kennedy Administration" (PhD diss., University of Wisconsin-Madison, 2000).
27 Richard Mahoney, *JFK: Ordeal in Africa* (New York: Oxford University Press, 1983), 243.
28 "International Reaction to Death of President Kennedy."
29 Schlesinger, *Thousand Days*, 1029.
30 Telegram, Guinean ambassador to the United States, Karim Bangoura, to Rusk, November 23, 1963, Box 2: "Office of West African Affairs, Country Files 1951-1963, Guinea," Folder "Communications & Records: General Correspondence," Bureau of African Affairs, GRDS, NARA.
31 Nkrumah, quoted by Rooney, *Nkrumah*, 242.
32 Williams, *Africa*, 160.
33 Nkrumah eulogy, quoted in ibid.
34 Rooney, *Nkrumah*, 230.
35 Schlesinger, *Thousand Days*, 1029; Airgram A-333, US ambassador to Algeria, William Porter, to Rusk, November 30, 1963, Folder "Reactions to Death, Miscellaneous," Box 430, NSF, JFKL.
36 Schlesinger, *Thousand Days*, 564.
37 Ahmed Ben Bella, quoted by Robert Merle, *Ben Bella* (London: Michael Joseph LTD, 1967), 137.
38 Ibid.
39 See *Visits by Foreign Leaders*, US State Department Office of the Historian. Available online: http://history.state.gov/departmenthistory/visits (accessed May 2, 2017); and List of Dignitaries at the State Funeral of John F. Kennedy. Available online: https://en.wikipedia.org/wiki/List_of_dignitaries_at_the_state_funeral_of_John_F._Kennedy (accessed September 12, 2017). Analysis by author. Fourteen foreign heads of state attended Kennedy's funeral, most from NATO member states. The only non-NATO heads of state attending were from Ethiopia, Japan, Jamaica, Israel, and the Philippines.
40 David Dacko, quoted in *West Africa*, November 30, 1963, 1359.
41 Charles Darlington and Alice Darlington, *African Betrayal* (New York: David McKay, 1968), 59.
42 "Telegram, Azikiwe to Johnson, November 24, 1963, Lot 68D8," Folder "Civil Rights," Box 3: "Classified Records of Assistant Secretary of State for African Affairs, G. Mennen Williams, 1961-1966," GRDS, RG 59, NARA.
43 "International Reaction to Death of President Kennedy." Interestingly, when the American ambassador handed Nkrumah a copy of the Warren Report, the Ghanaian president thumbed through it and pointed to the name of Allen Dulles as a member of the Warren Commission. He then handed it back abruptly, muttering, "Whitewash." See Jim DiEugenio, "Dodd and Dulles vs Kennedy in Africa," *The Probe* 6, no. 2 (1999). Additionally, several African leaders believed that Robert Kennedy was assassinated for the same reason: see Ambassador William Edmondson, oral history interview, April 5, 1988, Frontline Diplomacy, Manuscript Division, Library of Congress, Washington (Frontline Diplomacy).
44 William Attwood, *The Reds and the Blacks: A Personal Adventure* (New York: Harper & Row, 1967), 146.
45 Tom Mboya, recorded interview by Gordon P. Hagberg, March 10, 1965, JFKOHP, JFKL.
46 Robert Rakove, *Kennedy, Johnson, and the Nonaligned World* (New York: Cambridge University Press, 2013), xvii.

47 Anthony Nutting, *Nasser* (New York: E.P. Dutton & Co., 1972), 224.
48 Schlesinger, *Thousand Days*, 1029.
49 James Wine, recorded interview by John Stewart, January 26, 1967, JFKOHP, JFKL.
50 John Marcum, *The Angolan Revolution: Exile Politics and Guerrilla Warfare (1962-1976)* (Cambridge: MIT Press, 1978), 132.
51 *West Africa*, November 30, 1963, 1343.
52 Ibid., 1353.
53 Letter to the editor from M.A. Olubayo, ibid., 1353.
54 Letter to the editor from Lanre Awoniyi, ibid., 1353.
55 Williard De Pree, oral history interview, February 16, 1994, Frontline Diplomacy.
56 Stephen Paterson Belcher, oral history interview, April 7, 1988, Frontline Diplomacy. See also *West Africa*, November 30, 1963, 1343.
57 "International Reaction to Death of President Kennedy."
58 Sargent Shriver, *Point of the Lance* (New York: Harper & Row, 1964), 40.
59 Harris Wofford, *Of Kennedys & Kings: Making Sense of the Sixties* (Pittsburgh: University of Pittsburgh Press, 1992), 487.
60 Leland Barrows, recorded interview by William W. Moss, February 4, 1971, JFKOHP, JFKL.
61 Vince Farley, interview with author, December 10, 2003.
62 William Attwood, oral history statement, November 8, 1965, JFKOHP, JFKL.
63 Phillip Pillsbury, Jr., oral history interview, February 28, 1994, Frontline Diplomacy.
64 Harris Wofford, interview with author, November 5, 2003, Washington DC.
65 Johnson, quoted by Rooney, *Nkrumah*, 230.
66 Touré, quoted by Noer, *Soapy*, 272.
67 Julius Nyerere, quoted by William Smith, *We Must Run While They Walk: A Portrait of Africa's Julius Nyerere* (New York: Random House, 1971), 195.
68 Mahoney, *JFK*, 231.
69 David Newsom, interview with author, October 26, 2005, via telephone.
70 *U.S. Overseas Loans and Grants [Greenbook] Database.* Available online: http://gbk.eads.usaidallnet.gov/ (accessed July 7, 2010). Data analysis by author. See also David Newsom, oral history interview, June 17, 1991, Frontline Diplomacy.
71 Remarks of Kaunda toasting President Gerald Ford, April 19, 1975, Folder "4/19/75 Kaunda Dinner," Box 13, Robert Orben Files, 1973–77, Gerald R. Ford Presidential Library, Ann Arbor.
72 *West Africa*, November 30, 1963, 1343.
73 Vince Farley, interview with author, December 10, 2003.

3

"I Named My Son Kennedy": Rural Kenyan Perceptions of John F. Kennedy during Decolonization

Kara Moskowitz

In 1961, a Kenyan farmer petitioned American president John F. Kennedy for an agricultural loan. "I want to practice proper farming," Zebedeo Omwando explained, "but I do not know where to turn to get money."[1] Though Omwando's decision to solicit the US president for a small loan might appear artless, the timing of his letter suggests political acumen and a keen awareness of a shifting global context in which decolonization and international development had gained momentum, and in which American interest in Africa had swelled. Omwando sent his letter just as transnational organizations and foreign nations began funding development programs which delivered technical aid and disbursed loans to farmers. He penned his petition four months after Kennedy signed the executive order establishing the Peace Corps, following the Kennedy administration's provision of famine relief to Kenya, and shortly after the Kennedy Foundation financed the transportation of East African students to US universities. Omwando likely was not a naive actor but a shrewd one.

The American consul general Richard Freund replied some months later affirming Kennedy's interest in the challenges facing Africa. "Unfortunately," Freund continued, "it is not possible for President Kennedy personally to consider problems of individual citizens in foreign countries."[2] Omwando's decision to petition the president implies he had believed in the possibility of an altogether different outcome to this interaction. It seems that he not only anticipated the formation of a personal connection with the US president, but he hoped this relationship would, in turn, produce material benefit. Omwando was neither alone in his specific targeting of Kennedy as a potential patron nor unique in his broad ambitions to acquire development resources.

African independence coincided with the expansion of international development agencies into the newly postcolonial world. The 1960s moment ushered in changing development practices and political actors. This setting—of political transition, of new actors distributing resources—thus played a role in reconfiguring African worldviews and ideas of authority. Kennedy came into power at a particularly auspicious moment for US-Africa relations. It was a period of political excitement and broadening imaginaries. The Cold War and the shifting demographics of the UN freed American politicians from complete allegiance to European allies, allowing Kennedy to support African nationalist movements. Kennedy's support and his popular policies melded well with African desires for independence and development. Likewise, Kennedy cultivated personal relationships with leaders for his African diplomacy, and this integrated easily into Kenya's political culture of personalized authority.[3] Moreover, this was an era of expanding media distribution in Africa, and of greater global connections. Not only did Kennedy support independence, offer aid, and personalize his rule, but Kenyans had the necessary access to radios and newspapers to follow the American president's actions closely.

As a result, Kennedy made a favorable impression on Kenyans throughout the colony. Archival and oral evidence illustrate that many Kenyans came to believe that Kennedy supported Africa more so than any previous American president. Perhaps, most tellingly, in the years after his assassination, many Kenyans gave their children his name. Former American ambassador to Kenya, William Attwood, wrote that "there are many people in Kenya named after him" and, during an oral interview, Kenyan Gladys Kamonya said, "I named my son Kennedy after John F. Kennedy; he was the president and everybody was talking about him."[4] Even today, one frequently meets Kenyans with the name Kennedy.

Although there is a growing literature on the connections between decolonization and development in Africa, scholars have yet to fully explore how the entrance of new transnational actors shaped African political imaginaries at independence. The literature on international development has provided discursive analysis of the invention of "development," "technical expertise," and the "Third World."[5] Recent decolonization scholarship has highlighted deliberations among trade unionists, African leaders, grassroots activists, and local elites, emphasizing the possibilities and uncertainties of independence.[6] Both literatures have revealed—though perhaps overemphasized—the high modernist logic of developmentalist states.[7] In focusing on knowledge production, formal political actors, and top-down interventions, scholars have largely overlooked the actions of non-elites.[8] Yet, in the mid-twentieth century, the vast majority of African citizens resided in the countryside, and many vigorously scrutinized and participated in local, national, and international political processes.[9]

Some politically active rural Kenyans came to respect Kennedy, but the scholarship on this subject remains limited. Historians have paid little attention to Kennedy foreign policy outside Cold War and modernization frameworks and even less attention to how average Africans received and experienced these programs.[10] Though some scholarship has demonstrated the importance of Kennedy's relations with African leaders, the president also directed his personalized politics at non-elite Africans.[11] The perception of a friendly, intimate relationship with a US president, who also offered material aid, appealed to rural Kenyans and blended readily into established patron-client relationships.[12] Approaching this history both from below and from the African perspective reframes our knowledge of how the decolonizing world understood Kennedy. Postcolonial citizens certainly wanted greater global inclusion, and they valued Kennedy's personal consideration. They also deeply desired development, and there was immense pressure for politicians to deliver on development promises.

Africanist historians possess the ability to offer more locally grounded analysis on the impact of international relations. Yet, Africanists' focus on social histories of local areas has meant the creation of an, at times, parochial historiography seemingly divorced from global forces. This scholarship sometimes presumes that national and transnational institutions impinge on rural communities without scrutinizing the relationships between institutional actors and the populations they engage with.[13] Implicit in all of this is the assumption that average Africans remained disengaged from, and ill-informed about, international politics, a notion the evidence clearly counters.

Postwar Kenya saw an explosion in broadcasting and news publications. The expanding media landscape offered Kenyans greater access to national and global news. Increased media circulation, in turn, transformed the way Kenyans, and Africans more broadly, saw themselves in their community and colony, and in the world.[14] Africanist scholars have shown that vernacular communications help unify new ethnic collectivities and promote nationalist ambitions.[15] Yet, the postwar era was not marked simply by an uptick in ethnonationalism and nationalism, but also by flourishing internationalism. Kenyan political imaginations became both geographically narrower and broader than the boundaries of the soon to be nation-state. As they learned more about transnational organizations and foreign nations, Kenyans—like Zebedeo Omwando—looked outward to international actors for assistance and leadership.

Three interconnected historical lenses—Kenyan decolonization, growing American development assistance to Africa, and the politics of the US Civil Rights movement—reveal how Kennedy's discourse and his programs shaped Kenyan lives, and how Kenyans thus came to imagine Kennedy as a supporter and patron. Rural Kenyans were knowledgeable about the complexities of global politics, and they used the rhetoric and policy of foreign leaders to make sense of the decolonizing world and their place in it.

Background

Africans throughout the continent expected that independence would bring development. These expectations initially grew out of the postwar context and the enactment of metropolitan development and welfare acts in the 1940s, which introduced state-led development programs. The promises of African nationalist leaders further contributed to widespread expectations for development. Postwar development programs and rhetoric coincided with the establishment of the Bretton Woods institutions—the International Bank for Reconstruction and Development (the original World Bank institution) and the International Monetary Fund.[16] The UN proclaimed the 1960s the "Development Decade," which President Kennedy inaugurated at the UN in New York. The same decade witnessed the rapid decolonization of much of Africa.

In 1960, on the heels of decolonization in Asia and portions of Africa, Kenyan independence negotiations began. The most heated political debates revolved around the structure of the postcolonial government, which determined control over the distribution of land and development. In 1962, prior to the resolution of these issues, the UK, the World Bank, and West Germany commenced the largest land transfer and resettlement program in Kenya's history. Development programs would continue after independence on December 12, 1963, part of a broader set of mid-twentieth-century policies increasingly shaped by transnational institutions and foreign nations. Not only were decolonization and development coterminous and co-constitutive, then, but external actors played a central role in financing, planning, and implementing these programs.

The United States represented a fairly new player to this scene.[17] In 1953, the United States began offering loans and grants to Kenya to fund development programming.[18] Roughly a year later, American government officials worked out a five-point program for East Africa to: strengthen American consular representation; improve United States Information Service programming; develop exchanges with institutions of higher education; establish the Foreign Operations Administration, a relief agency, on the ground; and facilitate interest in East Africa among private foundations.[19] American policymakers aimed to use "visible projects" to make the United States "concrete and real" to East Africans.[20]

The general emphasis of this initial development programming, both its form and its function, would remain in place for the next decade. The intensity of American interest, on the other hand, would grow dramatically. By the mid-1950s, aggregate US economic aid to Kenya had not even reached $4 million, but a little over a decade later, the cumulative amount had extended to $30 million.[21] Economic aid of the United States to Africa, as a whole, followed similar patterns. From 1945 to 1955, Africa garnered less than one-sixth of 1 percent of total US foreign aid. By 1956, American aid to Africa had reached $10 million. In just a matter of four years that number had jumped to $100 million, though it still represented a negligible proportion of total American foreign aid spending.[22]

At the very moment that the United States sought to make its interest in Kenya evident, improved access to media made this goal more achievable. Just as East Africa received greater amounts of US aid, average Kenyans were more poised than ever before to learn about this assistance and its origins. The Second World War had transformed Kenya's media infrastructure. Prior to 1939, newspaper publication and radio broadcasting primarily served the European and South Asian population of the colony. With the outbreak of the war, the colonial state established a government information office to develop radio and print to recruit Africans and spread wartime propaganda.[23] The government supplied wireless sets to district commissioners, schools, and missions. Colonial information officers added a number of vernacular broadcasts to the limited Swahili broadcasting already in place. The British administration also published newssheets in vernacular languages.

The postwar era witnessed the unmatched growth of the vernacular press. In addition to the increasing number of mission and government newspapers aimed at African audiences, Kenyans started fifty-six newspapers in the decade following the war.[24] Though literacy rates were low at this time, a great deal of evidence from throughout the continent demonstrates that "virtually all newspapers were read by more than one person, and many more were read aloud, translated, summarized, amended."[25] The proliferation of the African-controlled, vernacular press ceased with the 1952 Mau Mau State of Emergency and government bans on these papers, but Kenya's newspaper culture continued to thrive. Indeed, state suppression of a vernacular press that focused on local politics might have had unintended globalizing consequences. When Kenyans turned, instead, to European and Indian run presses, they came across more international news.[26]

With the invention of the cheaper and more durable transistor in 1948, African radio purchases skyrocketed.[27] By the end of 1951, Kenya's southern neighbor, Tanganyika, had an estimated one thousand radio receivers. Yet, by 1960, a survey estimated 70,000 sets in use.[28] Eight years later, the number of radios in Tanzania had increased again by almost tenfold, up to over five-hundred thousand. In that same period, a survey of four rural Taznanian villages found that 82 percent of all men and 62 percent of all women listened to the radio at least some of the time.[29]

Radio listeners were not necessarily radio owners. Many likely listened at public events, local shops, or neighbors' houses. Radio listening, similar to newspaper reading, was a profoundly social event, which oral histories illustrate. Joseph Dugere Munge, a Kikuyu resident of Kenya's western Rift Valley, noted that "the whole village would listen to the radio together."[30] Others recounted visiting their neighbors to listen each evening, and those who managed to purchase radios described inviting friends over to listen.[31] Kenyans could list the precise programs—Radio Taifa, BBC, and Sauti ya Amerika (Voice of America)—and name the specific broadcasters for various vernacular programs.[32] Many recounted the excitement of listening to world news, "even from America," in the early 1960s.[33] Though both men and women enjoyed listening to the news, women often had too much domestic work to walk to a neighbor's house to hear broadcasts, so they listened less regularly.[34]

Improved media fostered global connections, molding more expansive ideas of authority. Kenyans began to hear about Kennedy, and they liked what they heard. Even during his campaign, Kennedy called attention to the continent's poverty, criticizing how the United States, deplorably, had "done little to provide the development capital . . . essential to a growing economy."[35] Kennedy continued to impress Africans with his attention to the "Third World," and by distancing himself from unpopular American policies. The *East African Standard*, one of two nationally distributed daily newspapers, put Kennedy's victory on its front page, carrying news of the president-elect promising "to work for the 'cause of freedom around the world.'"[36] In January 1961, Kennedy declared that his administration was "dedicated to supporting the legitimate rights to self-determination of Afro-Asian states."[37] This set him apart from his predecessor, Dwight D. Eisenhower, a point quite clear to Africans. Kenyan politician Tom Mboya noted the transformative significance of the Kennedy administration: "It was the beginning of a completely new era in our foreign relations with America. It also created a departure which Africa had always been looking for from the days when American foreign policy vis-à-vis Africa was conducted through Britain or France, through NATO allies and so on, to a more direct relationship."[38] Kennedy successfully dissociated his administration from disliked US policy and from imperial powers.

President Kennedy relied on more than discourse. He advocated for the enhancement of American development aid and earnestly courted African leadership. Under Kennedy, the United States established the Agency for International Development. Modernization theory served as an "intellectual framework as well as a political objective" for Kennedy.³⁹ Though modernization theory implicitly presumed "Third World" backwardness, it also produced tangible investments from the United States in the form of training centers, American volunteers, and infrastructure projects.

Still, Kennedy utilized a diverse toolkit for his foreign relations, which entailed far more than modernization theory. As Muehlenbeck has argued, "Kennedy devoted more time and effort toward relations with Africa than any other American president."⁴⁰ Kennedy pursued personal relationships with African leaders.⁴¹ Kenyans recognized this, and Mboya recounted that "this personal approach to things; contact with people at a personal level became one of the main stamps of the Kennedy Administration."⁴² Kenyans appreciated Kennedy's apparently genuine interest. They also respected his mode of diplomacy grounded in personal relationships, which had long been integral to their indigenous political institutions.⁴³

Kenyan familiarity with US politics and foreign policy shaped their political imaginations. Not only did Kenyans attempt to gain access to American aid, but they also began to imagine external funders as potential postcolonial patrons. As communities sought support and politicians distributed aid, they engaged in old practices of mutual reciprocity where dependents exchanged loyalty for a patron's protection. When Kenyan communities received US aid, they often perceived it as coming from Kennedy himself.

The airlift

Between 1959 and 1963, a set of assistance programs brought close to 800 East African students to America, where they pursued their higher education on scholarship.⁴⁴ In September 1960 alone, 289 East African students traveled to the United States on four chartered planes. No past or future program would match that of 1960.

In the years leading up to that airlift, Tom Mboya had worked tirelessly to assemble scholarships for Kenyan students in the United States, as he sought to educate future civil servants. Eighty-one students traveled to the United States in September 1959 on this first "airlift." While small in size, the initial program garnered attention in both the United States and Kenya. Jackie Robinson, Harry Belafonte, and Sidney Poitier were among the supporters. Though the first chartered plane departed from Nairobi's isolated airport in the middle of the night, "a crowd of five thousand gathered for the send-off and listened patiently to farewell addresses by Mboya, [Julius] Kiano, and others."⁴⁵

Following the success of the first airlift, the African American Students Foundation (AASF) and Mboya sought to expand the program, and close to 300 East African students were offered funding to enroll in 1960.⁴⁶ Given that the program had more than tripled in size, the AASF and Mboya had difficulty financing the students' airfare. They approached US government officials in the State Department but to no avail. Frank Montero and William Scheinman would write to the House Subcommittee on Africa in August 1960 that the State Department had "repeatedly turned a cold shoulder to the airlift-African program."⁴⁷ Seeking last minute funding, Mboya met with then-senator Kennedy. Mboya recounted spending a morning discussing the airlift, noting that Kennedy was "sympathetic." Kennedy then approached his brother-in-law, Sargent Shriver, who managed the family's foundation, and they offered $100,000 to charter four planes and to provide extra funding for the students.[48] Because of the role these actors played, the 1960 program would become popularly known as the "Kennedy airlift" or the "Mboya airlift."

The airlift took place at the height of the 1960 US presidential campaign. When the Kennedy Foundation's donation came to light, Republicans criticized Kennedy for politicizing aid and infringing on US government policy. However, Mboya set the record straight, commending Kennedy for realizing "that education is an urgent problem in Africa."[49] The *East African Standard* carried news of the airlift on its front page multiple times during August and September 1960. On August 19, the front-page headline read, "Grant for student airlift," while the following day, it was "Election row over E. African students."[50] When Kenyans learned about the controversy, they saw Kenya as central to an American election and to global political processes. They came to see Kennedy as a patron, who understood their desires for education and took the place of an unwilling US government. Senator Kennedy took offense at the allegation that he tried "to take over the functions of the Government," but the news may have been interpreted that way in Kenya, likely to Kennedy's benefit.[51]

Kenyans came to know of the airlift, not simply because of the controversy surrounding it, but also because of the deep impact it made on their communities. Local villages throughout the colony mobilized to support their brightest students. US visa stipulations required students possess $300 in cash, an amount beyond the means of average Kenyans.[52] Many villages held fundraising meetings to collect the money. When local residents attended, they learned more about the airlift and offered small donations. During a visit to Kenya, Theodore Kheel, Kennedy advisor and AASF board member, was particularly impressed by Kenyan commitment to education. He wrote to Sargent Shriver in September 1960, "I have pictures . . . of old women and little children contributing pennies to enable their sisters and brothers to come to the United States to study. In Machakos . . . 5,000 Africans sat for over four hours listening to a discussion of why they should give financial aid to educate some 20 students from their area."[53] Families, friends, and neighbors donated to the young scholars, and they hoped the airlift students would eventually return home and aid their communities. Mungai Mbayah, a 1959 airliftee, noted, "We will all be called upon to give public service when we go back to Kenya. Nothing short [of that] will be acceptable to our people and to those who enabled us to come here to study."[54]

More than 90 percent of airliftees returned to Kenya, and many of them played significant roles in postcolonial society.[55] For the next twenty-five years, airlift students would make up about half of Kenya's parliamentarians. They also took up positions as cabinet ministers, high-level civil servants, ambassadors, professors, doctors, conservationists, and businesspeople. Former airliftee George Saitoti would become Kenyan vice president, and Wangari Maathai would start the Green Belt Movement and become the first African woman to win a Nobel Prize.[56] The prominent positions of airlift alumni, in turn, generated greater knowledge of, and attraction to, Kennedy.

Many Kenyan students met President Kennedy in the United States. Tom Mboya noted that, when students interacted with Kennedy, "they were most impressed with his charm and simple manner and very human approach."⁵⁷ These impressions, in combination with appreciation for the foundation's assistance, seem to have improved US-Kenya relations before Kennedy even took office. AASF president Frank Montero wrote that the airlift "was taken as a great symbol of American concern," remarking how a professor working in Kenya told him "nothing has done more for the United States prestige than the Airlift."⁵⁸

The airlift came to permeate Kenyan politics at this time. During the 1961 election, Tom Mboya's ballot symbol—for illiterate voters—was an *ndege* or airplane to remind the electorate about the airlift. Mboya's campaign even chartered a plane to circle above his election rally, and they used the slogan "*uhuru na ndege*" (independence and airplanes).⁵⁹ J. Wayne Fredericks, Kennedy's deputy assistant secretary of state for African Affairs, credited the airlift with generating Kenyan awareness of Kennedy "because of his interest in Africa."⁶⁰ In three months, Kennedy would be elected president.

Food aid

The year 1961 was "disastrous" in the words of Rift Valley provincial commissioner J. A. H. Wolff.⁶¹ Heavy rains followed drought and armyworm, causing extensive damage to crops. Many parts of Kenya required famine relief.⁶² By this time, the United States had been steadily extending its food aid programs. In 1954, Eisenhower signed the US Agricultural Trade Development and Assistance Act, or PL-480, offering food relief while facilitating the purchase of surplus American agricultural produce. In September 1960, Eisenhower proposed a multilateral food aid agency to the UN General Assembly. When Kennedy entered office, he built upon Eisenhower's programs. He renamed PL-480 Food for Peace and, within the program, he emphasized development in the Global South over American agricultural disposal.⁶³ The Food for Peace committee recommended that "the food needs of Africa, which seem to have been neglected . . . demand immediate attention."⁶⁴ President Kennedy also became a public advocate for the Freedom from Hunger campaign.⁶⁵

In this setting, Kenya experienced its first postwar food shortage, and the United States offered assistance. Kenyans vividly recall receiving food aid in 1961, particularly, because the imported American yellow corn differed from the white maize they were accustomed to.⁶⁶ Philomon Tanai, a clergyman living in the western highlands, recounted receiving "yellow maize from the US" during "the worst famine I remember."⁶⁷ The importation of such curious maize indicated to Kenyans that they had received external assistance, as did the prominence of Kennedy and his public support of food relief programs.

Kenyans showed their gratitude to the United States, especially to Kennedy. White House correspondence details how, "in appreciation . . . for the recent gift of American corn," a Kamba chief presented Kennedy with a carved walking stick, "a symbol of authority" in Kenya.⁶⁸ Duruma chiefs sent "hearty congratulations" to the president, noting he had "saved many lives . . . during the time of famine which still haunts our people."⁶⁹ Ronald Ngala, leader of the House, wrote President Kennedy "to offer our most heartfelt thanks for all that your government has done to assist us in famine relief. The misery and suffering that has been caused by this terrible disaster has been greatly alleviated by the generosity of the United States of America."[70]

East Africans remembered US famine relief after 1961. Following Kennedy's assassination, in a letter to the editor, Nairobi resident Kabiru Deen commended Kennedy for his food aid: "The tragic death of President Kennedy is a great loss to all freedom loving people of the world. The US and its people have been most generous and kind towards this country in every way. They provided us with free food when it was so badly needed here."[71] Dave Zarembka, a former Peace Corps Volunteer in Tanganyika and Kenya, said that, in the late 1960s, Kenyans still attributed the 1961 famine relief to Kennedy.[72] Tanganyika also received American food aid in 1961, a year Tanzanians today not only mark as the anniversary of their independence, but also as the year of "Merika" or "Kenedi."[73]

When East Africans received food aid, they tended to acknowledge Kennedy rather than the US government, and when they did so, they made sense of the president's generosity through older political forms. The arrangement harkened back to precolonial times, when patrons offered their clients protection from starvation.[74] As the political context changed, Kenyans began crafting new expectations of international leaders to fulfill these roles, and of their own leaders to garner aid from external actors.

Though Kennedy might not have understood the intricacies of patron-client relations, he and his aids recognized the constitutive role of aid in fostering connections. Kennedy wrote a thank you note to the Kamba chief for his walking stick, and he acknowledged Ronald Ngala as well, noting the "American people were deeply moved by reports of suffering" and "are most happy to know that our food assistance were timely and did much to alleviate the intense hardship."[75] Such letters were not simply a product of presidential decorum. The American Consul General in Nairobi requested "a suitable picture" of the president posed with the walking stick to give to the Kamba chief as a way of obtaining "favorable publicity."[76] The Kennedy administration saw these communications as vital diplomatic tools.

Kennedy's administration sought positive publicity with many programs, and frequently made symbolic gestures to Africans. When the mayor of Nairobi wished to give President Kennedy a carved chess set with "African motifs . . . contained in an elephant-hide box" and the First Lady a "silk zebra design scarf," the US consulate in Nairobi recommended that it "would be [an] excellent gesture with just [the] right political and psychological touch for our relations with Kenya if Mrs. Kennedy could accept for [the] White House."[77] The administration's attention to these moments, and their promotion of African encounters with the president, helped ingratiate Kennedy to Kenyans.

Kenya's Kennedy fervor: In life and death

Kenyans were initially critical of Kennedy's civil rights policy, given the tumultuousness of American racial politics when he took office. Kenyans, as well as Africans broadly, saw the US Civil Rights movement as part of a global struggle against racism and discrimination. They not only identified with African Americans but watched US politics closely and criticized the government. In May 1963, Jomo Kenyatta wrote to Kennedy, "People of Kenya deplore continuing oppression of Negroes in Southern United States which belies US claim to true democracy."[78] Such criticism worried Kennedy, and his office took care to reply to Kenyatta privately and publicly.[79] Whether Kennedy ultimately responded more attentively to the Civil Rights movement because of Cold War politics or out of genuine concern for African Americans, his policy played well in Africa.[80] The press and African leaders increasingly praised Kennedy, directing their criticism at white Americans instead. After the 16th Street Baptist Church bombing, the international press excoriated white supremacists, but covered Kennedy's "expression of outrage."[81]

Kenyan tributes to Kennedy after his assassination illustrate how dramatically opinions had altered. In the National Assembly, the once critical Kenyatta lauded Kennedy for his civil rights efforts, his commitment to world peace, and his assistance with the student airlift.[82] Opposition leader Ronald Ngala echoed Kenyatta, commending Kennedy for his educational and economic projects in Africa and for working "to achieve equality among his citizens regardless of their colour or religion."[83]

Throughout Kenya, people mourned the passing of the president. The *East African Standard* dedicated five consecutive days of front-page space to Kennedy and Kenyan memorialization. Kenyans sent a "huge wreath containing 1,726 blossoms, one for each Kenyan student who has studied or is studying in the United States" to Washington for the funeral. Several hundred people marched through Nairobi to the American Consulate-General, where they presented "a note expressing sorrow at the President's death."[84] A rally at Eldoret stadium held a moment of silence for Kennedy and "agreed to send a telegram of condolence to Mrs. Kennedy."[85] Flags were flown at half-mast, and Catholic services were held. Over 6,000 people attended the service at the Holy Family Cathedral in Nairobi, including Kenyatta and Governor-General Malcolm MacDonald. At the mass, Father Njenga "praised Mr. Kennedy's personal generosity which had enabled men and women from Kenya to study in the United States and which would prove of inestimable value to the emerging nation."[86]

Most striking is the grief of ordinary Kenyans in rural areas, who could not attend the formal ceremonies in distant cities. Ambassador Attwood remarked upon the great "Kennedy legend" all over Kenya.[87] Tom Mboya recounted that Kennedy's death "registered so sharply. It was as though someone very close at home had died and people reacted spontaneously in practically every little town and village in this country."[88] Oral histories from the western highlands support these accounts. Ainea Alulu, a Maragoli farmer, said, "We were upset. We would have gone to the funeral if it was within walking distance."[89]

This grief underscores how beloved Kennedy had become. Frederick Kemboi arap Tum Kaptulus—a Rift Valley farmer of Nandi ethnicity—recounted, "Africans liked John F. Kennedy, because we were thinking that Kennedy had some relationship with Africa. Kenyan politicians said Kennedy was the best because he united the whites and the Africans."[90] Similarly, another Rift Valley resident, Jairo Murunga Libapu said, "Kennedy used to fight for Africans." Libapu—a Maragoli man who divided his time between carpentry and farming—had never seen Kennedy's image and only heard of him through radio broadcasts. In fact, he assumed the president was a *marekani mweusi* (African American), on account of Kennedy's perceived dedication to Africa and African Americans.[91]

Rural Kenyans largely agreed upon Kennedy's dedication to Africans, and they revered the president for it. The student airlift, famine relief, Kennedy's rhetorical attention to Africa, and his friendly engagements with African leaders impressed them. Kennedy's support for the Civil Rights movement further bolstered his image. Even so, Kenyan knowledge of Kennedy was uneven. Few women could recount much in detail about Kennedy, likely because they had less opportunity to listen to the radio with their domestic workload. Further, wealthier, educated Kenyans seem to have preserved more specific memories of Kennedy, as a result of media access.

Conclusion

Kenyan memorialization and admiration for Kennedy continues to this day. The election of Barack Obama, the son of a Kenyan who studied in the United States, brought renewed attention to the airlift.[92] The Kenya National Archives recently added an exhibit on Mboya, Kennedy, and the airlift. Students take field trips to the gallery and pose for photos in front of the display, ensuring that a future generation is familiar with this history. As Kenyans name their children Kennedy, they continue honoring the president. They do so, because of Kennedy's contributions to the airlift, famine relief, and civil rights.

Kennedy's personality and policy, along with his ability to understand and legitimate the aspirations of the developing world, were all key to his popularity. Kenyans saw Kennedy as a new patron, and often ascribed US aid to the president, personally. Decolonization and the dramatic growth of the Kenyan media were also central to Kennedy's popularity, as Kenyan worldviews expanded and they sought to participate in global politics. Further, his assassination occurred before some of the disillusionment about postcolonial politics and international aid set in, and before a period of economic decline. Local histories reveal why Kennedy's personality and policy appealed to Africans more specifically. Approaching this history from the ground up offers a more complex narrative of the changing geopolitics of the mid-twentieth century than Cold War and modernization paradigms reveal. Global politics became inflected, and remade, in local settings.

Notes

1 Zebedeo T. Omwando to His Highness the President, United States of America, "Farming Loan," July 15, 1961, BV/1/538, Kenya National Archives, Nairobi (KNA).
2 Richard Freund, US consul general, to Omwando, Catholic Mission, Kisii South Nyanza, March 8, 1962, BV/1/538, KNA.
3 Philip Muehlenbeck, *Betting on the Africans: John F. Kennedy's Courting of African Nationalist Leaders* (Oxford: Oxford University Press, 2012).

4 William Attwood, *The Reds and the Blacks: A Personal Adventure* (London: Hutchinson & Co., 1967), 234; Gladys Kamonya, interview by author, Lumakanda, June 8, 2015.
5 James Ferguson, *The Anti-Politics Machine: "Development," Depoliticization, and Bureaucratic Power in Lesotho* (Minneapolis: University of Minnesota Press, 1994); Arturo Escobar, *Encountering Development: The Making and Unmaking of the Third World* (Princeton: Princeton University Press, 1995); Leander Schneider, *Government of Development: Peasants and Politicians in Postcolonial Tanzania* (Bloomington: Indiana University Press, 2014).
6 Frederick Cooper, *Citizenship Between Empire and Nation: Remaking France and French Africa, 1945-1960* (Princeton: Princeton University Press, 2014); Kate Skinner, *The Fruits of Freedom in British Togoland: Literacy, Politics, and Nationalism* (New York: Cambridge University Press, 2015); Frederick Cooper, *Decolonization and African Society: The Labor Question in French and British Africa* (Cambridge: Cambridge University Press, 1996); Daniel Branch, *Kenya: Between Hope and Despair, 1963-2011* (New Haven: Yale University Press, 2011); Emma Hunter, *Political Thought and the Public Sphere in Tanzania: Freedom, Democracy, and Citizenship in the Era of Decolonization* (Cambridge: Cambridge University Press, 2015).
7 Most famously, James Scott, *Seeing Like a State: How Certain Schemes to Improve the Human Condition Have Failed* (New Haven: Yale University Press, 1998). Daniel Immerwahr has recently argued that historians have actually overstated the adherence to modernization policy and theory in the mid-twentieth century. Immerwahr, *Thinking Small: The United States and the Lure of Community Development* (Cambridge: Harvard University Press, 2015).
8 For an exception, see Priya Lal, *African Socialism in Postcolonial Tanzania: Between the Village and the World* (Cambridge: Cambridge University Press, 2015).
9 "World Development Indicators 2012," The World Bank. Available online: http://databank.worldbank.org (accessed February 7, 2013). Similar to other parts of Africa, 92.6 percent of the Kenyan population lived in rural areas in 1960.
10 See Odd Arne Westad, *The Global Cold War* (Cambridge: Cambridge University Press, 2007); Michael Latham, *Modernization as Ideology: American Social Science and "Nation Building" in the Kennedy Era* (Chapel Hill: The University of North Carolina Press, 2000); David Ekbladh, *The Great American Mission: Modernization and the Construction of an American World Order* (Princeton: Princeton University Press, 2010); Nils Gilman, *Mandarins of the Future: Modernization Theory in Cold War America* (Baltimore: The Johns Hopkins University Press, 2003). The only scholar who has specifically examined Kenya-US relations during the Kennedy administration is P. Godfrey Okoth. Okoth, *US Foreign Policy Impact on Kenya's Domestic and Foreign Policy* (Kampala: Makerere University, 1987); and Okoth, *United States of America's Foreign Policy towards Kenya, 1952-1969* (Nairobi: Gideon S. Were Press, 1992). For an American-centric analysis of American-Kenyan relations, see: Gerald Horne, *Mau Mau in Harlem? The US and the Liberation of Kenya* (New York: Palgrave Macmillan, 2009). Historians of Africa have examined Kennedy-era programs, but without analysis of their impact on foreign relations or on African imaginations: John Aerni-Flessner, "Development, Politics, and the Centralization of State Power in Lesotho, 1960-75," *JAfH* 55, no. 3 (2014): 401–21.
11 Muehlenbeck, *Africans*.
12 On patron-client relationships in Africa, see: Jean-Francois Bayart, *The State in Africa: The Politics of the Belly* (London: Longman, 1993); Bruce Berman, "Ethnicity, Patronage and the African State: The Politics of Uncivil Nationalism," *African Affairs*

97, no. 388 (1998): 305–41; Richard Joseph, *Democracy and Prebendal Politics in Nigeria* (Cambridge: Cambridge University Press, 1987); Crawford Young, *The Rise and Decline of the Zairian State* (Madison: University of Wisconsin Press, 1985).

13 Belinda Bozzoli, *Women of Phokeng: Consciousness, Life Strategy, and Migrancy in South Africa, 1900-1983* (Portsmouth: Heinemann, 1991); Laura Fair, *Pastimes and Politics: Culture, Community, and Identity in Post-Abolition Urban Zanzibar, 1890-1945* (Athens: Ohio University Press, 2001).

14 Steven Feierman, *Peasant Intellectuals: Anthropology and History in Tanzania* (Madison: University of Wisconsin Press, 1990), 252–59; David William Cohen and E. S. Atieno Odhiambo, *Siaya: The Historical Anthropology of an African Landscape* (Athens: Ohio University Press, 1989), 35.

15 Gabrielle Lynch, *I Say to You: Ethnic Politics and the Kalenjin in Kenya* (Chicago: University of Chicago Press, 2011), 38–39. See also: Monone Omosule, "Kalenjin: The Emergence of a Corporate Name for the Nandi-Speaking Tribes of East Africa," *Geneve-Afrique* 27, no. 1 (1989): 75; Ben Kipkorir, *People of the Rift Valley* (London: Evans, 1978), 2. There is a vast historical literature on the printing press and nationalism. Most famously, Benedict Anderson, *Imagined Communities: Reflections on the Origin and Spread of Nationalism* (New York: Verso, 1991).

16 For ease of understanding, I refer to the IBRD as the World Bank.

17 In fact, there is not a great deal written about the US-Kenya relationship prior to the 1950s.

18 Attwood, *Reds and Blacks*, 173.

19 Godfrey Okoth, "US Foreign Policy Toward Kenya, 1952-1960," *Ufahamu: A Journal of African Studies* 14, no. 1 (1984): 37–39.

20 Ibid., 38.

21 Ibid., 41; Attwood, *Reds and Blacks*, 173.

22 "Remarks of Senator John F. Kennedy (Dem.-Mass.), Chairman of the Senate Foreign Relations Subcommittee on African Affairs, before the Second Annual Conference of the American Society of African Culture, at Waldorf-Astoria Hotel, New York City, Sunday Evening 7 pm," June 28, 1959, Speeches and remarks by JFK, Democratic National Committee Press Releases, 1958–1960, Speeches and Press, Presidential Campaign Files 1960 (PCF), Pre-Presidential Papers (PPP), Papers of John F. Kennedy (PJFK), John F. Kennedy Presidential Library, Boston (JFKL).

23 Fay Gadsden, "Wartime Propaganda in Kenya: The Kenya Information Office, 1939-1945," *IJAHS* 19, no. 3 (1986): 408.

24 Fay Gadsden, "The African Press in Kenya, 1945-1952," *JAfH* 21, no. 4 (1980): 515.

25 Luise White, *Speaking With Vampires: Rumor and History in Colonial Africa* (Berkeley: University of California Press, 2000), 252. See also: J. Glassman, "Sorting out the Tribes: The Creation of Racial Identities in Colonial Zanzibar's Newspaper Wars," *JAfH* 41, no. 3 (2000): 395–428; Charles Ambler, "Mass Media and Leisure in Africa," *IJAHS* 35, no. 1 (2002): 124.

26 Gadsden, "African Press," 532.

27 Graham Mytton, *Mass Communication in Africa* (London: Edward Arnold Publishers, 1983), 3.

28 Ibid., 3.

29 Feierman, *Peasant Intellectuals*, 251.

30 Joseph Dugere Munge, interview by author, Mautuma, November 11, 2012.

31 Ainea Alulu, interview by author, Lumakanda, November 5, 2012; Aaron Juma Wechuli, interview by author, Lumakanda, November 14, 2012.

32 Frederick Kemboi arap Tum Kaptulus, interview by author, Leseru, July 21, 2016; James Musamusi Matunda, interview by author, Lumakanda, July 19, 2016.
33 Aaron Masista, interview by author, Lumakanda, July 20, 2016.
34 Nora Kasigene, interview by author, Lumakanda, July 18, 2016; Samson Sumba, interview by author, Lumakanda, November 13, 2012.
35 Michael Latham, *The Right Kind of Revolution* Modernization, Development, and U.S. Foreign Policy from the Cold War to the Present (Ithaca: Cornell University Press, 2011), 87.
36 "Kennedy Calls for Supreme US Effort," *East African Standard*, November 11, 1960.
37 Muehlenbeck, *Africans*, xii.
38 Thomas Mboya, recorded interview by Gordon Hagberg, March 10, 1965, 7, Oral History Program (OHP), JFKL.
39 Latham, *Right Kind of Revolution*, 2.
40 Muehlenbeck, *Africans*, xiii.
41 Ibid. This is the core of Muehlenbeck's argument, illustrated by the twenty-eight African heads of state Kennedy hosted in the Oval office.
42 Mboya, recorded interview, 7.
43 On personal relations and Kenyan political institutions, see: Bruce Berman and John Lonsdale, *Unhappy Valley: Conflict in Kenya and Africa: Book One: State and Class* (Athens: Ohio University Press, 1992); Sara Berry, *No Condition Is Permanent: The Social Dynamic of Agrarian Change in Sub-Saharan Africa* (Madison: University of Wisconsin Press, 1993); Branch, *Kenya*.
44 Tom Shachtman, *Airlift to America: How Barack Obama, Sr., John F. Kennedy, Tom Mboya, and 800 East African Students Changed their World and Ours* (New York: St. Martin's Press, 2009), 7.
45 Ibid., 101.
46 Ibid., 123.
47 Frank Montero, president, and William Scheinman, vice president to the honorable Charles Diggs, Subcommittee on Africa, House Committee on Foreign Affairs, Washington, August 16, 1960, re African Students Airlift, Press Secretary's Subject File, 1960, Speeches and the Press, PCF, PPP, PJFK, JFKL.
48 Tom Mboya, *Freedom and After* (London: Andre Deutsch, 1963), 145.
49 Cited from Muehlenbeck, *Africans*, 39.
50 "Grant for Student Airlift," *East African Standard*, August 19, 1960; "Election Row over E. African Students," *East African Standard*, August 20, 1960.
51 Senator Kennedy's Office, "The Facts on Grant to African Students Airlift Summary," African Students Airlift, Democratic National Committee Press Releases, 1958–1960, Speeches and Press, PCF, PPP, PJFK, JFKL.
52 Shachtman, *Airlift*, 92.
53 Theodore Kheel to Sargent Shriver, The Joseph P. Kennedy, Jr. Foundation, September 13, 1960, Michigan State University African Activist Archives, East Lansing (MSAAA).
54 Quoted in Shachtman, *Airlift*, 88.
55 Ibid., 226.
56 Ibid., 226–27.
57 Mboya, recorded interview, 4.
58 "Memorandum by Frank Montero, President of the African American Students Foundation, 'To See African Needs through African Eyes,'" 1960, MSAAA.
59 Mboya, *Freedom*, 149.

60 J. Wayne Fredericks, recorded interview by Joseph O'Connor, April 18, 1966, 1 OHP, JFKL.
61 Rift Valley Province Annual Report 1961, PC/RVP, KNA.
62 Ibid.
63 Amy Staples, *The Birth of Development: How the World Bank, Food and Agriculture Organization, and World Health Organization Changed the World, 1945-1965* (Kent: Kent State University Press, 2006), 110–11.
64 "The Food for Peace Program," Submitted by the Committee to the President-elect January 19, 1961, and "A Report of the Food for Peace Committee Appointed by Senator Kennedy," October 31, 1960, PC 2/CO 150 Kenya (Executive), Box 662, Series 39, White House Central Subject Files (WHCSF), JFKL.
65 Staples, *Development*, 111, 114.
66 Kaptulus, interview by author, Leseru, November 22, 2012; Theresa Ngososei, interview by author, Leseru, November 27, 2012.
67 Philomon Tanai, interview by author, Leseru, January 9, 2013.
68 Executive Secretary L.D. Battle to McGeorge Bundy, "Presentation to the President of a Carved Walking Stick from the Kamba Tribe of Kenya," August 29, 1961, Folder Kenya: General, 1961, Box 127, Series 01: Countries, National Security Files (NSF), JFKL.
69 District Officer, Hinterland, on behalf of the Hinterland Chiefs, to Kennedy, September 12, 1962, Folder: Kenya, Box 63, Series 07: Countries, WHCSF, JFKL.
70 The Hon. R.G. Ngala to The President of the United States of America, The White House, November 30, 1961, Countries: Kenya: November 1961–January 1962, President's Office Files (POF), JFKL.
71 Kabiru Deen, Nairobi, "Letters to the Editor: President Kennedy," *East African Standard*, November 26, 1963.
72 Dave Zarembka, e-mail message to the author, March 16, 2017.
73 Kristin Phillips, *Subsistence Citizenship: Hunger, Development, and the Politics of Precarity* (Bloomington: Indiana University Press, 2018).
74 James Giblin, *The Politics of Environmental Control in Northeastern Tanzania, 1840-1940* (Philadelphia: University of Pennsylvania Press, 1992).
75 Kennedy to Musyioki, chairman of the council, September 6, 1961 Box 269, Gifts (GI), Series 17, WHCSF, JFKL; Kennedy to the honorable Ronald Ngala, leader of the house, Nairobi, Kenya, January 19, 1962, Countries, Kenya: November 1961–January 1962, POF, Presidential Papers, PJFK, JFKL.
76 "Presentation of a Carved Walking Stick."
77 Nairobi to Department of State, March 13, 1963, Box 127, NSF, JFKL.
78 Jomo Kenyatta, KANU President to the US President, May 9, 1963, Box 127, NSF, JFKL.
79 Horne notes, "Kenyatta's Spring 1963 message questioning the severe maltreatment of demonstrating Negroes in Birmingham was accorded 'heavy play [in] all newspapers,' said the Nairobi Consulate." *Mau Mau in Harlem?*, 228.
80 Mary Dudziak, *Cold War Civil Rights: Race and the Image of American Democracy* (Princeton: Princeton University Press, 2011); Westad, *Cold War*, 135.
81 Mary Dudziak, "The 1963 March on Washington," *French Journal of American Studies* 107 (2006): 67.
82 Kenya, National Assembly Official Report (Hansard), November 15, 1963.
83 Ibid.
84 "Cathedral Service Tomorrow," *East African Standard*, November 25, 1963.

85 Ibid.
86 "6,000 Pay Tribute to Mr. Kennedy: Kenya Leaders Attend Requiem Mass," *East African Standard*, November 27, 1963.
87 Attwood, recorded interview, 11, OHP, JFKL.
88 Mboya, recorded interview, 5.
89 Alulu, interview by author, July 20, 2016.
90 Kaptulus, interview by author, June 9, 2015.
91 Jairo Murunga Libapu, interview by author, Lumakanda, July 19, 2016.
92 Barack Obama Sr. did not travel to the United States on the airlift, though he did benefit from AASF financial assistance while attending university.

4

Brazilian Public Opinion of John F. Kennedy and the Alliance for Progress in Cold War Brazil (1961–63)

Felipe Loureiro

In the early 1960s Brazil became a crucial Cold War battleground for the United States. The country presented serious economic problems and social upheavals. The recently inaugurated Kennedy administration feared that Brazil could experience revolution, following Fidel Castro's Havana, seen as an imminent threat to US national security.[1] Some even believed that if Brazil went red, it would become not another Cuba but another China, given its continental size, resources, strategic importance, and regional impact.[2]

It was no accident, then, that Washington considered Brazil key for the success of the Alliance for Progress, Kennedy's economic aid program to Latin America. Based on the so-called modernization theory, the alliance intended to employ aid to promote growth in "transitional" societies interpreted to be halfway between "traditional" and "modern," or on the edge of a "takeoff" stage, as MIT social scientist Walt Rostow had it. Modernization intellectuals and the US officials feared this transition, as its social and economic transformations might politically destabilize affected nations. The alliance hence sought to foster development to prevent radical revolution.[3]

The alliance also intended to modernize Latin American countries taking the US economy, society, politics, and culture as its ideal type.[4] Simultaneously, from the late 1950s the Soviet Union was offering Third World countries economic assistance too, presenting the statist Soviet model as the quickest and the safest path toward development. The perception that Moscow had modernized fast, turning a backward rural country into a world power in a few decades, and was competing head-to-head with the United States (if not surpassing it, for instance in space), seemed to prove that Nikita Khrushchev was right to assert the superiority of the Soviet model.[5]

Just as Moscow opened up to Third World countries, Washington's hegemony over Latin America, uncontested after the Second World War, ran into obstacles. The presidency of Kennedy's predecessor, Dwight D. Eisenhower, was not particularly good for the hemisphere. Washington supported right-wing dictators and, despite intense Latin American (especially Brazilian) lobbying, rejected any Marshall-Plan-like aid program.[6] The image of the United States deteriorated in the region. Venezuelans violently attacked Vice President Richard Nixon's goodwill tour motorcade in May 1958.[7] Cuba's increasing anti-Americanism and the sympathy it seemed to enjoy in the hemisphere reinforced the US perception that something had to be done in order not to lose the continent to Communism.[8]

Kennedy understood this well, as his Alliance for Progress showed.[9] Besides, few could have represented the winds of change better. He was a young, dynamic, and charismatic leader, as well as Catholic, as many Latin Americans. And he talked of the need for US citizens to help out their fellow brothers of the hemisphere in achieving development through democratic institutions, opening up a "New Frontier" there and elsewhere in the Third World.[10]

Even though the Alliance for Progress ultimately failed—the 1960s became "the decade of dictatorship" in Latin America, not the promised "decade of development"—it is unclear to what extent this happened because public opinion remained indifferent to Kennedy's image and policies. Nor is it clear whether a possible lack of public support pushed Washington to count on (and instigate) anti-communist Latin American militaries to take power.[11]

Brazil is a case in point. Kennedy and US officials recognized the country's regional importance and saw in it as "transitional" nation par excellence.[12] Indeed, rapid industrialization was transforming the Brazilian landscape. A traditionally rural society was urbanizing at a rapid pace. In twenty years, from 1939 to 1959, the number of city dwellers was quickly catching up with those living in the countryside.[13] However, poverty, income inequality, and poor public services persisted.[14] When the economy plummeted in the early 1960s, social tensions peaked. Urban and rural workers mobilized increasingly, some of them influenced by radical leftist leaders, including communists. Leftist leaders helped propel an unprecedented level of public demonstrations, urban strikes, and land invasions.[15] In Washington, many believed Brazil was on the verge of a revolution.[16] In March 1964 a US-backed coup overthrew Brazil's left-wing president João Goulart (1961–64), opening the door for a twenty-one yearlong military dictatorship.[17]

Taking this story as background, this chapter seeks to analyze how Brazilians perceived Kennedy, the United States, and the Alliance for Progress during Kennedy's administration. Implicitly, we seek to address whether US attitudes and policies toward the region, such as the launching of the Alliance for Progress (March 1961), the failed Bays of Pigs invasion (April 1961), the signature of the alliance charter in Punta del Este, Uruguay (August 1961), and Kennedy's handling of the Cuban Missile Crisis (October 1962) affected how Brazilians perceived the president, the United States, and the alliance. This in turn may help explain why Washington began to see a coup against president Goulart as a possible solution to the so-called Brazilian problem.

To study Brazil's public opinion in the early 1960s, we rely on three surveys conducted by two Brazilians polling institutes on behalf of the United States Information Agency (USIA), and under instructions of the US State Department: the *Instituto de Pesquisas de Opinião e Mercado* (IPOM [Market and Public Opinion Research Institute]), founded in 1952 as an affiliate of Elmo Wilson's International Research Associates (INRA), and the *Instituto de Estudos Sociais e Econômicos* (INESE [Institute for Social and Economic Studies]), an offshoot of IPOM founded three years later. Both specialized in providing opinion polls for the US embassy in Brazil and became models for good-quality polling research in the country.[18] Their surveys are not fully comparable, though; questions, methodology, and scope differed. Nonetheless, they constitute the only known surveys that polled Brazilians' perceptions of Kennedy, the United States, and the alliance. As a matter of fact, the December 1962 pool, carried out by INESE, was the second national opinion poll in Brazil's history.[19]

The chapter is divided into four sections. Section one presents a brief context of US-Latin American, and especially US-Brazilian relations during the Kennedy presidency, as well as of Brazil's economic and political outlook at the period. Section two discusses Brazilians' perceptions of Kennedy and the United States between January 1961 and November 1962. Section three does the same, but having the Alliance for Progress as the main focus. Finally, section four concludes.

Brazil and the United States during the Kennedy administration

During the short Jânio Quadros administration (January to August 1961), Washington showed great interest in assisting Brazil through the Alliance for Progress. In May, the Kennedy government approved a major financial package on Brazil's behalf, refinancing old debts and providing new money.[20] The situation changed radically when Jânio Quadros renounced the presidency in August, triggering a political crisis. Vice President João Goulart's links with leftist groups, particularly in the labor movement, made him unacceptable to parts of the Brazilian army. Some officers accused Goulart of being either a communist himself or a useful innocent, indirectly accepting communist infiltration of Brazil's trade unions in exchange for political support from workers.[21]

At least since the early 1950s Washington also nurtured a long-term distrust of "Jango," as Goulart was informally known. Even though Kennedy issued a declaration stating that the United States would not interfere in the August crisis, Washington secretly discussed whether to provide material support for anti-Goulart officers, backing away only when realizing that these officers would not prevail.[22] Eventually, to avoid a civil war, a compromise was reached: Goulart stepped in, but with limited powers. The Brazilian Congress approved an amendment to the country's constitution, setting up a parliamentary regime. A plebiscite was scheduled to take place six months before the end of Goulart's term (to be finished in January 1966), so Brazilians could decide whether to maintain the new political system.

Although Washington preferred Goulart out of power, US-Brazilian relations during his presidency started off better than one could have imagined. This was due mainly to Goulart's limited powers and his political moderation early on. But after less than a year, relations deteriorated, principally because Goulart struggled bitterly against the legislative for anticipating the plebiscite on the parliamentary amendment. He won after receiving the backing of the country's leftist labor leaders, who organized two national strikes in support of his demands and gained full presidential powers in January 1963.²³ In late 1962, to make things worse, Goulart threatened to sever relations with Washington and look for Soviet aid if the Kennedy administration did not provide sufficient economic aid in support of Brazil's economic development plan. The threat backfired, stiffening Washington's attitude toward the Brazilian president.²⁴

By mid-1963, relations between the two countries were dramatically strained. The Kennedy administration was providing alliance money only to friendly Brazilian states, a policy famously named by US ambassador Lincoln Gordon as "islands of administrative sanity."²⁵ Concomitantly, US contacts with the anti-Goulart officers and civilians increased. Supported by the Johnson administration—which continued and to some extent intensified Kennedy's strategy toward Brazil—the military toppled Goulart in March 1964, setting up what would turn out to be a twenty-one-year-long authoritarian regime in Latin America's largest country.

Given the Kennedy administration's key role in early 1960s Brazil and the impact of US attitudes and policies in Latin America, one may ask to what extent the perceptions of common Brazilians about the young, charismatic, and active Kennedy followed, or even influenced, the changing stages of US-Brazilian relations. How did Brazilians judge Kennedy and his leadership? And did Washington's incrementally toughening policy toward Goulart's Brazil impact Brazilians' view of the US president? The next sections seek to address these issues by looking at opinion polls.

Brazil's public opinion on President Kennedy

Before poring over Brazilians' evolving perception of Kennedy, we have to address two poll characteristics. One regards representativeness. The polls deal only with urban areas. The November–December 1962 poll, the broadest of the three, was based on all Brazil's municipalities with more than 10,000 habitants—the majority of Brazil's cities. The 55 percent of Brazilians living in the countryside in 1960 was excluded from the poll then. Representativeness was even trickier in the September 1961 poll. It was based only on Brazil's two biggest cities: Rio de Janeiro and São Paulo, the former Brazilian capital and the country's economic heart, respectively.²⁶

The second characteristic regards the polls' questions. Only the January and the September 1961 surveys contained specific questions about Kennedy. The latest poll, carried out in late 1962, inquired interviewees about the United States as a country, not about the president. This is not a major setback, though. Brazilians considerably personalized (and still personalize) politics.²⁷ It is reasonable to suggest that the way Brazilians rated Washington matched the image they nurtured about the US leader.

Taking these two considerations into account, the first question one needs to ask is to what extent (urban) Brazilians were even aware of Kennedy's existence in the early 1960s. The number was surprisingly low. In January 1961, just before the start of the Kennedy administration, only 41.7 percent of Brazilians who lived in the country's five biggest and richest cities (São Paulo, Rio de Janeiro, Belo Horizonte, Porto Alegre, and Recife) knew him.²⁸ This was not because he had not yet been sworn in. Eisenhower was leaving that month and only 44.1 percent had knowledge of him—a number just slightly higher than Kennedy's.²⁹

In Brazil's countryside, even fewer knew Kennedy. The January 1961 survey is the only of the three polls that contains a small (but very unrepresentative) rural sample: two rural municipalities, Limoeiro and Divinópolis, belonging to two of the most important and populous Brazilian states, Pernambuco and Minas Gerais, respectively. In both, 98 percent of the interviewees were unable to identify Eisenhower or Kennedy.[30] If this represents even vaguely Brazil's rural areas, it would mean that both US presidents were completely unknown to more than half of the Brazilian population.

This low level of awareness regarding a basic feature of international affairs certainly had to do with the country's underdevelopment. Brazil was the fourth worst nation in South America in terms of life expectancy (fifty-five years of life expectancy on average, against sixty-eight in Uruguay, sixty-five in Argentina, and fifty-seven in Chile); the third worst in illiteracy rate (40 percent of Brazilians could neither read nor write in 1960, against 9 percent of the Argentineans, 11 percent of the Uruguayans, and 16 percent of the Chileans); and the second worst in primary school enrolment (10.2 percent in 1960).[31] When one geographically disaggregates social indicators, the picture becomes even more dramatic. Of the twenty-one states in the Brazilian federation in the early 1960s, three-quarters had more than 50 percent of their municipalities without water supply and sewage treatment. The poorest and less urbanized states also presented the worst indicators in terms of life expectancy, illiteracy, and school enrollment. Although 40 percent of the Brazilian population was not able to read and write in 1960, in five states as many as 75 percent were illiterate when Kennedy became president.[32] It is not a great surprise thus that the majority of urban Brazilians (and almost the totality of those living in Brazil's countryside) did not know who the recently elected US president was in January 1961.

In just seven months, the situation had changed considerably, at least in Brazil's two most important cities. In the September 1961 survey, carried out in Rio de Janeiro and São Paulo, almost 70 percent of interviewees knew Kennedy, while back in January the figures had been considerably lower (Table 4.1). The emphasis of Kennedy's foreign policy agenda on Latin America, as well as the US government's considerable propaganda efforts promoting the Alliance for Progress and Kennedy himself, seems to have had an effect.[33] For the first time in the Cold War, Latin America had become a crucial region for the United States.[34]

Disaggregating the September 1961 poll by gender, age, and class yields interesting results. Men, young adults, and rich and middle-class people were considerably more likely to know Kennedy than others, particularly women, old people, and the poor. Variance is perhaps most striking regarding income. More than 90 percent of interviewees belonging to rich and medium-income classes, but less than half of those grouped as poor, knew Kennedy in September 1961 (Table 4.1).

If public knowledge of Kennedy increased in Brazil's greatest cities between January and September 1961, and if it is reasonable to think this had to do with the US leader's attention to Latin American issues and with the amount of direct and indirect references to Kennedy in Brazilian TV and radio stations and newspapers and magazines, one needs to ask next: How did Rio and São Paulo citizens perceive Kennedy? Put simply: As good or bad? Considering that the survey came out only a

Table 4.1 Awareness of Brazil's Public Opinion as to Who the US President Was, São Paulo and Rio de Janeiro, September 1961

	Kennedy		Other or Don't Know		Total	
	Number	%	Number	%	Number	%
Total	552	69.0	248	31.0	800	100.0
By City						
Rio de Janeiro	296	74.0	104	26.0	400	100.0
São Paulo	256	64.0	144	36.0	400	100.0
By Sex						
Men	312	78.0	88	22.0	400	100.0
Women	240	60.0	160	40.0	400	100.0
By Age						
18–24	135	67.5	65	32.5	200	100.0
24–44	295	72.0	115	28.0	410	100.0
44 or plus	115	60.5	75	39.5	190	100.0
By Social Class						
Rich	41	93.2	3	6.8	44	100.0
Medium Class	322	90.4	34	9.6	356	100.0
Poor	188	47.0	212	53.0	400	100.0

Source: INESE, "Brazil, Sept. 1961, Brazil in Crisis Attitudes," September 1961, RG 306, NARA.

few months after the Bay of Pigs fiasco (April 1961) and a few weeks after the official inauguration of the Alliance for Progress (August 1961), there were reasons to account for both possibilities.

Overall, Rio and São Paulo citizens saw Kennedy in a very positive light. More than 60 percent of those who had an opinion of him considered the US president a "good leader," grading him from eight to ten in a zero-to-ten rating scale. Less than 10 percent considered Kennedy a "bad leader." Once again, disaggregating numbers by gender, age, and income yields significant contrasts. Women, young adults, and poor people were least likely to evaluate Kennedy's leadership. And not coincidently, all these parameters correlate with low levels of formal education, higher illiteracy rates, and harder access to information. Income showed the greatest variance. Among the rich, almost 70 percent considered Kennedy a good leader. This suggests that those who constituted the alliance's main target, the poor, were less amenable to Kennedy's image and policies, at least in Brazil's two largest cities (Table 4.2).

Turning to the reasons behind Kennedy's good performance in Rio and São Paulo opinion polls, one finds surprisingly that it did not have to do with the alliance. Interviewees were asked to grade Kennedy's leadership at the moment of the interview, September, and before the August 1961 official launch of the alliance. Remarkably, results were almost the same: roughly 60 percent of the interviewees graded Kennedy as a good leader. Among the few whose opinion improved, only 1 percent pointed to

Table 4.2 Brazil's Public Opinion on John F. Kennedy, São Paulo and Rio de Janeiro, September 1961

	Bad (0–2)		Normal (3–7)		Good (8–10)		Don't Know	
	Number	%	Number	%	Number	%	Number	%
Total	56	7.0	184	23.0	380	47.5	180	22.5
By City								
Rio de Janeiro	24	6.0	80	20.0	212	53.0	84	21.0
São Paulo	32	8.0	104	26.0	168	42.0	96	24.0
By Sex								
Men	26	6.5	110	27.5	194	48.5	70	17.5
Women	24	6.0	74	18.5	186	46.5	116	29.0
By Age								
18–24	11	5.5	59	29.5	91	45.5	39	19.5
24–44	31	7.6	101	24.6	199	48.5	79	19.3
44 or plus	6	3.2	24	12.6	93	48.9	67	35.3
By Social Class								
Rich	2	4.5	11	25.0	28	63.6	3	6.8
Medium Class	23	6.5	93	26.1	221	62.1	19	5.3
Poor	22	5.5	80	20.0	138	34.5	160	40.0

Source: INESE, "Brazil, Sept. 1961, Brazil in Crisis Attitudes," September 1961, RG 306, NARA.

either US foreign aid policy to developing countries or US loans to Brazil. Importantly, months before, in May, the US government had offered a major financial package on Brazil's behalf using the alliance label, a move that had received substantial news coverage in Brazil and highlighted by US propaganda.[35] Regardless, it does not seem that Brazilians with the greatest access to news linked the alliance with the US leader. And if this was the case in Brazil's two biggest and richest cities, it was probably true in the country's most backward, rural areas.

If not for the alliance, what was the foundation for this good image? An interesting strategy is to examine how Rio and São Paulo citizens interpreted Kennedy's statement about the Brazilian political crisis of August 1961, sparked by President Quadros's sudden resignation. Even though Washington secretly considered supporting the anti-Goulart faction of the Brazilian army, in his statement Kennedy declared that Washington respected Brazil's right for self-determination. In spite of the fact that 76 percent of the interviewees were not acquainted with Kennedy's declaration, more than half thought he had been sincere when presented with the statement. Once again, men, young adults, and affluent citizens showed the greatest confidence in the US president (Table 4.3).

What interests us most, however, is the reason behind the faith that Rio and São Paulo citizens had in Kennedy, even though two-thirds did not know his statement in advance. Table 4.4 illuminates this matter. The largest portion, 35 percent, believed in Kennedy not because of what he did, but of what he was. They believed in the US leader for his perceived personal attributes, including honesty, sincerity, righteousness,

Table 4.3 Brazil's Public Opinion on Whether John F. Kennedy Was Sincere in His Declaration about the Brazilian August 1961 Political Crisis, São Paulo and Rio de Janeiro, September 1961*

	Sincere		Wasn't Sincere		Don't Know	
	Number	%	Number	%	Number	%
Total	434	54.3	90	11.3	276	34.5
By City						
Rio de Janeiro	226	56.5	28	7.0	146	36.5
São Paulo	208	52.0	62	15.5	130	32.5
By Sex						
Men	232	58.0	56	14.0	112	28.0
Women	202	50.5	34	8.5	164	41.0
By Age						
18–24	100	50.0	29	14.5	71	35.5
24–44	240	58.5	45	11.0	125	30.5
44 or plus	96	50.5	19	10.0	75	39.5
By Social Class						
Rich	28	63.6	2	4.5	14	31.8
Medium Class	236	66.3	50	14.0	70	19.7
Poor	172	43.0	40	10.0	188	47.0

Source: INESE, "Brazil, Sept. 1961, Brazil in Crisis Attitudes," September 1961, RG 306, NARA.

judiciousness, responsibility, good intentions, and friendliness. These traits were particularly emphasized by women (Table 4.4).

Regrettably, the September pool does not allow us to know what made interviewees conclude all this about Kennedy. It is reasonable to conjecture that United States Information Agency (USIA) propaganda and commercials—many promoting the alliance and Kennedy in person—might have been the main cause.[36] Brazilians' good if not heroically romanticized perceptions of Kennedy comprised *imagined* personal attributes. At least, this is a logical conclusion given that interviewees knew little about the alliance and Kennedy's actions and speeches. Instead of being drawing on well-grounded knowledge, Rio and São Paulo citizens seemed to perceive the US president based on his image, particularly his youthfulness, charisma, and the way he unwittingly projected the notion of white masculinity.

In fact, the concept that politics and public life naturally belonged to white males was widespread in postwar Brazil, even though black and women's movements became stronger and more vocal in the first half of the century, and small steps were taken toward equal rights. Women's right to vote, for example, came only in 1932, and as long as 1962, when Brazil's Civil Code was reformed, women were still considered legally incapacitated, alongside minors and the mentally ill. The perspective that women had to be constrained to the domestic sphere, as guardians of the family, acting as wife and mother, was dominant, carrying the weight of Brazil's patriarchal heritage and Catholic

Table 4.4 Reasons Expressed by Brazil's Public Opinion to Believe that John F. Kennedy Was Sincere in His Declaration about the Brazilian August 1961 Political Crisis, São Paulo and Rio de Janeiro, September 1961 (percent)

	Total	Rio	São Paulo	Men	Women
Kennedy is intelligent, sincere, judicious, responsible, a friend, a democrat, well-intentioned, honest, a man of peace	35.0	33.8	34.5	30.3	37.5
Kennedy did not interfere in our political crisis; because the United States usually doesn't interfere in Brazil	21.7	20.0	20.7	22.7	17.9
The United States is our friend; has been always our friend	8.3	7.7	8.6	9.1	7.1
The United States has given financial aid to Brazil; the United States is interested in Brazil's development; because the United States is aiding Latin America	6.7	6.2	6.9	9.1	3.6
Kennedy is Catholic; Kennedy has a Christian formation	3.3	6.2	3.4	3.0	5.4
Kennedy's political trajectory as defender of democracy	1.7	3.1	1.7	3.0	3.6
The United States has interests in Brazil; the United States has investments in Brazil	1.7	1.5	3.4	4.5	0.0
I don't see reason for Kennedy not being sincere	1.7	3.1	0.0	1.5	1.8
Other reasons	5.0	7.7	1.7	6.1	3.6
Don't know	15.0	10.8	19.0	10.6	19.6
Total	100.0	100.0	100.0	100.0	100.0

Source: INESE, "Brazil, Sept. 1961, Brazil in Crisis Attitudes," September 1961, RG 306, NARA.

formation. Public opinion pools carried out in Brazil's largest cities in the early 1960s confirm that not only men but also most women considered that politics and public life were basically men's business.[37] No wonder women stood out in pointing to imagined personal attributes to explaining their good opinion on President Kennedy in September 1961. As a white man, Kennedy was occupying a natural space in leading one of the world's great powers.

The second and third most common answers to the question why Rio and São Paulo citizens believed Kennedy was a sincere leader did not refer to actual US policies and/or actions in Brazil either. Rather, both related to perceived personal attitudes of Kennedy's or to a decades-old US-Brazilian friendship, even though bilateral relationship became gradually colder in the postwar period.[38] Fascinatingly, the fact that Kennedy was the first US Catholic leader was not as relevant. Neither was his presumed defense of democracy. Similarly, few named US economic aid to Brazil as their main reason to believe Kennedy was sincere. This was another clue that the

Alliance for Progress had a superficial impact on the perception of those living in Brazil's two most important cities.

A year later, in December 1962, Brazil's urban public opinion maintained the same good view on Washington, despite the poor effective results presented by the alliance by then. The November–December 1962 survey shows that half of urban Brazilians considered the United States "good or very good," similar to 1961 (Figure 4.1).

An interesting feature of the November–December 1962 survey is that it contains data on six other South American countries: Argentina, Bolivia, Colombia, Chile, Ecuador, and Venezuela. As Figure 4.1 makes crystal clear, the major contrast between them was the relatively high number of Brazilians without an opinion about the United States. This probably reflected Brazilians' lower level of instruction and access to information. Of the six surveyed countries, only Bolivia's illiteracy rates were higher than Brazil's. While Brazil had more citizens who did not have an opinion on Washington, the remaining five South America countries presented the inverse picture: more citizens who regarded Washington as "very good." To be aware of what Washington was doing at the time seems to have been correlated to approval.

A similar pattern is found looking at Brazil's and other South American countries' perception on whether Washington had the capacity to provide "wise leadership" in world affairs on behalf of the hemisphere. This question is particularly interesting given the timing of the survey: weeks after the Cuban Missile Crisis. Its resolution represented an enormous victory for the United States against the Soviet Union, demonstrated Kennedy's crisis management skills, and proved that Latin America was unquestionably a US zone of influence.[39] While two-thirds of South Americans believed Washington had either "very great" or "considerable" capacity to lead the hemisphere, less than half of Brazilians thought the same. Strikingly, the number of Brazilians who did not have an opinion on the issue matches those who regarded Washington as competent to perform the role of leader (Figure 4.2).

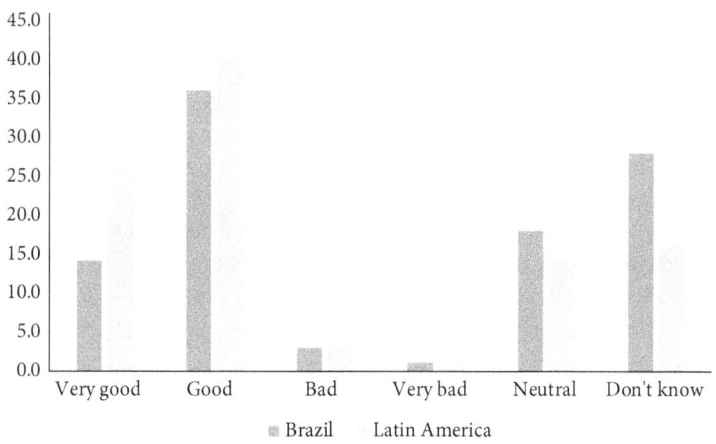

Figure 4.1 Brazilian and Latin American public opinion on the United States, urban areas, November–December 1962 (percent).

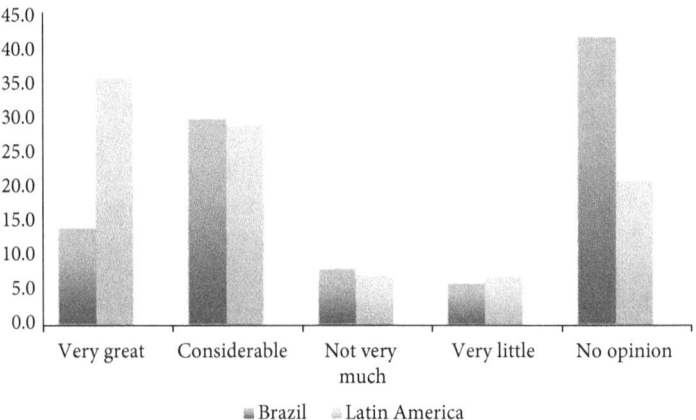

Figure 4.2 Confidence of Brazilian and Latin American public opinion on the US ability to provide wise leadership for other countries, urban areas, November–December 1962 (percent).

Although South Americans were much more confident in the US leadership after the Cuban Missile Crisis than the Brazilians, Brazil's urban public opinion continued to be, for the most part, in favor of Kennedy's United States. A quick comparison will do here. At the same time, in late 1962, only 12 percent of urban Brazilians had a "very good" or "good" opinion of the Soviet Union, with 48 percent nurturing a "bad" or "very bad" perception of Moscow. The same question regarding Fidel Castro, one of the main actors of the Cuban Missile Crisis, wielded similar results. Just 8 percent of urban Brazilians liked Castro in late 1962, while 45 percent had a "bad" or "very bad" opinion" of him. Clearly, Brazil was not becoming a safe haven for Soviet or Castro-like Communists, as some right-wing Brazilians, as well as some US policymakers, feared.[40]

Besides, the majority of Brazilians who had "very little" or "not very much" confidence in the US leadership did not know the reason for such feelings—a huge contrast with the rest of South America, where the absolute majority knew why they felt that way (Table 4.5). Brazilians with anti-US tendencies tended to be much more malleable to change than their Spanish-speaking South American counterparts, as the latter were able to identify concrete reasons for their bad perceptions of Washington.

An important feature of Table 4.5 is the number of Brazilians and other South Americans who did not trust the US leadership because of Washington's economic interests in the hemisphere, whether because the US government was only "interested in profits" and "in exploiting other countries," or because Washington faced "too many pressures from vested economic interests." In 1961, only 1.7 percent of Rio and São Paulo citizens had pointed to these issues. Even though the question and the survey are not the same, the fact that this number doubled by 1962, to 4 percent, is significant.

By the time of the November–December 1962 survey, Latin Americans' criticism of the alliance had become much more acute. The next section will focus on whether Brazilians were acquainted with Kennedy's aid program in late 1962.

Table 4.5 Reasons for the Lack of Confidence in the US Leadership by Brazilian and Latin American Public Opinion, Urban Centers, November–December 1962 (percent)

	Brazil	Latin America
The United States is only interested in profits; in exploiting other countries; too many pressures from vested economic interests	4.0	5.0
Because Americans are ignorant, lack experience; the history of US international relations shows them incapable of doing so	0.0	1.0
No country can direct other countries; other countries resist US leadership	2.0	1.0
Lack of US sincerity; the United States doesn't really have the desire or motivation to provide leadership in international affairs	1.0	1.0
US military interests prevent their providing wise leadership; only interested in military power	0.0	0.0
Other reasons	1.0	3.0
Don't know; not indicated	6.0	2.0
Not asked	86.0	87.0
Total	100.0	100.0

Source: INESE, "The Economic and Political Climate of Opinion in Latin America and Attitudes Toward the Alliance for Progress," June 1963, JFKL.

Brazil's public opinion on the Alliance for Progress

The only USIA survey carried out in Goulart's Brazil that asked specific questions about the Alliance for Progress was the November–December 1962 poll. By then, Kennedy's aid program for Latin America was almost two years old. In Brazil, it started off promisingly, saving the Quadros administration from financial bankruptcy in May 1961, and providing in April 1962 for the following two years $131 million in economic aid to Northeast Brazil, the country's poorest region.[41] Similarly to what happened in other parts of Latin America though, US policymakers put forward several conditions for disbursing aid, provoking criticism from Latin American leaders, including Goulart. By the time the Inter-American Economic and Social Council (IA-ECOSOC) took place in Mexico City in October 1962, to discuss what the alliance had accomplished, the general feeling, especially among Latin American representatives, was that the program needed to be reformed. As Washington's support for the alliance waned from 1963, so did the program.[42]

Despite the modest performance of the alliance during its first two years, and the low level of instruction and access to means of information that Brazilians had, it is still eye-opening, given the USIA's strenuous promotion of Kennedy's aid program in Latin America, that the majority of urban Brazilians were unaware of the very existence of the alliance by late 1962 (Figure 4.3). If rural areas had been taken into account, this

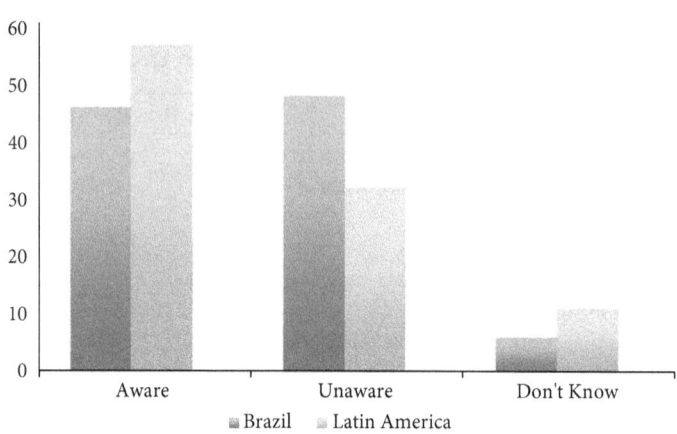

Figure 4.3 Awareness of Brazilian and Latin American public opinion on Kennedy's Alliance for Progress, urban centers, November–December 1962 (percent).

figure would certainly have been much higher. Elsewhere in South America, the level of awareness was greater, reaching almost 60 percent of the interviewees. But even there, no less than one in three did not know what Alliance for Progress meant in November–December 1962.

If it is clear, then, that the alliance was simply unknown to a great proportion of urban Brazilians in late 1962, what can be said about the perception of those who knew the program at least by name? Did they have a good impression? The answer is no. The number of Brazilians who "fully" approved Kennedy's aid program matched those who approved it "partially," did not care, or did not have an opinion about it. Being aware of the alliance in Brazil's urban areas in November–December 1962 did not mean being favor of it. A large proportion of Brazilians was simply uninterested, ignorant, or discontent about Kennedy's major policy initiative for Latin America (Figure 4.4). A different picture emerges when we look at South America as a whole. Two-thirds of those acquainted with the alliance fully approved it by late 1962—a percentage almost two times Brazil's. In South American countries, then, if one got to know the Alliance for Progress, one tended to be in favor of it (Figure 4.4).

The alliance's performance did not vary substantially among Latin American nations during the Kennedy presidency. And although US-Brazilian relations deteriorated sharply from mid-1962, until then Brazil was privileged in terms of aid allocation.[43] Therefore, the difference in support for Kennedy's program probably did not have to do with fund disbursements or, for that matter, with short-term US economic interests in disrupting the alliance's goals, the program's poor planning and results, or the lack of US accountability concerning its performance.

As Table 4.6 shockingly indicates, more than 75 percent of the urban Brazilians who did not fully approve Kennedy's aid program in late 1962 in fact did not know why they had such a view. Therefore, to have heard of the Alliance for Progress in Brazil's urban areas in November–December 1962 meant precisely (and only) that to have heard the name of the program, but not to be aware of its content and objectives,

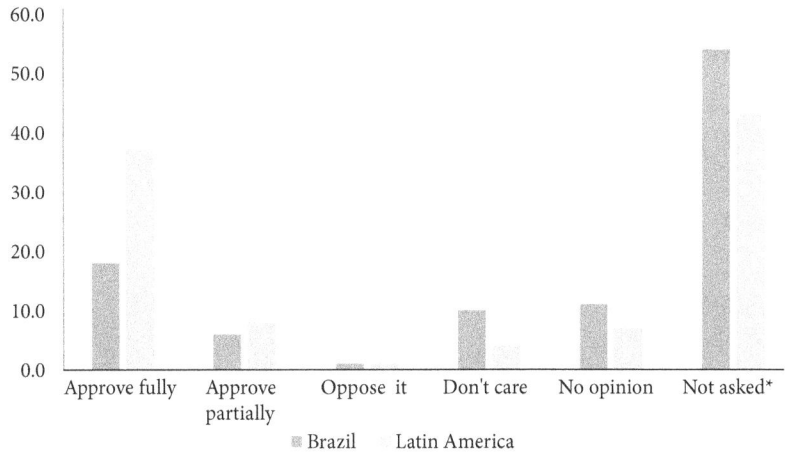

Figure 4.4 Level of approval of Kennedy's Alliance for Progress by Brazilian and Latin American public opinion, urban centers, November–December 1962 (percent).

Table 4.6 Reasons Stated by Brazil's and Latin America's Public Opinion for Not Fully Approving the Alliance for Progress, Urban Centers, November–December 1962 (percent)*

	Brazil	Latin America
The aims of the United States are not disinterested or completely sincere in giving aid; the alliance is being used to serve the interests of US capitalists; it is a political maneuver.	1.0	3.0
The public is not sufficiently informed as to the objectives and development of the program. It does not have popular support.	1.0	3.0
Because the alliance has not yet shown the results which were expected of it.	0.0	2.0
Government instability, inefficiency and poor administration hamper the progress of the program; they plan projects but don't carry them out.	0.0	0.0
Planning for the program is poor; the program is badly thought out.	1.0	0.0
Other reasons	1.0	2.0
Don't know, not indicated	13.0	6.0
Not asked	83	87
Total	100.0	103.0

Notes: * Total may exceed 100 percent because some respondents provided more than one answer.
Source: INESE, "The Economic and Political Climate of Opinion in Latin America and Attitudes Toward the Alliance for Progress," June 1963, JFKL.

let alone its results and limitations. This reinforces the idea that the good approval ratings that the United States and Kennedy garnered in early 1960s Brazil stemmed from imagined perceptions resulting from Kennedy's image as a leader and some long-term goodwill held by Brazilians toward the United States not because of actual US policies and actions.

Conclusion

The analysis of Brazil's urban public opinion in the early 1960s indicates that Washington's Cuba policy and the increasing deterioration of US-Brazilian relations did not greatly impact Brazilians' view on Kennedy and the United States. Most urban Brazilians rated Kennedy and Washington extremely well during the January 1961–December 1962 period, even though bilateral relations were strained from mid-1962. Besides, urban Brazilians were more aware of Kennedy than they have been of previous US leaders such as Eisenhower. Still, a good proportion was not acquainted with Kennedy, either.

Looking into the reasons that explain Kennedy's good image in Brazil, the main cause was not his concrete policies, such as the implementation of the Alliance for Progress, for which Brazil was a key country particularly during the Quadros administration and the first months of the Goulart government. Nor was Kennedy's Catholicism much of value, even though Catholic Brazilians made up the bulk of the country's population. The main cause rather seemed to be how Brazilians perceived his public persona: his sincerity, righteousness, responsibility, and friendliness. To interpret these perceptions, surveys would have to be much more specific, though, which was not the case. We can only conjecture that the causes might have to do with Kennedy's own projected attributes (charisma, youth, eloquence); with Brazilians' tendency to personalize politics, to evaluate political leaders through moral lenses, and to regard the public sphere as a natural realm for while males; and with the long-standing image of the United States as a Brazilian partner and ally.

The conclusion that Kennedy's good image was related more to his attributes than policies is reinforced by the fact that most urban Brazilians simply disregarded Kennedy's most important policy initiative for Latin America at the time: the Alliance for Progress. This showed in December 1962, a full year and a half after the program's inauguration, and despite strenuous efforts by the US government, particularly the USIA, to promote the alliance through various channels, such as TV, radio, newspapers, magazines, and billboards. Even among those that responded positively, indicating they had heard of the program, almost half did not fully approve it, although the vast majority could not explain why.

In general, then, Brazilians had a very superficial knowledge about the largest US policy initiative in Latin America. Still, they mostly approved Kennedy and/or held the United States in high esteem. This good perception was definitely not due to the alliance's promises or results, then. It is true that the picture is different when one takes South America as a whole: the United States rated higher, and more people knew of Kennedy's aid program. But this does not change the fact that Kennedy's and US approval rates in Brazil were still remarking high—contrasting with the Soviet Union and Fidel Castro's Cuba, for example—regardless their lack of knowledge about the alliance.

Another fascinating aspect one finds looking into Brazil's urban opinion during the Kennedy administration is that age, gender, and income counted. In general, men, young adults, and most importantly wealthy citizens registered the highest approval ratings of Kennedy and the United States. As the alliance focused on overcoming underdevelopment in Latin America, supporting an array of social programs, including the provision of housing, schooling, and basic infrastructure for the hemisphere's poorest areas, it is remarkable that middle-class and rich citizens constituted the bulk of the urban Brazilians who saw a good leader in Kennedy. The main reason was that wealthy citizens, due to better schooling and greater access to means of information, knew who Kennedy was, while more than half of the poor Brazilians who lived in the country's largest cities—probably even those affected by projects financed by the alliance—simply did not know the US president as late as September 1961.

In sum, it seems that the alliance in Brazil boosted Kennedy's image more among those who were less in need of US economic support—and thus less amenable to radical ideologies, according to modernization theorists. Vice versa, a significant number of the urban poor, who alongside the rural poor constituted the key target of US modernizing efforts, seemed to be unaffected by US actions and policies in Brazil, at least when it came to simply knowing the US president and judging what he stood for.

Notes

1 Lars Schoultz, *That Infernal Little Cuban Republic: The United States and the Cuban Revolution* (Chapel Hill: University of North Carolina Press, 2009).
2 For Brazil's importance to Kennedy's administration, see Jeffrey Taffet, *Foreign Aid as Foreign Policy: The Alliance for Progress in Latin America* (New York: Routledge, 2007), 95–97; Stephen Rabe, *The Most Dangerous Area in the World: John F. Kennedy Confronts Communist Revolution in Latin America* (Chapel Hill: University of North Caroline Press, 1999), 63–64; Rabe, *The Killing Zone: The United States Wages Cold War in Latin America* (New York: Oxford University Press, 2012), 110–11. For the China reference, see Peter Smith, *Talons of the Eagle: Dynamics of the US-Latin American Relations* (Oxford: Oxford University Press, 2000), 157.
3 For Brazil and the Alliance, see Felipe Loureiro, "The Alliance For or Against Progress? US-Brazilian Financial Relations in the Early 1960s," *JLAS* 46, no. 2 (2014): 326–33; Rabe, *Killing Zone*, 105–13; Taffet, *Foreign Aid*, ch. 5. For a broad analysis of the Alliance, see Jerome Levinson and Juan de Onís, *The Alliance That Lost Its Way* (Chicago: Quadrangle, 1970); and Michael Dunne, "Kennedy's Alliance for Progress: Countering Revolution in Latin America (Part II): The Historiographical Record," *International Affairs* 92, no. 2 (2016): 435–52.
4 Michael Latham, *The Right Kind of Revolution* (Ithaca: Cornell University Press, 2011), 44–53.

5 For Soviet approaches toward Latin America, see Tobias Rupprecht, *Soviet Internationalism after Stalin: Interaction and Exchange between the USSR and Latin America during the Cold War* (Cambridge: Cambridge University Press, 2015).
6 Stanley Hilton, "The United States, Brazil, and the Cold War, 1945-1960: End of the Special Relationship," *JAmH* 68, no. 3 (1981): 599–624; Stephen Rabe, *Eisenhower and Latin America* (Chapel Hill: University of North Carolina Press, 1988), chs. 1–2.
7 Michael Zahniser and Michael Weis, "A Diplomatic Pearl Harbor? Richard Nixon's Goodwill Mission to Latin America in 1958," *DH* 13, no. 2 (1989): 163–90.
8 Jeffrey Taffet, "Latin America," in *A Companion to John F. Kennedy*, ed. Marc Selverstone (Malden: John Wiley and Sons, 2014), 307–27.
9 Rabe, *Most Dangerous Area*, ch. 1; Taffet, *Foreign Aid*, chs. 1–2.
10 Arthur Schlesinger, *A Thousand Days* (New York: Fawcett, 1992), 184–93.
11 Thomas Field Jr., *From Development to Dictatorship: Bolivia and the Alliance for Progress in the Kennedy Era* (Ithaca: Cornell University Press, 2014), 3.
12 Schlesinger, *Thousand Days*, 117–18.
13 Felipe Loureiro, *Empresários, Trabalhadores e Grupos de Interesse: a Política Econômica nos Governos Jânio Quadros e João Goulart, 1961-1964* (São Paulo: Unesp, 2017), 30–31.
14 Ibid.
15 Cliff Welch and Sérgio Sauer, "Rural Unions and the Struggle for Land in Brazil," *Journal of Peasant Studies* 42, no. 6 (2015): 1113–17; Felipe Loureiro, "Strikes in Brazil during the Government of João Goulart (1961–1964)," *Canadian Journal of Latin American and Caribbean Studies* 46, no. 1 (2016): 76–94.
16 Joseph Page, *The Revolution That Never Was: Northeast Brazil, 1955-1964* (New York: Grossman, 1972), ch. 1.
17 The literature on the US involvement in the coup is vast. Key contributions include René Dreifuss, *1964: A Conquista do Estado* (Petrópolis: Civilização Brasileira, 1987); Ruth Leacock, *Requiem for Revolution* (Kent: Kent State University Press, 1990); and Carlos Fico, *O Grande Irmão. Da Operação Brother Sam aos Anos de Chumbo* (Rio de Janeiro: Civilização Brasileira, 2008), ch. 1. See also Anthony Pereira, "The US Role in the 1964 Coup in Brazil: A Reassessment," *Bulletin of Latin American Research* 37, no. 1 (2018): 5–17. For the impact on Latin America, see Tanya Harmer, "Brazil's Cold War in the Southern Cone," *CWH* 12, no. 4 (2012): 659–81.
18 In chronological order, the three surveys employed here are (a) IPOM, "Brazil, General Attitudes," January 1961, Country Project Files, compiled 1953–1965 (CPF), folder "Brazil, Jan. 1961, Several Attitudes," Box 11, Record Group (RG) 306, National Archives, College Park (NARA); (b) INESE, "Brazil, Sept. 1961, Brazil in Crisis Attitudes," September 1961, CPF, folder "Brazil, Sept. 1961, Brazil in Crisis Attitudes," Box 11, RG 306, NARA; and (c) INESE, "The Economic and Political Climate of Opinion in Latin America and Attitudes Toward the Alliance for Progress," June 1963, National Security Files (NSF), Regional Security Files (RSF), folder "Latin America, General, 7/63-11/63," Box 216, John F. Kennedy Presidential Library (JFKL). For IPOM and INESE, see Octávio da Costa Eduardo, "Pequena História Comentada da Pesquisa de Mercado e Opinião Pública no Brasil," *Revista da ESPM* 10, no. 1 (2003): 10–21. For USIA-led opinion surveys around the world during the Cold War, see Mark Haefele, "John F. Kennedy, USIA, and World Public Opinion," *DH* 25, no. 1 (2001): 63–84; and Alan McPherson, "U.S. Government Responses to Anti-Americanism at the Periphery," in *Foreign Policy at the Periphery: The Shifting Margins*

    of US International Relations since World War II, ed. Beval Sewell and Maria Ryan (Lexington: University Press of Kentucky, 2017), 77–101.
19 Eduardo, "História," 16.
20 Loureiro, "Alliance For or Against Progress," 329–30.
21 A good summary of the 1961 political crisis is Thomas Skidmore, *Politics in Brazil, 1930-1964: An Experiment in Democracy* (New York: Oxford University Press, 2007). For Goulart's links with the Brazilian labor movement, see Felipe Loureiro, "João Goulart e a cúpula do movimento sindical brasileiro," *História São Paulo* 36, no. 3 (2017): 1–23.
22 Loureiro, "Alliance For or Against Progress," 333.
23 Ibid., 337–38.
24 Felipe Loureiro, "The Alliance for Progress and President João Goulart's Three-Year Plan: The Deterioration of US-Brazilian Relations in Cold War Brazil," *CWH* 17, no. 1 (2017): 61–79.
25 Fico, *Irmão*, 78; Leacock, *Requiem*, 135–6. For an in-depth account of the "island of administrative sanity" policy, see Felipe Loureiro, "Making the Alliance for Progress for a Few: U.S. Economic Aid to Brazilian States in Cold War Brazil (1961-1964)," *Journal of Cold War Studies* (forthcoming).
26 Loureiro, *Empresários*, ch. 1.
27 A classic reference on this regard is Victor Nunes Leal, *Coronelismo, enxada e voto. O município e o regime representativo no Brasil*, 4th ed. (São Paulo: Companhia das Letras, 2012).
28 IPOM, "Brazil, General Attitudes," January 1961, RG 306, NARA.
29 Ibid.
30 Ibid.
31 Unless otherwise referenced, all social indicators were taken from the Montevideo Oxford Latin American Database (MOxLAD), and are available online: https://moxlad-staging.herokuapp.com/home/en (accessed November 8, 2018).
32 Instituto Brasileiro de Geografia e Estatística (IBGE), *Estatísticas Históricas do Século XX*. Available online: http://seculoxx.ibge.gov.br/ (accessed November 8, 2018).
33 Fernando Santomauro, *A atuação política da Agência de Informação dos Estados Unidos no Brasil (1953-1964)* (São Paulo: Cultura Acadêmica, 2015), 145–70.
34 Rabe, *Most Dangerous Area*, ch. 1.
35 See Loureiro, *Empresários*, ch. 4.
36 For how USIA employed Kennedy's image in official propaganda in Rio de Janeiro, see Renata Keller, "The Latin American Missile Crisis," *DH* 39, no. 2 (2014): 195–222. For the USIA's role in Brazil, see Santomauro, *atuação política*.
37 For the opinion polls, see Morris Blachman, "Eve in an Adamocracy: The Politics of Women in Brazil" (PhD diss., New York University, 1976), 65–69. Recent contributions include Andrea Allen, *Violence and Desire in Brazilian Lesbian Relationships* (New York: Palgrave, 2015); Benjamin Cowan, *Securing Sex: Morality and Repression in the Making of Cold War Brazil* (Chapel Hill: University of North Carolina Press, 2016). A classic is Thomas Skidmore, *Black into White: Race and Nationality in Brazilian Thought* (Durham: Duke University, 1992).
38 Hilton, "United States." For the birth of Brazil's historically good relations with the United States, see Bradford Burns, *Unwritten Alliance: Rio-Branco and Brazilian-American Relations* (New York: Columbia University Press, 1966).
39 James Hershberg, "The Cuban Missile Crisis," in *The Cambridge History of the Cold War*, vol. II, ed. Melvyn Leffler and Odd Westad (Cambridge: Cambridge University

Press, 2010), 65–87. For the crisis' impact on Latin American geopolitics, see Keller, "Missile Crisis."

40 Loureiro, "Alliance for Progress and President João Goulart's Three-Year Plan," 67–70.
41 For US aid to Quadros's Brazil, see Loureiro, "Alliance For or Against Progress," 333–34. For the US aid to Brazil's Northeast, see Riordan Roett, *The Politics of Foreign Aid in the Brazilian Northeast* (Nashville: Vanderbilt University Press, 1970).
42 For more information on the October 1962 IA-ECOSOC in Mexico City, see Taffet, *Foreign Aid*, 52–57.
43 Taffet, *Foreign Aid*; Dunne, "Kennedy."

Part II

Appropriation: Domestic Contexts

5

"An Example for Other Small Nations to Follow": John F. Kennedy, Ireland, and Decolonization

David P. Kilroy

Remembered by many observers as the highlight of his 1963 state visit, in an emotional address before the joint houses of the Oireachtas, John F. Kennedy referred to Ireland as "the first of the small nations in the twentieth century to win its struggle for independence." Kennedy promoted the young republic as an example of postcolonial modernization for emerging states in Africa and Asia to emulate.[1] Veteran Irish parliamentary reporter Brian Inglis noted that "hardened politicians wept in their seats" as Kennedy characterized Ireland's leaders as men who knew "the meaning of foreign domination" and praised them for now providing a voice for other small nations on the world stage.[2]

Kennedy's message resonated strongly with political leadership on both sides of the parliamentary aisle, most of whom were veterans of Ireland's armed independence struggle between 1916 and 1921. Officials in the Irish Department of External Affairs (DEA) drew particular satisfaction from the American president's praise for Ireland's activist role in the UN General Assembly and its commitment to peace "from Cork to the Congo . . . and Galway to the Gaza strip." Kennedy's four-day visit was greeted with overwhelming enthusiasm from all segments of Irish society. Huge crowds welcomed the American chief executive and were enthralled by the spectacle and symbolism of the great-grandson of a Famine-era emigrant returning to Ireland as the most powerful man in the world. Those four days in June 1963 were, in the words of one historian, "days of national celebration."[3]

The fact that Secretary of State Dean Rusk was not among Kennedy's large traveling entourage has prompted many scholars to conclude that the visit lacked policy significance for the United States and instead was motivated by a mixture of Kennedy's personal interest and a play for the Irish vote. Historians who have analyzed Kennedy's visit tend to conclude that the Irish government alone sought to frame a policy agenda for the visit, with Dublin aiming to secure US backing for Ireland's application for EEC membership and to attract direct foreign investment from the United States for an ambitious government Programme for Economic Expansion launched in 1958. While Kennedy and Taoiseach Seán Lemass did hold private talks when they met in Dublin, many scholars have concluded that there were few pressing concerns in US-Irish relations in 1963 and so no defining issues with which to frame the event. Most studies of Irish foreign affairs and US-Irish relations in this era therefore tend to gloss over President Kennedy's visit to Ireland.[4]

Contemporary American observers were equally dismissive, with the press initially panning the trip as an unnecessary distraction from the president's more pressing challenges. Kennedy personally overruled objections from the State Department officials who feared that Ireland would distract from the important foreign policy agenda behind the larger trip to Europe that included a historic visit to West Berlin and stops in key NATO capitals, London and Rome. Both scholars and contemporary observers alike, however, have too often overlooked the extent to which Kennedy sought to infuse a foreign policy narrative into the Irish visit, one that reflected his desire to portray US foreign policy and American interests as consistent with the hopes and aspirations of anti-colonial nationalists and peoples emerging from colonial rule in Africa and Asia.

Unpacking this point, this paper makes three key arguments. First, Kennedy saw in Ireland's non-communist struggle for independence a useful frame of reference for Third World countries in the process of, or on the way to, decolonization. In his famous 1957 Algeria Speech, Kennedy asserted that the "single most important test of American foreign policy today is how we meet the challenge of imperialism, what we do to further man's desire to be free."[14] During his four-day visit to Ireland, Kennedy repeatedly emphasized Ireland's pioneering role in the process of decolonization and the value of its experience as a model for the orderly dismantling of empire. Kennedy had long admired the role of Éamon de Valera, Ireland's octogenarian president, in leading the Irish nationalist struggle for independence and later, as prime minister, in guiding the country peacefully through the rocky transition from colony to stable independent democracy. Kennedy's reading of Irish history informed his thinking on the challenge of decolonization. The visit provided an ideal platform for him to articulate his views on the issue.

Secondly, Kennedy saw Ireland as an exemplar of postcolonial liberal-capitalist success in a world where, from a US perspective, communism appeared too often to be winning the race for the hearts and minds of people in the Global South. Ireland's independent role at the UN, together with Kennedy's understanding of the Irish nationalist cause as an anti-colonial struggle and his portrayal of Ireland in 1963 as a country in the midst of a modernization transformation, made it a perfect "example for other small nations to follow."[5] Kennedy emphasized this theme repeatedly in his public remarks during the trip; the Kennedy administration's key Irish policy initiative that resulted from the visit was to facilitate Dublin's ongoing modernization efforts.

Thirdly, and finally, both the Irish government and the Irish public at large embraced Kennedy's characterization of Ireland as a model for decolonization and an exemplar of postcolonial modernization, because this was consistent with how they understood their country's history and its place in world. As noted above, Kennedy's views on decolonization drew on his sympathetic reading of Irish history and his admiration for the leadership of De Valera. As president of the League of Nations in 1938–39 De Valera had been a vocal champion of the rights of small nations, and this philosophy, together with active support for decolonization, was a key factor behind the activist role Ireland had played at the UN since joining in 1955. For the Irish government and the majority of the people, the country's history made it a natural ally of anti-colonial causes across Africa and Asia. At the same time, Ireland was deeply anti-communist and committed to a democratic-capitalist path of development, and so the message that Kennedy brought in 1963 was one already deeply embedded in the country's political culture.

Kennedy, Ireland, and decolonization

Kennedy, in contrast to his father and most of his siblings, was genuinely interested in his Irish ancestry. During a 1947 trip to Ireland, he drove the back roads of County Wexford to track down distant cousins in the tiny hamlet of Dunganstown. He made two other trips to Ireland, in 1945 and 1955, before returning as president. As a young journalist on his way to the 1945 Potsdam Conference, Kennedy stopped for several days in Ireland during which time he interviewed several leading Irish politicians, most notably then Taoiseach De Valera. De Valera was a veteran of the failed 1916 Easter Rising and leader of the Sinn Féin movement that led Ireland to independence in 1921. After refusing to accept the terms of the treaty with Britain that granted Ireland dominion status in the British Empire and partitioned off the northeast corner of the country, De Valera and his fellow republicans briefly went into self-imposed political exile before realizing the futility of their protest. De Valera formed the Fianna Fáil party in 1927, quickly making it the dominant force in Irish electoral politics. He first became prime minister in 1932, beginning a twenty-five-year period of almost unbroken political dominance during which time Ireland completely transformed its relationship with Britain. Under De Valera, Ireland sought to reduce its continued economic dependence on Britain, took back the treaty ports held by the Royal Navy after independence, declared neutrality in the Second World War and the Cold War, and adopted a new constitution that effectively made it a republic. He was a towering political figure and a recognized symbol of anti-colonial nationalism in the early twentieth century.

As one De Valera biographer notes, there were few leaders of his kind in that era with whom Kennedy was more familiar.[6] De Valera's declaration of Irish neutrality during the Second World War met with unvarnished resentment in both London and Washington. Nonetheless, writing for Hearst's *New York Journal-American* in 1945, Kennedy praised De Valera's pragmatism and defended the logic of Irish neutrality as the only viable option that a small state had in a great power struggle. Kennedy informed readers that, given Winston Churchill's role as Minister for War during the Irish war of independence, De Valera had good reason to be skeptical about the British prime minister's views on Irish independence.[7] In the European diary he kept in 1945, Kennedy pushed back against American criticism of De Valera's wartime leadership, noting that he "has fought politically in the Dáil the same battle he fought militarily in the field—a battle to end partition, a battle against Britain." Kennedy was impressed by the "brilliant" De Valera's stubborn determination, forged in English prisons, and sympathized that only "independent Ireland, free to go where it will be the master of its own destiny" could put to rest its quarrels with Britain.[8]

Kennedy met with De Valera again when he returned to Ireland in 1947, and arriving as president in 1963 it was De Valera, now occupying the ceremonial office of Irish president, who greeted him at Dublin Airport. In what was perhaps the most symbolically significant moment of the 1963 visit, Kennedy laid a wreath at Arbour Hill cemetery where the executed leaders of the Easter Rising were interred. Kennedy aides recalled that at a dinner hosted by De Valera that evening, Kennedy asked the Irish president why his sentence of death for his role in the rising had been commuted. Kennedy was reportedly "spellbound" as De Valera explained that the British spared his life because he was born in the United States.[9] The next day in Limerick, Kennedy told his audience how moved he was to participate in the wreath laying ceremony in the company of De Valera "whose life is so tied up with the life of this island."[10]

Kennedy's interest in De Valera and the Irish nationalist struggle hint at a possible foundation for his views on decolonization. There are clear parallels between De Valera's anti-colonial nationalism and philosophy of the rights of small nations and Kennedy's views on decolonization and anti-colonial nationalism. Kennedy's exposure to Irish history and politics offered an early example of anti-colonial nationalism and postimperial independence. It would therefore have provided one of the key areas of context for the conclusion he reached by the time he was in the US Senate that "the revolt against colonialism [and] the determination of people to control their own destinies" was the great moral issue of the age.[11]

During his brief tenure on Capitol Hill, first as a congressman and then as a senator, Kennedy's position on the partition of Ireland ran strongly counter to the official view of the State Department, which held that it was entirely a matter of British internal affairs. As a reporter Kennedy had defended Irish neutrality in the Second World in part because of what he concluded was the impermanent nature of partition. Partition and the "age-old quarrel with England," Kennedy wrote, were key motivating factors in Irish politics, and uniting the country was a cause for which "all Irishmen of the south are united."[12] During a hearing before the House Committee on Foreign Affairs in 1950, Kennedy spoke in favor of an all-Ireland plebiscite on the issue, while in the Senate six years later he cosponsored a failed resolution in support of Irish reunification. While electoral politics in the Massachusetts's heavily Irish American 18th district, or even in the state as whole, likely factored in to his thinking, Kennedy's views on partition cannot be completely divorced from the context in which they were formed. Kennedy's assertion that justice in Ireland depended on giving all the people on the island "the opportunity to choose their own form of government" was more than a self-serving political ploy. Kennedy's rhetoric on partition was rooted in his experiences in Ireland and consistent with his call for the United States to show more concern for aspirations of colonized peoples.[13]

In his 1957 Algeria speech Kennedy asserted that the "single most important test of American foreign policy today is how we meet the challenge of imperialism."[14] Kennedy's position challenged the assumption that the US response to decolonization should accommodate its European Cold War allies.[15] Indeed, distancing US policy from historic Western imperialism would better enable Washington to call attention to the evils of Soviet imperialism in Eastern Europe. On this issue too, Kennedy turned to Irish history as a frame of reference. In 1955 then Senator Kennedy stopped off in Dublin on his way back from a fact-finding mission to Poland and accepted an invitation to speak to students at a Vincentian seminary, All Hallow's College, on Communist repression of Catholicism.[16] The address he gave in Ireland was essentially a stump speech developed for Irish American and US Catholic audiences in which he drew a connection between Ireland's historic pursuit of liberty and the struggle against communist tyranny. "All of us of Irish descent," he told an Irish American audience, "are bound together by the ties that come from a common experience." It was from this common past that the Irish diaspora drew sympathy for the nationalist "aspirations of all people everywhere." Ireland's "long and ultimately successful fight for independence," he intoned, "offers encouragement and hope to all who struggle to be free."[17] For Kennedy this was the link between the Irish nationalist struggle and his understanding of Americanism. When he came to Ireland as president, he was visiting a country that had long served as an inspiration for his views on empire, nationalism and anti-colonialism.

Kennedy, Ireland, and modernization

In his inaugural address Kennedy pledged to "those new states whom we welcome to the ranks of the free" that the US would do all in its power to ensure "that one form of colonial control shall not have passed away merely to be replaced by a far more iron tyranny."[18] Providing a credible blueprint for postcolonial development was central to that effort. Leading figures in the Kennedy administration embraced the modernization model, which emphasized reforming economic organization, political structures, and social values in newly independent states with a view to transforming traditional societies into modern states. Modernization informed much of the thinking behind programs like the Alliance for Progress and was the key to the administration's strategy for stemming the tide of Marxism in the Third World.[19] Ireland served as a useful object lesson for the White House's vision. The Lemass government's Programme for Economic Expansion conformed on many levels to the modernization model, and Kennedy hinted as much when he praised Ireland's transformation from a colony once haunted by famine to a modern capitalist nation. Kennedy characterized this process as a "revolution" that would lead eventually to the Irish people fully sharing in "world prosperity."[20]

Kennedy portrayed Ireland as a society at the midpoint on the linear scale of modernization, still in the process of shedding its skin as a traditional, underdeveloped society, just starting to show the dynamic signs of a modern state. Kennedy repeatedly praised Irish government efforts to transform Ireland from an impoverished colony to a stable capitalist democracy. He demonstrated US support for the Irish government's economic reform program by facilitating a high-profile return visit by Lemass to the United States and endorsed the Taoiseach's campaign to court US investors. Kennedy also went against the advice of the State Department in offering support for Irish membership in the EEC, a key strategic goal of the Lemass government.[21] Kennedy lauded Lemass's efforts to move Ireland away from the cultural insularity of the De

Valera years, going so far as to urge a reluctant Taoiseach to abandon the campaign to revive the Irish language which Kennedy dismissed as a "waste of national energy."[22] Kennedy accepted that the Irish people "look to the past with pride" but emphasized the greater importance of looking to the future with the expectation of "building a vigorous, new country."[23]

Shortly after Kennedy returned from Ireland, Lemass featured on the cover of *Time* magazine and in a lengthy article inside, under the Cold War themed title "Ireland: Lifting the Green Curtain." The article, which Kennedy personally called to Lemass's attention, highlighted many of the themes that Kennedy focused on in his Ireland speeches: Lemass's success in revitalizing a dormant economy, Dublin's desire to join the EEC, Ireland's anti-colonial credentials, and its cordial relations with the emerging nations of Africa and Asia.[24] It offered a ringing endorsement of the Taoiseach's agenda and echoed in the clearest terms Kennedy's reading of modern Ireland.[25] For Lemass, it provided a perfect entrée for his October investor recruitment visit to the United States, a multicity tour with stops in Chicago, Boston, Philadelphia, and New York. Kennedy personally intervened to facilitate Lemass's efforts, encouraging American investors to take note of Ireland's modernizing economy.[26]

Kennedy's support for Lemass's economic agenda was matched by his administration's encouragement for Ireland's active role on the world stage. Relative to other European states Ireland enjoyed a positive reputation in the Global South, thus enhancing its significance as symbol of modernization. The State Department background notes for Kennedy's visit placed particular emphasis on the role played by Ireland at the UN.[27] The US Mission at the UN reported in 1962 that Ireland was one of a group of unaligned Western European states that served as a moderating force in the General Assembly on issues pertaining to decolonization. Ireland in particular was willing to counteract the "take it or leave it" tendency of many positions emanating from the emerging Afro-Asian bloc, as long as the US put pressure its Western allies to "come up to date on colonial matters."[28] In both his public remarks and his private conversations with Lemass, Kennedy praised Ireland's role in the UN, citing in particular Irish peacekeeping in the Congo, and Ireland's mediation role in the Kashmir crisis, the sort of crises where the legacy of empire complicated the US response. For Kennedy, a combination of Ireland's colonial past, its long struggle for independence, its newness as a nation, and its strong democratic-capitalist credentials, translated into significance on the world stage in the era of decolonization. Kennedy spoke of "this island . . . which was the first country in the twentieth century to lead what is the most powerful tide of the century" now having a special mission to "join with other countries of the free world" and lead the drive for "independence and peace."[29] "Ireland's hour has come," Kennedy told the Oireachtas, before elaborating on his vision for Ireland's role:

> To the extent that the peace is disturbed by conflict between the former colonial powers and the new and developing nations, Ireland's role is unique . . . Ireland has excellent relations with both the new and the old, the confidence of both sides and an opportunity to act where the actions of greater powers might be viewed with suspicion.[30]

Ireland, decolonization, and the Kennedy message

This articulation of Irish exceptionalism was wholly consistent with how Ireland's political leadership understood the country's place in the world. In 1963, the Republic of Ireland was just four decades removed from British rule and partition remained for many an unwelcome reminder of the nation's colonial past. In the early years of independence, the narrative of the Irish nation shaped a foreign policy aimed largely at distancing Ireland from its former colonial master. This was particularly true after Fianna Fáil took power in 1932 on a platform of removing the last remnants of the British Empire and uniting the country. Fianna Fáil's policies of neutrality and economic nationalism, though politically popular in Ireland, left the country isolated from Europe and struggling economically. The maintenance of neutrality during the Second World War and the early Cold War also placed a serious strain on Ireland's relationship with the United States. The Soviet Union compounded Ireland's isolation by repeatedly vetoing Irish applications to join the UN until 1955.

Once UN membership was secured, however, the Irish delegation at the General Assembly quickly carved out a prominent and largely independent role for itself on a range of issues, including decolonization. In this "golden era" of Irish foreign policy, Dublin actively promoted an ideal vision of an international order based on collective security, international law, self-determination, and anti-colonialism.[31] In forging what Ben Tonra refers to as the "global citizen" narrative of Irish foreign policy, policymakers drew on the history of Ireland's colonial past and embraced a pragmatic approach to preserving the rights and independence of small states in a world dominated by great powers.[32] It was a vision that first took shape during Ireland's brief but active membership in the League of Nations in the 1930s and was embraced across the Irish political spectrum. Successive Irish governments after 1955 took the position that Ireland, as both a former colony and a Western European republic, was uniquely positioned to act as a bridge between the West and the emerging states. Conor Cruise O'Brien, who served as special UN representative during the Congo crisis in the early 1960s, asserted that Ireland's global outlook "was not just a question of brooding on the past . . . but of a present day contrast rooted in history."[33] In a 1960 speech before the UN General Assembly, Minister for External Affairs Frank Aiken stressed that the Irish people "know what imperialism is and what resistance to it involves . . . we do not hear with indifference the voices of those spokesmen of African and Asian countries who passionately champion the rights of millions who are still . . . under foreign rule."[34] An *Irish Times* editorial on the date of the country's admission to the UN echoed these sentiments and emphasized the pragmatism of this approach, noting that "by doing good for others we will do even greater good for ourselves."[35]

Kennedy was not the first visiting head of state to endorse Ireland's "global citizen" foreign policy. In May 1960 Kwame Nkrumah made a brief visit to Ireland after attending the Commonwealth Conference in London, where he formally announced Ghana's new status as a republic. In an address to the Irish UN Association in Dublin, Nkrumah spoke of his admiration for the Irish people and noted the parallels between the Irish and the African struggle for independence. The Ghanaian president told his Irish audience that "the struggle of Ireland for independence was not the struggle of one country alone, but part of a world movement for freedom." Former Minister for External Affairs and future Nobel Laureate, Seán MacBride, also addressed the gathering and noted that by virtue of their history, the Irish people intrinsically understood the desire for "emancipation of peoples who had been subject to colonial rule" and "watched with sympathy ... the struggle of people in Africa for national freedom."[36] The next day the *Irish Press* editorialized that Nkrumah could not but find a sympathetic audience in a country that "had known the rigours, bigotry and stupidity of colonial rule."[37] These sentiments reflected the conscious image that Ireland projected for itself on the world stage, and it was in this context that Kennedy's message about modernization and decolonization was received in 1963.

The Nkrumah visit serves to illustrate the historic tendency for Ireland to be "cited as paradigmatic ... by a range of other early anticolonial nationalisms."[38] This is most evident in the case of Indian anti-colonial nationalism. Whether it was the interest of nineteenth-century moderates in the Home Rule movement or inspiration drawn by radical elements from the republican struggle for independence between 1916 and 1922, there is a considerable history of Indian nationalist interest in the Irish story.[39] Irish leaders such as De Valera and Michael Collins were well known in Indian nationalist circles, and in instances such as the Easter 1930 Chittagong Armory Raid Irish republicanism served as both a symbolic and strategic source of inspiration.[40] After independence, radical activists such as Subhas Chandra Bose and other Indian nationalists traveled to Ireland where they met with De Valera and other leaders of the Irish independence struggle. Even as India transitioned to independence, a delegation traveled to Ireland to consult with De Valera about India's future constitutional status vis-à-vis the British Empire.[41] Such visits reinforced Irish notions of exceptionalism with regard to the issue of decolonization.

Irish claims to a unique understanding of the anti-colonial struggle in the Global South were tempered, however, by the geographic and economic reality of Ireland's place in Europe. The "global citizen" narrative in Irish foreign policy existed side by side, often uneasily, with what Tonra characterizes as the "European republic" narrative.[42] Ireland was at once both an advocate of the rights of small nations and an ideologically and culturally Western European state. When Ireland's independent role at the UN ruffled feathers in the Western alliance, Irish leaders were quick to reassure the United States and the Western European powers that its small nation advocacy was compatible with their interests. Dublin considered such reassurances necessary in order to maintain hopes of persuading the United States to intervene on partition and to secure support for both Lemass's economic program and Ireland's EEC application. The fact that there was still considerable resentment in the State Department over Irish neutrality, made such reassurances imperative from Dublin's point of view.

Kennedy's election provided a welcome opportunity for a reset in US-Irish relations that might allow for an easier balance between the country's dual European and global identity. The Irish public followed Kennedy's campaign for the White House closely. For many people he served as a symbol for the rise of exiled nineteenth-century Irish Catholics from the despair of the Famine to the promise of the American dream. They were, in De Valera's words, "overjoyed when he was finally declared elected."[43] Framed photographs of the new president became a fixture on the walls of Irish Catholic households, sandwiched between the Pope and the Sacred Heart, a phenomenon *Look* magazine dubbed "the Kennedy Cult."[44] Kennedy's Catholicism as much as his Irish ancestry made him a symbol of triumph over persecution and marginalization in Ireland. As the first Irish Catholic to hold the office of American chief executive, he was a powerful symbol of triumph for the Gaelic nationalist tradition.

Lemass spoke for many when he asserted that it was "a source of joy to us that a man of Irish blood has been elected to that very high office."[45] In the small town of New Ross, County Wexford, close to his ancestors' home that Kennedy had visited in 1947, a victory party was scheduled for election night. However, in a tragic reminder of Ireland's activist foreign policy, the celebration was postponed out of respect for nine Irish soldiers killed while on duty with the UN peacekeeping mission in the Congo. Instead, 5,000 people packed the streets of New Ross on inauguration day, and were rewarded with a taped thank you message from the new president in which he paid homage to his family's roots in the area, recalled his 1947 visit and promised to return soon.[46]

Soon after Kennedy entered the White House, the Irish government began to lobby for a presidential visit. Having failed to interest any previous US presidential administrations in taking up the cause of Irish unity, there was a brief surge of optimism in Dublin that an Irish American president might be persuaded to leverage American power to bring to an end the remaining link to the British Empire in Ireland. However, it quickly became apparent that the support for ending partition that Kennedy had expressed as a legislator was far more difficult to reconcile with his role as president. Irish officials probed to see if Kennedy might privately press Britain on partition, but were forced to conclude that pushing the administration too hard on the issue might jeopardize the very idea of a visit altogether.[47] Officials at the DEA later acknowledged that Kennedy, despite his personal goodwill on the issue, could not do anything that would undermine the US strategic partnership with Britain. The issue did come up in Kennedy's and Lemass's private talks in Dublin, but, despite his numerous references to Ireland's colonial past, Kennedy did not make a single public mention of partition during his four days in Ireland.[48] This omission was evidence of the reality that Kennedy's critique of colonialism was cautious at best and would never extend to the point where it challenged vital US strategic interests in Europe.

Kennedy's silence on partition did not go wholly unnoticed. A group calling itself the Border Protest Committee hand-delivered a letter for the president to the US embassy in Dublin calling on him to honor his "stated policy to end Colonialism wherever it can be found" and to address the issue of "British occupied Ireland."[49] Kennedy arrived in Ireland at a time of significant transition in Irish border politics and the atmosphere was more muted than at any time since partition. Lemass had concluded that prioritizing partition, as De Valera had done, unduly complicated Irish relations with the United States, and the policy of his government toward Northern Ireland had begun to shift from neglect to engagement. Whereas previous Irish governments had tended to dismiss the concerns of the unionist population in the north, Lemass adopted a strategy of "winning over the hearts and minds of our fellow Irishmen in the North."[50] Were Kennedy to take a public position on the issue during his visit, it would complicate the back channel efforts already underway between Dublin and Belfast to build a cross border dialogue. Nationalists on both sides of the border did draw some encouragement from Kennedy's refusal to accept an invitation from the Unionist prime minister Terence O'Neill to visit Northern Ireland, which Kennedy recognized would have been an embarrassment for Lemass.[51] That, however, was the extent to which Kennedy became involved in the issue. The Irish government had come to accept that the United States, even with an Irish American president who had previously spoken out against partition, was not going to alter its position on the matter.

Lemass's ready acceptance of the Kennedy administration's geostrategic rationale for avoiding the issue is illustrative of the degree to which Dublin broadly sympathized with the Cold War agenda of the United States. For most Irish people there did not appear to be any inconsistency between Ireland's neutrality and its activist foreign policy on the one hand, and sympathy for the West in the Cold War on the other. The *Irish Times*, for example, praised the "noble realism" of Kennedy's Oireachtas speech "that echoed his recent pronouncements on the Cold War."[52] Arriving in Ireland directly from his triumphal visit to West Berlin, Kennedy reminded his Irish audience that world was divided "between those who believe in self-determination and those ... who would impose upon others the harsh and oppressive Communist system." Though Ireland charted an "independent course in foreign policy ... it is not neutral between liberty and tyranny and never will be."[53] The Irish anti-colonial struggle, Kennedy asserted, was a reminder to those behind the Iron Curtain that the quest for freedom was often a long and painful process but one that was ultimately attainable. Kennedy's comments were largely in line with public opinion in Ireland and in Lemass he found a particularly sympathetic ear.

Lemass worked from the assumption that the maintenance of world peace and stability depended on US leadership. In defending his government's decision to conduct weapons searches of Czech planes refueling at Shannon Airport en route to Cuba during the missile crisis, Lemass asserted that just because it was not a member of NATO did not mean that Ireland was neutral when it came to the outcome of the Cold War.[54] Faced with questions in the Dáil on Ireland's future relationship with NATO, Lemass asserted that "the existence of NATO is necessary ... for the defence of the countries of Western Europe, including this country ... [and] we are in full agreement with its aims."[55] While Lemass may have been more willing than many of his colleagues to reevaluate Ireland's commitment to neutrality, anti-communist sentiment was widespread in Catholic Ireland and the natural sympathies of the majority of people lay with the United States in the Cold War. Kennedy's anti-imperialist message resonated in Ireland, not just because of his praise for Irish nationalism and Irish foreign policy but also because in 1963 most Irish people believed the United States to be on the right side of history.[56]

Kennedy's failure to address partition was largely offset by what most Irish observers at the time felt was the depth of his sympathy for and the sincerity of his rhetoric about Ireland. The wreath laying ceremony at Arbour Hill, described by the *Irish Times* as a somber and dignified episode amid an otherwise boisterously enthusiastic schedule, was of particular symbolic significance to Ireland's nationalist leaders.[57] Lemass recalled that for the president of "the greatest nation in the world" to honor the revolutionary nationalists whose self-proclaimed blood sacrifice had begun the process of the dismantling of the British Empire, was an event of "great emotional significance" for the Irish people.[58] It was a moment of validation for the Irish republic and magnified the impact of Kennedy's message on the correlation between Ireland's nationalist struggle and its role on the world stage in the 1960s. The crowds that flocked to see the visiting president in 1963 were thrilled by Kennedy's assertion that Ireland now had a special mission to help guide peoples fighting oppression to do "what Ireland did in the early part of this century and, indeed, has done for the last 800 years—and that is associate intimately with independence and freedom."[59]

Kennedy tied this mission directly to Ireland's commitment to the UN. He praised Ireland's role in the General Assembly, which he said gave Ireland far more influence than its relative size. Other small nations could learn from Ireland's example the value of active membership in the UN and its role in providing collective security and "a forum for an equal chance to be heard, for progress towards a world made safe for diversity." Kennedy paid tribute to the "twenty-six sons of Ireland" killed while serving with the UN peacekeeping force in the Congo (ONUC) and the sacrifice the Irish people had made in the cause of world order.[60] The Irish public took great pride in the service of Irish troops in the Congo, a role for which the DEA believed Ireland was ideally suited because of its colonial past.[61] The financial and human cost of Ireland's participation in the four-year ONUC operation strained but did not break Ireland's commitment to an active UN role. When Kennedy emphasized the importance of the sacrifice Irish soldiers had made in the Congo he echoed a sentiment expressed in an *Irish Times* editorial three days after nine Irish soldiers had been killed in Niemba in 1960. The editorial asserted that the tragedy had not altered "the outlook of our people" who continued to embrace the mission as a "symbol of the very real help that we—in our unique position as a white nation which knows the meaning of oppression—can hope to offer the new nations of the world."[62]

For the editors of the *Irish Times* it was clear that race, in addition to geography and history, was a factor in Ireland's "unique position" when it came to the politics of decolonization. Race was undoubtedly a factor in Ireland's ability to cultivate its dual identity as "global citizen" and "European republic," and perhaps also in its appeal to an American audience as a symbol of successful decolonization and modernization. While his great-grandfather was part of a generation of Irish Americans who had struggled to overcome prejudice and discrimination, by the time JFK arrived in Ireland the Irish in America had been fully assimilated into the racial hierarchy of the United States. Thus for a great many of the white Americans who tuned in to watch television footage of the visit, the throngs of people who came out to welcome the American president would have looked comfortingly familiar. Ultimately, however, Kennedy's conception of Ireland as a model postcolonial state had less to do with race than it did with his reading of Irish history and his own personal connections with Ireland. His familiarity with the story of Ireland's independence struggle provided him with a frame of reference for the unfolding process of decolonization and he found in Ireland in 1963 a convenient model of modernization in action that conformed to his administration's blueprint for stability in the postcolonial world.

Conclusion

In his public remarks in Ireland in 1963, Kennedy made decolonization and modernization major of themes of his state visit. Kennedy's familiarity with the politics and history of Ireland enabled him to utilize it as a stage from which to address a wider global audience on what his administration understood to be some of the critical issues of that era. Kennedy's message resonated in Ireland because it reinforced how the Irish people saw themselves at that time and where they saw themselves going in the future. The president's visit boosted Irish national pride, validated the country's republican traditions, and engendered pride in Irish foreign policy. Kennedy's anti-colonial rhetoric served as an endorsement of the internationalist foreign policy championed by the DEA, while references to modernization resonated strongly with Lemass and his fellow economic reformers. Kennedy's visit helped dispel the long, dark shadow of the Famine era in Ireland, and his youth and vigor was particularly attractive to the new, postrevolutionary generation.[63]

Kennedy's rhetoric on colonialism, couched as it was within the broader dynamic of the Cold War struggle, was largely consistent with Ireland's position on decolonization, which was ultimately quite cautious and moderate. Both the Lemass government and the Kennedy administration, while consistently expressing public support for self-determination, favored a gradual and orderly transition from empire to independence. The Irish government favored decolonization as matter of principle but also as a pragmatic means of preserving international stability. The Irish UN delegation repeatedly emphasized that conditions must be right for self-rule and that the process must "minimize grievances among both the coloniser and the colonised."[64] Such a position was directly in line with US National Security Council directive on West Africa that called for "orderly economic development and political progress by the countries of the area in cooperation with the metropoles or former metropoles and other free world countries."[65] Similarly, while Assistant Secretary of State George Ball recommended a "commonwealth relationship" to Portuguese dictator Antonio Salazar as model for Lusophone Africa, De Valera had urged the Indian delegation that visited Dublin in 1947 to push for external association within the British Commonwealth, a concept his government had put into effect in 1936.[66] The commonwealth had been the vehicle by which Ireland transitioned from empire to independence, and the government in Dublin clearly favored it as model for orderly decolonization and a means of avoiding political turmoil like that which had ensued in the Congo. Kennedy's rhetoric in favor of decolonization and his praise for the role of Ireland in the UN signaled to the Lemass government American support for such an orderly process.

Notes

1 John F. Kennedy, "Address to the Joint Houses of the Oireachtas, Dáil Éireann," Dublin, June 28, 1963, reprinted in *A Memory of John Fitzgerald Kennedy* (Dublin: Wood Printing Works, 1963), 18–19.
2 Brian Murphy, "JFK: More than Words," *Irish Independent*, June 17, 2013.

3   Dermot Keogh, *Twentieth Century Ireland: Revolution and State Building* (Dublin: Gill & McMillan, 2005), 252.
4   Maurice Fitzgerald, "Ireland and the US in the Post-War Period," *The Lost Decade: Ireland in the 1950s,* ed. Dermot Keogh, Finbar O'Shea, and Carmel Quinlan (Cork: Mercier Press, 2004), 88, 200; Ronan Fanning, *Independent Ireland* (Dublin: Helicon, 1983), 203; Keogh, *Twentieth Century Ireland*, 252; Sylvia Ellis, "The Historical Significance of President Kennedy's Visit to Ireland in June 1963," *Irish Studies Review* 16, no. 2 (2008): 114–15.
5   Kennedy, "Address to the Joint Houses," 18–19.
6   Owen Dudley Edwards, "The American Identity of de Valera," in *De Valera's Ireland*, ed. Gabriel Doherty and Dermot Keogh (Cork: Mercier Press, 2003), 13–14.
7   Edwards, "de Valera," 12; Arthur Mitchell, *JFK and His Irish Heritage* (Dublin: Moytura Press, 1993), 100–4.
8   Eric Freedman and Edward Hoffman, eds., *John F. Kennedy in His Own Words* (New York: Citadel Press, 2005), 180.
9   Kenneth O'Donnell and David Powers, *Johnny, We Hardly Knew Ye: Memories of John Fitzgerald Kennedy* (New York: Little & Brown, 1976), 426. Most scholars agree that De Valera's reprieve had little to do with his American birth but rather was prompted by British concern over the public mood in Ireland. The story nonetheless became part of the public folklore about the Rising: Brian Barton, *Secret Court Martial Records of the Easter Rising* (Belfast: Blackstaff, 2002); Robert Schmuhl, *Ireland's Exiled Children: Americans and the Easter Rising* (New York: Oxford University Press, 2016).
10 Kennedy, "Remarks at a Reception in Limerick," June 29, 1963, reprinted in *A Memory of John Fitzgerald Kennedy*, 28.
11 Remarks of Senator John F. Kennedy at the Western Pennsylvania Columbus Day Banquet, Pittsburgh, October 14, 1956, John F. Kennedy Presidential Library (JFKL). Available online: https://www.jfklibrary.org/archives/other-resources/john-f-kenned y-speeches/pittsburgh-pa-19561014 (accessed December 13, 2018).
12 Kennedy, "Eire Ulster Union Lies at the Base of Irish Politics," *San Antonio Light*, July 29, 1945, 8.
13 Ellis, "Kennedy's Visit," 120.
14 Remarks of Senator John F. Kennedy in the Senate, Washington, July 2, 1957, JFKL. Available online: https://www.jfklibrary.org/archives/other-resources/john-f-kenned y-speeches/united-states-senate-imperialism-19570702 (accessed December 13, 2018).
15 Anders Stephenson, "Senator John F. Kennedy: Anti-Imperialism and Utopian Deficit," *JAS* 48, no. 1 (2014): 17.
16 Mary Denzer, "A Generation Remembers the Kennedy Assassination," *The Catholic Key*. Available online: http://www.catholickey.com/index.php3?gif=news.gif&mode =view&issue=20081128&article_id=5413 (accessed February 6, 2016).
17 Remarks of Senator John F. Kennedy before the Irish Fellowship Club of Chicago, March 17, 1956, JFKL. Available online: https://www.jfklibrary.org/archives/other-res ources/john-f-kennedy-speeches/chicago-il-irish-fellowship-club-19560317 (accessed December 13, 2018); Remarks by Senator John F. Kennedy at Irish Institute, New York City, January 12, 1957, JFKL, https://www.jfklibrary.org/archives/other-resources/joh n-f-kennedy-speeches/irish-institute-nyc-19570112 (accessed December 13, 2018).
18 Kennedy, Inaugural Address, January 20, 1961, online at APP. Available online: https:/ /www.presidency.ucsb.edu/documents/inaugural-address-2 (accessed December 13, 2018).

19 Michael Latham, *Modernization as Ideology: American Social Science and "Nation Building" in the Kennedy Era* (Chapel Hill: University of North Carolina Press, 2000), 7, 30, 57.
20 Kennedy, "Address to the Joint Houses," 18–19.
21 Ellis, "Kennedy's Visit," 123.
22 Seán Lemass, Oral Interview conducted by James O'Connor, August 8, 1966, John F. Kennedy Oral History Collection (JFKOHC), JFKL.
23 Exchange of Remarks between Kennedy and Lemass, October 15, 1963, Speech Files, Papers of John F. Kennedy (PJFK), JFKL.
24 "Ireland: Lifting the Green Curtain," *Time*, July 12, 1963, 28–40.
25 Kennedy to Lemass, July 23, 1963, Trips: Ireland, 1963, PJFK, JFKL.
26 Kennedy, Joint Statement Following Discussions with the prime minister of Ireland, October 17, 1963, online at APP. Available online: https://www.presidency.ucsb.edu/documents/joint-statement-following-discussions-with-the-prime-minister-ireland (accessed December 13, 2018).
27 Ellis, "Kennedy's Visit," 114.
28 US Mission to the United Nations to the US State Department, April 19, 1962, *FRUS*, 1961–1963, vol. XXV, doc. 201.
29 Kennedy, "Remarks at City Hall, Cork," June 28, 1963, reprinted in *A Memory of John Fitzgerald Kennedy*, 11.
30 Kennedy, "Address to the Joint Houses," 18–19.
31 Fitzgerald, "Ireland and the US"; Joseph Morrison Skelly, *Irish Diplomacy at the United Nations: National Interests and International Order* (Dublin: Irish Academic Press, 1997).
32 Ben Tonra, *Global Citizen and European Republic: Irish Foreign Policy in Transition* (Manchester: University of Manchester Press, 2012), 34.
33 Kevin O'Sullivan, *Ireland, Africa and the End of Empire: Small State Identity and the Cold War, 1955-1975* (Manchester: University of Manchester Press, 2012), 12–34.
34 Stephen Howe, *Ireland and Empire: Colonial Legacies in Irish History and Culture* (London: Oxford University Press, 2000), 155.
35 *Irish Times*, December 16, 1955, 7.
36 *Irish Times*, May 19, 1960, 4.
37 O'Sullivan, *Ireland*, 1.
38 Elleke Boehmer and Bart Moore-Gilbert, "Introduction to Special Issue: Postcolonial Studies and Transnational Resistance," *Interventions* 4, no. 1 (2002): n7, 17.
39 See Howard Brasted, "Indian Nationalist Development and the Influence of Irish Home Rule, 1870 to 1886," *MAS* 14, no. 1 (1980): 37–63; Richard Davis, "The Influence of the Irish Revolution on Indian Nationalism: The Evidence of the Indian Press, 1916-1922," *South Asia* 9, no. 2 (1986): 55–68; Kate O'Malley, *Ireland, India and Empire: Indo-Irish Radical Connections, 1914-1964* (Manchester: University of Manchester Press, 2008).
40 Michael Silvestri, *Ireland and India: Nationalism, Empire and Memory* (London: Palgrave Macmillan, 2009), 46–47.
41 O'Malley, *Ireland*, 100–2; Deirdre McMahon, "Ireland, Empire, and the Commonwealth," in *Ireland and the British Empire*, ed. Kevin Kenny (London: Oxford University Press, 2004), 213.
42 Tonra, *Global Citizen*, 51–66.
43 Éamon de Valera Oral Interview, conducted by Joseph E. O'Connor, September 15, 1966, JFKOHC, JFKL.

44 J. Roddy, "The Kennedy Cult," *Look*, November 17, 1964, 66.
45 Lemass Oral Interview, JFKL; Mike Cronin, "'Ireland is an Unusual Place': President Kennedy's 1963 Visit and the Complexity of Recognition," in *Turning Points in Twentieth-Century Irish History*, ed. Thomas Hachey (Dublin: Irish Academic Press, 2011), 119.
46 *Irish Times*, November 10, 1960, 11; *Irish Times*, January 21, 1961, 9.
47 Frank Aiken Oral Interview, conducted by Joseph O'Connor, September 15, 1966, JFKOHC, JFKL; Thomas Kiernan Oral Interview, conducted by Joseph O'Connor, August 5, 1966, JFKOHC, JFKL.
48 Hugh McCann Oral Interview, conducted by Joseph O'Connor August 8, 1966, JFKOHC, JFKL; Kiernan Oral Interview; Ellis, "Kennedy's Visit," 121–22.
49 Leo McCann and George Kennedy Scott to Kennedy, June 26, 1963, White House Central Files, JFKL.
50 McCann Oral Interview; Kiernan Oral Interview.
51 Terence O'Neill to Kennedy, May 6, 1963, National Security Files, JFKL.
52 *Irish* Times, June 29, 1963, 11.
53 Kennedy, "Address to the Joint Houses," 18–19.
54 Maurice Fitzgerald, "The Mainstreaming Irish Foreign Policy," in *The Lemass Era*, ed. Brian Girvin and Gary Murphy (Dublin: University College Dublin Press, 2005), 88; Skelly, *Irish Diplomacy*, 241.
55 Dáil Debates, vol. 193, vols. 6–8, February 14, 1962. Available online: https://www.oireachtas.ie/en/debates/debate/dail/1962-02-14/5/ (accessed December 13, 2018).
56 Public opinion in Ireland would shift significantly in the wake of the Vietnam War as evidenced by widespread protests against US foreign policy during the presidential visits of Richard Nixon in 1970 and Ronal Reagan in 1984.
57 *Irish Times*, June 29, 1963, 8.
58 Lemass Oral Interview.
59 Kennedy, "Remarks at City Hall, Cork," 11.
60 Kennedy, "Address to the Joint Houses," 18–19.
61 O'Sullivan, *Ireland*, 36, 41.
62 *Irish Times*, November 22, 1960, 11.
63 James Carroll, *One of Ourselves: John Fitzgerald Kennedy in Ireland* (Boston: Images from the Past, 2003), 16, 180–81; Ellis, "Kennedy's Visit," 125.
64 O'Sullivan, *Ireland*, 21.
65 National Security Council Report, NSC 6005/1, April 9, 1960, *FRUS*, 1958–1960, vol. XIV, doc. 27.
66 Embassy in France to Department of State, August 31, 1963, *FRUS*, 1961–63, vol. XIII, doc. 357; McMahon, "Ireland," 213.

6

Global Media, Emotions, and the "Kennedy Narrative": Kennedy as Seen from the "Global South"

Sönke Kunkel

In March 1962, an international passenger flight took Peruvian citizen Armando Pazos from Lima, Peru, to Los Angeles. Seated next to him was an unusual traveler: a life-sized bronze bust of President John F. Kennedy. The work of famous Peruvian sculptor Carlos Pazos, the bust was on its way to Inglewood, California, where the sculptor was visiting his daughter and son-in-law. The day before, Pazos had learned that President Kennedy, too, would soon visit the area, and so he had ordered his son back in Lima to quickly rush in the other Kennedy by plane. The bust arrived too late, however, forestalling a California meeting of the two presidents. Yet, a few days later, Pazos managed to get an audience in the White House instead. White House photographers and a film crew stood by in the Cabinet Room when, on March 29, 1962, the artist and a Peruvian delegation finally presented the bust to US chief of protocol Angier Biddle Duke.[1]

One year into the Kennedy era, Latin Americans found themselves struggling to redefine their relationship to the US presidency, and the strange travels of the bronze Kennedy, echoing those struggles, demonstrated what new emotional bonds they had begun to form toward its current incumbent. Latin Americans, observed *LAT* correspondent Robert Hartman after an extended fact-finding tour through South America, liked Kennedy: "They like his youthful vigor, his religion, his beautiful wife, his gracious gestures toward them, his style of speech." There was a "mystic faith in President Kennedy and his genuine interest in them" among Latin Americans, Hartman found, evident not only in the many conversations that he had with ordinary Latin Americans but also on streets in the "remote mountains of Colombia" where he had seen a jeep "with a faded Kennedy campaign sticker proudly displayed on its windshield."[2] Summing up his experiences after his travels across the continent, Hartman noted that he could "honestly report having heard nothing but praise and admiration for President Kennedy. His campaign song, 'High Hopes,' has not replaced the native Latin rhythms but its spirits animated everyone with whom I talked from Panama to Patagonia, presidents and peons."[3]

As in many parts of Latin America, the Kennedy presidency also raised great expectations throughout Asia and Africa. Among urban middle and upper classes in

Bombay, Tokyo, Manila, Bangkok, and Singapore, Kennedy got high scores in opinion polls as "the world figure most admired" and the "statesman making the greatest contribution to the advancement of peace."[4] Students from Asia and Africa, being invited to the White House Rose Garden with their international peers in the summer of 1961, collectively thronged, pushed, and overwhelmed Kennedy with their elbows to get a handshake, cheering as if they were "movie fans greeting a matinee idol," as the *NYT* reported.[5] Kennedymania even extended to rural peasants in the far deserts of the state of Rajasthan, India. On the election day, villagers living some 50 miles from Jaipur assembled around a community radio set and tuned in to world news. When news broke that Kennedy was about to win, listeners clapped their hands and patted themselves on the shoulders. Asked by a puzzled newsman why they would do so, one farmer explained: "Somehow most of the people here think that Kennedy is another Nehru. If Kennedy is defeated the only happy persons will be the handful of local Communists who are afraid that his victory will mean closer collaboration between the American administration and Nehru's Congress Party up in Delhi."[6] More than a US-Latin American affair, then, the Kennedy era rallied hopes and political emotions around the whole globe, helping to transform the US presidency into a truly *global* institution.

What made Kennedy so popular in what is now commonly referred to as the "Global South"? One explanation, often put forward by historians—though much less researched—is that Kennedy entered the White House during a moment of transformative change in global mass communications, perhaps reflected best by the global rise of television and the stunning advances in satellite communications.[7] In a country like Argentina—as indeed in many countries throughout Latin America— the advance of television reshaped the local media landscape, and made watching the president a thrilling new experience. Of the four channels serving the over 500,000 TV sets in 1961 Argentina, three had commercial agreements with American TV stations, and while shows like *I Love Lucy* or *Bonanza* usually scored the highest ratings, news footage provided by US stations assured that Argentineans would also frequently see President Kennedy in their living rooms.

Kennedy was the first president of the "global village":[8] Television offered new forms of participatory involvement across time and space, and in this sense stood for a new sensational sense of global interconnectedness. But it was not just television that made Kennedy popular, partly for the simple reason that television was not yet a global medium in the early 1960s. While it established itself quickly in countries like Argentina, Colombia, or Mexico, populations across large parts of Africa and Asia still had to do without it in the Kennedy years. In Nigeria, for example, television served the bigger cities, but hardly reached into the countryside. India's television station only broadcasted to a limited number of TV community sets around New Delhi. Tanganyika had no TV service at all. What made Kennedy popular in those countries were media transformations of a different kind, culminating in an expanding reach and social use of mass media throughout the "Global South" more generally. In India, a "newspaper boom" tripled circulation figures of dailies, weeklies, and monthlies since the late 1950s,[9] and in many other countries across Asia, Africa, and Latin America new picture magazines, illustrated weeklies, and fashion journals began to flourish, among

Figure 6.1 Peruvian Sculptor Carlos Pazos presents his Kennedy bust to US chief of protocol Angier Biddle Duke in the Cabinet Room, White House, March 29, 1962. Picture credit: Abbie Rowe, White House Photographs, John F. Kennedy Presidential Library, Boston (JFKL), Digital Identifier: JFKWHP-AR7130-B, https://www.jfklibrary.org/Asset-Viewer/Archives/JFKWHP-AR7130-B.aspx (accessed March 3, 2018).

them Africa's *Drum Magazine*, Latin American *Panorama*, or the *Illustrated Weekly* in India. Typically abounding with extensive advertisements for fashion, movies, cosmetics, cars, and the latest consumer gimmicks, those magazines introduced long photo spreads showing stars and celebrities, but they also frequently featured the new US president.

Historians have often commented on the ways Kennedy exploited and capitalized on the global rise of mass media and the 1960s "culture of images"[10] in particular. We know, in the words of Michael Hogan, that Kennedy aimed at creating "what marketers would call a 'brand,'" in the process fashioning "carefully constructed idealizations that exemplified the highest qualities of American life."[11] Far less attention, however, has been paid to the agency and the underlying motives that postcolonial and global media themselves had in constructing and projecting Kennedy images to their audiences. Serving the entertainment desires of their postcolonial readers (and viewers), those media often had their own stakes in the Kennedy imagery. By the early 1960s, many had just begun to merge political reporting with the narrative techniques of entertainment into new forms of "politainment."[12] Pictures ranked high under this new approach, so did human-interest stories that offered a personal touch on politics and allowed postcolonial readers to imagine new and "modern" lifestyles. Unlike Nikita Khrushchev or Konrad Adenauer, Kennedy fit the bill. The US president offered style, he offered fashion, and he offered pictures that global media could appropriate and adapt to cater to the emotional longings of their readers. Thus, when *Primera Plana* launched its first issue in Argentina, it did not feature an Argentinean celebrity on its cover, but Kennedy. And when the new illustrated weekly *Siete Días Ilustrados* attempted to boost its sales, it advertised its services with local sports and culture celebrities, but also with a photograph of Kennedy. In Mexico, too, Kennedy was featured frequently on magazine covers, and throughout postcolonial countries photo stories as much as cartoons of him flourished.[13] "It is as if I knew President Kennedy personally," remarked a newspaper reader from Tanzania after Kennedy had been assassinated: "I have read about him so often."[14]

Jumping at the photo opportunities and stories that Kennedy offered, global media typically fashioned their own readings of Kennedy. Those readings were often framed by local political concerns and expectations. Thus, in India press commentaries on Kennedy rose and fell with his stances on Kashmir and the Chinese threat. West African readings of Kennedy were shaped to a large extent by his civil rights policies. Latin Americans looked for signs of Pan-American solidarity. Beyond the political commentary usually found in editorials and opinion pieces, however, global media also often fashioned more apolitical accounts of Kennedy, offering narratives that personalized the collective wants, self-images, and fantasies of their own readers (and viewers) through the image of Kennedy.

Two themes often stood out in media across Africa, Asia, and Latin America: Kennedy, the family man, and the glamour of the White House, a theme that media usually emotionalized for their readers by focusing on the First Lady. Kennedy, during a state visit to France in May 1961, once quipped that he was "the man who accompanied Jacqueline Kennedy to Paris,"[15] and in light of the First Lady's unprecedented global popularity he did indeed have a point. In the emerging media landscapes of Africa, the First Lady often ranked high along with Elvis Presley, American Jazz artists, or with Western fashion, and in Asia, too, illustrated weeklies, fashion magazines, and the yellow press featured her regularly.[16] In late 1961, the popular *Illustrated Weekly of India* twice ran a feature story of the First Lady and her life in the White House, so did India's leading tabloid *Blitz* which came out with a three-part series on Jacqueline Kennedy in March 1962.[17] "The President and I," *Blitz* claimed, had been written exclusively for Indian audiences by Jacqueline Kennedy and would reveal "her choices and the things she likes best—about her appearance, her dress, hair, house, children, husband, her hopes, fears and doubts."[18]

The popularity of the First Lady reflected changes in the global media environment and its hunger for human-interest stories, but it also had a way of opening new emotional vistas through which people could relate to the US presidency. Jackie's fashionable style, her elegance, her struggle between the dual responsibilities of mother and First Lady, loyal housewife and independent mind, spoke directly to the desires and struggles of early 1960s "modern" women, and invited readers of *Blitz*, the *Illustrated Weekly of India*, or similar human-interest magazines in Asia, Africa, or Latin America to engage with the institution she represented. Meanwhile, men, too, fell under Jackie's spell. Indian prime minister Nehru, reported then ambassador Galbraith from India, was "deeply in love" with her and had a "picture of himself strolling with J.B.K. displayed all by itself in the main entrance hall of his house."[19] In Colombia, Peace Corps director Sargent Shriver observed during a visit that Jackie Kennedy had become "the new, pin-up queen of the Latinos" as "her pic[ture] appear[ed] on many a wall." Latin Americans, Shriver found, had also given her a new name: "La Reina" (the queen).[20]

Given the First Lady's global popularity, it came as no surprise that TV shows featuring her, too, usually drew large audiences outside of the United States. The first of these, the CBS show "A Tour of the White House with Mrs. John F. Kennedy," was widely circulated abroad after it had aired in the United States in February 1962, and was an instant success. According to some counts, hundreds of million viewers saw it, and United States Information Agency (USIA) posts reported enthusiastic responses: In Karachi, Pakistan, the film was shown no less than forty-four times to an overall audience of 27,000. Particularly Indian women seemed to like it. As USIA's New Delhi post registered, film showings were packed with women's groups, leading the post to also schedule special night screenings. In Iran, a special showing was arranged for Empress Farah Diba the day the film arrived and for Muhammad Riza Shah Pahlavi the next day, and in Africa, too, posts considered the show "useful in conveying a picture of the White House and Mrs. Kennedy's personality." Around the world, foreign commentators lauded the show for demonstrating "Mrs. Kennedy's youthful enthusiasm, intense interest in history and the arts, her natural charm and national pride."[21]

Catering to postcolonial wants for glamour and politainment through carefully arranged picture tableaus and home stories, the Kennedy White House changed the way global populations came in touch with the presidency and created new emotional bonds between the Kennedys and their global media consumers. And yet, to see the popularity of the Kennedys throughout the "Global South" only in terms of their picture making and their glamour, would mean to miss another essential aspect of the Kennedy presidency. What made Kennedy so appealing to populations across the Global South was not only that he was a gifted maker of images—he also had a powerful story for those living in Latin America, Africa, and Asia, a new narrative that he crafted skillfully over his presidency, and that reshaped his relations with the decolonized world. That story stressed Kennedy's genuine compassion for the sufferings and needs of the decolonized world, promised its uplift from mass poverty, and thereby reconnected the United States to the aspirations for social and economic "progress" that marked the decolonizing world of the 1950s and 1960s. In the end, it was that narrative which accounted for much of the Kennedy appeal in the "Global South."

The global spread of the Kennedy narrative rested to no little degree on the work of the USIA. Set up in 1953 to nourish America's image in the world, USIA had become a powerful media provider in its own right by the early 1960s and operated in practically all countries throughout the "Global South." USIA furnished stories about America across the whole spectrum of media channels—from pamphlets, publications, and cartoons handed out to local populations through mobile exhibits to radio broadcasts on its own station, the Voice of America. In many parts of Latin America, Africa, and Asia, USIA also ran its own local information centers. Offering exhibits, films, concerts, seminars, lectures, evening entertainment, and a library, those centers usually drew large audiences per year. USIA also furnished its own news articles and photographs for local news media, arranged for live radio broadcasts of Kennedy speeches, tried to place film clips of Kennedy press conferences on local television and cinema screens, and even produced its own films and TV shows. Thus, as USIA concluded by mid-1962, in a country like Argentina chances were high that everybody who had "a radio or television set" had "sometime during the year been exposed to a USIS program,"[22] a finding that truly applied to most parts of the "Global South" in the early 1960s.

If USIA furnished the infrastructure for the global dissemination of the Kennedy narrative, Kennedy's foreign aid program furnished the actual story, framed as a new promise already in his inaugural address: "To those peoples in the huts and villages of half the globe struggling to break the bonds of mass misery, we pledge our best efforts to help them help themselves, for whatever period is required."[23] Ten days later, in his State of the Union address, Kennedy reiterated his commitment to fighting poverty in the "whole southern half of the world," announcing as one of the goals of his administration "a new and more effective program for assisting the economic, educational and social development of other countries and continents."[24] After his 1957 Senate speech on Algerian decolonization, Kennedy had for a long time argued for such a program, attacking the "lamentable lack of concern" that the Eisenhower administration had demonstrated vis-à-vis the decolonizing world and Latin America in particular. Those policies, Kennedy charged during a campaign stint to Florida, had not only laid the groundwork for Castro's takeover of Cuba and an outburst of anti-Americanism throughout the hemisphere, they had also created a great disconnect between the United States and the social, economic, and material aspirations of Latin Americans. "The people of Latin America," Kennedy argued, "have not felt we are concerned about freedom. They fear we are really concerned about them only as pawns in the cold war. We are more interested, they think, in our investments in those countries than in the people." It would therefore be "incumbent on the next President of the United States," Kennedy concluded, "to, at the beginning of his term of office, indicate by action and word his belief in the solidarity of the Western hemisphere (. . .) his belief that the people of this hemisphere can provide through freedom a better life (. . .) his belief that the cause of freedom and the cause of people identifying themselves and developing their own resources is the great cause of the 1960's."[25] The United States, as ambassador Chester Bowles summed up the general feeling among Kennedy's staff, had done too little "in the sphere of giving of ourselves to the peoples of the underdeveloped world" in the Eisenhower years. "In achieving a sense of identification" of America's "cause with that of the indigenous peoples," it therefore lagged behind.[26]

In March 1961, dramatizing his commitment to the developing world, Kennedy eventually rolled out his new foreign aid program, asking Congress for the creation of the Peace Corps and a concerted effort in foreign aid under the wings of a newly established Agency for International Development.[27] In a White House speech that was transmitted live on radio to Latin America, Kennedy on March 13 also officially proclaimed the Alliance for Progress: "a vast cooperative effort, unparalleled in magnitude and nobility of purpose, to satisfy the basic needs of the American people for homes, work and land, health and schools—*techo, trabajo y tierra, salud y escuela*." Under the alliance, sketched out as a ten-year plan for the Americas, the United States would immediately make available a $500-million fund to fulfill the Act of Bogota, step up its Food for Peace program aid, work toward a Central American common market and free trade areas throughout the Americas, provide assistance to Latin American universities and research institutions, and promote cooperation and exchanges in the fields of higher education and culture. The United States, Kennedy told his audience in the White House and in front of radio sets throughout Latin America, had "not always grasped the significance" of the "hemisphere's mission" to "lift people from poverty and ignorance and despair." But it was now prepared to "turn from these mistakes" and "from the failures and the misunderstandings of the past" by committing itself to a "bold" new approach that, by the end of the decade, would have the "living standards of every American family (...) on the rise," made "basic education (...) available to all," and rendered hunger "a forgotten experience."[28]

Reports of Kennedy's compassion for the "Global South" soon suffused media landscapes from Latin America to Asia, in press comments and editorials, radio broadcasts, and TV shows. With its operations in full swing throughout the Global South, USIA, too, promoted the story. Voice of America broadcasts, scheduled immediately after Kennedy's address on the Alliance for Progress, provided background information on the initiative and were later extended into a broadcast series on "modernization around the world." Wall posters and pamphlets distributed throughout the developing world publicized Kennedy's speeches.[29] Picture stories and exhibits on the foreign

Figure 6.2 An example of a typical cartoon on the Alliance for Progress as USIA disseminated them by the millions in Latin America. "Unidos en la Alianza," Entry 53, Box 9, RG 306, NARA.

Figure 6.3 Another example of a typical cartoon on the Alliance for Progress as USIA disseminated them by the millions in Latin America. "Unidos en la Alianza," Entry 53, Box 9, RG 306, NARA.

aid program more generally showcased specific aid projects and demonstrated, in the words of a USIS official, how the program would "benefit the viewers."[30] By 1962 and 1963, films, too, often had a heavy emphasis on foreign aid and drew attention to the multitude of new aid projects underway, from housing over school construction to dam building.[31] USIA even introduced its own cartoon program which dramatized Kennedy's commitment to helping the poor and served to "engender support" for the alliance through "direct, graphic, and easily understood appeals to Latin American workers and farmers."[32] Until late 1964, USIA exported almost thirty-eight million cartoons to Asia and Latin America where they began to compete with Walt Disney's Donald Duck.[33] Among rural readers "of low educational level," the agency found in a media impact study on Colombian *campesinos*, the format worked well in getting the message across and was "extremely effective, understandable and acceptable."[34]

In practice, Kennedy's foreign aid program reflected the intellectual currents of "modernization as ideology"[35] and put social engineering at the center, but it also connected exceptionally well with the broader social aspirations of decolonizing and developing societies. Kennedy, noted Venezuelan Radio-TV commentator Jose Nahr in response to the president's address on the Alliance for Progress, was the first US president to fully grasp the needs and concerns of Latin America,[36] and most Latin Americans shared that assessment.[37] Studies and polls done by the USIA's research branch explained why: When asked about their "basic hopes" and long-term values, "nearly all of" the "ordinary human beings" asked in developing countries had the same "predictable priorities. First, they want a chance to make a good living for themselves and their families. Close behind in ranking come adequate housing and good education for their children." To the surprise of USIA analysts, "neither 'peace' nor 'avoiding Communism'" appeared "among the top six values in developing countries" such as Brazil, India, or the Philippines. By a "large margin," the "top aspiration" throughout those countries was "prosperity."[38]

In striking contrast to the cold-blooded and calculated Cold War move that actually stood behind the foreign aid program, global media and populations from Latin America to Asia widely believed in Kennedy's commitment to improving their living standards and saw it as coming out of a genuine, heartfelt, and deeply personal concern for the needs and aspirations of the developing world. As *El Tiempo* in Bogotá put it: "One of the great complaints of Latin America has been the lack of comprehension of its problems by officials of the United States. Now President Kennedy declares that the fundamental requirement of political life is freedom. And (. . .) he looks to our needs of economic development and social advance with the same concern that the shortcomings of his own country arouse in him."[39] Media outside of Latin America often voiced similar views, and in India ordinary citizens stressed their belief in Kennedy's "absolute honesty of purpose"[40] long after he had been assassinated. Indian citizens therefore also flooded the *Illustrated Weekly of India* with letters when, in 1965, it asked its readers to explain "What, in your opinion, was the secret of Kennedy's unique hold on the imagination of people the world over?" The answers: It was Kennedy's "youthful dynamism" and "passion for human welfare" (Morarji Desai), his "overmastering desire for the common man" (Ramaswami Aiyar), "his earnest devotion to the cause of humanity" (Shalini Abhyankar, Ahmedabad), his "happy home life (. . .). He brought new hope to a fear-ridden, frustrated and poverty-stricken world" (Mrs. Nijhawan, Jamshedpur), "his courage and resolution in times of crisis, his sustained faith in democracy, his dynamism in economic policies, his fight against racial discrimination, his love and sympathy towards the underprivileged people of the whole world" (M. Chickannaiyappa, Tumkur).[41] The same perceptions marked a commemorative volume on "Kennedy through Indian Eyes" that had come out a year earlier and assembled the voices of politicians, journalists, and intellectuals along with a selection of Kennedy's speeches. Tributes throughout stressed that Kennedy not only worked toward assuring wealth and prosperity in the United States but had added to this "a deeper human and moral outlook which embraced in its scope the peoples of the world" (Prime Minister Nehru), that he had been a "leader who could season his country's unmatched strength with human understanding" (*Thought*, New Delhi) and that India had lost a "sincere friend who understood our difficulties and appreciated our aspirations" (Speaker's tribute in Indian Parliament on November 25, 1963).[42] Those were idealizations, to be sure, but they did move along the lines of a foreign imaginary of Kennedy that had evolved since 1961.

The hopes and beliefs that people in the Global South pinned on Kennedy had much to do with the promises that Kennedy made, but there was more behind them. To millions of those living in Africa, Asia, and Latin America, the Kennedy narrative also recognized the sense of historical agency that they had formed in the age of decolonization. Kennedy, postcolonial and Latin American media audiences sensed, gave a voice and new meaning to their struggles for a better life. Thus, media audiences often responded with great enthusiasm when being shown films about their own modernizing efforts and American aid, at one point, as USIA reported, leading rural audiences on "opposite sides of the globe" in Pakistan and Costa Rica to break out into strikingly similar and "spontaneous shouts of 'Long Live Kennedy.'"[43] Others flooded local US posts with requests for Kennedy's writings.[44] Populations also turned out in record numbers every time the Kennedys' visited, whether in Venezuela and Colombia in 1961, in Pakistan, India, and Mexico in 1962 (India and Pakistan getting the First Lady alone) and in Costa Rica in 1963. Long before Kennedy's much famed trip to Berlin in June 1963, those travels were mass-mediated, mass-staged, and mass spectator events, but also occasions for ordinary people to openly express their emotions for the Kennedys. Nearly half of Bogotá turned out on the streets when the Kennedys visited in late 1961, a crowd of 500,000 and the biggest that had ever welcomed Kennedy. It was a most "tumultuous welcome," as a US correspondent noted, the streets packed with people that waved handkerchiefs, threw ticker tape, shouted bravo, and pushed forward once the Kennedys passed in their open limousine, being stopped only by the guards "from crushing the President and the First Lady with affection."[45] The welcome, noted *La Nación* in Costa Rica, stressed "the sentiment of solidarity uniting all the peoples of America in this hour (. . .) to powerfully stimulate the material and cultural progress of all the inhabitants of our hemisphere," and as Bogotá's Radio Cadena Nacional seconded, the great enthusiasm shown in the streets not only expressed Colombian gratitude for US aid, but represented their "adherence to the leader of democracy, to the defender of liberty and human dignity, and to a Christian chief of state who wants to impose in a shattered world the standard of union justice, and solidarity with those who struggle and suffer."[46] Crowds in the streets had a simpler reading, welcoming the Kennedys with signs and banners saying "Welcome Kennedy and Jacqueline," "Welcome Jackie," and "Welcome Sir John Kennedy, President and Lady the Choice of the [World]."[47] Weeks after the Kennedys had departed, related correspondent Richard Massock, "some of the US flags displayed for the occasion still fluttered from lamp posts" in Colombia and Venezuela, and "not even the Communists bothered to tear them down."[48]

There were also limits to the global Kennedy appeal, however. A few days before the Kennedys' visit to Bogotá, a number of likely protestors had been put into jail temporarily by local police to guarantee an unmarred visit, a move that pointed to the local resistance against the Kennedys. In Mexico, too, radical students threatened to disrupt Kennedy's visit, but were eventually kept on a leash by local police. There were also frictions within local and global media landscapes. Within the left radical press around the world, Kennedy rarely scored applause for his policies. Sometimes populations also simply didn't know him. In the hinterlands of Nicaragua, as a survey turned out, 33 percent of the rural *campesinos* asked were able to name Kennedy as the president of the United States, but 67 percent had no clue who Kennedy was and what he represented.⁴⁹ Anti-Kennedy campaigns, too, were a fact of the times in some countries—often organized locally by socialist or communist student groups. In China, the Communist Party even produced its own anti-Kennedy film: "Kennedy in his true colors." The film dwelled widely on Kennedy's policy failures and was a box office success in Chinese cinemas, but remained a local affair.⁵⁰ Not least, global sympathies for Kennedy often diminished considerably in the wake of controversial foreign policy decisions, including the failed Bay of Pigs invasion attempt of April 1961, the resumption of nuclear testing or defoliation in Vietnam—events that each time led to temporary drops in Kennedy's global approval ratings.

Perhaps the greatest challenge to the ways foreigners viewed Kennedy, however, came from within the United States. The problem was, of course, segregation, a matter that moved massively into the national spotlight with the drama of the freedom rides, the riots against the integration of the University of Mississippi, the protest marches in Birmingham, and the 1963 clash with Governor Wallace in the school door of the University of Alabama. More than a domestic affair, those events were widely covered in global media and each time exposed the Kennedy administration to allegations of moral hypocrisy, particularly in Africa. Reports sent in from US posts frequently stressed the "whole raft of adverse headlines and editorials"⁵¹ printed in African media on America's racial strife. In the wake of the Birmingham crisis, many within and outside of the administration also pointed to the dramatic impact that pictures of police dogs attacking protestors had among African audiences.⁵² To African viewers, explained Russell Howe, longtime African correspondent of the *Washington Post*, "U.S. news pictures of bloodstained demonstrators and mass arrests" not only looked "similar to the sort of (much bloodier) colonial clashes" that Africans had experienced in Kenya, Senegal, or Madagascar some years ago. They also fixed in African minds the notion of "White resentment at African independence."⁵³

Most strikingly, some media also attacked Kennedy personally. "President Kennedy," as the *Morning Post* in Nigeria put it, "must be feeling quite small, not only in the eyes of the Russians who have always been taught to disbelieve every American anyway, but before all the world to whom he has always represented his country as the champion of liberty. The brutes of Alabama, after all, knocked the bottom out of all these preachments about the free world which America regards as its image."⁵⁴

Historians have often emphasized Kennedy's restrained and passive approach to civil rights which led him to act only under the pressures of dramatic crisis situations. Kennedy, notes John Hellmann in his ground-breaking study of the *Kennedy Obsession*, "typically responded to specific problems by shaping them into crisis situations," using his narrative talent to chart out his own plot in order to "position himself as hero figure."⁵⁵ Kennedy's response to the civil rights struggle was no exception. To his credit, however, once those crisis situations were there, Kennedy did not take chances and sent in federal marshals and national troops in all major confrontations with Southern segregationists between October 1962 and June 1963. On June 11, 1963, finally, Kennedy also went live on television to announce that he would introduce new civil rights legislation to desegregate all facilities which were open to the public. The United States, he told the nation, was facing a "moral crisis as a country and as a people." It was now "time to act in the Congress, in your State and local legislative body and, above all, in all of our daily lives."[56]

Ending Kennedy's long wavering on civil rights, the June 11 address was symbolic politics at its best, primarily intended to offset the cracks that the pictures of racist violence during the Birmingham marches had left on America's Cold War image.[57] Nonetheless it had a significant impact. In their immediate responses, African media stressed Kennedy's courage to take on segregation and his moral commitment against racial discrimination, with some media in Nigeria even going as far as to cherish him "as one of the greatest champions of the rights of man that ever lived."[58] By July, Kennedy also ranked number one among African students in the United States "as the most admired political leader outside of Africa," and while 62 percent had an adverse opinion of US race relations, 69 percent of them felt they were improving.[59] All in all, surveys showed, Kennedy's response to the Birmingham marches and his June 11 address had registered well with global audiences, and many of them thought that the administration was doing a good job on civil rights.[60]

What new perspectives does an inquiry into such responses open on the history of the Kennedy presidency? Kennedy's global popularity, as responses to his civil rights policies and the foreign aid program show, rested not alone on Kennedy's ability to fashion appealing images, but also on the fact that the actions he offered responded to aspirations and political expectations of populations across the "Global South." In this story, global media and postcolonial populations were not passive recipients of the Kennedy message. They evaluated Kennedy's actions in terms of their own concerns, formulated expectations, and thereby created the pressures which led Kennedy to act in the first place. Kennedy's great talent, in turn, lay in framing his responses to such expectations in narratives that spoke to the concerns and aspirations of global audiences. Kennedy's political life, as Jacqueline Kennedy once put it, therefore "had more to do with myth, magic, legend, saga, and story than with political theory or political science,"[61] and much political work, as a broad historical scholarship has shown, indeed went into fabricating those stories and myths.

In the end, the history of the Kennedy presidency is therefore not only a history of political decision-making and new diplomatic advances in an age of decolonization. It is also embedded in a broader history of global media transformations, changing postcolonial entertainment desires, popular political concerns, and collective aspirations for better living standards. Kennedy offered the promises global media audiences were looking for. Therewith, he not only popularized the institution of the US presidency within the United States but also globalized it around the world in ways that only few US presidents have done before or after him.

Notes

1 The episode is covered in "Will Somebody Please Take this Man to Our Leader?" *LAT*, March 22, 1962; "Peruvian Sculptor Plans Tardy Gift to President," *LAT*, March 27, 1962.
2 "'Si Kennedy' Becomes Latin Nations' Theme," *LAT*, March 26, 1961.
3 "South America Looks to Kennedy for Magic," *LAT*, March 10, 1961.

4 USIS India to USIA Washington, Middle and Upper Class Opinion in Bombay, Tokyo, Manila, Bangkok, and Singapore on Political and Social Issues in July 1963, November 1, 1963, Box 49, Country Project Files, Office of Research, Record Group (RG) 306, National Archives, College Park (NARA).
5 See "Foreign Students Stampede at White House to Shake Kennedy's Hand," *NYT*, July 14, 1961; "Foreign Students Engulf President," *NYT*, July 12, 1962; "Kennedy Mobbed by Foreign Students at White House," *NYT*, July 19, 1963.
6 "Nehru's Visit Comes at Time of 'Disenchanted Relations,'" *Washington Post*, November 2, 1961.
7 On the broader impacts and implications for US foreign policy, see Sönke Kunkel, *Empire of Pictures: Global Media and the 1960s Remaking of American Foreign Policy* (New York: Berghahn, 2018).
8 Marshall McLuhan, Quentin Fiore, and Jerome Agel, *War and Peace in the Global Village* (Toronto: Penguin, 2003 [1968]), 17.
9 Shankarlal Chandulal Bhatt, *Indian Press since 1955* (New Delhi: Publications Division, Ministry of Information and Broadcasting, 2000), 1.
10 David Lubin, *Shooting Kennedy: JFK and the Culture of Images* (Berkeley: University of California Press, 2003).
11 Michael Hogan, *The Afterlife of John F. Kennedy: A Biography* (Cambridge: Cambridge University Press, 2018), 17.
12 Andreas Dörner, *Politainment: Politik in der medialen Erlebnisgesellschaft* (Frankfurt: Suhrkamp, 2001).
13 See for an example of a picture story "Inside the White House," *Illustrated Weekly of India*, July 30, 1961. On examples for Kennedy cartoons, see *Sunday News*, Tanzania, *Times of India*, passim.
14 "Shock Shared by All," *Sunday News* (Tanzania), November 24, 1963.
15 Kennedy, "Remarks and Question and Answer Period at the Press Luncheon in Paris," June 2, 1961, Public Papers of the Presidents, online at APP. Available online: http://www.presidency.ucsb.edu/ws/?pid=8170.
16 On Africa, see "County Girl, Studying in Africa, Writes Views of Dark Continent," *LAT*, April 1, 1962.
17 See "The First Lady of America," *Illustrated Weekly of India*, September 3, 1961; "Personalities: Jacqueline Kennedy," *Illustrated Weekly of India*, December 10, 1961; "The President and I. Exclusive to Blitz in India. By Jacqueline Kennedy," *Blitz*, March 3, 1962.
18 Blitz ad for the series quoted in New Delhi to Secretary of State, February 23, 1962, Box 3110, Central Decimal File, 1960-1963, RG 59, NARA.
19 Galbraith to Kennedy, March 2, 1962, Box 29a, Special Correspondence, President's Office Files (POF), JFKL.
20 Sargent Shriver to Kennedy, October 27, 1961, POF. Available online: https://catalog.archives.gov/id/193719 (accessed March 6, 2018).
21 *The Statesman* (New Delhi), quoted in Wilson to Salinger, June 21, 1962, Papers of John F. Kennedy, Presidential Papers, POF, Departments and Agencies, US Information Agency (USIA), JFKL. On the foreign reception of the show, see also Caroline Schwalbe, "Jacqueline Kennedy and Cold War Propaganda," *Journal of Broadcasting and Electronic Media* 49, no. 1 (2006): 111–27.
22 USIS Buenos Aires to USIA Washington, Annual USIS Assessment Report: 1961, July 31, 1962, Entry 1047, Box 5, RG 306, NARA.
23 Kennedy, "Inaugural Address," January 20, 1961, APP. Available online: http://www.presidency.ucsb.edu/ws/?pid=8032 (accessed March 07, 2018).

24 Kennedy, "Annual Message to the Congress on the State of the Union," January 30, 1961, APP. Available online: http://www.presidency.ucsb.edu/ws/?pid=8045 (accessed March 7, 2018).
25 Kennedy, "Speech of Senator John F. Kennedy, Tampa, Hillsborough County Courthouse," October 18, 1960, APP. Available online: http://www.presidency.ucsb.edu/ws/?pid=74098 (accessed February 26, 2018).
26 Bowles to Murrow, March 3, 1961, quoted in Jason Parker, *Hearts, Minds, Voices* (New York: Oxford University Press, 2016), 118–19.
27 Kennedy, "Special Message to the Congress on Foreign Aid," March 22, 1961, APP. Available online: http://www.presidency.ucsb.edu/ws/?pid=8545 (accessed March 7, 2018).
28 Kennedy, "Address at a White House Reception for Members of Congress and for the Diplomatic Corps of the Latin American Republics," March 13, 1961. Available online: http://www.jfklibrary.org/Research/Ready-Reference/JFK-Speeches/Address-at-a-White-House-Reception-for-Members-of-Congress-and-for-the-Diplomatic-Corps-of-the-Latin.aspx (accessed May 11, 2011). On the Alliance for Progress, see most recently: Jeffrey Taffet, *Foreign Aid as Foreign Policy: The Alliance for Progress in Latin America* (New York: Routledge, 2007).
29 Wilson to Goodwin, March 6, 1961, Box 1, USIA, JFKL; McKnight to Wilson, Second Day Handling of President's Latin American Address, March 15, 1961, Box 1, USIA, JFKL; McKnight to Murrow, USIA Support for the Alliance for Progress, November 27, 1961, Box 1, USIA, JFKL.
30 Waldman to Szekely, Project 63-068: Alliance for Progress Exhibit, November 13, 1962, Entry 1039, Box 1, RG 306, NARA.
31 See "United in Progress" or "The School at Rincon Santo."
32 USIA, 20th report to Congress, January 1-June 30, 1963, Library, NARA. On the cartoon program, see Matthew Jacobs, "Reformists, Revolutionaries, and Kennedy Administration Public Diplomacy in Colombia and Venezuela," *DH* 42, no. 5 (2017): 859–85.
33 Rowan to President, Weekly Report, December 15, 1964, Box 12, Chronological Files of the Director, RG 306, NARA.
34 Review of USIA Research, March 4, 1963, Papers of John F. Kennedy, Presidential Papers, POF, Departments and Agencies, USIA. Available online: https://www.jfklibrary.org/Asset-Viewer/Archives/JFKPOF-091-007.aspx (accessed March 4, 2018).
35 Michael Latham, *Modernization as Ideology: American Social Science and "Nation-Building" in the Kennedy Era* (Chapel Hill: University of North Carolina Press, 2000).
36 McKnight to Wilson, Third Day Handling of President's "Alliance for Progress," March 16, 1961, Box 1, USIA, JFKL.
37 For many more examples, see McKnight to Wilson, Second Day Handling of President's Latin American Address, March 15, 1961, Box 1, USIA, JFKL; and McKnight to Wilson, Third Day Handling.
38 Review of USIA Research.
39 Quoted in "Si Kennedy."
40 Ram Singh/M. K. Haldar, *Kennedy through Indian Eyes* (New Delhi: Vir, 1964), 18.
41 See "Homage to Kennedy I"; "Kennedy's Dream"; "Reader's Tributes," all in *Illustrated Weekly of India*, May 23, 1965, and May 30, 1965.
42 Quotes in Singh/Haldar, *Kennedy*, 23–25.
43 Wilson to Kennedy, Weekly Report, September 24, 1963, Office of the Director (OD), Chronological Files (CF) 1953-1964, Reel 63, RG 306, NARA.

44 Wilson to Kennedy, Weekly Report, March 6, 1962, OD, CF 1953-1964, Reel 59, RG 306, NARA.
45 "Throngs Hail Kennedys in Colombia," *LAT*, December 18, 1961; "500 000 in Bogota Greet President on Alliance Tour," *Special to the NYT*, December 18, 1961; Office of Operations to President, Foreign Radio and Press Reaction to President Kennedy's Latin American Trip, December 18, 1961, Box 128, Papers of Pierre Salinger, White House Staff Files, JFKL.
46 Ibid., December 19, 1961.
47 "Kennedy's Latin Tour Is Personal Triumph," *Wall Street Journal*, December 18, 1961; "Throngs."
48 "U.S. Prestige: It's in Good Shape," *LAT*, January 21, 1962.
49 Murrow to Kennedy, Weekly Report, June 18, 1963, OD, CF 1953–1964, Reel 65, RG 306, NARA.
50 Murrow to Kennedy, Weekly Report, March 13, 1962, OD, CF 1953–1964, Reel 59, RG 306, NARA.
51 Wilson to Schlesinger, October 11, 1962, OD, CF 1953–1964, Reel 52, RG 306, NARA.
52 Wilson to Kennedy, Weekly Report, May 14, 1963, OD, CF 1953–1964, Reel 66, RG 306, NARA.
53 Russel Howe, "Average African Confused on U.S. Racial Issue," *Washington Post*, July 22, 1963.
54 Reaction to Racial Tension in Birmingham, Memorandum, IRS, May 14, 1963, Box 96a, POF, JFKL.
55 John Hellmann, *The Kennedy Obsession. The American Myth of JFK* (New York: Columbia University Press, 1997), 99.
56 Kennedy, "Radio and Television Report to the American People on Civil Rights," June 11, 1963, APP. Available online: http://www.presidency.ucsb.edu/ws/?pid=9271 (accessed March 16, 2018).
57 On this point, see Michael Krenn, ed., *Race and U.S. Foreign Policy during the Cold War* (New York: Garland, 1998); Mary Dudziak, *Cold War Civil Rights: Race and the Image of American Democracy* (Princeton: Princeton University Press, 2000); Thomas Borstelmann, *The Cold War and the Color Line: American Race Relations in the Global Arena* (Cambridge: Harvard University Press, 2001).
58 Murrow to Kennedy, Reactions to June 11 speech, June 14, 1963, OD, CF, 1953–1964, Reel 15, RG 306, NARA.
59 Wilson to Kennedy, Weekly Report, July 9, 1963, OD, CF, 1953–1964, Reel 64, RG 306, NARA.
60 On India, see Wilson to Kennedy, Weekly Report, July 16, 1963, OD, CF 1953–1964, Reel 64, RG 306, NARA.
61 Quoted in David Heymann, *A Woman Named Jackie* (Secaucus: Carol, 1989), 418.

7

From Hope to Disillusionment: Moroccan Perceptions of the Kennedy Presidency

David Stenner

Introduction

Less than two months after the inauguration of John F. Kennedy, on March 3, 1961, Hassan II ascended the Moroccan throne following the surprise death of his father, King Mohammed V. He was twelve years younger than his American counterpart and certainly much less prominent outside of his own country. But despite receiving only a fraction of the foreign media coverage of his US counterpart, the elaborate ceremony— which included a display of the royal umbrella, a parade of dignitaries kissing the young ruler's right hand, and a horseback ride in the company of his black elite soldiers— proved no less spectacular. Hassan II would soon emerge as an influential player in Africa and the Middle East during his thirty-eight years on the throne despite ruling only a medium-sized North African kingdom. Pitiless toward his opponents, charming to those dear to him, and closely aligned with the United States, he represented the ultimate Cold Warrior whose friendship politicians in Western capitals desired.

The political role of the United States in the world, and Hassan II's rule, constituted the overlapping lenses through which the Moroccan population perceived global affairs during the 1960s. The country's political elites had already been aware of the international political situation for a long time before obtaining independence from France and Spain in March 1956. Inspired by the liberation of countries like India, in 1947, and Indonesia, in 1949, as well as the brutal war in neighboring Algeria from 1954 to 1962, many Moroccans had come to understand foreign and domestic politics as inherently intertwined. The members of the nationalist *Hizb al-Istiqlal* (Independence Party) organized their campaign for independence both at home and abroad after its establishment in January 1944, culminating in a successful propaganda campaign that spanned from Cairo via Paris to New York. Their global network of supporters put significant international pressure on the colonizers and thus proved pivotal in the struggle to end the two, French and Spanish, protectorates.[1] International affairs constituted a central aspect of Moroccan politics from its very inception, because many of the Istiqlal's leaders had spent more time abroad than at home during the late colonial era.

It is from this vantage point that we must understand Moroccan perceptions of the presidency of Kennedy, who self-consciously portrayed himself as an outspoken anti-colonial politician willing to work with the peoples of Third World to build a world of peace and prosperity. After all, Kennedy had risen to international prominence following his now-famous "Algeria speech" on the Senate floor in July 1957, in which he had condemned imperialism as "the great enemy of . . . freedom" and suggested that France "get out of North Africa completely."[2] These words had been extremely well received by the peoples of the Maghrib, who welcomed this clear distancing from the Eisenhower administration's pro-French attitude. Many in the region hoped that the United States would finally become a truly emancipatory force following Kennedy's win in the 1960 presidential election.

Yet by the time of Kennedy's funeral in November 1963, this initial enthusiasm for his anti-colonial credentials had largely abated. Now, Moroccans spent little time talking about his emancipatory politics, focusing instead on his fight against segregation and for tax cuts at home as well as the important symbolism of his youth. They no longer displayed the same excitement as in previous years, despite remaining sympathetic toward Kennedy as a man and politician. Having realized that his policies were muss less revolutionary than originally anticipated, the US president had long ago lost his saint-like aura in the eyes of many Moroccans, despite the fact that they sincerely mourned his tragic death. Hope had given way to disillusionment.

An additional factor behind the transformation of Kennedy's image can be found in Moroccan domestic politics. Although the Istiqlal had dominated the anti-colonial movement during the last decade of foreign occupation, the royal palace had successfully sidelined the nationalist party from the reins of power following independence. Hassan II's ascendance to the throne further aggravated the political situation, as he quickly established a fully authoritarian regime. The country's first constitution, of December 7, 1962, legitimized his role as "commander of the faithful, symbol of the unity of the nation, head of the cabinet of ministers . . . [and] commander of the armed forces." He maintained the right to "dissolve the parliament . . . [and] announce laws," and most importantly, his very person was "sacrosanct and holy."[3] Moreover, he built a close alliance with the United States that strengthened and legitimized the monarchy at home.[4] The CIA concluded in August 1962 that although "the King publicly espouses nonalignment . . . his policy in practice is to stay within easy reach of the Western umbrella."[5] A different report confirmed that he had clearly established his "pro-Western proclivities," and this shift in foreign policy also impacted Morocco's fragmented field of local politics.[6] Thus, if we want to analyze Moroccan perceptions of Kennedy, we must read them from the standpoint of domestic events. By 1963, the US president appeared not only like a youthful politician of increasingly questionable anti-colonial credentials abroad but also as an enabler of an ever more authoritarian regime at home.

One way to gain a more in-depth understanding of Kennedy's perception in the decolonizing world is by looking at the Moroccan press, especially the two organs of the conservative Istiqlal, the country's most important political party. Published since September 1946 and thus Morocco's oldest independent daily newspaper, the Arabic-language *al-'Alam* ("The Banner") represented the viewpoints of the Istiqlal during the immediate postindependence period that lacked a vigorous independent press. Widely circulated and often read communally in coffee shops, it reached an important sector of the population, though widespread illiteracy (80.2 percent of men in 1960) significantly narrowed its potential readership to the educated elites and parts of the urban working class.[7] Until July 1963, the party also published the francophone weekly *al-Istiqlal*, which "addressed itself primarily to French readers" interested in the viewpoints of the nationalist movement.[8] It had a more left-leaning editorial line since many of its journalists had spent their formative years at French universities during the late colonial period. In the absence of legal protections guaranteeing the freedom of the press, the few nongovernmental newspapers had to tread extremely carefully when discussing domestic issues so as to not run afoul of the unofficial censorship rules. Despite these serious limitations, *al-'Alam* and *al-Istiqlal* constitute useful windows into the ideational landscape of the country's politically conscious elites during the tumultuous postindependence period.

Anticipating the Kennedy presidency

Al-'Alam followed the electoral campaign between Kennedy and Richard Nixon closely. In September 1960, the newspaper quoted the Democratic candidate regarding his plans to increase US support for non-Western nations: "The intent of our aid is not to buy the friendship of other states or to make them our dependencies. We want to help them ... to the degree that they can be independent from any foreign control, including our control."[9] On the eve of the election, columnist Abdelatif Ahmed Khalis approvingly explained that "it was known that the Democratic candidate supports the case of the Algerian people and demanded its freedom and independence."[10] The journalist admitted that Kennedy's stance on Algeria "was more zealous before than it is today," but added that it was "certain that his initial pledges will be victorious over the political environment" he would encounter as president.

In the weeks following Kennedy's victory, *al-'Alam* reminded its readers that the president-elect had repeatedly promised to "give special attention to the wave of independence that is engulfing the African continent" and that "the US will work to spread freedom across the entire world."[11] Especially his bold inaugural address received substantial attention. Asians and Africans consequently "registered with great relief—without a doubt—his resolve not to permit the exchange of the old colonialism for a new colonialism and ... to present the necessary aid to the states in order to help the people rid themselves of misery," because "the future belongs to freedom, and if the young president wants to preserve the tradition of his country, he must participate in the name of the United States."[12]

Al-Istiqlal offered a much more somber assessment of the potential for change embodied by Kennedy. Initially, the newspaper had expressed its hope for a Kennedy victory because he would "ally America with African nationalism."[13] A different article published in mid-December remarked that "Kennedy had expressed the hope ... that US foreign policy will be ... not only anti-communist, but also a symbol of 'liberty.'"[14]

But the francophone weekly nonetheless remained skeptical regarding Kennedy's nascent presidency. Despite his flowery rhetoric, "neither Kennedy's [inauguration] speech nor his first press conference have provided the least indication . . . that the United States will recognize its past mistakes."[15] While Kennedy might have rhetorically offered the recently liberated countries to "defend their liberty" and promised "the loyalty of a true friend," it seemed quite difficult to take such statements seriously "if one is aware . . . of the US intervention in the Congo for example."

Kennedy's anti-colonialism

One litmus test for deciphering Kennedy's true intentions was his attitude toward the revolutionary anti-colonial regimes. "Will the relations between the People's Republic of China and the United States develop?," asked Abdelatif Khalis in *al-ʿAlam* in March 1961.[16] Referring to Kennedy's recent statements on global affairs, the columnist concluded that the president might actually "reach an understanding with the People's Republic of China" in order to "reduce the degree of international tensions." But this honeymoon between the Moroccan press and the Kennedy administration came to an abrupt end in the wake of the disastrous Bay of Pigs Invasion of April 17, 1961, the failed attempt by US-backed counterrevolutionary forces to overthrow the Castro regime. A long op-ed article by Khalis condemned the "assault against Cuba" and praised the revolution of 1959 as a "victory over feudalism and despotism."[17] Referring to Kennedy's harsh anti-Communist rhetoric during the election campaign, he criticized the commonplace but "unfounded assumptions" that the new president would actually change Washington's stance toward the Western Hemisphere. The saintly aura surrounding Kennedy had already evaporated.

Still, Kennedy's personal engagement with Third World politics continued to fascinate Moroccans. Throughout the spring of 1961, the US administration repeatedly signaled its sympathy toward the Third World. "We support the African states from the bottom of [our] heart[s]," declared Kennedy in a telegram to the Conference of African states.[18] Especially his willingness to receive the leaders of recently decolonized nations in the White House underlined his interest in the fates of the non-Western peoples.[19] Kennedy also publicly called upon Britain to reform its colonial regime in Kenya and supported the autonomy of Northern Rhodesia, thus distancing himself from the passing age of European rule.[20] Even more satisfying in the eyes of North African observers was Kennedy's engagement with Arab leaders to find a just solution for the Palestine question; for example, he exchanged a number of amicable letters with Egypt's Gamal Abdel Nasser.[21] Kennedy's reception of Ahmed Ben Bella just three months after Algeria's independence in July 1962 further underlined his commitment to the postcolonial world.[22] The United States even provided the transport for the Algerian delegation traveling back home to North Africa after the successful conclusion of the peace talks with France in March 1962.[23]

Kennedy's most ambitious foreign policy project was the promise of increased economic aid. The unveiling of the Alliance for Progress in March 1961 demonstrated his willingness to spend billions of dollars in order to "raise the standard of living and end the dictatorial regimes in Latin America" and create "a world society that is peaceful [and] made up of free and independent states."[24] His assurances of economic support went beyond Latin America and included countries like the Congo.[25] Such reports on Kennedy's foreign policy depicted him as a well-meaning world leader, who sought to live up to his reputation by cooperating with the nations of the Third World within the ideological boundaries of liberal capitalism.

Yet al-ʿAlam also featured articles that provided critical assessments of the US administration. "Why do [the United States] wage a feverish war against the non-aligned states?," asked one article in November 1961.[26] Instead of accepting the principle of Cold War neutrality, Kennedy's aggressive foreign policy stance allegedly paralleled those of his two predecessors and thus constituted "a new sign . . . that foretells serious dangers and necessitates the outmost precaution." A different op-ed published two years later scolded the Kennedy administration for its intention to veto UN Security Council resolutions condemning Portuguese colonialism in southern Africa as well as the apartheid regime in Pretoria. "Those who are astonished by this do not understand the spirit which drives US politics," explained the article.[27] Washington seemed to hope that all colonial regimes would inevitably collapse under their own weight, making it unnecessary to alienate two crucial Cold War allies. "America does not look beyond this [issue]," which would mean embracing the aspirations of the peoples of Africa and Asia. By positioning itself as "the guardian of Christian culture and Western progress," the US inevitably sided with white minority rule. Kennedy's gradualism and focus on containing Communism trumped the interests of the decolonizing world.

Al-Istiqlal, by contrast, always remained skeptical regarding Kennedy's rhetoric. When Indonesian President Sukarno and Modibo Keita of Mali came to the White House as emissaries from the recently concluded Belgrade Conference in September 1961, Kennedy provided his guests with "the best welcome" but did not discuss any details of US foreign policy.[28] One year later, the newspaper printed a front page that featured four equally large pictures of Fidel Castro, Nehru, Chou en-lai, and Kennedy. Rather than as the leader of the "free world," the US president appeared as a coequal of his Third World counterparts.[29] The context was quite serious. At the height of the Cuban Missile Crisis, *al-Istiqlal* advocated for Havana's right to defend itself against "extreme interference in its internal affairs."[30] What might superficially appear as a conflict between the world's two leading superpowers actually became an act of anti-imperialist resistance when seen from the Global South. "Can we permit . . . that we remain at the mercy of the pressing of a button in the East or West, which risks bringing death to a large portion of our planet?," an editorial rhetorically asked the reader, before concluding that the Cold War is "a struggle that does not concern us." Kennedy certainly did not appear as a guarantor of liberty as he and his Soviet counterpart's "egoistic reflex[es]" threatened the very survival of the human race.

Amid such critical assessments of Kennedy's role toward the decolonizing world, ʿAllal al-Fassi published a lengthy editorial in defense of the US administration in both *al-ʿAlam* and *al-Istiqlal* in July 1963. Kennedy had decided to organize "a remarkable campaign" in the United States that will incite the population "against the existence of states subject to foreign rule," according to the president of the Istiqlal party.[31] Al-Fassi furthermore praised America's return to its "proclaimed liberal principles"—

after all, "nothing is as noble as a man fighting for the liberty of others." Yet even the party's most prominent conservative member did not unequivocally embrace the US president. Kennedy's recent policy changes, al-Fassi explained, "have luckily begun to adopt the attitude of the Soviet Union regarding the necessity to end colonialism." The US president, rather than being a world leader, seemed to have finally fallen in line with the inevitable march of history.

Kennedy the Cold Warrior

Central to Kennedy's image as a Cold Warrior was his determination to confront the Soviet Union. Immediately following his inauguration, al-ʿAlam wrote that "Mr. Kennedy will only negotiate with the Kremlin from a position of strength."[32] After his first visit to Paris in May 1961, the newspaper commented, "The US president . . . confirmed that he was not afraid of the future and that the situation is calling for manifestations of patience, resolve, and audacity."[33] Kennedy's passionate anti-communist rhetoric went so far as to claim that the nonaligned states "had a responsibility before history" to take a stance when confronted with "the shared . . . communist threat."[34] Neutrality was not an option. The youthful Kennedy also appeared as the guardian of an aging Europe.[35] During the Vienna summit on June 4, 1961, Kennedy had vigorously defended the interests of Western Europe vis-à-vis the Warsaw Pact through his unwavering stance on the issue of Berlin.[36] His personal commitment to West German security had "put Adenauer and German politicians at ease."[37] The US president had also provided the necessary "moral support" to Charles de Gaulle in his struggle against "the military fanatics and their rebellious movement in Algeria" following the putsch orchestrated by French settlers in April 1961.[38] In an article explaining the project of European unification, al-ʿAlam commented that since the Second World War, "power has been transferred from Old Europe to New America"—a large picture of a smiling Kennedy indicated that he personified this geopolitical transformation.[39]

Two editorials capture the evolving Moroccan attitudes toward his role as a Cold War leader. Abdelatif Khalis explained in February 1961 that "the differences between the Eastern and Western blocks in international affairs are serious," making it very difficult to secure a "rapprochement between the [two] viewpoints."[40] However, Kennedy's nascent presidency increased the possibility of "prudence triumphing over the spirit of egoism and fanaticism," paving a path "for an understanding . . . [between] the two blocks" that might benefit the international situation and allow Third World countries to prosper. A cartoon published just one year later indicated the sobering mood in Morocco with regard to the Cold War: it depicted Kennedy and Khrushchev sitting on the moon and looking back at our planet with a caption reading: "look at how peaceful the earth is now that we have left it!"[41] The drawing humorously expressed an increasing disenchantment with the Kennedy presidency.

Even with regard to Kennedy's Cold War policies, al-Istiqlal adopted a much more critical line than its arabophone sister publication. Of course, the US president's role as the leader of the West became clear during pivotal world events such as the Berlin crisis, when he received his German counterpart in the White House to deliberate on the political situation in central Europe just as the Berlin Wall was being constructed.[42] Kennedy also asserted his leadership through "calm and firmness" in the weeks leading up to the Cuban Missile Crisis in October 1962.[43] The US president subsequently used a speech at the NATO command headquarters in Naples to express "the determination of his country to defend the liberty of Europe."[44] But the newspaper also offered a very pessimistic assessment concerning the Alliance for Progress, proclaiming that "Latin America is disappointed by John F. Kennedy."[45] He had only offered "vague promises . . . without specifics" instead of a concrete roadmap outlining a project of the same magnitude as the Marshall Plan "that benefitted Europe following the end of the [last] war." It appeared that "the United States are not about to retake the initiative in South America" at a time when many countries in the Western Hemisphere were "flirting more and more with communism." Kennedy's administration put the narrowly defined national interest before the welfare of other countries.

The newspaper's criticism also attacked the discrepancy between the image and reality of Kennedy as a global statesman; the president's trip to Europe on the eve of the Vienna summit caused a particularly acerbic commentary. After briefly describing his diplomatic achievements in Paris, the article focused on the "romantic stopovers" that the presidential couple had enjoyed across the continent ("good wine, waltzes . . . and theater, and clothing stores as well as animal nurseries for Jacqueline") before rendering a devastating verdict: at a time when "millions of human beings are starving" the world "demands result, nothing but results" from international diplomacy.[46] "These millions of [hungry] beings, will they be enticed by this young couple that one could easily see . . . in [a movie like] *Gone with the Wind*?," the article asked sarcastically. The personal aspects that regularly fascinated audiences around the world about the Kennedys—their ability to project an almost magical aura of a seemingly perfect youthful couple dominating world politics—was now used against the president. He suddenly seemed out of touch with the harsh realities of the world surrounding him.

Civil rights

Apart from these global issues, it was Kennedy's attitude toward the civil rights movement at home that shaped his image in Morocco.[47] Already early into his presidency, a high-ranking official at the Department of State had pointed out that American influence in Africa would remain limited as long as the United States did not grant full citizenship rights to its own citizens.[48] Khalis concurred. "Segregation . . . demolishes the United States' reputation abroad," he held, admonishing that the United States "cannot play an important role on the international stage" and "lead the free world" unless it resolves this issue.[49] Especially his readiness to challenge segregation in Alabama during the summer of 1963 with the help of federal troops shaped the image of a strong leader willing to tackle this pivotal domestic issue with determination.[50] Kennedy's willingness to receive African and African American visitors at the White House further bolstered his anti-racist credentials.[51] Moreover, his meeting with black students from the University of Alabama and his speech to US mayors in Honolulu in which he outlined his support of the civil rights movement cemented his image as a great emancipator.⁵² Khalis celebrated that "Kennedy was not one of the men who hesitated before these events," because "he was an opponent to segregation and thus ordered his brother [the Attorney General] to use all legal means to suppress this rebellion" by a few southern states.⁵³

The struggle against institutionalized racism in the United States thus stood at the intersection of US domestic politics, anti-colonialism, and the Cold War. In a speech before the UN in September 1963, Kennedy promised to end racial discrimination at home while forcefully denouncing the apartheid regimes in southern Africa.⁵⁴ Capturing this complicated dynamic, al-ʿAlam explained that Kennedy's "resolve" in executing the court order to integrate all American universities was not only based on "humanitarian" concerns but also took place in "consideration of foreign policy."⁵⁵ Without such forceful actions against segregation "it would have been impossible for the United States to bring to life a successful international policy towards the African continent." It was both a question of racial justice and a publicity issue. "There is no doubt that his victory in this important humanitarian sphere will help him overcome obstacles in other states," al-ʿAlam wrote at the height of Kennedy's presidency. The president's progressive domestic policies permitted him to maintain some of his popularity in Morocco.

Al-Istiqlal, too, embraced Kennedy regarding his fight against segregation, this "scandal of the civilized world."⁵⁶ As James Meredith's struggle to enter the University of Mississippi caught international attention in the fall of 1962, Kennedy "took firm measures to impose federal law in order to eradicate this scourge, which causes great harm to the reputation of the country."⁵⁷ "President Kennedy has won his battle in Alabama against the segregationists," the newspaper cheered after the federal government had successfully forced another state to desegregate its higher education system in June 1963.⁵⁸ It also applauded "his victory over the racist Governor [George] Wallace," which the president had achieved "with a courage and loyalty that one must acknowledge." After reporting that the American press had described the president's efforts as "courageous" and "admirable," *al-Istiqlal* drew a straight line from Abraham Lincoln's emancipation of the country's slaves one hundred years earlier to Kennedy's efforts on behalf of racial equality.⁵⁹ By describing it as a "legacy of the colonial system," the newspaper linked the current situation in the United States to the past era of foreign occupation in North Africa and other parts of the world.⁶⁰ Thus, at least on this issue, his presidency had delivered the kind of social progress that the peoples of Asia and Africa had been expecting for a long time.

Hassan II's visit to Washington and the US military bases

A main area of friction between the United States and Morocco resulted from the US naval base at Kenitra, which had been granted by the French protectorate authorities in the aftermath of the Second World War.⁶¹ The presence of foreign soldiers symbolized the continuation of the colonial era in the eyes of many Moroccans, given that it was based solely on an agreement between two Western powers and thus ridiculed the notion of their country's sovereignty. Just two weeks after his inauguration, al-ʿAlam proclaimed enthusiastically, "Kennedy gave the order to create a list of US military bases abroad . . . from which he might withdraw."⁶² Eight months later, the tone had changed considerably as a different editorial depicted the ongoing US military presence as a violation of Moroccan independence. Written shortly after the departure of the last French soldiers, it explained that "the citizens are now opening their eyes towards a new age, the age of freedom," because "the people's nationalist awareness" now called for "a hastening of the elimination of these bases which are symbols of a bygone age."⁶³ Yet it eventually became clear that the pragmatic foreign policy pursued by the royal palace did not fully accommodate such passionate nationalistic appeals.⁶⁴

Hassan II eventually traveled to the United States for an official state visit in March 1963 amid increasing tensions over the military installations. After arriving by ship at the port of New York, he took a train to Washington where Kennedy and his spouse personally received their guest at Union Station before driving in an open-roof limousine past "more than 250,000 Americans that crowded the streets of the city" to welcome him.⁶⁵ While the US media would later reduce the number of spectators to 100,000, many of whom had primarily come to see their own president, this warm reception nonetheless constituted a great publicity success for Hassan II. The Moroccan delegation's goal was quite simple—in the words of the king himself it was the establishment of a "new age of friendship for the sake of freedom, peace, and dignity in the world." Al- 'Alam added that the "King hopes [US] financial aid will increase and that US businessmen will do a greater amount of investments" in Morocco.⁶⁶ Taking place in the immediate aftermath of the adoption of the constitution of 1962 that centralized most powers in the hands of the king, the state visit also suggested American approval of this highly controversial project that cemented Hassan's authoritarian rule.

Al- 'Alam's coverage of this event remained somewhat scarce and eventually included some indirect criticism. Upon his return to Morocco, the monarch proclaimed that he had permitted the US Navy to continue using its base in Kenitra as a communication hub beyond 1963.⁶⁷ The announcement obviously enraged the nationalist-minded journalists. "The foreign bases are nothing but an occupation and remnants from the age of colonialism," thundered a front-page editorial.⁶⁸ Criticizing the eternal "threat to Morocco and violation of its sovereignty" constituted the best line of attack for a party that had few venues to oppose the increasingly authoritarian monarch. For the king, the deal with the Kennedy administration was a brilliant move since it gave him "considerable leverage to help ensure a continuing flow of US military aid and economic assistance," as an American diplomat would note a few years later.⁶⁹ From the viewpoint of the political opposition, however, it provided ultimate evidence for the increasingly close relationship between Rabat and Washington. The Kennedy administration clearly did not hesitate to cooperate with authoritarian regimes abroad, which damaged the president's image as "liberator" of the peoples of the Third World.

Concerning Hassan II's visit to Washington, *al-Istiqlal* showed itself even more critical than its sister publication. While the United States were certainly "a friendly country" and had offered financial support "to fight against underdevelopment" in Africa, the continent's peoples had "not appreciated the more or less direct intervention in the Congo prior to [Prime Minister Patrice] Lumumba's assassination [in January 1961] or the half-heartedness of US diplomacy in the Algerian case prior to . . . independence."⁷⁰ The editorial then pivoted to the issue closest to its readers' hearts, namely the importance of "evacuating the military bases within the assigned period" as a sign of "respect for our sovereignty." The already quite low expectations had not improved after the king's return.

On April 7, *al-Istiqlal* offered a detailed assessment that did not look too kindly upon Hassan's diplomatic mission. While Morocco "occupies a strategic location in Africa with regard to the United States," it was much less clear that Washington had understood the importance to not "make Morocco deviate from its policy of non-alignment" despite the fact that the king had "explained his country's interest . . . in peace and freedom."[71] In additional to this barely disguised criticism of the monarch, the newspaper pointed out that Hassan II had obtained "nothing concrete" with regard to a "US contribution to the economic development of Morocco." *Al-Istiqlal* also showed itself dismayed that both sides had agreed to a future "constructive use of the military bases," which indicated that the installations might remain open to the US military indefinitely. The newspaper's editorial board displayed little confidence in Hassan II's willingness to defend the popular will on this important issue.

Kennedy's assassination

Kennedy's assassination, on November 22, 1963, sent shock waves across the entire world and Morocco was no exception. *Al-'Alam* proclaimed that "the world has lost a great leader" whose death would "influence the entire world";[72] a few days later, it reported that hundreds of thousands of Americans had paid their last respects at the wake organized in the Capitol building.[73] The newspaper also honored the late president by printing the speech he was supposed to have given in Dallas.[74] Inundated by a flood of condolences that reached the White House from across the globe, Congress granted several assistants to his widow Jacky in order to help her respond to them. "The women of the world envied her . . . now they are crying for her sake," the same article explained.[75]

Yet surprisingly few articles dealt specifically with the accomplishments of the man that had led the United States for almost three years. "'What has happened is painful,' . . . said the average person here in Morocco and on all five continents," explained *al-'Alam* to its readers in a caption underneath a large portray of the deceased.[76] Instead, the newspaper focused on Kennedy's youthful appearance as a source of inspiration. One article offered an overview of the prevalent mood around the world after summarizing the global impact of his energetic appearance, "The Kennedy disaster touched the buttons of affection in the hearts of every man and woman, every youth and old person."[77] In contrast to all other major countries "ruled by old men," Kennedy's youth had caused many to expect "the deliverance of the world from the thinking and the politics of the old" as he sought to "tear down the barricade between East and West and terminate the politics driven by hatred." By late December, *al-'Alam* explained that Kennedy's "belief in liberal democracy" was the basis for understanding his entire worldview.[78] His achievements were threefold: passing "laws against segregation" and supporting "the right to vote of all blacks in America and [their] equality with whites," his active role in increasing "foreign aid," and "lowering taxes . . . for the middle class." But no article celebrated him as a hero of the decolonizing world.

What does this coverage of the Kennedy assassination tell us about local perceptions of the thirty-fifth president of the United States? At first, it might seem quite strange that his attitude toward the Third World received so little attention by *al-'Alam*, especially given the enthusiastic reception his electoral victory had originally caused inside the North African kingdom. Yet three years later his mixed foreign policy record toward the Third World had notably reduced that enthusiasm in Morocco. Just as importantly, domestic political considerations had also contributed to a general disappointment with the American politician. The most obvious example can be found in the struggle over the continuing presence of US military installations on Moroccan soil. Less than four weeks after Kennedy's assassination, an editorial in *al-'Alam* reminded its readers of the importance of the enduring struggle for complete national sovereignty in light of the continuing presence of foreign soldiers on Moroccan soil, explaining that "the agreement between King [Mohammed V] and [US President] Eisenhower in 1959 to return the bases . . . symbolized independence and sovereignty" and thus has to be honored.[79] Yet the article did not mention the late US president, despite the fact that he had successfully convinced Hassan II to keep the bases open for the foreseeable future. Neither a hero nor a villain, Kennedy's image in Morocco had undergone a dramatic transformation during his brief tenure in the White House.

Conclusion

Kennedy was the first US president willing to publicly support the aspirations of the peoples of Africa and Asia, which endeared him to millions of men and women around the world. But his actual record in office rarely lived up to his lofty rhetoric. Despite numerous African heads of state visiting the White House as well as a substantial increase in US foreign aid, the constraints of the Cold War caused him to adopt foreign policies that did not coincide with the interests of the decolonizing world. Thus, a much more nuanced image of Kennedy emerged already during his lifetime, one that acknowledged Kennedy's achievements as president, while nonetheless lacking the enthusiasm that had engulfed parts of Moroccan society following his electoral win in November 1960.

A comparative study of *al-'Alam* and *al-Istiqlal* also grants us new insights into Morocco's political landscape. Perhaps surprisingly, the two publications interpreted Kennedy's tenure somewhat differently. Whereas the arabophone daily initially offered a predominantly optimistic portrayal of the president, the francophone weekly maintained a very skeptical attitude throughout his three years in the White House. The theme of anti-colonial solidarity featured prominently in both publications, but *al-Istiqlal* embraced the burgeoning Non-Aligned Movement wholeheartedly long after its left-leaning members had left the party to establish the socialist UNFP (*Union nationale des forces populaires*) in 1959. Even center-right Moroccans apparently believed in the liberatory potential of radical anti-colonialism to a degree that might surprise us, given that historians have usually associated this ideological current with the far Left—at least in the context of Western countries.[80] These preferences might not have had a major impact on Moroccan diplomacy during the Cold War, since the monarchy maintained a monopoly over the nation's foreign relations. But we begin to understand that skepticism toward the foreign policy pursued by Hassan II prevailed across the kingdom's political spectrum.

An analysis of the country's two leading conservative newspapers also presents us with further insights into both Moroccan and American history. While it would certainly be incorrect to view these newspapers as mass mediums, they did express the viewpoints of the largest and most popular political party in the country. Because his presidency overlapped with a highly volatile period in Moroccan politics, the "leader of free world" was not only a foreign statesman engaging with the global issues of his time but also a politician involved in domestic politics. Especially Hassan II's decision to move beyond his predecessor's preference for nonalignment and instead become an ally of the United States politicized Kennedy's image in Morocco. His support for the monarchy, though mainly for pragmatic reasons, clearly contradicted Kennedy's claims to be a forceful voice for freedom around the world. It is only by applying both of these lenses—domestic politics and international affairs—that we can comprehend contemporary perceptions of Kennedy in Morocco in particular and across the Third World in general.

We thus have to question some of the assumptions driving both practitioners and students of US foreign relations. Too often, the absence of reliable data—and ideological blind spots—prevent us from correctly assessing the image of the United States abroad. Kennedy's presidency is a case in point. While many of his political companions and scholars have taken his carefully crafted image as the "secretary of state of the Third World" at face value, the historical record tells a very different story. In the specific case of Morocco's conservative party, few viewed him as a champion of global liberty by the time of his untimely death in November 1963; he had become just another representative of the unacceptable status quo characterizing international relations at the height of the Cold War. The way that Americans wanted to be seen, and the way Washington's policies were actually perceived abroad, diverged quite drastically even in a nation that remained extraordinarily friendly toward the United States. We are in utter need of more studies of perceptions of the United States from the outside-in—and not from the inside-out—to obtain even a basic understanding of how the world views this country.

Acknowledgments

I would like to thank Jessie Stoolman for her invaluable research assistance in Morocco.

Notes

1 David Stenner, *Globalizing Morocco: Transnational Activism and the Postcolonial State* (Stanford: Stanford University Press, 2019).
2 "Remarks of Senator John F. Kennedy in the Senate, Washington DC," July 2, 1957. Available online: https://www.jfklibrary.org/Research/Research-Aids/JFK-Speeches/United-States-Senate-Imperialism_19570702.aspx (accessed March 27, 2017).

3 "Constitution of the Kingdom of Morocco, Published December 14, 1962," in *al-Dasatir fi al-'alam al-'arabi, 1839-1987*, ed. Yusif Qazmakhuri (Beirut: Dar al-Hamra, 1989), 609–16.
4 Rabat to Department of State: Meeting with King, May 5, 1962, RG59/771.56/5-462, US National Archives, College Park, MD.
5 CIA Current Intelligence Weekly Summary: The Royal Regime in Morocco, August 24, 1962, Special Articles p. 4, Central Intelligence Agency Freedom of Information Act (FOIA) Electronic Reading Room (CIA-ERR).
6 CIA Special Report: Morocco under King Hassan, March 22, 1963, 2, CIA-ERR.
7 Maâti Monjib, *La monarchie marocaine et la lutte pour le pouvoir* (Paris: L'Harmattan, 1992), 231.
8 "From *L'Opinion du Peuple* to *al-Istiqlal*," *al-Istiqlal*, October 12, 1951, 1.
9 "Comparison between Foreign Policies of Kennedy and Nixon," *al-'Alam,* September 25, 1960, 6.
10 "US Presidential Election Campaign Intensifies," *al-'Alam*, November 4, 1960, 5.
11 "Kennedy Wins Presidential Election and Hopes to Make His Country Spread Freedom in the World," *al-'Alam*, November 10, 1960, 6; and "The Principles of JFK's Foreign and Domestic Policies," *al-'Alam*, November 10, 1960, 6.
12 "The Responsibilities of the New President," *al-'Alam*, January 22, 1961, 2.
13 "On the Eve of the American Elections: Kennedy Proposes that America Allies Itself to African Nationalism," *al-Istiqlal*, October 15, 1960, 13.
14 "The New Administration of the United States and the Underdeveloped Countries," *al-Istiqlal*, December 17, 1960, 10.
15 "A Disappointing Past . . . An Uncertain Future," *al-Istiqlal*, January 28, 1961, 7.
16 "Will the Relations between Popular China and the United States Develop?," *al-'Alam*, March 16, 1961, 2.
17 "The Assault against Cuba," *al-'Alam*, April 19, 1961, 2.
18 "Kennedy: 'We Support the African States from the Bottom of Our Hearts,'" *al-'Alam*, February 10, 1961, 2.
19 "Kennedy and Sukarno Condemn Colonialism in Asia and Africa," *al-'Alam,* April 27, 1961, 2; and "Kennedy Receives Mauritanian Ambassador," *al-'Alam*, May 18, 1961, 1.
20 "Kennedy Receives African Leaders from Kenya and North Rhodesia in White House," *al-'Alam*, April 21, 1961.
21 "Kennedy's Project to Solve the Case of Palestine," *al-'Alam*, May 28, 1961, 1; "Nasser Prepares Response to Kennedy's Letter on Palestine," *al-'Alam*, June 17, 1961, 2; and "Letters between Abdel Nasser and Kennedy on International Problems," *al-'Alam*, July 8, 1962, 2.
22 "Kennedy Greets Ben Bella at the Door of the White House [picture caption]," *al-'Alam*, October 18, 1962, 2.
23 "Why Were They Delayed in Geneva?," *al-'Alam*, March 22, 1962, 1–2.
24 "Will Kennedy Head towards the Soviet Union?—$600 Million Aid to Latin America in Twenty Years," *al-'Alam*, March 15, 1961, 2; and "Kennedy Speaks before Congress," *al-'Alam*, January 12, 1962, 2.
25 "Important Talks between Kennedy and Adoula," *al-'Alam*, February 6, 1961, 1–2.
26 "Why Do They Wage Such a Feverish War against the Non-aligned States?," *al-'Alam*, November 30, 1961, 2.
27 "The Citizen's Opinion," *al-'Alam*, July 18, 1963, 1.
28 "Kennedy and Khrouchtchev: Will they Negotiate Regarding the Status of Berlin as Demanded by the Non-Aligned States?," *al-Istiqlal*, September 18, 1961, 14.

29 "Peace: Neither Gamble nor Blackmail," *al-Istiqlal*, October 27, 1962, 1.
30 "Cuba: An Anger that Should Not Concern Us," *al-Istiqlal*, October 27, 1962, 3.
31 "Allal al-Fassi, 'Resistance to Neo-colonialism,'" *al-Istiqlal*, July 14, 1963, 8; and "The Citizen's Opinion," *al-'Alam*, July 9, 1963, 1.
32 "Echo to Kennedy's State of the Union Speech in Moscow," *al-'Alam*, February 1, 1961, 2.
33 "Kennedy Is Not Afraid of the Future," *al-'Alam*, June 8, 1961, 2.
34 "Test Ban Treaty Must Encompass All Nuclear States," *al-'Alam*, January 26, 1963, 1.
35 "Kennedy's Speech on Berlin," *al-'Alam*, July 27, 1961, 2.
36 "Discussion between Kennedy and Khrushchev," *al-'Alam*, June 4, 1961, 1, 5.
37 "US-Soviet Talks on Berlin Fail," *al-'Alam*, May 19, 1962, 2.
38 "De Gaulle Meets with Kennedy," *al-'Alam*, June 1, 1961, 2.
39 "The European Common Market and the US-Soviet Economic Struggle," *al-'Alam*, May 22, 1962, 5.
40 "Signs of Optimism," *al-'Alam*, February 1, 1961, 2.
41 "Russia and America in Space," *al-'Alam*, March 9, 1962, 2.
42 "Chancellor Adenauer in Washington," *al-Istiqlal*, November 25, 1961, 14.
43 "Is It for Cuba or Berlin?" *al-Istiqlal*, September 15, 1962, 14.
44 "Assessment of a Trip to Europe: Kennedy Affirms that the United States will Defend Europe," *al-Istiqlal*, July 7, 1963, 13.
45 "Latin America Disappointed by Kennedy," *al-Istiqlal*, March 18, 1961, 18.
46 "Mr. Kennedy Has Emptied the Bottle, but will Dance Waltz in Vienna without a Purpose," *al-Istiqlal*, June 3, 1961, 13.
47 "Kennedy Works to End Segregation in the United States," *al-'Alam*, March 8, 1961, 2.
48 "US Policy towards Africa," *al-'Alam*, February 1, 1961, 2.
49 "Segregation in the United States," *al-'Alam*, May 27, 1961, 2.
50 "The Complexity of the Higher Principles that Control the Behavior of Whites towards Black People," *al-'Alam*, June 5, 1963, 6.
51 "Kennedy with African: Kennedy Stands with African Visitor," *al-'Alam*, November 14, 1963, 6; and "250,000 Blacks Protest before the White House," *al-'Alam*, August 27, 1963, 6.
52 "Kennedy Reveals Five Points to Abolish Segregation in America," *al-'Alam*, June 11, 1963, 2; and "Kennedy: 'The United States Won't Be Free Until All of Its Citizens Are Free,'" *al-'Alam*, June 13, 1963, 2.
53 "Segregation in the United States," *al-'Alam*, May 27, 1961, 2.
54 "Kennedy Holds Speech before UN General Assembly," *al-'Alam*, September 21, 1963, 1.
55 "Segregation in the US and Its International Impact," *al-'Alam*, October 4, 1962, 2.
56 "The Black Problem, a Scandal of the Civilized World," *al-Istiqlal*, June 9, 1963, 13.
57 "The Oxford Affair Should Be the Last Twitches of the Greatest Scourge of Our Time: Racial Segregation," *al-Istiqlal*, October 6, 1962, 10.
58 "The USA at a Time of Self-criticism: One Century after Abraham Lincoln . . .," *al-Istiqlal*, June 16, 1963, 12.
59 "Mr. Kennedy and the 'Charter of the Blacks': This Is Far from Being over . . .," *al-Istiqlal*, June 23, 1963, 13.
60 "The Oxford Affair should be the Last Twitches of the Greatest Scourge of Our Time: Racial Segregation," *al-Istiqlal*, October 6, 1962, 10.
61 I. W. Zartman, *Morocco: Problems of New Power* (New York: Atherton Press, 1964), 23–60.
62 "The US Bases in Morocco," *al-'Alam*, February 2, 1961, 1.

63 "The Age of Freedom Requires Elimination of the US Bases," al-'Alam, October 1, 1961, 1–2.
64 "The US Military Bases Abroad," al-'Alam, December 15, 1962, 4.
65 "King Hassan Arrives in Washington, Joint US-Moroccan Statement will be Published Today," al-'Alam, March 28, 1963, 1.
66 "King Finishes His Visit to America," al-'Alam, March 30, 1963, 1.
67 "Senate Unit Finds U.S. Has Secret Base in Morocco for Navy Communications," NYT, July 28, 1970, 4.
68 "After the Return: The US Bases," al-'Alam, April 4, 1963, 1.
69 "Intelligence Note RAFN-49 Prepared in the Bureau of Intelligence and Research," November 3, 1970, FRUS, 1969–1976, vol. E-5, Part 2, documents on North Africa, 1969-1972. Available online: https://history.state.gov/historicaldocuments/frus1969-76ve05p2/d107 (accessed November 19, 2018).
70 "The Trip of Hassan II to the United States of America," al-Istiqlal, March 24, 1963, 3.
71 "With Regard to the Joint Statement," al-Istiqlal, April 7, 1963, 4.
72 "Kennedy Has Died," al-'Alam, November 23, 1963, 1.
73 "Yesterday . . . the United States Bid Farewell to Its Deceased President," al-'Alam, November 26, 1963, 1.
74 "Kennedy was Ready to Explain His Foreign Policy Philosophy . . . But!!!," al-'Alam, December 2, 1963, 6.
75 "Congress Grants Jackie Kennedy Several Assistants to Help Her Answer the Letters She Received," al-'Alam, December 4, 1963, 2.
76 "What Has Happened Hurts," al-'Alam, November 26, 1963, 6.
77 "Only His Youth Remains to the World," al-'Alam, November 27, 1963, 6.
78 "The Book Kennedy Never Published: A Nation of Immigrants," al-'Alam, December 23, 1963, 6.
79 "Converting the US Bases in Morocco," al-'Alam, December 19, 1963, 1.
80 Christoph Kalter, *The Discovery of the Third World: Decolonization and the Rise of the New Left in France, c. 1950-1976* (New York: Cambridge University Press, 2016); Jürgen Dinkel, *The Non-Aligned Movement: Genesis, Organization and Politics (1927-1992)* (Leiden: Brill, 2018).

8

Foreign Gifts and US Imperial Ambiguities: The Kennedy Years

Cyrus Schayegh

Mrs FAKHRI GARAKANI
C/O Mr. A. MALEKI
Ferdowsi Street
Teheran- Iran.

Tehran 16th December 1961.

H.E. The President of The United States,
White House,
Washington,
U.S.A.
Dear Mr. President,
　　During 62 years of my active life, I made a few portrait of well known international figures, amoung them,

> The late Reza Shah the great,
> The president Shahanshah of Iran,
> Jesus Christ,
> Mahatma Gandhi,
> Abraham Lincoln,
> Pope John XXIII.

　　The portrait of Mahatma Gandhi, was presented by H.I.M. the Shahanshah of Iran during his state visi to India, to the Government and people of India.
　　I have always desired to present my work of art in an International Show in U.S.A. and as I am getting too old, and I have not the chance to come over to U.S.A. I am sending you one of my work.
　　As the Christmass coming you may be interested for a present for his Holy Pope John XXIII, so I am sending his portrait which is made of silk embrodery with total working hours of 3,200.
　　I hope, you find my work interesting, and I leave the value of it to your own judjment. If you really don't like my work, it could be arranged to be returned to me in Iran.

I deeplu apologise for the trouble which I am making,

> Very respectfully Yours.
> F. Garakani (Mrs)[1]

Fakhri Garakani was born in 1898 in the northern Iranian town of Rasht. The child of a Francophile merchant and an educated mother, she learned French. Aged fourteen, she was married. She gave birth to four children, of whom one died early; soon widowed, she self-confidently insisted they bear her name. Her granddaughter, Alaleh Garakani, remembers that Fakhri "and her mother were close" to the Americans at Rasht's US Presbyterian missionary hospital and school, founded in 1906, where both taught handicraft and confectionery and learned English, as the above letters, some mistakes notwithstanding, patently show. While they did not convert, Garakani was not a devout Muslim either. Around 1937, she moved to Tehran, opening a tailor shop; soon returned to Rasht, where she ran a tailor shop, too; and, middle-aged, followed her children to Tehran, where she passed in 1992. She had picked up embroidery as a

Figure 8.1 Fakhri Garakani, portrait of Jesus.

child from her mother, eventually coloring her pictures' threads herself. "Flower and portrait embroidery was her great love" and her art.[2] "It almost literally lived," is how Jesseman Robert Pryor, one of Rasht's Americans, described her papal portrait. "The colors used were only shades of black, grew and white. In my opinion it was a three-dimensional masterpiece."[3] While I have not found the portrait, Garakani's family sent me an image of a portrait of Jesus she created (Figure 8.1).[4]

Garakani's art was exceptional; her interest in embroidery was not. Embroidery had been known already in premodern Iran. By the late nineteenth century, some new state primary schools included it in home economy courses' sowing lessons. So did US missionaries, whose "agenda emphasized providing 'modern,' high quality social services such as health care and education . . . to the urban middle and upper classes."[5] A 1939 issue of the *Torch*—the magazine of the Rasht Presbyterian Girl School, where Garakani taught—noted, "during the past two weeks we have had hand-sown articles (novelty) and embroidered towels in the 'show case.' The girls have gotten many patterns from the display and are now sowing some for themselves."[6] Furthermore, enterprising Iranian women other than Garakani, too, elevated what educational manuals defined as a housewifely skill to a female art.[7]

As for her papal portrait, Garakani did not hear back from Kennedy. After three months, her patience ran out.

> Mrs. FAKHRI GARAKANI
> C/O Mr. A. Maleki
> Ferdowsi Street
> Tehran Iran.
>
> Tehran 19th March 1962.
>
> H.E. The President of the United States,
> White House,
> Washington,
> U.S.A.
>
> Dear Mr. President,
>
> I refer to my letter 16th December 1961 and avail myself of the opportunity of enclosing herewith, a copy of my previous letter, together with the relative receipt from the Luft Hansa Office, here in Tehran, indicating that the delivery of our parcel to the White House has taken place on the 22nd of December 1961.
>
> Although a considerable time has elapsed since the dispatch of the a/m parcel, but we profoundly regret for not having heard as yet, anything from you with regard to this matter.
>
> With best compliments,
> Respectfully yours,
> F. Garakani[8]

The same month she sent this second letter, Garakani devised another way of reaching the American president, Iran's patron since the US-British-Iranian royalist coup d'Etat of 1953, which had deposed Prime Minister Mohammad Mosaddeq and re-empowered

Mohammad Reza Shah Pahlavi (r. 1941–79).[9] She recalled that in 1961, at the house of Pryor and his wife Mary Louise, she had run into a former Presbyterian missionary, T. Cuyler Young, a Princeton professor of Iranian Studies who from 1927 to 1936 had served in Rasht, and his American wife Helen, who had served there, too; she must have known them from that time. She asked Pryor to contact Young. Pryor agreed, enclosing copies of her letters.[10] Young responded. "I shall tuck [your letter] into my pocket when I go down to Washington on Friday night for Secretary Rusk's dinner in honor of the Shah," incidentally on a state visit.[11] In May, he received a letter from Harold Saunders, an acquaintance at the executive office of the president's National Security Council. "The White House mail room tells me they sent Mrs. Garakani's embroidered portrait of Pope John XXIII to our embassy in Tehran on February 20th, asking that it be returned to her with thanks."[12]

Garakani indeed received the portrait back[13]—which is where this story ends, and our questions begin.

Why did Garakani send Kennedy a portrait? One explanation is character. Sentences like "If you really don't like my work" radiate self-confidence. A related second explanation is Garakani's remark that "I have always desired to present my work of art in an International Show in U.S.A"—"My grandmother always desired to put her works in a museum," as her granddaughter remembers.[14] This wish materialized in a telling detail in Garakani's Jesus portrait. While in Persian she merely signed with her first and last name, in the portrait's bottom left corner, in English she also included year and place. And unlike her Persian signature, the English note was not sown into the portrait but stitched to its bottom right corner later on, to internationalize her *oeuvre d'art*.

These two factors make clear why Garakani sent nothing less than a "child," as she put it, across the Atlantic, and why she doggedly tracked it.[15] What they do not explain is why she deemed her act feasible in the first place.

What we need to do, then, is to reflect on the assumptions underpinning her action. We can discern three. Garakani believed her papal portrait was likely to reach Kennedy quickly and reliably. She assumed he knew her portrait's papal subject and genre, embroidery, and would recognize it as a suitable gift. And, finally, she hoped the US president would be interested in a reciprocal gift transaction—for this was what she was proposing, as we will see—with an ordinary non-US citizen. For reasons of space, this chapter will focus on that last assumption.

The argument

The fascination of Garakani's story aside, its deeper interest lies in its ambiguities, uncertainties, and contradictions, and in the tentative nature of her assumptions. She wagered that the US president would exchange gifts with a foreigner following, as we will see, the Iranian *pishkesh*-versus-*en'am* (a gift to one's superior versus a gift to one's inferior) pattern of gifts traded between unequals—as if he were her president. Also, he at first view was not interested in her—but ultimately was. Moreover, as Kennedy intensified Washington's "engagement" with the Third World,[16] and presented himself as young, open-minded, and approachable,[17] hundreds of foreigners sent him gifts—but these were ambiguous, too. Nonpolitical givers sought to get physically close to Kennedy and his might by way of a gift—again, as if he were their leader. And politically explicit gifts insisted on nations' equality—yet the very act of sending them recognized the US president's extraordinary power.

These ambiguities, uncertainties, and contradictions were characteristic of the type of imperial polity the United States grew into following the Second World War. This argument is built on the view that postwar Washington assembled an "international empire" that "achieve[d] imperial ends" importantly though not exclusively "by working through the states of others."[18] While rooted in prewar practices and firmly in place by the late 1940s, this modus operandi became truly worldwide in the early 1960s. "The United States' advent as a world power coincided with the opening of the second wave of decolonization, when the nation emerged . . . as the only legitimate state form in the 'international' order."[19] Kennedy's presidency coincided with the peak of that wave. Affirming that "the great battleground for the defense and expansion of freedom today, is the whole southern half of the globe,"[20] he responded to this historic juncture. Sure, already his predecessor, Dwight D. Eisenhower, felt compelled to somehow deal with this issue and, related, with US race relations, from the mid-1950s. But he did so grudgingly, even with "anger."[21] Not so Kennedy. Concerned with the nonwhite world from the 1940s, and taking "office at the moment in time when America's optimism was at its zenith," he engaged the many new nation-states of the Third World head-on, demonstrating genuine interest and considerable knowledge.[22] Policy wise, meanwhile, he and his administration advanced often authoritarian economic development programs, expanded counterinsurgency, and organized opinion polls worldwide and tried feeding postcolonial media more US news.[23] In Iran, the US Information Service (USIS) for instance pursued the "heavy coverage by all media, especially radio and TV" of Kennedy speeches, influencing media reports that Garakani likely consumed.[24]

The fact that postwar imperial Washington worked with nation-states while simultaneously circumscribing their sovereignty made it an ambiguous, contradictory polity, and bred uncertainty about its nature. And as Washington's international imperial modus operandi became truly worldwide in the early 1960s, so did ambiguity. The fact that the peak of postwar decolonization coincided with Kennedy's presidency, together with the tension between his outsize power and global ambition and his ability to be (seen by many as) an open-minded, fresh leader sympathetic to hopes for greater equality between nations, revealed the US international empire's inherent ambiguity like never before and, perhaps, after.

Asking what gifts ordinary non-US citizens sent to somebody who was not their leader, interpreting why, and examining the White House's reactions, helps us study that ambiguity. That's because gifts, though voluntary, imply reciprocity, and emerge from and cement, and thus reflect, a sociopolitical order, whether desired or existing. The view that gift exchanges underpin relationships just about everywhere was first conclusively developed in 1923 by Marcel Mauss in *Essai sur le don [The Gift]*.[25] Using anthropological sources, mainly on native North Americans and Pacific islanders, ancient European and Hindu legal documents, and some other sources, this sociological-anthropological text by Emile Durkheim's nephew has remained the touchstone of its subject matter.[26] Mauss held that reciprocal gift giving constitutes a complex, all-encompassing "system of total services."[27] Embodying the donor's identity and hence possessing a "soul," according to Mauss, gifts help cement relationships in presumably "primitive" societies—a term whose normative implications he rejected[28]—but in ways also in the commercialized contemporary West.[29] The significance of gifts means, Mauss argued, that although respective "exchanges and contracts . . . in theory . . . are voluntary, in reality they are given and reciprocated obligatorily." Put differently, gifts are inherently ambiguous. This also means that though voluntarily given, a gift, if not reciprocated, triggers rancor and even symbolic or physical violence.[30] It becomes *Gift*, German for poison.[31] Disinterested gifts do not exist, Mauss concluded[32]—which is why every gift (we are coming full circle here) is reciprocal and why it underpins, and in this sense reflects, a sociopolitical relationship.[33] It's this insight that explains why so many foreigners sent Kennedy gifts, and why most hailed from regions that were very closely tied to Washington: Latin America, Western Europe, and East Asia.

The Iranian pishkesh-enʿam gift exchange

"The giving of gifts, though not peculiar to Persian society, is particularly common in that society," famous late British historian of Iran Ann Lambton once stated with a touch of exaggeration.[34] Safavid Empire (1501–1722) historian Rudi Matthee has called gift exchanges between subjects and rulers "a conspicuous part of traditional social and political life. . . . Subordinates presented gifts to their superiors to express their fealty or to propitiate them, acknowledging past favors and anticipating future ones. The gift giving of superiors, by contrast, was designed to secure their subordinates' continued loyalty, but it also symbolized the munificence and magnanimity of the donor. . . . Generally, the gift that a social inferior gave to a superior was referred to as *pīškaš*, while a gift in the reverse direction was called an *enʿām* . . . often given in money."[35] The Qajars (1785–1925) revived some Safavid practices.[36] "Gift exchange was a vital component of Qajar administration and political life," serving manifold functions, Assef Ashraf has stated—while insisting that this was not exceptional.[37]

General patterns of gift giving assume concrete form in contingent "historical circumstances":[38] what Ashraf affirmed for Qajar Iran holds also for the Pahlavi era (1925–79). Exceptions aside,[39] Muhammad Riza Shah (and his fellow royals) did not gift objects but handed out favors and *enʿam*s, gratuities, to cement and symbolize dominance. In this sense, the shah acted quite like the Qajars. The Pahlavi court paid subsidies to lesser clergymen.[40] Some were one-time payments. The court minister from 1966 to 1978, Asadollah Alam, snickered in his diary that on December 31, 1969, "I received various mullahs [clergymen], falling over themselves to lavish praise on HIM [His Imperial Majesty]; clearly in expectation of some sort of hand-out."[41] High-ranking officials, too, like Prime Ministers Fazlollah Zahedi (1953–55) and Amir Abbas Hoveyda (1965–77), used *enʿam*s as a personal political tool.[42] The shah also gifted "'Pahlavi' sovereign gold coins to select officials and individuals at Nowruz [New Year] or at some official ceremonies": a perfect blend of object, value, and self-representation.⁴³ Other, nonmonetary, nongeneric favors representing the shah were royal medals and orders and signed photographic portraits, asserting his dominance while simultaneously raising the recipient's status, symbolically transferring a smidgen of royal power. Officials hung the photos in their office; some cried when unexpectedly awarded a high honor.⁴⁴

In exchange for *en'am*s, the shah received *pishkesh*s. Take Garakani, for instance. As she told Kennedy, she had given Iran's ruler a portrait of Gandhi and, Pryor noted, of Nehru. In exchange, the Presbyterian wrote, the shah "gave her 10,000 tomans."⁴⁵ Although we possess no further details, Garakani most likely did not name a price, as in Kennedy's case. Ten thousand tumans were not the price of a good, then, but a royal gratuity for a subject's gift.

More important to the shah than material *pishkesh*s was political consent, by voicing support or at least withholding critique. Although he coveted political dominance from his inauguration in 1941 and attained it by the early 1960s, becoming an autocrat with far-reaching powers, he remained "haunted, and to an extent driven, by the stigma of illegitimacy, made more acute in his case by the popular view that he had been restored to the throne by foreign powers" in the 1953 coup.⁴⁶ Intersecting with this individual anxiety was a quest to legitimize modernizing socioeconomic reforms—a twin concern unknown to the Qajars. It showed in a particular favor to individuals: educational opportunity. Following the coup, the shah ordered that "the children of those convicted of treason under Mosaddeq be given a proper education, and fully offered 500,000 rials for the purpose." And in a fascinating case, he in 1958 gifted Ahmad Shams, a six-year-old prodigy from Chalus, close to his north Iranian honeymoon destination of Ramsar, a full education up to an MA degree for his impressive smarts and memory.⁴⁷ The twin concern was manifest, too, in how the shah framed signature policies: as his gift to the nation he believed to embody. He praised his own magnanimity; loyalists lauded him for "spending his own money and property to [ensure the] people's well-being and the country's development"; and stamps depicted him granting land deeds (Figure 8.2).⁴⁸

Figure 8.2 The Shah gifting land deeds to peasants. Source: Roman Siebertz, *Die Briefmarken Irans als Mittel der politischen Bildpropaganda* (Wien: ÖAW, 2005), Abb. 80.

Garakani's papal portrait as an attempted pishkesh

Garakani's attempted contact with Kennedy was patterned on the Iranian *pishkesh-en'am* exchange. Her expectation of a monetary compensation did not contradict, but was congruent with, her papal portrait being a *pishkesh* gift, rather than a commercial transaction. This reading is affirmed by the fact that her first letter's conclusion, "I deeply apologize for the trouble which I am making," translated a Persian expression that, however rhetorically, signaled a power relationship. Further, she did not state a price; did not say how much the shah had paid for her Gandhi portrait; and did not indicate in which currency and how (by check? cash transfer? etc.) Kennedy may pay her. Neither did she set a payment deadline—and "temporal deferral is the essence of the gift."[49] Apropos timing: she sent the portrait as a Christmas *pishkesh*, congruent with the Iranian habit of giving rulers a *pishkesh* at particular occasions, including religious celebrations. And to cite Mauss, her object had a "soul."[50] She lived in and through it. Tremendously invested, she called it a "child." On a related note, its papal motif turned a generic object into a personalized gift for Kennedy, the first Catholic president of the United States.

Why did Garakani think Kennedy may be interested in a relationship with *her*, an Iranian from the provinces, by giving *her* an *en'am*? Whatever the answer, she must have thought he has a political stake in a non-American like her. But what political stake? I begin my answer by zooming out.

Other foreign gifts to Kennedy

As it turns out, Garakani was not the only non-American who sent Kennedy a gift, in exchange for an *en'am* or not. Documents kept at the John F. Kennedy Presidential Library contain references to 717 gifts to Kennedy and/or his wife Jacqueline and their children from foreign citizens.[51] The real number was higher. The files are "incomplete"—Garakani's gift for example is absent—and do not list all addresses.[52]

The variety of gifts was mind boggling. Some represented virile presidential powers—a cast metal buffalo from the USSR, an Austrian wooden Hercules, and a Venus for Jacqueline[53]—or were depictions: a Swiss scrapbook of pictures, some from Kennedy's inauguration; canceled stamps portraits of the presidential couple, from Turkey, and of him, from India; an embroidered needle portrait by the Harvard Society of Taipei, Taiwan; an Iranian carpet bearing his face; a wood carving of the couple, gifted to the First Lady while visiting Italy; portrait paintings from Brazil, from Mexico, of daughter Caroline, and from Togo, of him in native cloths.[54] Others represented the donors' home: a tiny Colombian flag; pictures of Cologne and Berlin.[55] Yet others blessed—a Brazilian mother-of-pearl crucifix of Our Lord of Bonfim, Bahia's patron saint; a small painting of the Holy Virgin, from Mexico—or transferred religious powers: the white socks of a monsignore, from a sister in the Dominican Republic.[56] Most gifts were from individuals, a few from groups: Spanish children sent Caroline a doll; Sicilian artisans handcrafted a ceramic space-capsule-shaped cradle; and the village of Utete, in Tanganiyka, sent a canoe, a stuffed alligator, a mortar and pestle, a water jug, and three bamboo reels.[57] Some gifts were for daily use: a Colombian embroidered bedspread and pillow case; a hand painted china plate with bird design from Mexico.[58] Others were immaterial: the honorary membership awarded by a Barcelona swimming club, say, or the musical compositions "Carolina" and "The Great Alliance for Progress," from El Salvador.[59] A few gifts were antiques, for instance a 2000-year-old amphora from Turkey, while some mirrored current events: after the mayor of Mexico, DF, had symbolically given Kennedy the city's keys, the president received keys to El Paso; to "the hearts of all Mexicans"; and to San Remo, Italy.[60] Almost no donor asked for an *en'am* sort of exchange, but a few did, explicitly or not. Mrs. Deolinda Martinez Pavon, a Paraguayan, sent a white embroidered shirt for the president and noted "she would like to send a similar shirt to Mrs. K. and children." Ismail Alpaslan, from Ankara, stated he had "spent 177 hours, completing the work done on [a] goose egg [that] has 29 letters, and 78 holes for riveting letters cut out of lead." And when Kennedy visited Rome in 1963, a local tailor, Angelo Ritrico, sent him ties and asked for permission to visit him in his hotel, take his measurements, and tailor a suit and coat for him.[61]

Gifts hailed from seventy-two states on all inhabited continents, from Third World, capitalist democratic, and communist countries like Nigeria, New Zealand, and Poland. Even the frontrunners were geographically, economically, and religiously mixed. Measured by gifts per capita, the top twenty-five gift-giving countries sending at least five gifts were Costa Rica followed by Venezuela, Mexico, Ireland, Greece, Austria, Guatemala and Israel, Colombia, Switzerland, El Salvador, The Netherlands, Ecuador, Italy, Chile, Canada, Spain, Peru, Australia, Japan, South Korea, France, Turkey, Taiwan, and West Germany. In absolute numbers, Mexico's 138 gifts were followed by Italy (57), Japan (46), Colombia (39), India (31), Venezuela (30), Greece and West Germany (23), France (22), Austria and Spain (19), Canada (15), The Netherlands (14), Brazil, Costa Rica, and Turkey (13), South Korea (12), Switzerland (11), Britain (11), Guatemala (10), Chile and Ireland (9), The Philippines (8), Iran (7), and Australia, Ecuador, El Salvador, Pakistan, Peru, and Poland (6).[62]

Differences notwithstanding these frontrunners, except Catholic Poland and populous India, shared a crucial commonality. The Latin American, European, and East Asian countries in the above list all entertained tight economic and/or political-military relations with Washington. Beneath this commonality, however, gifts reflected different types of tight political relationships. Some symbolized alliance: a German "desk set carved in metal, gilded with wood base . . . called the Berlin Brandenburg gate, and on top of it, the American Eagle." Others invoked Pan-American equality. Consider the wool shawl "with white fringes appliqued flags of the countries meeting in Costa Rica for a conference" of American presidents, including Kennedy, in 1963. And yet others called for universal equality, for instance a Neapolitan priest's poem entitled "The Universal Fatherland."[63]

Whether a gift's political message was explicit or not, donors hoped to obtain something in return. Their sentiment reflected on the ambiguities and contradictions inherent in Washington's international empire. Those whose gifts lacked an explicit political message still recognized Kennedy as a figure whose power matters also to citizens other than "his" own; but they did not explicitly refer to him as an imperial ruler. Many struck this balance as they were trying—by way of a gift that, so Mauss, embodies them—to get physically close to Kennedy, in order to partake of his might or add to it.[64] The afore-cited Dominican socks and Paraguayan shirt were for Kennedy to wear; a Colombian bedspread was to sleep under;[65] and Ritrico assured Kennedy that taking his measurements would make him, the Roman tailor, "the most happy of all the Italians you will meet" and called him "*My* Hon. President."[66] Songs were meant for Kennedy's ears.[67] For his eyes was the "piece of cloth with many signatures on it," nothing else, from the "Peasant Federation of La Libertad [in] the Valley of Viru, Trujillo, Peru."[68] And the "wine and a keg of brandy" he received in Wiesbaden were literally to be absorbed by him. In response, Kennedy played with the aura of the physical proximity to power and with Washington's global presence, joking that "when he leaves the office of president he will leave an envelope in the desk for his successor that says "To be opened only in saddest moments," and inside will be written, "Go visit Germany."[69] A subset of gifts lacking an explicit political message was images of Kennedy: the afore-noted scrapbook, painting, and portraits made of canceled stamps, embroidered textile, carpet, and wood, for instance. "We see you, you matter to us," their message was; "you are one of us," detailed the portrait of Kennedy dressed as a Togolese. In exchange, these donors hoped to be recognized by Kennedy, if "only" through their portrait of him.

Donors of explicitly political gifts, too, hoped for something in return: the chance to be heard by a most powerful man. Many invoked non-imperial aims, rejecting political hierarchies. The afore-noted Italian poem "The Universal Fatherland" called for mankind's equality; the Costa Rican shawl featuring flags of American countries conjured up Pan-American cooperation; the German desk set of the Brandenburg gate and the American eagle evoked binational friendship. But such egalitarian messages notwithstanding, those gifts were ambiguous and contradictory, too. The very act of sending them to Kennedy implied that he, as the US president, had particular powers to promote non-imperial, egalitarian politics. Else, why bother sending him these gifts at all? What is more, the very nature of these gifts hinted at inequalities, rendering them ambiguous in their own right. The poem was sent not only in Italian but also in the United States' official language, English, lest it will not be understood. The shawl was sown on the occasion of Kennedy's visit to Costa Rica. And the American eagle sat right on top of the German gate. These gifts expressed a hope for equality in the world while implicitly recognizing that the US president had a great say in this matter and, hence, was unequal to others.

Garakani's attempted gift exchange as a reflection of ambiguity

This brings us back to Garakani's *pishkesh*. Like the afore-noted gifts, it was ambiguous. The response to our earlier question—"what political stake did Garakani think Kennedy may have in her, prompting him to send her an *enʿam* for her *pishkesh*?"—is that she was not sure. Her overture was a trial balloon.

On the one hand, Kennedy was a president-emperor to Garakani; the man at the helm of the state that was Iran's patron; a, if not *the*, world leader; in short, a man who should have a political stake in recognizing her and her gift. Hence, her overture was patterned on the inferior-superior *pishkesh-en'am* exchange. Hence, she stressed that the shah possessed one of her portraits: as a model for her overture to the US president. And hence, too, her afore-noted deferential language; the absence of a price tag and of a payment deadline and modus; the ceremonially charged timing of Christmas; the way in which she put her soul into her gift; and the personalized nature of her gift. This side of Garakani's understanding of Kennedy was likely formed by the Iranian press, all the more because she was literate and by the early 1960s lived in Tehran. The capital's daily *Ettela'at*, for example, covered the 1960 presidential campaign, Kennedy's election, his inauguration, and his subsequent work at much greater depth than any other third country's domestic politics. It described Kennedy as a regular man, approachable and normal, often by way of his wife and young children, and often through pictures: Caroline "smiling into the future" with her mother and president-elect father; the newborn John with his mother; Caroline's shenanigans at church and her father's attempts to calm her (Figure 8.3).[70] At the same time, *Ettela'at*'s Kennedy was tough as nails—he wore neither hat nor coat on a freezing election day in Boston, it reported—and super-humanly committed, working twenty hours his first day as

Figure 8.3 Caroline Kennedy with her father at church.

president.⁷¹ His election was historic, worldwide "the most important post-war event since Stalin's death"; as for the new First Lady, she had motherly "advice to the women of the entire world."⁷² He launched "the era of the new frontier," and did so from a mansion, the White House, whose architecture, and the First Lady's redecoration of it, was covered in detail.⁷³ *Ettela'at* also ran a daily serialized translation of Kennedy's Pulitzer-winning book *Profiles in Courage*.⁷⁴ And it repeatedly depicted gifts: the First Lady with a gift by Austrian citizens, for instance; a painting for her thirty-second birthday from a Parisian gallery; and a painting of Kennedy in traditional Chinese garb from Taiwan (Figure 8.4).⁷⁵

Figure 8.4 "Kenedi-ye chini!" (The Chinese Kennedy!).

On the other hand, the fate of Garakani's *pishkesh* to Kennedy exemplifies that gifts carry risks. They are "probes into uncertainty."⁷⁶ Her first letter's mention of her exchange with the shah may be read also as an explanation, to Kennedy, of how her gift exchange proposal actually functions, lest he does not understand. Further, she recognized he may not see her portrait as a gift or simply not want it: "If you really don't like my work, it could be arranged to be returned to me in Iran." And while insisting "I leave the value of [the portrait] to your own judjment," her note that its production took 3,200 hours was meant to help estimate compensation. Finally, her second letter can be interpreted as her turning her gift into a commercial object, or as an example of an unreciprocated gift becoming *Gift* (poison). This turn showed in her second letter's language, too. Unlike the first, it was terse; and Garakani had solicited aid.⁷⁷ There was barely a mistake here. Gone were the Persianisms, the "I deeplu [*sic*] apologise for the trouble which I am making." The language was advanced. And not just any language, but that of the world's new leading empire: English. It's as if the certainty of proper English counterbalanced Kennedy's behavior. Garakani told Kennedy in his very own language that she was his equal, that she demanded certainty.

But certainty never came. The Iranian *pishkesh-en'am* exchange did not work with Kennedy. The US president did not have a political stake in Garakani after all.

The White House's reaction to Garakani and US aid as a gift

Or did he? The White House's reply to Young's inquiry about Garakani's gift was ambiguous: an ambiguity that in effect mirrored Garakani's. Having explained that her gift had been returned, Saunders concluded "I'm sure you understand the necessity for handling such items this way and can put the best possible face on it in replying to your friend in Rasht." He also expressed his pleasure "to be of some help with this little problem in 'people-to-people diplomacy.'"⁷⁸ This referenced an initiative, in 1956, by Eisenhower, who had insisted that the United States needs "millions of individual Americans acting through person-to-person communication in foreign lands" to win the Cold War.⁷⁹ Saunders's note was ironic, then. As noted earlier, Kennedy presented himself as young and stylish *and* as open and accessible. But he evidently was not an ordinary citizen. He could not take up Garakani's offer precisely because he was the US president: he would have shown an official stake in her.

And yet, his administration did have a stake in her. This is why Saunders asked Young to "put the best possible face on it." Kennedy's administration felt it ought to keep its face vis-à-vis a sixty-two-year-old woman from a provincial town one ocean and two continents away from Washington.

On a final note, Washington's own gift to foreign countries—aid—and the ambiguity of this, as any, gift—self-less yet self-interested—reflected the US international empire's ambiguities and contradictions, too.⁸⁰ Robert Packenham's classic text on the matter put it well. While in his "1961 Foreign Aid Message to Congress President Kennedy spoke of the goals of 'an enlarged community of free, stable, and self-reliant nations,'" in practice aid programs pursued "anti-Communist, pro-American political stability."⁸¹ On the one hand, US aid was meant to create goodwill, sending US taxpayers' money abroad. Its anti-communism was shared by allies' and clients' governments; the 1947 US Marshall Plan is one example of many.[82] And it considered sovereign governments' political and developmental wishes. France insisted on spending Marshall's money in Algeria; and Iran cajoled Washington into cofinancing a dam that US engineers had criticized.[83] On the other hand, US aid sought to immunize sovereign countries against real or imaginary communist inroads, helping Washington to contain Moscow.[84] More broadly, it symbolized and deepened Washington's ability to influence sovereign countries. It was unilateral, and sometimes even surprised recipients; the Marshall Plan certainly did.[85] And as it often could not be repaid directly, and carried expectations of fealty, it could become poisonous. Many French resented Marshall money, and the shah was "tired of [still] being treated like a schoolboy" even when US aid, massive after the 1953 coup, had waned.[86] In sum, a reflection by Bruce Grant on Tsarist imperial gift giving matters to the US case, too: "As Bourdieu . . . recalls, [the] naturalness [of the gift] comes in the form of 'censured, euphemized . . . violence.' At is most fundamental symbolic level, gift giving is deeply ambiguous, exerting a violence that binds, keeping both loved ones and enemies close at hand."[87]

Conclusion

The Garakani-Kennedy gift exchange attempt and other foreign gifts tell us a thing or two about how certain postcolonial (and some other non-US) citizens thought of Camelot's king in particular and of the postwar United States in general. Ambiguities, uncertainties, and contradictions characterized this encounter in both directions. Garakani was unsure whether Kennedy had an imperial sort of political stake in people outside the US metropole, and Kennedy's administration returned her portrait yet did not want her to get a wrong impression. This twin reality; the Iranian gift exchange pattern between unequals that guided Garakani's overture to a foreign president; the fact that most foreign gift givers treated Kennedy as their own while underlining their independence; and the circumstance that most came from regions closely tied to Washington: all this shows that foreign gifts to Kennedy were ambiguous.

This was not exceptional. Empires other than the United States have produced ambiguities, uncertainties, and contradictions, too.[88] It did, however, reflect the tension distinctly fundamental to the postwar US *international* empire, which accepted nation-states while simultaneously working through them. This approach peaked during Kennedy's presidency, who embraced many decolonizing movements and acknowledged their historic nature while striving to hold and expand Washington's global power.

Notes

1 Copy of Garakani's letter, folder 2, box 4, group AC164, Seeley Mudd Manuscript Library, Princeton University, Princeton (SMML).
2 E-mail, Alaleh Garakani, October 22, 2018. I thank her for her biographical information, and Tatiana Garakani, a grandniece of Fakhri's, for connecting me with Alaleh and providing information, too.

3   Robert Pryor to T. Cuyler Young, Resht, March 31, 1962, folder 2, box 4, group AC164, SMML. For missions, see http://www.iranicaonline.org/articles/christianity-viii (Yahya Armajani, "CHRISTIANITY viii"). The Pryors served in Iran from 1957 to 1970, the wife, Mary Louise, working principally as a nurse: "Pryor, Rev. Jesseman Robert," RG360, and "Pryor, Mary Louise Rennice," RG360, Presbyterian Historical Society, Philadelphia (PHS).
4   Image: courtesy of Alaleh and Tatiana Garakani.
5   Quotes: Jasamin Rostam-Kolayi, "From Evangelizing to Modernizing Iranians," *Iranian Studies* 41, no. 2 (2008): 214. For home economics, see ibid., 222–23. See also 'Ala Firouz, "Needlework," in *A Survey of Persian Handicraft*, ed. Jay and Sumi Gluck (Tehran: Bank-e Melli Iran, 1977), 217–64; Ministry of Education, *Ketab-e Honaramuz-e Dushizegan* (n.p. [Tehran]: Nehzat-e Sharq, 1924), 29–31. I thank Pamela Karimi for this text; also, see her *Domesticity and Consumer Culture in Iran* (London: Routledge, 2013).
6   "Now Let's Look Back," *The Torch*, April 1939, n.p., RG91-20-4, PHS.
7   One Fakhr al-Zaman Askarpur Khodadad exhibited embroideries in Brussels, and taught the Shah's first child, Shahnaz: "Naqashi ba suzan wa-nakh," *Kh'andaniha* 36 (1955): 34. From 1959, Queen Farah Diba patronized crafts including embroidery and commissioned artists to embroider state gowns: Firouz, "Needlework," 256.
8   Folder 2, box 4, group AC164, SMML.
9   For postwar Iran, see Ali Ansari, *Modern Iran since 1921* (London: Pearson, 2003), 75–165; Ervand Abrahamian, *A History of Modern Iran* (Cambridge: Cambridge University Press, 2008), 123–54.
10 Pryor to Young. For Young's missionary life in Rasht, see "Young, Theodore C.," RG360, PHS.
11 Young to Pryor, Princeton, April 10, 1962, folder 3, box 4, group AC164, SMML. Young, who had served at the Office of Strategic Services in the Second World War and in 1944–46 became the first US public affairs officer in Tehran, was involved in Washington's Iran policy as a voice rather critical of the shah's policies. Claudia Castiglioni, *Gli Stati Uniti e la modernizzazione iraniana* (Milan: Mondadori università, 2015), 46–47, 52–54; Matthew Shannon, "Reading Iran," *Iranian Studies* 52, no. 2 (2018): 289–316.
12 Saunders to Young, May 23, 1962, folder 3, box 4, group AC164, SMML.
13 E-mail, Tatiana Garakani to author, October 28, 2013.
14 E-mail, Alaleh Garakani, October 28, 2013.
15 Pryor to Young.
16 Robert Rakove, *Kennedy, Johnson, and the Nonaligned World* (Cambridge: Cambridge University Press, 2013), xxi; Stephen Rabe, *John F. Kennedy: World Leader* (Washington: Potomac, 2010).
17 Mark White, *Kennedy: A Cultural History of an American Icon* (London: Bloomsbury, 2013); Lee Konstantinou, "The Camelot Presidency: Kennedy and Postwar Style," in *Cambridge Companion to John F. Kennedy*, ed. Andrew Hoberek (Cambridge: Cambridge University Press, 2015), 149–63.
18 Paul Kramer, "Power and Connection: Imperial Histories of the United States in the World," *AHR* 116, no. 5 (2011): 1366. US *modi operandi* varied: Geir Lundestad, "Empire by Invitation?" *Journal of Peace Research* 23, no. 3 (1986): 263–77, on Europe; Greg Grandin, *The Last Colonial Massacre* (Chicago: University of Chicago Press, 2004), on Latin America. Washington also worked through international institutions it helped create—Victor Bulmer-Thomas, *Empire in Retreat* (New Haven: Yale

University Press, 2018), 129–58—and military dominance of the seas, air, and outer space and control of small non-sovereign spaces, many islands, mattered greatly, too: Barry Posen, "Command of the Commons," *International Security* 28, no. 1 (2003): 5–46; Ruth Oldenziel, "Islands: The United States as a Networked Empire," in *Entangled Geographies*, ed. Gabrielle Hecht (Cambridge: MIT Press, 2011), 13–42.
19 Kramer, "Power," 1368.
20 Quoted in Vaugh Rasberry, "JFK and the Global Anticolonial Movement," in *Cambridge Companion*, 128.
21 Thomas Borstelmann, *The Cold War and the Color Line* (Cambridge: Harvard University Press, 2003), 88. See also Jason Parker, "Cold War II: The Eisenhower Administration, the Bandung Conference, and the Reperiodization of the Postwar Era," *DH* 30, no 5 (2006): 871.
22 Stephen Ambrose and Douglas Brinkley, *Rise to Globalism*, 8th ed. (London: Penguin, 1997), 171.
23 Mark Haefele, "John F. Kennedy, USIA, and World Public Opinion," *DH* 25, no. 1 (2001): 63–84; Bradley Simpson, *Economists with Guns* (Stanford: Stanford University Press, 2008), on Indonesia; Thomas Field, *From Development to Dictatorship* (Ithaca: Cornell University Press, 2014), on Bolivia.
24 USIS Tehran, "Country Assessment Report for Calendar Year 1963," January 30, 1964, 3, folder 7, container 51, Country Files 1950-1966, Record Group 306, National Archives, College Park.
25 Marcel Mauss, "Essai sur le don," *L'Année sociologique* 1 (1923–24): 30–186; *The Gift*, trans. W. Halls (London: Norton, 1990).
26 Marcel Fournier and Jean-Christophe Marcel, ed., "Les présences de Marcel Mauss," special issue of *Sociologie et sociétés* 36, no. 2 (2004): 5–245, esp. "Présentation," 5–14; James Siegel, "False Beggars: Marcel Mauss, The Gift, and Its Commentators," *Diacritics* 41, no. 2 (2013): 60–79 at 63; Marcel Fournier, *Marcel Mauss* (Paris: Fayard, 1994). Introduction include Mark Osteen, "Introduction," in *The Question of the Gift*, ed. Mark Osteen (London: Routledge, 2002), 1–42; Aafke Komter, ed., *The Gift* (Amsterdam: Amsterdam University Press, 1996); Marcel Hénaff, "Mauss et l'invention de la réciprocité," *Revue du MAUSS* 36 (2010): 71–86.
27 Mauss, *Gift*, 5–6.
28 Hénaff, "Mauss," 83.
29 Mauss, *Gift*, 66.
30 Mauss, *Gift*, 3 (quote), 5.
31 Ibid., 62–63.
32 Many agree: Jacques Derrida, *Given Time* (Chicago: University of Chicago Press, 1992); James Laidlaw, "A Free Gift Makes No Friends," *Journal of the Royal Anthropological Institute* 6 (2000): 617–34.
33 Among historians, such relationships have interested modernists—see the fascinating Eva Giloi, *Monarchy, Myth, and Material Culture in Germany, 1750-1950* (Cambridge: Cambridge University Press, 2011), a monograph on gifts I am thankful Matthew Unangst pointed out to me—and especially pre-modernists: Natalie Zemon Davis, *The Gift in Sixteenth-Century France* (Madison: University of Wisconsin Press, 2000); Felicity Heal, *The Power of Gifts* (New York: Oxford University Press, 2014); Anthony Cutler, "Significant Gifts: Patterns of Exchange in Late Antique, Byzantine, and Early Islamic Diplomacy," *Journal of Medieval and Early Modern Studies* 38, no. 1 (2008): 79–101; Linda Komaroff and Sheila Blair, eds., *Gifts of the Sultan* (New Haven: Yale University Press, 2011).

34 Ann Lambton, "Pīškaš," *Bulletin of SOAS* 57, no. 1 (1994): 145–58.
35 Rudi P. Matthee,"GIFT GIVING iv. In The Safavid Period," Encyclopaedia Iranica X/6: 609–14. Available online: http://www.iranicaonline.org/articles/gift-giving-iv (accessed December 30, 2012).
36 Lambton, "Pīškaš," 156. See also Willem Floor, "GIFT GIVING v. In the Qajar Period," Encyclopaedia Iranica X/6: 615–17. Available online: http://www.iranicaonline.org/articles/gift-giving-v (accessed December 30, 2012).
37 Assef Ashraf, "The Politics of Gift Exchange in Early Qajar Iran," *CSSH* 58, no. 2 (2016): 553–54.
38 Ibid., 554.
39 Asadollah Alam, *The Shah and I* (London: Tauris, 1991), 178, on souvenirs: Queen Farah Diba bringing from "a tour of Russia . . . gifts for all her admirers."
40 Ibid., 116n2.
41 Ibid., 116.
42 Ibid., 509; Ardeshir Zahedi, *Khatirat* (Bethesda: Ibex, 2006), II, 72; Abbas Milani, *The Shah* (New York: Palgrave, 2011), 250, on SAVAK founder Teymur Bakhtyar.
43 Hence, regular people gifted cheaper Pahlavi cold coins, too: Anne Betteridge, "Gift Exchange in Iran," *Anthropological Quarterly* 58, no. 4 (1985): 192. Quote: E-mail, Ali Gheissari to author, July 18, 2018. E-mail, William Beeman to author, August 2, 2018, stated that "during the Festival of Arts, the frequent gift given to local performers were gold pahlavi coins."
44 Alam, *Shah*, 174 (on deputy foreign minister Abbas Ali Khalatbary), 201 (on Finance Minister Jamshid Amuzegar).
45 Pryor to Young.
46 Quote: Ansari, *Iran*, 126. See also Milani, *Shah*, 104.
47 Quote: Ansari, *Iran*, 132. E-mail, Alex Shams to author, July 23, 2018; he is writing a biography of his father.
48 *Hammeh behtar zendegi konim* (Tehran: Nashriyeh-ye edareh-ye koll-e amuzeshi-ye bozorgsalan, 1964), 101. See also Ansari, *Iran*, 132; Milani, *Shah*, 280.
49 Osteen, "Introduction," 15.
50 Mauss, *Gift*, 66.
51 The relevant files' digital identifiers, all in https://www.jfklibrary.org/archives/search-collections/browse-digitized-collections, John F. Kennedy Presidential Library, Boston (JFKL), are JFKPOF-138-015, -016, -017, and -018 (all digital identifiers were accessed July 17, 2018).
52 JFKPOF-138-015, JFKL.
53 JFKPOF-138-017-p0013, JFKPOF-138-017-p0071, JFKL.
54 JFKPOF-138-015-p0072, JFKPOF-138-015-p0024, JFKPOF-138-017-p0012, JFKPOF-138-016-p0047, JFKPOF-138-017-p0045, JFKPOF-138-017-p0061, JFKPOF-138-018-p0034, JFKPOF-138-018-p0043, JFKL.
55 JFKPOF-138-018-p0040, JFKPOF-138-018-p0053, JFKPOF-138-018-p0060, JFKL.
56 JFKPOF-138-018-p0055, JFKPOF-138-018-p0041, JFKPOF-138-016-p0059, JFKL.
57 JFKPOF-138-015-p0095, JFKPOF-138-018-p0134, JFKPOF-138-016-p0082, JFKL.
58 JFKPOF-138-016-p0047, JFKPOF-138-018-p0057, JFKL.
59 JFKPOF-138-015-p0040, JFKPOF-138-018-p0057, JFKL.
60 JFKPOF-138-018-p0047, JFKPOF-138-018-p0120, JFKPOF-138-017-p0021 (quote), JFKPOF-138-018-p0105, JFKL.
61 JFKPOF-138-018-p0040, JFKPOF-138-015-p0044, JFKPOF-023-002-p0055, JFKL.
62 Author's calculation.

63 JFKPOF-138-018-p0060, JFKPOF-138-018-p0117, JFKPOF-138-017-p0059, JFKL.
64 There is an imperial dimension here, too. One may reflect on this pattern while keeping in mind Ernst Kantorowicz, *The King's Two Bodies* (Princeton: Princeton University Press, 1957) and Michael Hogan, *The Afterlife of John F. Kennedy* (New York: Cambridge University Press, 2017).
65 JFKPOF-138-016-p0047, JFKL.
66 JFKPOF-023-002-p0055 (my italics), JFKL.
67 JFKPOF-138-018-p0057, JFKL.
68 JFKPOF-138-015-p0051, JFKL.
69 JFKWHA-198-005, JFKL.
70 "Siyasat-e jadid-e Amrika," *Ettela'at*, November 10, 1960, 1; "Nakhostin 'aks az nawzad-e ra'is-e jomhuri-ye montakhab-e Amrika," *Ettela'at*, December 1, 1960, last page; "Dokhtar-e Kenedi kelisa-ra behem zad," *Ettela'at*, November 28, 1960, 1. I thank Ekaterina Pukhovaia for collecting *Ettela'at* issues; all translations are mine.
71 "Hayajatangiztarin entekhabat dar Amrika enjam shod," *Ettela'at*, November 9, 1960, 3; "Kenedi dar awwalin ruz 20 sa'at kar kard," *Ettela'at*, January 22, 1961, 4.
72 "Kenedi, Rusewelt-e dowwom," *Ettela'at*, November 15, 1961, 6 (first two quotes); "Tawsieh-ye khanum-e Kenedi be-zanan-e khaneh-dar," *Ettela'at*, February 20, 1961, 2.
73 "Kenedi dawran-e 'marz-e jadid'-ra aghaz kard," *Ettela'at*, January 21, 1961, 1; "Banu-ye Kenedi qiafeh-ye kakh-e sefid-ra taghiir khʷahad dad," *Ettela'at*, November 21, 1960, 4; "160 sal dar kakh-e sefid," *Ettela'at*, January 21, 1961, 5; photo of Jacqueline Kennedy shopping for the White House in New York, *Ettela'at*, March 27, 1961, 3.
74 "Sima-ye shoja'an," *Ettela'at*, December 25, 1960, 9 – February 5, 1961, 9. The original is John F. Kennedy, *Profiles in Courage* (New York: Harper, 1956).
75 "Zhaklin Kenedi," *Ettela'at*, June 7, 1961, 10; "Hediyeh beh-Zhaklin Kenedi," *Ettela'at*, August 8, 1961, 11; "Kenedi-ye chini!," *Ettela'at*, March 27, 1961, 5.
76 Stephen Gudemann, "Postmodern Gifts," in *Postmodernism, Economics and Knowledge*, ed. Stephen Cullenberg, Jack Amariglio, and David Ruccio (London: Routledge, 2001), 467.
77 E-mail, Tatiana Garakani to author, October 25, 2013, relates that some in the Garakani family say "the letter was actually written by . . . Fakhri's nephew . . . Fereydun Garakani. He was an author, and was translating books, plays to [Persian], was very interested in Pakistan and India, where he spent a bit of time. He also had a radio show."
78 Saunders to Young, May 23, 1962, folder 3, box 4, group AC164, SMML.
79 www.eisenhower.archives.gov/research/online_documents/people_to_people/BinderT.pdf (accessed November 25, 2018).
80 The question of war reparations was a key background to Mauss' *Le don*: Grégoire Mallard, "'The Gift' Revisited," *Sociological Theory* 29, no. 4 (2011): 225–47. See also Mallard, *Gift Exchange: The Transnational History of a Political Idea* (Cambridge: Cambridge University Press, 2019).
81 Robert Packenham, "Political Development Doctrines in the American Foreign Aid Program," *World Politics* 18, no. 2 (1966): 211, 213.
82 Odd Arne Westad, *The Cold War* (London: Penguin, 2017), 113–14.
83 Cyrus Schayegh, "Iran's Karaj Dam Affair," *CSSH* 54, no. 3 (2012): 612–43.
84 Packenham, "Doctrines"; Tony Judt, "Introduction," in *The Marshall Plan*, ed. Martin Schain (Houndsmill: Palgrave, 2001), 3.
85 Ibid., 2.

86 Quote: Andrew Johns, "The Johnson Administration, the Shah of Iran, and the Changing Pattern of US–Iranian Relations, 1965-1967," *Journal of Cold War Studies* 9, no. 2 (2007): 64. For France and Europe, see Westad, *Cold War*, 112, 115; Volker Heins and Christine Unrau, "Gift-Giving and Reciprocity in Global Society," *Journal of International Political Theory* 14, no. 2 (2018): 131.

87 Bruce Grant, *The Captive and the Gift: Cultural Histories of Sovereignty in Russia and the Caucasus* (Ithaca: Cornell University Press, 2009), 156–57.

88 Antoinette Burton, *The Trouble with Empire* (New York: Oxford University Press, 2015); Daniel Brückenhaus, *Policing Transnational Protest: Liberal Imperialism and the Surveillance of Anticolonialists in Europe, 1905-1945* (New York: Oxford University Press 2017).

Part III

Appropriation, Cont'd: Antagonisms and Contestations

9

Watching, Countering, and Emulating Peaceful Evolution: PRC Responses to Kennedy Administration Cultural Diplomacy and Global Strategy

Matthew D. Johnson

The years of US president John F. Kennedy's administration loom large in the history of the People's Republic of China, though not for reasons which are linked to Kennedy or his policies. These were the years of post-Great Leap Famine retrenchment and ongoing economic crisis during which institutions were downsized and urban populations systematically reduced. Ideological and strategic rivalry between the PRC and Soviet Union—the Sino-Soviet split—intensified and spilled into the open. Mao Zedong, politically weakened, was temporarily overshadowed by presumed successor Liu Shaoqi, and other more seasoned leaders, such as Zhou Enlai, stepped to the fore as figures of stability and prudence. Despite severe domestic setbacks, PRC influence in Africa and Asia seemed to grow, creating anxiety and concern in Washington.[1]

Relations between the United States and PRC were deeply strained during this period, not just because of competition within the Third World. PRC leaders sought to expand their sphere of influence within the intermediate zone of countries between the socialist camp and capitalist-imperialist West.[2] This grand strategy of maintaining sovereignty while expanding international power and standing created complex challenges. Starting on August 23, 1958, People's Liberation Army units in Fujian shelled the Jinmen (Quemoy) islands continuously over six weeks, a challenge to America's policy of supporting Chiang Kai-shek's government on Taiwan and possibly a test of the Soviet Union's commitment to "revolutionary" struggle against an international status quo which reflected American power. The US response was to intensify commitment in Asia, not just across the Taiwan Strait (for instance the US-Taiwan Mutual Defense Treaty) but also in Vietnam and vis-à-vis Tibet.[3] On the PRC side, perceptions that the strategic environment was deteriorating significantly led to a push for "new initiatives" and a new, pragmatic approach to diplomacy.[4] USSR-PRC relations improved somewhat, tensions on the Sino-Indian border were defused, and Beijing sought peaceful resolutions to border disputes and proxy conflicts involving Asian neighbors.

Scholarship of the past decade has begun to highlight how the Cold War-era contest between the United States and PRC was played out in the realms of propaganda and psychological influence as well as diplomacy and military affairs. The "battle for hearts and minds" in Asia, and indeed around the world, began during the 1950s—though in actuality the Chinese Communist Party had been at war in this way with the American government far earlier—and continued into the 1960s.[5] This point strengthens another key theme concerning US policy toward China during the Kennedy years: Kennedy, like previous US presidents, was preoccupied by the PRC's growing role in Asia and understood the US-PRC rivalry as a contest between distinct militaries and developmental-ideological models.[6] Another notable point at which the US and PRC policy narratives converge is in shared assessments of the significance of Africa and Asia as zones of rivalry, particularly with respect to postcolonial "emerging countries."

In addition, Mao's perception of the United States during the Kennedy years was informed by decades of observation of US policy, including the Cold War strategic vision of hastening communist government collapse through values change known as "peaceful evolution." His view of Kennedy as a cultural manipulator was shared widely in PRC mass media and fundamentally informed how other PRC leaders, such as Zhou Enlai, understood US power to work in both international and domestic settings.[7] Indeed, Mao's internal assessments of American policy before and during Kennedy's presidency, which were closely read and discussed by his inner circle, indicated that peaceful evolution may have been viewed as the gravest long-term threat to the socialist camp.

PRC perceptions of Kennedy were thus framed by two linked dynamics, as this chapter argues. One was political turbulence in the socialist camp believed to stem from US peaceful evolution strategy; the other, the emergence of cultural relations in Cold War diplomacy as an innovation linked to power and influence, particularly with regard to expansion of American influence in the middle zones of Africa and Asia. These perceptions had momentous consequences. They created a minor revolution in the conduct of PRC diplomacy, with cultural relations and training in foreign languages coming to the fore of how junior embassy staff were prepared for service, and led to a wider internationalization of the PRC education system at a national level. How the United States was presented abroad under Kennedy impacted how the PRC was presented abroad under Mao, and vice versa. In the struggle to win influence through cultural relations, the Kennedy administration's approach to foreign engagement became a template for PRC diplomatic work.

Peaceful evolution as strategic threat: The background of China's Kennedy encounter

During the mid-1950s, US secretary of state John Foster Dulles issued a series of statements concerning the desirability and inevitability of socialism's collapse, an outlook later described in Chinese documents as "peaceful evolution" (和平演变) or "peaceful victory" (和平取胜) strategy. Chinese Communist Party (CCP) high political official Bo Yibo, who until 1953 held the title of Minister of Finance, recalled Dulles' words as signaling the US intention to destroy socialism through a combination of mental pressure (meaning, in this context, triggering a crisis of ideological conviction) and propaganda.[8] By the mid-1950s, then, it appears that CCP leaders were at least tangentially aware of a new strategic approach being taken by US counterparts: conflict with the socialist world was to be fought in the spheres of ideology, popular consciousness, and information.

Mao was becoming aware of Dulles' comments, which began to appear in the international media with some regularity from 1957 onward.[9] Mao was, of course, also aware of what were perceived as internal threats to socialism, both in the Soviet bloc and at home. Dulles' words suggested that communist parties were in real danger, and that the United States and allies sought to accelerate its disappearance. Mao may have seen these assessments reflected in Nikita Khrushchev's "secret speech" and attack on Stalin's legacy at the 20th Congress of the CPSU held in 1956; in anti-communist uprisings in Poland and Hungary; and in internal attacks on the CCP by rightists, including figures within the party, again during 1957. Mao believed that peaceful evolution represented a greater threat to the socialist camp than post-Stalin Soviet leaders acknowledged, saying to USSR ambassador to the PRC Pavel Yudin on July 22, 1958:

> Although we support the Soviet Union, we won't endorse its mistakes. As for [the differences over] the issue of peaceful evolution, we have never openly discussed [these differences], nor have we published [them] in the newspapers. Cautious as we have been, we choose to exchange different opinions internally. I had discussed them with you before I went to Moscow. While in Moscow, [we assigned] Deng Xiaoping to raise five [controversial] issues. We won't openly talk about them even in the future, because our doing so would hurt Comrade Khrushchev's [political position]. In order to help consolidate his [Khrushchev's] leadership, we decided not to talk about these [controversies], although it does not mean that the justice is not on our side.[10]

Warnings against internal ideological enemies ("enemies without guns") were not new in Maoist politics after 1949. However, Mao's concerns with rightism and infiltration of the CCP, contradictions between the CCP and the rest of PRC society, and "erosion" of values by degenerate capitalist thought ("sugar-coated bullets") had already begun to reach a new height on the eve of the Kennedy presidency.

Beginning in 1960, the PRC media began regularly publishing stories which reflected Mao's belief that the United States was carrying out a strategy of victory through peace (和平取胜的战略) meant to overthrow, corrupt, and internally divide countries within the socialist camp. This "sinister and poisonous" agenda was portrayed as a fundamental challenge to more genuine peace and progress.[11] It "numbed" the will to struggle against imperialism and promoted "internal collapse" leading to capitalist restoration.[12] From 1960 to 1964, across successive US presidencies, the *People's Daily* sought to link the United States to policies meant to overthrow the governments of socialist countries; revival of imperialism in Africa, Asia, and Latin America; and, more specifically, "peaceful evolution" as part of a concerted effort to undermine Soviet influence in Eastern Europe.

Propaganda carried in the *People's Daily* wasn't the only means by which CCP leaders sought to combat peaceful evolution forces. Threat perceptions of internal degeneration and dissolution leading toward capitalism were also manifested in warnings about "contemporary revisionism" which, in turn, led to actual efforts to counteract both foreign and domestic assaults on socialism. An April 16, 1960, editorial in the theoretical journal *Red Flag* titled "Long Live Leninism" made these connections plainly—imperialism, coupled with the belief among revolutionaries, that Marxist-Leninism was becoming "outmoded," made socialist countries internally vulnerable to change.[13] Mao wanted to build resistance to these pressures. The plan to resist revisionist forces represented by the United States and the USSR, and remove revisionists within the CCP from power, gained urgency in 1959–60, when the possibility of peaceful evolution at a global scale seemed most acute, as symbolized by Khrushchev's meeting with US president Dwight D. Eisenhower in September 1959 at Camp David. This urgency had not abated when, in January 1962, PRC chairman Liu Shaoqi gave the CCP Central Committee's report at the Seven Thousand Cadres Conference. He cited Mao to indicate that without a socialist economy, the PRC ran the risk of becoming revisionist, fascist, and reactionary. (Mao would later claim that this report represented his first statement that the CCP was in danger of being overthrown by domestic revisionism.[14]) At the CCP leadership's meeting in Beidaihe and at the Eighth CCP Central Committee Tenth Plenum, Mao again urged the CCP to be vigilant about going in the "opposite" direction toward capitalism and stressed the importance of "class struggle" against revisionism and dogmatism.[15] Polemic exhortations to the population to "never forget class struggle" and warnings against "contemporary revisionists" in the socialist camp—the latter indicating deepening friction with the Soviet Union which would spill out into the open in July 1963—thus emerged as a result of internal assessments that CCP rule was under serious, multidirectional attack.

Mao, Kennedy, and the American "Two Policies" strategy

Mao Zedong's diplomatic writings, which include conversations and articles published under Mao's name, placed Kenney within a broader context of US foreign policy as understood by Mao and, by extension, other PRC leaders and theorists. During the early 1960s, the United States was the PRC's greatest enemy. The United States and allies Japan and Taiwan threatened PRC sovereignty and claims in the Far East region, and the PRC was still unrecognized by the UN. Opportunities existed in the form of civil conflict in Japan and the emergence of potential supporters in Africa and other "middle zone" regions. On the other hand, the PRC was threatened by the American nuclear advantage and the build-up of a Tibetan armed force in adjacent Nepal.[16] Within this anomic regional and global order, Mao viewed Kennedy with wariness and hostility.

During an October 22, 1960, discussion with Edgar Snow, who had visited the CCP's major military base at Yan'an during the 1930s and won international acclaim for his account of that experience, Mao focused on US policy in the Far East.[17] Mentioning Kennedy and Nixon, both of whom were then presidential candidates, by name, Mao declared that Americans were "afraid of war."[18] At the same time, he recognized that the United States and Taiwan had blocked the PRC's ability to enforce claims to sovereignty over island clusters Mazu, Jinmen, and Penghu—and, indeed, over Taiwan itself. "We want all of the territory . . . it is our country's sovereign territory," he declared to Snow. Regardless of which presidential candidate won, Mao's appraisal was that the United States would remain hostile to the PRC's sovereignty claims and to recognition by the UN. Mao said little publicly about Kennedy following the latter's election victory. However, in an August 8, 1963 article, first published in *People's Daily*, he accused Kennedy of using "secretive tactics" to manipulate the "domestic struggle between classes and ethnicities."[19] These secret tactics consisted of discrimination, suppression, and use of military force against black Americans while, at the same time, deploying a public language of "safeguarding of human rights," "protection of rights for black Americans," and asking black Americans for "patience" to cheat them and numb their will to struggle.

Mao's assessment of Kennedy's tactics sounded familiar notes of CCP concern over US peaceful evolution strategy as posing an existential threat to the socialist camp. Fears of the spread of values of "bourgeois freedom" by US officials to thwart revolutionary politics was echoed in allegations that Kennedy's government used rights-based discourse to suppress and cheat black Americans. However, Mao's criticism of US military suppression of riots in the Panama Canal Zone, written less than two months after Kennedy's assassination, extended his broader analysis of US grand strategy as comprised of two, intertwined policies: a "war policy" of worldwide military invasion, and a "peaceful evolution policy" of capitalist restoration, primarily within the socialist camp.[20] According to Mao's speech, given to a *People's Daily* reporter on January 12, 1964, the American "invasion plan to rule the world [has been] continuous from Truman to Eisenhower to Kennedy to Johnson."[21]

Even after 1963, Kennedy never left Mao's mind, his name even becoming synonymous with a more subtle turn in American statecraft which blended the "war" and "peaceful evolution" approaches. In another interview with Snow, Mao suggested that Kennedy's strategy in the Southern hemisphere, with its reliance on "special forces warfare" and "local warfare," may have been influenced by his own, Mao's, writings on military operations.[22] By extension, Kennedy was the initiator of a new, neo-imperialist war against the Third World which incorporated tactics of people's wars of liberation, including the ideological dimension, though Mao claimed that these would be "useless" in an anti-people's war. (In the same interview, Mao also described himself and the rest of the Chinese people as "surprised" at the news that Kennedy had been killed.) If Kennedy represented anything to Mao, it was the image of a United States as a global power—and threat—whose techniques of domination were increasingly localized, fine-tuned, and subtle.

Whether this image also led to a turning point in Mao's thinking, toward the dawning recognition that the United States would be a more complex and enduring challenge than he had hoped, is difficult to conclude. However, it does seem to be the case that Mao perceived Kennedy as elusive, even shadowy, in his methods of pursuing power. In conversation with Egypt's president Gamal Abdel Nasser, on December 19, 1963, PRC State Council premier Zhou Enlai stated:

> At present the United States seeks hegemony over the entire world, an ambition which Britain, France, and other countries do not have. Such policies as Dulles' brinkmanship and Kennedy's New Frontier illustrate this issue. Against socialist countries, the United States engages in peaceful evolution. *Kennedy in comparison to Eisenhower is more cunning and has an even more reactionary policy of double dealing. He speaks on the one hand of peace, and on the other he speaks of the status of power.* It was precisely because the United States has powerful groups that did not permit him to engage in double dealing that they got rid of him in the end. Kennedy was reactionary, but a revolutionary people opposes assassination. Your film [*Saladin*], too, calls for a contest of arms, not schemes and intrigues.[23]

Zhou's words are likely to have reflected the prevailing views of the CCP high elite at the time. Though doubtless also intended to justify the anti-US position of PRC foreign policy, and tilt other leaders, such as Nasser, firmly toward the PRC side, the sense of American policy as simultaneously flexible and hostile—and, under Kennedy,

Figure 9.1 A recently elected Kennedy listens intently to CIA director Allen Dulles' "Cold War" instructions.

mercurial—resonates with Mao's fairly consistent sense of US strategy as grounded in both power politics and the manipulation of values and sentiment.

In the PRC mass media, articles and caricatures in the *People's Daily* likewise emphasized Kennedy's agenda of building up the power position of United States in military terms, even as a presidential candidate.[24] Kennedy was strategically anti-communist, a self-appointed defender of the Western Hemisphere, and paired offers of aid with the backing and threat of military strength.[25] His policies relied on special agents and border provocations; he was a tool of Allen Dulles (Figure 9.1). His mentality was seen as no different from that of previous Cold War-minded American presidents who viewed the PRC as an enemy. Kennedy was not portrayed as youthful per se, but rather as a rich, vain, and worried dandy whose manifold war schemes were constantly in danger of being thwarted by his country's moribund economy. In other images he was made to appear sadistic and inhuman (Figure 9.2). Further into Kennedy's presidency, as tensions between the United States and China increased in Southeast Asia, he was cast as a complex, deceptive figure—a chameleon-like manipulator and liar (Figure 9.3). Kennedy preaching peace while scheming for war and profit was one recurrent motif; his brutal mistreatment of African Americans, a metaphor for Jim Crow, was another.

Such representations were firmly within a Sino-Soviet tradition of caricaturing American presidents as hypocritical warmongers who served the interests of powerful, oligarchic elites while attempting to make other world leaders their puppets. (It is perhaps for this reason that PRC cartoonists seemed to take particular delight in showing Kennedy humiliated by Charles de Gaulle's forthright stance of pro-European

Figure 9.2 Kennedy serving fragrant "peace strategy" buns from a grisly kitchen. The ingredients are "invasion of Vietnam," "invasion of Congo," "interference in Laos," and "A"(-bomb) seasoning.

Figure 9.3 Kennedy binds the wrists of a kneeling African American (rendered, by contrast, in heroic socialist realist style) with restraints of "civil rights" and "legal acts," aided by a ferocious police dog.

Figure 9.4 Kennedy, as a perfected bodhisattva-like figure, is shown surrounded by symbols of coercive and noncoercive power.

autonomy vis-à-vis the United States.) They did, however, also seem to reinforce the more specific image of Kennedy as a particularly dangerous and duplicitous figure who was deft at employing both military and nonmilitary stratagems in his pursuit of American power (see Figure 9.4), which in some images was likened to the technique of an actor or painter. Photographs of Kennedy were rarely shown in the *People's Daily*.

Confronting American values abroad: The Ministry of Foreign Relations and PRC diplomatic perspectives

From at least the late 1950s onward, news watchers and analysts within the PRC Ministry of Foreign Relations had been observing trade and cultural relations (贸易和文化关系) between the United States and Soviet Union as a means of gauging the degree of rapprochement between the two superpowers. Beginning in 1958, the Soviet side's "positive" and "active" policy with respect to reestablishing normal economic ties was perceived as a possible sign that forces in Moscow might be engaged in a "struggle" to end the Cold War.[26] Soviet exhibitions held in New York and American exhibitions in Moscow, along with preparations of joint artistic performance activities, signified that the United States, too, led by Eisenhower, would be "enthusiastic" in making preparations to engage through both commercial and cultural means.[27]

PRC observers were likewise aware that the US exhibition in Moscow, planned by representatives of forty companies and with 250 corporate participants, would be used to exhibit "the living conditions of American workers," in order to demonstrate "that the lives of American workers are rich."[28] They also expected that the Soviet Union would do as much as possible to prevent the American exhibition from becoming too influential, in part by attempting to overshadow it with their own New York exhibition and planned August 1959 Moscow Film Festival. PRC assessments of evolving US-Soviet ties took a vivid interest in the impact of exhibitions and cultural events on public opinion. PRC Ministry of Foreign Relations internal memos stated that Soviet authorities were opposed to US jazz performances and literature and that the United States was "afraid" of Soviet performances and efforts to "break through the iron curtain." The Soviets were observed to have organized containment and analysis activities to figure out how to curb the expansion of American propaganda, while American customs authorities blocked the import of Soviet films and police were dispatched to cultural events.[29]

American integration of cultural agreements and exchange into foreign relations activity were forecast to accelerate into the early 1960s. "The US is afraid [of establishing cultural relations with the Soviet Union], but finds it difficult to refuse," reported PRC consular observers based in Moscow.[30] Global public opinion was seen to demand warming of ties; it was hoped that the Soviet Union would then use this opening to contain and marginalize the spread of capitalist culture and education. Confirming these expectations, US cultural reach seemed only to lengthen under the Kennedy administration. On March 30, 1962 the Embassy of the PRC in Ghana reported a flurry of US investments and agreements for a dam, smelting facility, and enhanced cultural and educational exchange.[31] American organizations were observed distributing publications; consulting on matters related to journalism and education; and making philanthropic donations. Embassy staff attempted to track the activities of the US Peace Corps, Carnegie Corporation, and Coca-Cola Company, as well as several British cultural associations believed to be contributing to the "Westernization" of Ghanaian culture.

Reports on both American and Soviet cultural and propaganda activities written later that year highlighted the dawning recognition that diplomacy in the Cold War global order had changed, and that PRC efforts to woo the "middle zone" of Africa and Asia were at an increasingly visible disadvantage. US news agency offices in Accra distributed books, soda, and inflatable balls to children; these "American cultural imperialism activities," coupled with more direct forms of American aid, were cited as explanations for the Ghana government's increasingly vocal international support for other pro-US positions, even on seemingly unrelated issues such as high-altitude nuclear testing.[32] Using the Red Cross, students on homestays, Peace Corps volunteers, pen pal programs, and derelict properties converted into new facilities for cultural dissemination, the United States was expanding influence while reducing similar opportunities for socialist countries. Likewise, the Soviet Union was also reported to be engaged in sponsorship of film festivals, youth activities, and cultural performances, a level of activity which far exceeded that of the aspirational PRC.

The status and mystique of "culture" in PRC assessments of American international influence thus rose considerably during the Kennedy period. Cultural agreements were a "reflection of politics," could "warm the tense international situation," erode the power of rival governments, and serve as cover for espionage and counterespionage operations.[33] Further evidence of use of culture as an important weapon of influence along the New Frontier came from Guinea where, as in Ghana, the United States dispatched Peace Corps volunteers alongside other trade, journalism, youth, and university student groups to establish a firm American presence in the newly independent country.[34] Embassy report writers identified two main methods employed by American organizations: economic aid and cultural exchange. Overseas teachers and students, in particular, were cited as exerting the greatest influence: impacting student values, distributing revolutionary literature, and building personal relationships with students. American students were of numerous races and genders, according to the report. Their initial arrival preceded the Kennedy administration by roughly six months; a second batch, however, had arrived in July 1961, seemingly prepared in advance to argue that conditions in the United States were "good," and against the PRC's positions with respect to Taiwan, Tibet, and the UN. American efforts were not always well received—some African officials and students resisted and found the influence efforts condescending—but, gradually, the American presence spread. PRC officials even lodged their own complaints, with leading diplomat Huang Hua writing to the Ghanaian government to protest the excessive and objectionable screening of American films in theaters.[35]

Countering and emulating Kennedy's United States through cultural relations

During the Kennedy administration, the sense among PRC foreign affairs experts that the United States was winning the contest of cultural relations (文化关系) ultimately resulted in a series of institutional changes within the Ministry of Foreign Relations and the PRC's main overseas culture and media body, the External Cultural Liaison Committee (对外文化联络委员会). These changes can be understood as driven by perceptions analogous to Zhou's posthumous assessment of Kennedy as "cunning" in the manipulation of values to serve American interests abroad and defeat socialism.[36] Wherever the PRC sought to gain a foothold beyond the socialist camp, the United States was already present through its cultural and economic efforts to contain the ideological influence of competitors. PRC consular staff wrote detailed and concerned descriptions of American cultural relations with Sweden in an effort to diagnose and understand the nature of their disadvantage.[37] In India, materials compiled by the PRC embassy throughout 1963 closely tracked the "very large strengthening of cultural activities and penetration of Indian educational circles."[38] More than fourteen professors and students were observed providing "cultural aid" (文化援助); US diplomatic missions and personnel were more engaged in Indian academic events. Cultural and academic exchange relations since 1962 had also included, for Indian scholars, scholarships for study and the involvement of a myriad of institutions, whose names were scrupulously documented in English by the report writers: the American Studies Research Center, American Workshop, American Field Service, World University Service, Project India, National Council for Educational Research and Training, Office of Education, and Students Service Union. The analysis concluded: "The [American] objective is to bring Indian youth closer to the United States, train new running dogs, and pursue a new plot for imperialist invasion."[39]

New operational approaches for countering American strategy were needed. The PRC response, unambiguously defined, was to begin strengthening diplomatic institutions of the State Council to combat this unprecedented "penetration" of countries of important to the PRC's own strategic designs. Within the Ministry of Foreign Relations, plans were designed and implemented to "meet the needs of the daily development of overseas cultural work" by recruiting and grooming a new cohort of middle-ranked diplomatic cadres specifically for functional roles in cultural areas.[40] Students were to be selected from the national International Relations Institute (国际关系学院) and trained in international diplomacy, cultural and artistic knowledge, and foreign languages; foreign language competency represented the focal point of the three-year curriculum. Once graduated, they would be expected to be able to read foreign periodicals, engage in high-level discussions with foreign counterparts, and fill internal roles as section heads and overseas cultural secretaries. By 1961, approximately 1,900 students were receiving foreign languages training in national diplomacy and foreign languages higher institutions within Beijing.[41]

Increasing capacity in foreign language instruction invariably required the recruitment of foreign staff who were fluent in key languages (in mid-1961 the targets were Spanish, Hindi, Tamil, Urdu, English, French, Arabic, and Swedish, and by 1962 included Japanese and Indonesian) as well as politically sympathetic to the CCP. Recruitment of linguistic experts from capitalist countries was carried out through the Ministry of Foreign Relations and CCP International Liaison Department; on paper, these recruits were either current or past members of foreign communist parties, or members of "fraternal" foreign parties and organizations.[42] Initially, many foreign experts were drawn from existing party-state broadcasting, journalism, and international relations institutions, and had been in the PRC from 1959 to 1960.

Competing with Kennedy's United States thus had two important consequences for the People's Republic of China. First, domestic enrollments in educational institutions devoted to diplomacy, international relations, and foreign languages increased. In this respect, international rivalry underpinned the internationalization of the PRC education system. The Ministry of Foreign Relations Education Section (教育司), together with the Ministry of Education, managed the training of students in translation and interpretation work through the Diplomacy Institute (外交学院) and Beijing Foreign Languages Academy.[43] In 1962, the Ministry of Education communicated plans to the CCP Central Committee Propaganda Department concerning the establishment of foreign language classes and a foreign languages academy system across the PRC's large- and medium-sized cities.[44] Student recruitment reached into secondary schools, with further plans to expand to the elementary level.

The educational changes were not, in practice, sweeping, nor was implementation wholly successful. Foreign language learning remained largely confined to larger cities such as Beijing, Shanghai, Chongqing, Guangzhou, Changchun, and Xi'an.[45] Learners were primarily secondary students and diplomatic cadres and, even within the academy and institute system, translation took up the majority of teacher and student time. "Translation tasks are numerous and urgent with so much struggle in the international system . . . the struggle is diplomatic," recorded members of the Ministry of Foreign Relations Education Section involved in planning work.[46] Plans to increase foreign language learning at the national level dragged on into 1963. Students sent abroad for further study did not always behave in politically acceptable ways, and in 1961 the Ministry of Foreign Relations received numerous reports detailing students attending forbidden political rallies, making their own political speeches, falling in love with citizens of other countries, or attempting to flee and defect.[47] Others simply failed to succeed in their studies or, in more extreme cases, were caught spying on behalf of foreign governments. By mid-1963, however, nearly 600 students from the PRC were abroad in twenty-seven countries, including those within the socialist camp, Asia, Africa, Latin America, and capitalist West.[48]

The second major consequence of competition with American cultural "cunning" in the diplomatic sphere was that PRC cultural activities abroad intensified. From 1961 onward, selected diplomatic trainees received specialized cultural training prior to assignment overseas. The External Cultural Liaison Committee sent a special delegation abroad to eight African countries. In Asia, Laos became one of the PRC's more active cultural and economic missions abroad. International agreements deepened cultural, artistic, and intellectual ties, particularly with familiar exchange partner countries such as Germany (GDR) and Poland. Led by a board comprised of well-known authors and artists, the Chinese People's External Cultural Association (中国人民对外文化协会) established ties with twenty-two foreign countries by early 1963.[49] Similar ties had existed from the 1950s. But they had been more limited, and in the early 1960s several distinctively new trajectories emerged: an increased emphasis on Asia and Africa, a more distinct role for sport (e.g., the First Games of the New Emerging Forces, held in November 1963 in Djakarta), and the pairing of cultural diplomacy with loans and technical aid.[50]

Overall, the result was an increasingly important role for culture in PRC diplomacy, especially with regard to the Africa-Asia-Latin America cluster of middle-zone countries prioritized by Mao. During the early 1960s, the frequency with which cultural and theater groups were dispatched to other Asian countries increased; among the more notable destinations were Vietnam, Indonesia, Cambodia, Pakistan, Nepal, Afghanistan, and Syria.[51] Cultural exchange programs and agreements were established with Mongolia, North Korea, Vietnam, Myanmar, Indonesia, and Syria. In addition to theatrical performances (some by the People's Liberation Army), cultural activities included photographic exhibitions, folk song and dance, and acrobatics. In Laos, the PRC created an entire exhibition of "socialist construction achievements" using photograph, arts and crafts, and film. Across Africa, the period from 1961 to 1964 also saw a marked increase in cultural cooperation agreements between the PRC and Algeria, Ghana, Tanzania, Somalia, Mali, Zimbabwe, Central African Republic, Guinea, and Congo.[52] Following a Zhou Enlai-led official tour of the region in 1963, additional economic aid agreements to African countries included theater construction in Somalia, Mali, and Guinea. Mass media also entered the picture, with PRC films shown as part of another China Economic Construction Exhibition held in Santiago de Chile in 1964.[53] That same year a China Film Week was held in Algeria, and throughout the early 1960s the PRC participated in approximately 50 international film festivals, with the China Film Corporation establishing business ties with over 600 companies in 84 countries, and exporting over 2,000 feature film, documentary, and newsreel titles.[54] Broadcasting activity increased as well, with more agreements signed with countries outside the Eastern Bloc, including transmission of "Voice of Beijing" programming via Mali.[55]

Competition with the United States was not the sole driver of the PRC's cultural diplomacy push, and Kennedy's policies alone do not explain the timing. The emerging Sino-Soviet split, already visible at the 1960 Bucharest Conference of the World Communist and Workers' Parties, also drove CCP efforts to urgently court international allies, as did bellicose statements from Chiang Kai-shek and the Republic of China government on Taiwan in 1962.[56] Cultural exchange with the Soviet Union diminished during this period, as did engagement with India after the 1962 Sino-Indian War. As CCP leaders opted for a more independent national course, diplomatic strategy and style followed suit. Other transregional mechanisms, such as the China-Latin America Friendship Association, established in March 1960, preceded the Kennedy presidency and signaled that the PRC was already moving in a more middle-zone-oriented direction, propelled as much by security needs for external recognition and normalization of relations as by grand strategic rivalry. (According to one historian, Mao was particularly enamored of the Castroist approach to cultural diplomacy, which emphasized folk music and dance.[57]) Even contact with "capitalist" European countries had been steady, if sparse, throughout the previous decade. However, there does seem to be historiographical consensus that the focus on Africa-Asia-Latin America increased during the early 1960s, and that culture—in particular stage performance, mass media, and youth and educational exchange—emerged as a notable dimension of engagement if measured in terms of new agreements and cooperative programs.[58] The parallels with cultural diplomacy under Kennedy do not seem to have been accidental for, as this chapter has shown, CCP understandings of culture as a powerful tool for building support in middle-zone countries, and as a tool of turning back the forces of "peaceful evolution," reached a new level of depth and urgency during what were, for the United States, the Kennedy years.

Conclusion: Mao's Kennedy, China's America

Scholarship on the Kennedy administration has focused on the flexibility of its foreign policy, particularly with respect to the Third World. An equally important wave has looked closely at less-studied aspects of Kennedy's diplomacy: propaganda, economic statecraft, and clandestine operations. But looking at Kennedy and his administration from the perspective of the PRC, starting with Mao Zedong, these distinctions between these aspects of Kennedy's statecraft begin to break down. US leaders were not ideologically flexible, yet Kennedy was a tactically sophisticated opponent—"cunning." American interests represented a threat to PRC sovereignty and international standing. The pursuit of American interests through cultural relations represented a challenging, far-flung, and unpredictable manifestation of that threat, one which required an urgent response. Throughout the years of the Kennedy administration, PRC leaders like Mao worried about the likelihood of values change through peaceful evolution, while foreign affairs institutions like the Ministry of Foreign Relations observed, countered, and emulated Westernization abroad. Ironically, through tactics that suggest strong parallels and learning across the "imperialist" and "socialist" camps.

Notes

1 See most recently, Gregg Brazinsky, *Winning the Third World: Sino-American Rivalry during the Cold War* (Chapel Hill: University of North Carolina Press, 2017).
2 See Chen Jian, *Mao's China and the Cold War* (Chapel Hill: University of North Carolina Press, 2001), 5.
3 Noam Kochavi, *A Conflict Perpetuated: China Policy during the Kennedy Years* (Westport: Praeger, 2002). On US-PRC relations, see Rosemary Foot, *The Practice of Power: U.S. Relations with China since 1949* (Oxford: Oxford University Press, 1995). On Tibet, India, and Kennedy, see Bruce Riedel, *JFK's Forgotten Crisis: Tibet, the CIA, and the Sino-Indian War* (Washington: Brookings, 2015).
4 Niu Jun, "1962: The Eve of the Left Turn in China's Foreign Policy," *Cold War International History Project Working Paper* 48 (2005): 9–10.

5 See Zheng Yangwen, Hong Lu, and Michael Szonyi, eds., *The Cold War in Asia* (Leiden: Brill, 2010).
6 Kochavi, *Conflict*, 27. See also Robert Rakove, *Kennedy, Johnson, and the Nonaligned World* (Cambridge: Cambridge University Press, 2013).
7 See also He Di, "The Most Respected Enemy: Mao Zedong's Perception of the United States," *The China Quarterly* 137 (1994): 144–58. He Di argues that Mao's respect for the United States came primarily from his assessments of U.S. military power, whereas this chapter takes a different approach by emphasizing Mao's understanding of US strategy, including peaceful evolution.
8 As quoted in Deng Liqun, "Mao Zedong fandui heping yanbian zhengzhi zhanlue de xingcheng yu fazhan" [The Formation and Development of Mao Zedong's Political Strategy to Oppose Peaceful Evolution]. Available online: http://www.qstheory.cn/politics/2016-01/29/c_1117923265.htm (accessed January 29, 2016), originally in Deng Liqun, *Zhengzhi zhanluejia Mao Zedong* [Political Strategist Mao Zedong] (Beijing: Central Ethnicities University Press, 2004).
9 Ibid.
10 "Minutes of Conversation, Mao Zedong and Ambassador Yudin," July 22, 1958, Cold War International History Project. Available online: http://digitalarchive.wilsoncenter.org/document/116982/. Source: Zhongguo renmin gongheguo waijiao bu and Zhong-Gong zhongyang wenxian yanjiu zhi, *Mao Zedong waijiao wenxuan* [Selected Works of Mao Zedong on Diplomacy, SWMZD], trans. and annotated by Zhang Shu Guang and Chen Jian (Beijing: Zhongyang wenxian chubanshe, 1994), 322–33.
11 "Weihu heping de juedingxing liliang" [The Decisive Force in Safeguarding Peace], *Renmin ribao* [*People's Daily*] (*RMRB*), February 6, 1960, 2.
12 "Zai Huasha tiaoyue diyue guo zhengzhi xieshang weiyuanhui huiyishang—Kang Sheng tongzhi tan muqian guoji xingshi" [At the Warsaw Pact Political Consultative Conference—Comrade Kang Sheng Discusses the Current International Situation], *RMRB*, February 6, 1960, 6; "Liening guanyu heping yu zhanzheng de lilun" [Lenin's Theories of Peace and War], *RMRB*, April 25, 1960, 7.
13 See Editorial Department of *Red Flag*, *Long Live Leninism!* 3rd ed. (Peking: Foreign Languages Press, 1960), 1–55. Available online: https://www.marxists.org/history/international/comintern/sino-soviet-split/cpc/leninism.htm (accessed December 1, 2018). Originally printed in *Red Flag*, April 16, 1960, 8. On the connection between contemporary revisionism and peaceful evolution as communicated to a mass audience, see "Liening de geming jingshen wan-gu-chang-qing" [Lenin's Revolutionary Spirit Will Remain Fresh Forever], *RMRB*, April 23, 1960, 8.
14 Deng, "Mao Zedong's Political Strategy."
15 Mao Zedong, "Speech at the Tenth Plenum of the Eighth Central Committee," September 24, 1962, *Selected Works of Mao Tse-tung*, vol. 8. Available online: https://www.marxists.org/reference/archive/mao/selected-works/volume-8/mswv8_63.htm.
16 On Tibetan forces in Nepal, see John Garver, *Protracted Contest: Sino-Indian Rivalry in the Twentieth Century* (Seattle: University of Washington Press, 2001), 148.
17 Edgar Snow, *Red Star over China* (New York: Random House, 1937).
18 Mao Zedong, "Tong Sinuo tan Taiwan wenti ji qita" [Discussing the Taiwan Issue and Other Matters with (Edgar) Snow], October 22, 1960, in SWMZD, 448–54.
19 Mao Zedong, "Zhichi Meiguo heiren fandui zhongzu qishi douzheng de shengming" [Declaration of Support for American Blacks in Their Struggle against Racial Discrimination], August 8, 1963, in SWMZD, 493–96; Originally published in *RMRB*, August 9, 1963.

20 Mao Zedong, "Zhongguo renmin jianjue zhichi Banama renmin de aiguo zhengyi douzheng" [The Chinese People Resolutely Support the Panamanian People in their Patriotic Righteous Struggle], January 12, 1964, in SWMZD, 510–12; Originally published in *RMRB*, January 13, 1964.
21 Ibid.
22 Edgar Snow, "Interview with Mao," *The New Republic*, February 26, 1965. Available online: https://newrepublic.com/article/89494/interview-mao-tse-tung-communist-china.
23 "Record of the Third Conversation between Premier Zhou Enlai and President Nasser," trans. Stephen Mercado, December 19, 1963, Cold War International History Project. Available online: http://digitalarchive.wilsoncenter.org/document/165430. Source: PRC Ministry of Foreign Relations (MFR) 107-01027-07; emphasis added.
24 "Meiguo liang dang zongtong houxuanren jingxiang fachu haozhan jiaoqi" [The Presidential Candidates of America's Two Parties Competitively Put Forth Warmongering Yells], *RMRB*, August 9, 1960, 5.
25 "Cong Kennidi de yanlun kan Kennidi zhengce" [Using Kennedy's Speeches to Look at Kennedy's Policies], *RMRB*, November 10, 1960, 6.
26 "Guanyu Sulian he Meiguo maoyi de wenhua guanxi de cailiao" [Materials Concerning USSR-USA Trade and Cultural Relations], October 10, 1959, MFR 109-01933-06(1).
27 "Su-Mei huban zhanlan zhong de douzheng" [The Soviet-American Exhibition Struggle], Embassy of PRC in USSR Cultural Department to MFR, April 13, 1959, MFR 109-01933-06(1).
28 Ibid.
29 "Su-Mei huban daxing zonghe zhanlanhui de douzheng" [The Soviet-American Struggle to Mutually Establish Large-Scale Comprehensive Exhibitions], Embassy of PRC in USSR Cultural Department to MFR, June 5, 1959, MFR 109-01933-06(1); "Sulian da juyuan zai Meiguo yanchu sheng kuang kongqian" [Unprecedented Victory for Soviet Theater Performed in America], Embassy of PRC in USSR Cultural Department to MFR, June 6, 1959, MFR 109-01933-06(1).
30 "Su-Mei 1960-1961 niandu wenhua xieyi jinxing chubu cuoshang" [Progress in Preliminary Planning for Soviet-American Cultural Agreements in 1960-1961], n.d., MFR 109-01933-06(1).
31 "Yijiuliusan nian di yi jidu Jiana wenhua dongtai" [Cultural Trends in Ghana, First Quarter, 1962], Embassy of PRC in Ghana to MFR, March 30, 1962, MFR 108-00812-01.
32 "Meiguo, Sulian zai Jiana de wenhua xuanchuan huodong qingkuang" [Condition of US, USSR Culture and Propaganda Activities in Ghana], Cultural Embassy of PRC in Ghana to MFR, July 9, 1962, MFR 108-00811-05.
33 "Sulian yu Meiguo zai wenhua, kexue funu jie lianxi qingkuang" [Condition of Contacts between Soviet and American Cultural, Scientific, and Women's Circles], Embassy of PRC in USSR Cultural Department to MFR, August 4, 1962, MFR 109-02417-04.
34 See "Meiguo zai Jinaya jinxing wenhua shentou qingkuang" [Conditions of American Cultural Infiltration in Guinea], Cultural Department of Embassy of PRC in Guinea to MFR, December 29, 1962, MFR 108-00807-01.
35 "Zhongguo waijiao bu he Duiwai wenhua lianluo weiyuanhui jiu Jiana shangying Meiguo fan-Hua yingpian 'Zhan huo' xiang Jia zhengfu jiaoshe shi huifu zhu Jia shiguan" [PRC Ministry of Foreign Relations and External Cultural Liaison

Committee Negotiations with the Ghana Government Concerning the Screening of American anti-China Films], Embassy of PRC in Ghana to MFR, June 1, 1963, MFR 108-00928-01.
36 "Record of the Third Conversation between Premier Zhou Enlai and President Nasser."
37 "Ruidian he Meiguo de wenhua guanxi qingkuang" [Conditions of Cultural Relations between Sweden and the United States], April 5, 1963, MFR 110-01704-02. This report totaled 133 pages.
38 "Meiguo jiaqiang zai Yindu jiaoyu jie de huodong qingkuang" [Conditions of US Strengthening of Activities within Indian Educational Circles], Embassy of PRC in India, January 17, 1964, MFR 105-01641-04.
39 Ibid.
40 "Duiwai wen wei guanyu zai Guoji guanxi xueyuan fushe duiwai wenhua ganbu zhuanxiuban (xi) de baogao ji chuli yiuian" [External Cultural Committee Report and Views on Handling Added Training Classes for External Cultural Cadres at the International Relations Institute], August 31, 1961, MFR 122-00171-03.
41 "Jiaoyu bu guanyu tongyi jianshao Beijing waiguoyu xueyuan he Guoji guanxi xueyuan 1961 nian zhaosheng zhibiao de han" [Letter from the Ministry of Education Concerning Agreement to Reduce 1961 Student Recruitment Targets for the Beijing Foreign Languages Academy and International Relations Institute], July–August 1961, MFR 122-00171-05.
42 "Duiwai wenhua lianluo weiyuanhui guanyu waiji jiaoyuan pingqing jihua ji guanli fangmian de yijian he xiangguan guiding" [Views and Related Regulations from the External Cultural Liaison Committee Concerning Planned Recruitment and Management of Foreign Instructors], PRC (State Council) External Cultural Liaison Committee, October 21, 1961, MFR 122-00177-03.
43 "Guanyu Jiaoyu si huiyi zhidu, Jiaoyu si de renwu, Fanyi chu gongzuo renwu, Xuexiao guanli chu de renwu, yeyu xuexiao renwu de taolun wenjian" [Discussion Documents Concerning the Education Section Meeting System and Tasks, Translation Department Work Tasks, School Management Department Tasks, and Part-Time School Tasks], January 1962, MFR 122-00067-02.
44 "Jiaoyu Bu dang zu guanyu sheli waiguo yu xuexiao de chubu yijian" [Preliminary Views from the Ministry of Education Leading Party Group Concerning Establishment of Foreign Languages Schools], March 17, 1962, MFR 122-00089-04.
45 "Jiaoyu bu guanyu zai ruogan da chengshi sheli waiguo xuexiao de jianyi" [Recommendation from the Ministry of Education Concerning Establishment of Foreign Language Schools in Several Large Cities], August 24, 1962, MFR 122-00089-17.
46 "Jiaoyu si 1962 nian gongzuo gaikuang he 1963 nian gongzuo guihua yaodian" [Education Section 1962 Work Situation and 1963 Work Plan Outline], January 28, 1963, MFR 122-00230-02.
47 See folio "Keji bu, Jiaoyu bu he Waijiao bu guanyu liuxuesheng gongzuo fengong wenti de tongzhi" [Ministry of Science, Ministry of Education, and Ministry of Foreign Relations Circular Concerning the Division of Responsibility Regarding Overseas Student Work], March 1961—June 1961, MFR 109-02991-01.
48 See folio "Zhongyang guanyu paiwang guo wai liuxuesheng guanli jiaoyu gongzuo de liang ge wenjian" [Two Central Documents Concerning Education Control Work for Students Sent Overseas], November 1963-March 1964, MFR 109-03477-01.

49 See "Zhongguo renmin duiwai wenhua xiehui he Zhongguo dui ge guo youhao xiehui mingce" [The Chinese People's External Cultural Association and List of Chinese People's Friendship Associations Established with Other Countries], January 1963, MFR 122-00284-02.
50 On PRC sport diplomacy in Africa, see Amanda Shuman, "Friendship Is Solidarity: The Chinese Ping-Pong Team Visits Africa in 1962," in *Sport and Diplomacy: Games within Games*, ed. J. Simon Rofe (Manchester: Manchester University Press, 2018), 110–29.
51 Zhou Lijuan, *Duiwai wenhua jiaoliu yu xin Zhongguo waijiao* [External Cultural Exchange and New China's Diplomacy] (Beijing: Wenhua yishu chubanshe, 2010), 55–56.
52 Ibid.
53 China Film Distribution and Exhibition Corporation, China Film Export and Import Corporation, *On the 35th Anniversary of China Film Distribution and Exhibition Corporation (1951-1986)* (Beijing: CFDEC & CFEIC, 1986), 106.
54 Ibid., 126.
55 Zhongyang renmin guangbo diantai tai shi bianxie zu, *Zhongyang renmin guangbo diantai tai shi ziliao huibian (1949-1984)* [Compiled and Edited Historical Materials of the Central People's Broadcasting Station (1949-1984)] (n.p., 1985), 713.
56 Zhou, *Duiwai wenhua jiaoliu yu xin Zhongguo waijiao*, 53.
57 Ibid., 62–63.
58 On the youth dimension of PRC diplomacy in Europe, see Perry Johansson, "Mao and the Swedish United Front against the USA," in *The Cold War in Asia*, ed. Zheng Yangwen, Hong Liu, and Michael Szonyi (Leiden: Brill, 2010), 231.

10

Whose Revolution? López Mateos, Kennedy's Mexican Visit, and the Alliance for Progress

Vanni Pettinà

Introduction

At around 11:00 a.m., on June 29, 1962, US president John Fitzgerald Kennedy, accompanied by his wife Jacqueline Lee Bouvier Kennedy, disembarked from an US Air Force Boeing 707 in Mexico City Central Airport, kicking off a three-day official visit to Mexico.[1] The presidential couple's renowned glamour did not disappoint the expectant Mexican crowds, gathered in large numbers outside the airport. Kennedy walked down the aircraft stairs wearing an elegant single breasted two-button grey suit, a blue long sleeve shirt, and a blue tie with white stripes, a set of clothing which Mexican newspapers proudly labeled as a typical example of the so-called Kennedy style. Jacqueline wore a matching coat in leaf green silk gazar, designed by the First Lady's personal couturier—the glamorous fashion designer Oleg Cassini. A twenty-one gun salute heralded their arrival as the Mexican president, Adolfo López Mateos, and his wife, Eva Sámano—joined by a crowd of twenty-five thousand shouting "Arriba Kennedy! Arriba Jaquelina!"—welcomed them. From there, the presidential motorcade departed to Los Pinos, the Mexican president's official residence, driving for 15 km through what a Mexican newspaper depicted as a "giant human fence" composed of workers, teachers, students, and common citizens cheering the convoy from both sides of the road. While some newspapers calculated that more than one million people accompanied the motorcade, others just declared the impossibility of estimating the exact number.[2] The Chilean ambassador to Mexico, Juan Smitmans López, trying to explain such a strong popular reaction to Kennedy's arrival, pointed to the 80,000 bureaucrats mobilized by the Partido Revolucionario Institucional (PRI) and the Confederación de Trabajadores de México (CTM), controlled by PRI, which had transported its affiliated members in trucks and paid them extra salaries in order to "facilitate their presence."[3]

At 12:40 p.m. the Kennedys and the Mateos entered Los Pinos where, finally freed from the official protocol and the cheering masses, the two presidents held their first private conversation, addressing the thorny issues which had marked Mexican-US relations during the two previous years.[4] The visit had begun.

Drawing on US, Mexican and other Latin American countries' primary sources and newspapers accounts, this piece aims to retrace Kennedy's visit to Mexico, addressing some of its political implications. Of particular interest are the sources collected in the General Directorate of Political and Social Investigations (Dirección General de Investigaciones Políticas y Sociales, DGIPS) of the Mexican National Archive (Archivo General de la Nación, AGN). DGIPS files show that the Mexican government generated a rather powerful system of propaganda around the visit, which came to include even the creation of an ad-hoc newspaper, *The Daily Good Neighbor*, published in English, which covered Kennedy's trip, trying to shape the public discourse surrounding it. The fact that the newspaper was published in English suggests that Mexican state propaganda efforts were not limited to its own citizens but aimed to shape the narrative of the visit at the international level.

The analysis of these sources shows that, while Kennedy's trip aimed to strengthen Mexico's engagement with the Alliance for Progress (AFP), the Mexican government, led by President López Mateos, used the visit rather successfully to frame the AFP as an offshoot of the 1911 Mexican Revolution. During the 1910s and the 1920s, a homogenous revolutionary program never existed. In fact, different contending political interpretations of the revolution cohabited at least until the late 1930s. However, by the early 1940s, these coalesced into a political project which hinged on the idea of state-led industrialization and—even if at times more rhetorically than practically—on a social reformist approach which drew on the extremely advanced 1917 Constitution.[5] Discursively subsuming the AFP's developmental goals under this specific idea of the Mexican Revolution allowed the Mexican government at least rhetorically to impose the primacy of the latter over the former. Assuming that the AFP represented a continuation of the Mexican Revolution's transformative process facilitated the Mexican embrace of Kennedy's hemispheric flagship program, avoiding the impression of forsaking the country's traditional attempts to defend its sovereignty and maintain an independent political stand in the region.[6] In addition, the trip, rather than weakening the hemispheric prestige of the country, showing Mexico as a remissive actor with regard to the United States, enhanced its status as an independent and legitimated foreign policy player at regional level.

Background and trip arrangements

Despite the heavy Ivy League glamour shown off at their arrival, the Kennedys' trip to Mexico was not meant to be just a pleasant, touristic tour of a country whose beauty had already enchanted the presidential couple during their honeymoon spent, in September 1953, in Acapulco. In point of fact, Kennedy's decision to visit the southern neighbor of the United States came as an attempt to directly address and possibly fix an array of thorny problems that had emerged between the two countries during the previous two years. US-Mexican relations were upset in particular by a clear disagreement about how to best handle the triumphant Cuban Revolution's destabilizing effects in the Western Hemisphere from January 1959.[7] Bilateral relations were also strained by President

López Mateos's attempts to reduce Mexico's political and economic dependence on the United States.[8] Mexico's search for a more independent position was reflected by the country's cold response to the AFP, the program which the Kennedy's administration announced during his inaugural address, on January 20, 1961, and launched formally in August 1961 at Punta del Este, Uruguay.[9] Before the trip was definitively scheduled for the end of June, the diplomatic frictions surrounding the Cuban quagmire made Kennedy cancel his visit to Mexico twice, in April and early December 1961.[10]

Like Washington, the Mexican government saw the visit as an important opportunity to release accumulated tensions and, more specifically, hoped it would help stabilize economic conditions, a crucial concern. Indeed, one of the most problematic effects of Mexico's cautious diplomatic approach to the Cuban Revolution had been economic. As a 1961 International Bank for Reconstruction and Development's paper analyzing Mexico's economic position highlighted, after decades of rapid expansion (6.2 percent per year), the year 1961 "was characterized by a lower rate of growth (3.5 percent), some uncertainty and reduced business confidence and by a heavy capital flight which resulted in a considerable loss of gold and foreign exchange reserves."[11] The challenging situation Mexico's economy was facing was in part rooted in the structural problems the country's process of industrialization begun experiencing in the late 1950s.[12] However, as US ambassador to Mexico, Thomas Mann, suggested in several reports, Mexico's mild reaction to the Cuban hemispheric challenge and, more in general, López Mateos's slacking reaction to the problem of international and domestic communism, had also generated concerns among national and foreign investors, increasing the volatility of the economy[13]. Mexico was not yet facing a situation of explicit crisis, but the economic slowdown the country was experiencing for economic and political reasons suggested to the López Mateos administration extreme prudence and made Washington's political and economic support particularly crucial in the summer of 1961. The Mexican president was therefore looking forward to using the political legitimation the trip could bestow on his government and the economic aid it hoped to negotiate directly with Kennedy.

Some of these concerns emerged in an interview that the newspaper *Excelsior* conducted, on the eve of Kennedy's trip, with Roberto Zapata, the director of Mexico's main corporative hotel conglomeration, Nacional Hotelera. In particular, Zapata highlighted that the presence of the American president in Mexico offered an opportunity for clarifying those political misunderstandings which, he insinuated, were responsible for generating economic tensions in Mexico: "I consider," he stated, "that President Kennedy's visit will help in a definitive way to restore the friendship ties between Mexico and the United States, whose friendship and identification lay far above of bad calculations that may exist."[14] The expression "bad calculations," used by Zapata, most probably referred to a critic assessment of López Mateos's Cuban policy and its consequences on the country's economy, a perception which was largely shared by the Mexican business community.

At the same time, for a country like Mexico, which during the 1920s had proudly adopted so-called revolutionary nationalism as the state's official ideology and the defense of its sovereignty as a national mantra, a too fast, too warm rapprochement with the powerful neighbor implied perils and challenges to the legitimacy of the PRI's political system. The Mexican government had to manage Kennedy's visit so to reaffirm the two countries' closeness but without giving the impression of renouncing to the basic principles of independence and autonomy that had marked Mexico's foreign policy since the triumph of the revolution.

The first step to achieve such potentially contradictory goals was assuring that Kennedy's visit developed without incidents or unwelcomed surprises. For that reason, as reported by the Chilean ambassador in Mexico City, Smitmans López, the Mexican government planned it down to the smallest detail. In the weeks previous to the trip, to avoid any relevant disturbance during Kennedy's visit, the federal government undertook a "cleaning" of Mexico City and increased its efforts at pacifying some of the most unrestful regions of the country. According to the Chilean ambassador, the Mexican government, using its almost dictatorial powers, had "cleaned the capital city and the countryside of all discontents, extremists or anti-Americans which existed and whose actions it is feared could generate problems during the visit of the illustrious guests." While the government seemed able to give a quick brushstroke of fresh paint to Mexico City, so as to offer an image of peace and cleanliness, Smitmans López highlighted how the tense situation that characterized the countryside has forced López Mateos to redouble policing efforts—with uncertain results. The government had sent fresh troops to Morelos, where the recent murder of a storied agrarian leader, Rubén Jaramillo, had stoked social tensions between peasants and the federal authorities accused of being responsible of his death. Additional troops were also sent to the southern states of Guerrero and Chiapas, which had also experienced vivid episodes of social unrest.[15] Although the CIA considered that Mexican security measures had been effective, General Chester V. Clifton (C. V. Clifton), military aide to the president, was put in charge of a contingency plan aimed to "establish military security with US forces for the President in Mexico" authorized "by verbal instructions only" and known only to a very limited number of general officers in the Pentagon and the White House staff.[16]

The program of the trip was also carefully studied and planned. Besides the bilateral talks with López Mateos and his staff, which would focus on political and economic issues, Kennedy personally requested that the program of his stay in Mexico included a visit to a Mexico City housing project and an agricultural communal land (*ejido*). Indeed, as Secretary of State Dean Rusk communicated to Mann, "President would like (. . .) visit rural development project (ejido) near Mexico City and see low cost housing projects. Purposes such visit demonstrate President's interest in lower income groups."[17] While the final program actually included a tour of a Mexico City project house, the Unidad Habitacional Independencia, the requested excursion to an *ejido* disappeared from the program, replaced by a visit to the Basilica of Our Lady of Guadalupe, the recognized symbol of Catholic Mexicans. Apparently, the decision to cancel the visit to the *ejido* and to the cooperative sugar mill of Zacatepec, three hours driving distance from Mexico City, was canceled due to Kennedy's back pain, which made long car trips impossible.[18] From Washington's point of view, the selection of the visit's main hotspots was made with the intention of offering Kennedy a comfortable ground to show his personal commitment to a progressive solution to Latin American and Mexican social problems.

But as we shall see, such places also granted Mexico a particularly favorable scenario to consolidate Mexico's image as a modern country and, above all, to promote the idea that the Mexican Revolution and its social programs represented the base of such advancements. Affirming that social reforms had been at the root of the country's rapid achievements, the Mexican government attempted, rather successfully, to establish the Mexican Revolution as the great precursor of the AFP, thus facilitating a more fluid interaction with Kennedy's flagship program for the Americas.

Kennedy's visit brief

The background paper on Mexico, prepared by the presidential staff and which Kennedy read before undertaking his trip, depicted Mexico City as "located in the large, bowl-shaped Anahuac Valley (. . .) at an altitude of 7.350 feet above sea level, making it the highest major city in the world." The dossier also highlighted that the city's extraordinary altitude was not its only peculiarity. Mexico City was "also the oldest metropolis on the American continent," built "on the site of the old Aztec capital and named after an Aztec chieftain." Besides the attractive geographic setting and an ancient, mythical past, Mexico City was also a vibrant spot, offering "amusements and entertainments for every taste." Mexico City was becoming "a gourmet center" while "the ballet was developing its own modern dance forms." Sunday afternoon bullfighting was certainly an attraction worth being mentioned, balanced by the more sophisticated and renowned musical events, "particularly in the summer, with an opera season featuring Mexican and Metropolitan Opera stars." The paper then listed some of the most important historical places of the city such as Mexico City's main plaza, the so-called Zocalo, the cathedral, depicted as "the oldest and largest church in the American continent" built "on the remains of the Great Aztec Temple." The National Palace, with Diego Rivera's 1931 "famous frescos," the Palace of Fine Arts (Palacio de Bellas Artes), Los Pinos, the "modest presidential residence (. . .) located at the end of the Chapultepec Park, described as one of the most beautiful natural parks in the world," were all listed, along with the Basilica of Guadalupe, among the most important highlights offered by the city.[19]

The sketch portrayed a city which blended a great, ancient past with a stroke of modernity that, in point of fact, resulted in a partial description, insofar as it did not include, for example, the slums generated by a breakneck urbanization process and the social imbalances of Mexico's development model which the city embodied. However, the dossier also showed a certain degree of accuracy. It emphasized that the city epitomized the social and cultural dynamism that the country's economic boom— the so-called Mexican Miracle, with an astonishing 6 percent average rate of economic growth between the late 1940s and the late 1950s—had unleashed in the city and the nation as a whole.

In this sense, crucially, Kennedy's paper reflected the image that at least some Mexicans had of their own country and capital city and that they were eager to show to the world. A letter sent by a reader, Ramón C. Cervantes, to the newspaper *El Universal*, summarized this pride for the modernity achieved by his country. Concluding his piece, he stated that he wished Kennedy had enough time to appreciate "how far we have arrived in our progress. Contemporary Mexico is a long way from that of fifty years ago!"[20]

The first day of the visit

During their three-day trip, the Kennedys had actually a chance to visit a good number of the captivating places which Mexico City offered, following a program that balanced old and modern locations. On Friday, after leaving Los Pinos, the Kennedys had lunch at the National Palace. Mrs. Kennedy then departed toward the National Museum of Anthropology, where she visited a crypt containing a Mayan tomb recently brought to Mexico City form the Palenque ruins and "the famous Aztec Calendar stone." The Kennedys met again at the end of the evening at the Palace of Fine Arts (Palacio de Bellas Artes) for a gala performance of the Ballet Folklórico de México.[21]

Mexican newspapers summed up the political gist of the first day of the Kennedys' trip in a quite straightforward way. *El Universal*'s main headline, on Saturday morning, declared in big type that "Mexico and the US walks similar revolutionary paths," while *Novedades* certified that the Mexican Revolution had finally been understood by Mexico's northern neighbor.[22] As the Chilean ambassador in Mexico underlined, it did not matter that Mexican newspapers were exaggerating in their reporting of the trip's political implications, because "it is evident that the quoted headlines mirror the feelings expressed in Mexico."[23]

It was indeed evident that Mexican newspapers, in a country where the national press was politically and financially dependent on the state, were responding to the government's attempt to steer the public narrative of the trip and its political meaning in a particular direction.[24] While a good part of the press accounts highlighted the astonishing warmth with which the Mexican people had welcomed the Kennedys, many papers also focused on the convergence between the Mexican revolution's social goals and the Alliance for Progress' aims, which Kennedy had come to promote in Mexico. As we will see, this reading implied that somehow, after decades of misunderstanding in which the United States had inconsistently and wrongly perceived the Mexican Revolution as a chaotic, anarchic, or even a communist process, Washington was finally acknowledging its historical importance as a project producing much needed social transformations.

The second day of the visit

The idea of a supposed continuity between the Mexican Revolution and the AFP reached its climax in the public discourse during the second day of Kennedy's visit, when the US president realized his first and unique incursion into Mexico's experiment in social policies. On Saturday, after placing a floral wreath at the Monument of

Independence, Kennedy drove to the Independencia Housing Project, a vast social housing complex built by the Mexican Social Security Institute (IMSS), a governmental agency founded in the early 1940s and responsible for granting Mexican citizens public health, pensions, and social security, including social housing.25

The Mexican political police's archives kept records of the newspaper, *The Daily Good Neighbor*, which the López Mateos government created on purpose just to cover Kennedy's visit. The paper offers a precise sense of the message which, according to the Mexican government, the US president's presence in Mexico and, in particular, at the Unidad Independencia, should convey to both national and international audiences. Published in English and edited by Coronel Jose García Valseca, a news tycoon with strong connections to several Mexican governments since the late 1940s, the *Daily Good Neighbor* meticulously covered the entire Kennedy's visit. An important section of the second-day issue was dedicated to magnifying the relevance of the housing project built by the IMSS. "The Unidad," proclaimed the short-lived newspaper, "is neither a city nor a housing project but something in between that combines the best features of both." Independencia was built to address housing problems related to the process of urban sprawl common to the United States and Mexico, which in the latter case was exacerbated by the high volume of domestic rural migration to cities. Designed to accommodate more than 10,000 people, the housing complex was inaugurated in September 1960. Directly inspired by a functionalist architectural approach and, as the *Daily Good Neighbor* reminded its audience, by the 1933 Athens Charter on Urban Planning elaborated by the Swiss architect Le Corbusier, it integrated gardens and playgrounds, medical facilities, nurseries, schools, supermarkets, and a theater. Among the many urban innovations portrayed in the Athens Charter, Independencia recovered an important concept put forward by Le Corbusier in his essay "La Ville Radieuse" (The Radiant City): class-free urban and housing planning. As the promotional newspaper reported, "There will be no class separation in the housing developments.... Manuel [*sic*] and white collars workers, professionals, businessmen and artisans will be included." What is more, "that former status-symbol of the rich, the tower apartment, is intended, in the UNIDAD, for occupancy by families of worker or white-collar affiliates who work in shops, offices or factories."26

The Daily Good Neighbor's description of the housing complex tellingly revealed what image of Mexico López Mateos's government sought to project. The idea of a utopian, class-free society embodied by Independencia broadly dovetailed with Kennedy's ambitious plan—rooted in modernization theory; implemented as a regional sprout in the AFP—to drive "backward" societies to a more advanced stage of development, marked by the absence of class conflict.27 Independencia offered an opportunity to show that the Mexican path to a more advanced stage of development relied on a strategy of social reforms without socialism. In the context of the Cuban socialist challenge to the hemispheric order, such an approach was particularly attractive for the Kennedy's administration as an alternative example to Cuba for the Americas.

The compatibility between the social reforms carried out by the Mexican Revolution and the AFP's goals was not the only aspect that the *Daily Good Neighbor* highlighted in its description of Unidad Independencia. The newspaper also translated a fragment of Instituto Mexicano del Seguro Social (Mexican Social Security Institute, IMMS)

Director General Benito Coquet's official description of Independencia: "A part of a social works program of the government which guarantees the freedom and security of its citizens, and which they won in their secular struggles in order to insure the individual and common well-being and happiness of all Mexicans." Portraying Independencia as a typical product of the Mexican government's social policy, which finally addressed the Mexican people's secular fight for social justice that had culminated in the Mexican Revolution, *The Daily Good Neighbor*, and thus the Mexican government, was trying to establish the primacy of the country's revolution over similar, more recent attempts, such as Kennedy's AFP, to promote and carry out social reforms in the region.

Kennedy's tour of Independencia and his speech at the end of his visit echoed the *Daily Good Neighbor*'s argument. The president, accompanied by Coquet, other senior IMMS officials, and Ambassador Mann, took a car tour of the project and got acquainted with its functioning and features. He then walked for a block "going from person to person, shaking hands with men, women and children." Rehearsing almost by heart a script that had been prepared well in advance of the trip, the president finally entered a ground floor apartment, without photographers and journalists, and came out to be eventually photographed with the family occupying the apartment.[28] According to *El Universal*, the house Kennedy had visited belonged to the worker Roberto Sahagún Hernández, thirty-nine years old, married to Magdalena Maldonado and father of eleven children. Sahagún Hernández worked as a textile worker, earning a daily salary of $4, to which he added the non-specified income of his two eldest daughters, and paying a $24 monthly rent for the apartment they occupied.[29] This family represented a perfect example of the social policies whose impact the Mexican government wanted to show off.

It could of course be, as the Chilean ambassador maliciously asserted, that Kennedy had not visited a social housing complex meant for workers but, in reality, for well-connected public employees.[30] Then again, Sahagún Hernández's life story showed that the project was a quite well-accomplished example of functionalist architecture, built by the state for its own citizens, including those with little economic resources, at rather affordable prices. In any case, the success of Mexico's efforts at weaving a public narrative of the visit favorable to its own interests surfaced in Kennedy's own speech (Figure 10.1): "I have been in many places with housing which has been developed under government influences," he stated in English, "but I have never seen any projects in which governments have played their part which have fountains and statues and grass and trees, which are as important to the concept of the home as the roof itself."[31] Even more importantly, at the end of his speech, Kennedy pointed to the fact that political freedom was inseparable from social justice and that Mexico's social housing policies, epitomized by Unidad Independencia, showed that the Mexican Revolution had understood this indissoluble connection. It was time for all the other Latin American countries as well to realize the absolute importance of this principle, to move forward following the goals set by "that great hemispheric movement called 'Alianza para el Progreso'"[32] (Figure 10.1).

In sum, three interlinked elements emerged with clarity from Kennedy's visit and speech at Independencia. There were alternatives to the Cuban model for social change; Mexican social reformism, embodied by Independencia, was a case in point;

Figure 10.1 Kennedy, at the microphones, delivers remarks during his visit to the Unidad Independencia (Independencia Housing Project) in Mexico City, 30 June 1962.[33]

and, finally, the AFP pointed in the selfsame direction as the Mexican model. Although Kennedy must have found this line of reasoning useful for himself, especially to market the AFP, it is clear that the connections drawn in the speech fully satisfied Mexico's goals, too.

The second day of the trip concluded with Jacqueline Kennedy visiting the Instituto Nacional de la Protección de la Infancia (INPI) factory, producing and dispensing packaged and dehydrated milk for Mexican schoolchildren. On his side, Kennedy concluded a day entirely focused on promoting AFP's goals driving back to Los Pinos, where he and López Mateos, signed an agricultural credit agreement. The loan, $20 million disbursed under the AFP by USAID, was aimed to raise income and opportunities in rural areas. Along with assisting farmers through supervised low-interest rate credits, the loan supported the construction of small irrigation works, self-help farming, water treatment facilities, farm to market roads, and rural electrification.[34] It represented less than 8 percent of existing credits to Mexican farmers from private and government institutions, an indication of Mexico's reluctance to join in full AFP's programs. Although originating in the US embassy and having primarily a social objective, the loan was jointly designed by US and Mexican officers to increase production on economically viable farms. And interestingly enough, it was modified by Mexican officers, who argued successfully that to increase campesinos' living standards, it was first necessary to raise agricultural productivity.[35]

The Mexican press, with the *Daily Good Neighbor* leading the way, celebrated that the $20 million, "almost interest free, seal US pledge to help agrarian reform."[36] As for Kennedy himself, it was telling that at the end of the ceremony that followed signing the loan, he once again paid homage to Mexico. "As your own Mexican Revolution has so vividly demonstrated—until all the campesino*s* of the hemisphere have the opportunity to own the land they till, until they are given the resources to till that land productively (...) until that day the peaceful revolution of the Americas will not be completed."[37] If we take seriously Kennedy's declarations, it was rather evident that by the end of the second day of his visit, the Mexican government had been able to impose its own narrative of the trip, portraying it as a US acknowledgment of the Mexican Revolution rather than just a successful promotion of the AFP.

The third day of the visit

On the last day of their stay in Mexico, the Kennedys had a chance to display their faith and their closeness to the Mexican people by attending mass in the Basilica de Guadalupe. In Ambassador Mann's words, this was "the emotional apex of the visit as far as the Mexican public was concerned.... News of the President of the United States worshipping at the shrine of the 'Virgen Morena' (Dark Virgin), venerated as Mexico's national miracle even by nominal or 'anti-clerical' Catholics of this country, has reached every corner of the Mexican countryside."[38]

Mann was right in arguing that the fact that the Basilica represented a public space, in which Mexican "religion and nationalism are intermixed," allowed Kennedy to garner the approval of vast sectors of the Mexican population. However, as Mexican newspapers correctly argued, visiting the Dark Virgin could also be read as another proof of the president's obeisance to Mexico's history and traditions. *Excelsior* explained the polysemic meaning of Kennedy's attendance of the mass in the Basilica well. "For the first time in history, an US President, kneeled, with affection, in front of the Virgen Morena."[39] With the usual exaggeration, but reinforcing the narrative of the Kennedys' visit during the three days, *El Nacional*, the PRI's official newspaper, closed its coverage of the visit by headlining "Mexico's national interest prevailed."[40]

Conclusion: Whose revolution?

We probably should not take this headline too seriously. In fact, at the end of his trip, Kennedy could declare himself quite satisfied with what he had achieved. The US president could proudly claim that he had been warmly welcomed by the largest Spanish-speaking country in the world and one of the most influential in the region. During his stay, Kennedy was able to strengthen his image as a social reformer, committed to a progressive solution of Latin American economic and social problems with important, positive consequences for his stand in the region. From the trip,

Kennedy's flagship program, the AFP, emerged stronger and in better shape. Even so, as this article has shown analyzing this important moment in US-Mexican relations, according to several privileged observers and actors involved in the visit, Mexico had probably obtained more from Kennedy's trip than what it had given in return. In a letter sent to Mexico's minister of Interior, Gustavo Díaz Ordaz, the day after the conclusion of Kennedy's visit, the Mexican ambassador to London, Antonio Armendáriz, vividly expressed his amusement about the benefits his country had achieved. "What impresses me more," he wrote, "has been our president's capacity to obtain Kennedy's acknowledgment that the ideas of our Revolution' represents the base of his program for an Alliance for Progress."[41]

Neither did Kennedy's symbolic and material concessions to Mexico escape the attention of Chilean ambassador Smitmans López who, as seen, had followed the US president's trip with interest and some bitterness. Commenting on the results of the visit, he affirmed that "there is no doubt that for Mexico, for its touristic, industrial and economic development future in general, as for the US policy of investments in this country, this trip represented the highest hope and it had an extraordinary magnitude and meaning." In this sense, he continued, "the visit has represented for Mexico the greatest advertising, political, economic and touristic achievement that the country could hope for." The Mexican politicians, he thought, had shown to have skills "extraordinarily superior" to those of their neighbors. They had achieved important practical results but, above everything, offered an image of political and social cohesiveness that presented Mexico as one of the most important countries and, in Latin America, "the one of major hierarchy." The proof par excellence of Mexico's achievements lay in Kennedy pronouncing the word "revolution" innumerable times during his stay, even more than López Mateos himself. Willingly and consciously or not, the US president had done Mexico's bidding, conveying an image of the Mexican Revolution as "the inspiration for his Alliance for Progress." This showed also in López Mateos and Kennedy's final joint communique. It asserted that "the fundamental goal of the Mexican Revolution is the same as the Alliance for Progress—social justice and economic progress within the framework of individual freedom and political liberty."[42] This was a clear diplomatic victory for Mexico's positions in the Chilean ambassador's eyes.[43] And he was not alone. Kennedy's reliance on the word "revolution" had been such that during a reception, the Soviet ambassador to Mexico, Vladimir Bazikin, joked to Smitmans López that now Latin American countries could choose between two revolutionaries, Kennedy and Nikita Khrushchev, both committed to deep social changes in the world.[44]

Smitmans López's bitterness knew no limits. A few days after Kennedy's departure, he visited US ambassador Mann to "congratulate" him on the good results achieved by Kennedy's visit. Poking his counterpart, he asked, with simulated naivete, if there was any private text complementing the final declaration: "I thought that the published text was the Mexican version and that yours was kept secret." "There is no such thing," Mann replied, "and if you are saying this because the Declaration clearly favors Mexico let me tell you that this is a country that receives a lot and gives back nothing."[45]

The trip was over.

Notes

1 "Las once horas de hoy, el momento histórico," *El Nacional*, June 29, 1962, 1; "Ambos mandatarios viajaron juntos de pie a bordo de un automóvil descubierto," *El Nacional*, June 30, 1962, 4.
2 "Clara demostración de simpatía y afecto," *El Universal*, June 30, 1962, 11.
3 Embajada de Chile en México, Confidencial 56, "Visita del Presidente Kennedy," July 2, 1962, 4, Oficios Confidenciales 1962, E-R, vol. 7 (OC/1962/E-R/7), Embachile Mexico (EM), Archive of the Chilean Ministry of Foreign Affairs (ACMF).
4 Archivo Genaro Estrada de la Secretaría de Relaciones Exteriores (AGESRE), "Schedule President Kennedy," XIV-615-1, Septima Parte, no date.
5 On the history of the process of revolutionary consolidations see, Paul Gillingham and Benjamin Smith, ed., *Dictablanda: Politics, Work, and Culture in Mexico, 1938-1968* (Durham: Duke University Press, 2014); Soledad Loaeza, "Modernización autoritaria a la sombra de la Superpotencia, 1944-1968," in *Nueva Historia General de México*, eds. Erik Velásquez García et al. (México: El Colegio de México, 2010), 1936–72; Luis Medina Peña, *Hacia el nuevo estado: México, 1920-1993* (México, D.F.: Fondo de Cultura Económica, 1994); Alan Knight, *The Mexican Revolution* (Cambridge: Cambridge University Press, 1986); Blanca Torres, *Hacia la Utopía Industrial: Historia de la Revolución Mexicana*, vol. 21 (México, D.F.: El Colegio de México, 1984).
6 On Mexico's idea of national sovereignty and its defense, see Christy Thornton, "A Mexican International Economic Order? Tracing the Hidden Roots of the Charter of Economic Rights and Duties of States," *Humanity* 9, no. 3 (2018): 389–421.
7 On the impact of the Cuban Revolution in Mexico and on US-Mexican relations, see Olga Pellicer, *México y la Revolución Cubana* (México, D.F.: El Colegio de México, 1972); Ana Covarrubias, "Las Relaciones Mexico-Cuba: Caribe, 1959-2010," en *Historia de las relaciones internacionales de México, 1821-2010*, vol. 3, ed. Mercedes de Vega (México, D.F.: Secretaría de Relaciones Exteriores, Dirección General del Acervo Histórico Diplomático, 2011); Renata Keller, *Mexico's Cold War: Cuba, the United States, and the Legacy of the Mexican Revolution* (New York: Cambridge University Press, 2015).
8 On Mexico's attempts to develop an autonomous foreign policy, see Vanni Pettinà, "Global Horizons: Mexico, the Third World, and the Non-Aligned Movement at the Time of the 1961 Belgrade Conference," *IHR* 38, no. 4 (2016): 741–64.
9 Scholarship has largely neglected the history of Mexico's interaction with the AFP. There is no monograph on this topic and general references can be found in time-worn works such as Mario Ojeda, *Alcances y límites de la política exterior de México* (México, D.F.: El Colegio de México, Centro de Estudios Internacionales, 2001). On the AFP, see Stephen Rabe, *The Most Dangerous Area in the World: John F. Kennedy Confronts Communist Revolution in Latin America* (Chapel Hill: University of North Carolina Press, 1999); Jeffrey Taffet, *Foreign Aid as Foreign Policy: the Alliance for Progress in Latin America* (New York: Routledge, 2007). On Mexico's reluctance to join the AFP, see "Politico-Economic Assessment," April 3, 1962, 9, 712.00/4-362, Record Group (RG) 59, National Archives, College Park (NARA).
10 "Memorandum for Ralph A. Dungan, Subject: Visit of López Mateos," April 11, 1961; Outgoing Telegram, Department of State, January 6, 1961; Embassy Telegram 1633 and 1634, December 6, 1961; Embassy Telegram 1633 and 1634, December 6, 1961; Incoming Telegram 1744, Mexico City to Secretary of State, December 17,

1961; Incoming Telegram 1759, Mexico City to Department of State, December 19, 1961; Outgoing Telegram, Department of State, Embtel 1832, December 29, 1961; all in Box 141, National Security Files / Countries (NSF/C), John Fitzgerald Kennedy Presidential Library (JKFL). See also: Outgoing Telegram, Department of State "re Presidential Visit," April 9, 1962.
11 International Bank for Reconstruction and Development, "Current Economic Position and Prospects of Mexico," April 10, 1961, I.
12 On Mexico's economic structural problems, see Enrique Cárdenas, "La economía en el dilatado siglo xx, 1929-2009," in *Historia económica general de México*, ed. Sandra Kuntz Ficker (México, D.F.: El Colegio de México, 2010).
13 See Incoming Telegram, n. 54, Mexico City to Secretary of State, July 8, 1961, Box 141, NSF, JFKL; President's Visit to Mexico, Scope Paper, no date, approx. June 1962, Classified Subject File, WH-41, 8/52/A/7/5, White House Files, Papers of Arthur M. Schlesinger, Jr., JFKL; Incoming Message, American Embassy Mexico City to White House, December 2, 1961, Box 141, NSF, JFKL. On Mexico's problematic economic situation, see Vanni Pettinà, "Global Horizons."
14 "La pregunta de hoy: ¿Qué opina usted de la visista del Presidente Kennedy y su esposa a México?" *Excelsior*, June 11, 1962.
15 Chilean Embassy in Mexico to the Ministry of Foreign Affairs, "Preparativos para la visita de J.F. Kennedy: Empréstitos; problema protocolar; limpieza; pacificación," June 23, 1962, OC/1962/E-R/7, EM, ACMF.
16 CIA, "Security Conditions in Mexico," June 28, 1962, Box 236, Trips and Conferences, NSF, JFKL; Joint Chief of Staff, "Memorandum for the President," June 28, 1962; "Memorandum for the Record. Visit of Major General C. V. Clifton to J3 re: Presidential Visit to Mexico," June 21, 1962.
17 Outgoing Telegram, "Presidential Visit," April 9, 1962, Box 237, Trips and Conferences, NSF, JFKL.
18 "Cerimonial," XIV-613-12, Segunda Parte, May 8, 1962, AGESRE.
19 "The President Trip's to Mexico: Background Paper: Items of Interest about Mexico City and Environs," June 19, 1962, Box 237, Trips and Conferences, NSF, JFKL.
20 "Una gran labor," *El Universal*, June 30, 1962, 2.
21 "Visit of the President of the United States and Mrs. John F. Kennedy to Mexico City, June 29-July 1, 1962," September 13, 1962, 6, Box 237, Trips and Conferences, NSF, JFKL.
22 "Marchan Mexico y EU por afines rutas revolucionarias," *El Universal*, June 30, 1962, 1; Embajada de Chile en México, Confidencial 56, "Visita del Presidente Kennedy," July 2, 1962, 4, OC/1962/E-R/7, EM, ACMF. For "Novedades," see ibid., 3.
23 Ibid., 4.
24 On the connections between the Mexican press and state, see Karine Bohmann, *Medios de comunicación y sistemas informativos en México* (México: Alianza Editorial, 1997).
25 On the IMMS, see Guillermo Farfán, *Los orígenes del Seguro Social en México: un enfoque neoinstitucionalista histórico* (México, D.F.: Universidad Nacional Autónoma de México, 2009).
26 *The Daily Good Neighbor*, July 1, 1962, 7, Box 2936 Exp 1, Archivo General de la Nación, Investigaciones Políticas y Sociales, México, D.F. (IPS).
27 On the theory of modernization and its impact on Kennedy's foreign policy, see Nils Gilman, *Mandarins of the Future: Modernization Theory in Cold War America*

(Baltimore: Johns Hopkins University Press, 2003); Michael Latham, *The Right Kind of Revolution* (Ithaca: Cornell University Press, 2011).

28 "Visita del Excelentisimo Señor Presidente Kennedy a la Unidad Independencia del Instituto Mexicano del Seguro Social," sin fecha, XIV-613-2, Segunda Parte, AGESRE; "Visit of the President of the United States and Mrs. John F. Kennedy to Mexico City, June 29-July 1, 1962," September 13, 1962, 7, Box 236, Trips and Conferences, NSF, JFKL.
29 "Visitó casa de modesta amilia," *El Universal*, July 1, 1962, 25; translation into Spanish of "Estados Unidos y México hacia una nueva era," *Chicago Sunday Tribune*, July 1, 1962, Box 2936 Exp 1, IPS.
30 Embajada de Chile en México, "Preparativos para la visita de J.F. Kennedy: Empréstitos; problema protocolar; limpieza; pacificación," June 23, 1962, 3, OC/1962/E-R/7, EM, ACMF.
31 "Ciudad para vivir," *El Universal*, July 1, 1962, 15.
32 Jacobo Zabludowsky, *J. F. Kennedy, López Mateos y América. Resumen de tres días de visita del Presidente J. F. Kennedy a México* (Mexico: Costa-Amic, 1962), 84.
33 Kennedy Visits Independencia Housing Project, Mexico City, KN-22510, Digital Identifier JFKWHP-KN-C22648, Folder Digital Identifier JFKWHP-1962-06-30-B, JFKL.
34 "Background on Agricultural Credit Loan Signed during the Visit of President John F. Kennedy to Mexico," no date, Box 236, Trips and Conferences, NSF, JFKL.
35 Telegram, Mexico City to State Department n. 3617, "Presidential Visit," June 13, 1962, Box 236, Trips and Conferences, NSF, JFKL.
36 *The Daily Good Neighbor*, July 1, 1962, 1, Box 2936 Exp 1, IPS.
37 "Comments by President Kennedy when the Agricultural Credit Agreement was Signed," no date, 2, Box 236, Trips and Conferences, NSF, JFKL.
38 "Implications of President Kennedy's Visit to Mexico," September 13, 1962, 5, Box 236, Trips and Conferences, NSF, JFKL.
39 "Se prostraron él y su esposa ante la Virgen," *El Excelsior*, July 2, 1962, 1A.
40 "Se impuso el interés de México," *El Nacional*, July 2, 1962, 1.
41 "EmbaMex GB informa opiniones prensa británica sobre visita Kennedy a Mex," July 3, 1962, Box 2936 Exp 1, IPS.
42 "Joint Communique Issued Between President John F. Kennedy and President Adolfo López Mateos Following Discussions in Mexico City," June 29–30, 1962, Box 236, Trips and Conferences, NSF, JFKL.
43 Embajada de Chile en México, Confidencial n. 56, "Visita del Presidente Kennedy. Su Extraordinaria Importancia para México (. . .)," July 2, 1962, OC/1962/E-R/7, EM, ACMF.
44 Ibid.
45 Ibid.

Camelot in Korea: The Paradox of John F. Kennedy in Authoritarian South Korea, 1961–63

Inga Kim Diederich

Introduction: Cold War image-making and charismatic leadership

The ubiquitous popularity of John F. Kennedy in Cold War authoritarian South Korea (Republic of Korea [ROK]) presents a paradox for the clear-cut political affinities that otherwise divided domestic Korean political forces. This chapter examines how Kennedy's presidential administration was received in South Korea, and how different Korean actors deployed his political and social symbolism toward conflicting ends. Specifically, it focuses on the tension between the Kennedy administration's considerable political authority as inheritor of the clientelist US-ROK alliance, on the one hand, and the charismatic promise of postcolonial ideals that Kennedy as a person symbolized in the Third World, on the other. Particularly in the first years of Park Chung Hee's military rule, state actors and non-state actors alike called on the liberal aspirations of Kennedy's "Camelot" to support their separate agendas of, respectively, shoring up Park's political authority and agitating against authoritarian rule. Whether Kennedy was invoked to legitimate Park's rule, as in Park's highly publicized 1961 White House visit, or appealed to as a symbol of liberal egalitarianism by anti-regime advocates in 1962 demonstrations agitating for a Status of Forces Agreement, his persona remained sacrosanct.

Alongside detailed analyses of state documents and popular periodicals, this chapter also examines Kennedy's symbolic power through visual representations, ranging from photographs to political cartoons. Such textual and visual evidence demonstrates the paradoxical place Kennedy occupied in a specific locale, South Korea, in a moment of flux between democratic promise and authoritarian reality. This case was a variation of a global trend—contradictory representations of the Kennedy ideal and the realities of American empire—and hence has broader implications for understanding the changing position of the United States in the early 1960s, ambiguously caught between sympathy for Third World decolonization and Cold War realpolitik.

Kennedy in Korea: Legitimacy and material support

Although characterized by temperamental differences that affected their leadership styles, a number of overlaps nonetheless marked the personal backgrounds and professional trajectories of Kennedy and Park Chung Hee. Both were born in 1917, had served in the military, and were committed to reformatory missions that carried them into power.[1] In 1960, Kennedy's "new frontier" mission won him the US presidential election, while in 1961 Park's zealotry for a "new age" inspired the military coup that secured him a position of political primacy as chairman of the Supreme Council for National Reconstruction (SCNR).[2] The two also shared a keen awareness of the power of image and perception in politics. In spite of his illness, Kennedy famously presented himself as the quintessence of youthful energy, invoking the "unfilled hopes" of liberal domestic policies and the "unknown opportunities" of international horizons. In contrast to Kennedy's open smile, Park circumspectly hid behind his trademark sunglasses and military attire, but nonetheless projected an indomitable will to propel his country from war-torn poverty into a new age of economic prosperity.[3] Both leaders forcefully presented themselves as the embodiments of watershed moments in their respective national histories and as heralds of a new age for the US-Korean alliance.

When Kennedy entered office, US planning in Korea was undergoing a shift away from a strict military focus toward a new emphasis on political, economic, and cultural persuasion. Since 1945, US involvement in Korea had been driven by military imperatives such as the ongoing lack of resolution to the Korean War (1950–53).[4] In the late 1950s, however, American policymakers began to reconceptualize containment as a matter of political, economic, and cultural persuasion, as much as military coercion.[5] This reassessment of South Korea's place in American Cold War strategy coincided with the emergence of a new form of liberal internationalism that sought to reshape the image of an internationally engaged America into one of necessary engagement and paternal benevolence.[6] US interests in postcolonial nations were sentimentally repackaged as a natural sympathetic outgrowth of a shared colonial past and an inextricably entwined future in the emerging globalized free world.[7]

As part of this general shift toward an integrationist vision of America's place in the global order, the late 1950s and early 1960s were marked by a growing consensus among American officials that it was high time for a serious reconsideration of US policy in Korea. Shortly after his inauguration, Kennedy received a memorandum from Walt Rostow warning that "all hands agree that the situation in Korea is not good" and urging that the "fresh look" promised in the 1960 American presidential election be applied in Korea as well.[8] State Department representative Donald Macdonald reported consistent failings in US programs in Korea since 1945, marked by an emphasis on stopgaps, attention to "petty detail" rather than the broader picture, and excessive bureaucracy.[9] Meanwhile Hugh D. Farley, deputy director of the US Operations Mission (USOM) in Seoul, found the conjunction of the embedded corruption in Korean institutions, the precipitous deterioration of political stability, and the incompetency of USOM leadership sufficient to "warrant emergency consideration and immediate action" and recommending a "crash program" redirecting the energies of both Republic of Korea Government (ROKG) and United States Forces Korea (USFK) personnel.[10] While his strategic recommendations were dismissed as alarmist, there was general agreement with his characterization of the "Korean picture" as one with "which we have failed to come to grips for eight years."[11] "In short," an exploratory investigation report concluded, "South Korea is basically so weak economically and unsteady politically that internal crisis or threat of crisis will be the norm, not the exception, over the years ahead."[12]

Meanwhile, in South Korea itself, Kennedy enjoyed a prominence equal to that of his stature in the United States. His popularity there was boosted by the fortuitous coincidence of his election with a wave of youth-led political populism. In April 1960, as Kennedy's presidential campaign was picking up steam in the States, a massive popular movement spearheaded by students was ousting the authoritarian Syngman Rhee government from power and installing South Korea's first true parliamentary democracy: the April 19 Revolution. The "Second Republic" lifted government restrictions on the press, resulting in an explosion of new outlets at precisely the moment of the 1960 US presidential race.[13]

While the liberated press was quick to exercise its newfound right to critique subjects like domestic political corruption and the ongoing US military presence in Korea, it also ardently believed in the potential for meaningful reform. General papers and specialized monthly journals alike seized on Kennedy as the personification of the ideals of the April Revolution and reported every detail of his political goals and personal background. Newspapers like *Chosŏn Ilbo* reprinted AP daily briefs on his schedule, intellectual journals like *Sasanggye* editorialized on his leadership qualities, and women's magazines like *Yŏwŏn* highlighted his desirability as a husband and father.[14] Demand for information about Kennedy was so high that James Macgregor Burns's biography of Kennedy, *John Kennedy: A Political Profile*, released in the United States in January 1960, was immediately translated into Korean and available for purchase ahead of Kennedy's inauguration in January 1961.[15] At the heart of this extensive coverage was a deep investment in an American president who would be a sympathetic partner in South Korea's sociopolitical transformation, sharing with Korean reformists the key qualities of youthful innovation, practical intellectualism, and committed idealism.

While South Korea's First Republic had conformed to a culture that venerated the wisdom of age rather than the vitality of youth—personified in President Syngman Rhee—the Second Republic eschewed the traditional age hierarchy in favor of student revolutionaries. In the wake of the uprising, newspapers ran previously unprintable cartoons pillorying the age veneration system, like a *Chosŏn Ilbo* panel captioned "Now read after me" that showed students teaching their elders the meaning of "democracy." Korean press coverage of Kennedy was in line with this new public approbation for the positive qualities of youth. Prior to Kennedy's inauguration, a profile in the journal *Saebyŏk* introduced him as the young scion of a family with an impeccable political pedigree, whose "New Frontier" was the most promising political agenda since Franklin Roosevelt's "New Deal."[16] Meanwhile, an article in *Sasanggye* anticipated the concerns of more conservative readers, assuring them that Kennedy's youth was an asset by noting that "America is a new country . . . and Kennedy's youth gives him his vision, and the energy needed to carry out his plans."[17]

To assuage concerns over the impetuosity and inexperience that might hamper the young president, intellectual journals highlighted Kennedy's intelligence and education. A *Saebyŏk* editorial immediately after his election described him as an expert in international affairs, "particularly respected in Europe, where his Harvard thesis is widely read," and "more interested in the situation in the Far East than his predecessors."[18] Intellectuals were particularly impressed by Kennedy's "brain trust," resulting in a 1961 *Sasanggye* series profiling each member individually.[19] According to this series, the brain trust brought academic theory and the scientific method to practical economic, social, and political problems. Its commitment to "rationality" presaged a desirable objectivity in Kennedy's international policy and showed that Kennedy himself was, despite his youthful idealism, a "man of reason."[20]

As a Cold War outpost, however, it was also important to Koreans to have a US president capable of taking decisive action. The prospect of a "New Frontier" was invigorating, but its realization posed a daunting task that demanded not just the inspiration of youth or knowledge of an academic, but the experienced wherewithal of a man of action. According to the newspaper *Kyŏnghyang sinmun*, "The United States today faces the greatest period of political, diplomatic, and economic trial in its history."[21] Reports on Kennedy's academic record were therefore always paired with his military record. A *Sasanggye* review on his performance during his first two months described him favorably as the inheritor of Theodore Roosevelt's resolve to "Walk softly and carry a big stick," editorializing that this made Kennedy an ideal patron for Korea in the face of China's growing threat. *Saebyŏk* noted in agreement that Kennedy's "pose" was partly thanks to his youth, but also expressed a distinctly American "Yankee" spirit of resolve.[22]

South Korean papers frequently drew favorable comparisons between Kennedy and his presidential predecessors, likening his intellectual reformism to Franklin Roosevelt and his aggressive resolve to Theodore Roosevelt. In terms of the history of Korean-American relations, however, the more apt parallel might have been Woodrow Wilson. There is a striking likeness between South Korean celebrations of the promise of Kennedy's idealism for the decolonizing world in 1960, and Korean intellectuals' excitement over the significance of Wilson's Fourteen Points for the colonized world in 1919[23] (Figure 11.1).

Just as colonial Korean perceptions of Wilsonian internationalism soured quickly with Wilson's failure to practice what he preached, however, changes in South Korean domestic politics soon forced Kennedy to choose between the liberal ideal preached by Kennedy, the charismatic symbol, and the Cold War realpolitik practiced by Kennedy, the state leader. On May 16, 1961, military troops commanded by Park Chung Hee wrested control of the country from the democratically elected Chang Myŏn government. Park's military coup forced Kennedy to choose between two competing demands: Would he be the defender of democracy or the stalwart against communism? On the one hand, not recognizing the junta would risk plunging a crucial corner of the Cold War containment boundary of the United States into catastrophic political instability. On the other hand, recognizing a military group that had overthrown a democratically elected government might seriously undermine the ideological credibility and attendant cultural capital that Kennedy commanded in Korea in

Figure 11.1 Advertisement for the Korean edition of *John Kennedy: A Political Profile*.

particular and the Third World in general. The coup shone a spotlight on a central contradiction in Kennedy's symbolic leadership: his aspiration to be both boldly anti-colonial and stridently anti-communist.

Meanwhile, for Park and his new government, acquiring American support was crucial to establishing themselves as the legitimate US sanctioned and internationally recognized new power in South Korea. Kennedy's recognition of the coup was not an immediate given. As Abraham Michael Rosenthal of the *NYT* perceptively noted, the junta had "established an authoritarian military regime and presented the United States with a new time of decision."[24] On the one hand, the ideological cast of the US as protector of democracy seemed to demand that the US stand on behalf of the rudely recalled first true democratic South Korean government. On the other, Washington's rhetorical commitment to self-determination—especially in the decolonizing and postcolonial Third World—as well as its determination to combat communism required it to recognize the new regime. Aware of Kennedy's dilemma, junta officials pitched themselves to US officials as both anti-communists and nationalist standard-bearers of postcolonial self-determination.

And so, despite continued reservations, Kennedy accepted Park's authority and issued a diplomatic invitation for November 1961.[25]

The military government's exploitation of Kennedy's image

Upon taking power, Park's junta immediately revoked the press freedoms expanded under the Second Republic, particularly restricting representations of Park and junta officials.[26] Military authorities screened all journalistic endeavors prior to publication and directly distributed photographs that represented Park favorably to government-controlled organs like *Tonga Ilbo*.[27] At the same time, Park's administration drew on Kennedy's charisma to solidify the standing of its new government. During his American tour six months after taking power the Korean press ran photographs of him and Kennedy at the White House, taken by junta publicists, which visually backed the claim that the new military government enjoyed the support of the American government.

Park's White House visit, although brief, consolidated his new regime's and the Kennedy administration's interests. It was also a major media moment that produced a steady stream of photographs that served the ideological and political needs of both administrations. For Kennedy, the photographs reasserted his personal cosmopolitanism and political internationalism. For Park, the photographs of his diplomatic sojourn through Japan and the United States elevated his image in South Korea from military strongman to political advocate for Korean interests in a perilous Cold War world (Figure 11.2).

In the iconic image of Kennedy and Park's first meeting, the two leaders gesture outward together. To be sure, Park's body is shut off and partially hidden while Kennedy angles open to the viewer, embodying what the Korean press admired as his "casual self-confidence."[28] But despite their stylistic contrast, both men are pictured as visionaries focused on a shared future. As a Korean newspaper said in a sentiment widely propagated in the domestic press at the time, "Their differences are less important than their shared purpose."[29]

By maintaining Kennedy's and Park's individual characters but creating a shared focus, such images also allowed the US-ROK alliance to renew its commitment to a shared developmental ambition of "Nationalist Modernity." This concept embodied the paradox of Kennedy's anti-colonial and anti-communist dilemma, and was reproduced in the Park regime's goals of development through integration into the global economy and the assertion of ROK sovereignty. Self-determination and integration therefore marked the shared agenda and dilemma of the two administrations.

In talks with US officials stationed in Korea, Park and his military compatriots took care to offer assurances that the coup was primarily an act of self-determination that expressed the wishes of the Korean people. They stressed points of political alignment with Kennedy's Cold War political agenda and assuaged concerns about antidemocratic tendencies by promising to hold democratic elections in two years' time.[30] The Park administration would also continue to employ this strategy of collapsing the contradictory aspects of the Kennedy administration to accrue the

Figure 11.2 President Kennedy and General Park Chung Hee. November 14, 1961, KN-C19432, Collection "White House Photographs," John F. Kennedy Presidential Library, Boston (JFKL).

material capital of US aid and the cultural capital that came with the political support of a charismatic American president. Park's calculation of the significance of Kennedy's support was borne out by Ambassador Samuel Berger, who was confident enough by December 1961 to assure Secretary of State Dean Rusk of the secure state of Korean politics thanks partly to popular confidence in Park himself, but more decisively to the support of the United States. He recounted the words of an unnamed Korean to him, following Park's November reception in Washington by President Kennedy, that "since the United States is impressed with Park, we Koreans value him more."[31]

Behind every man . . .: Two first ladies

This shared space of "Nationalist Modernity" was distinctly masculine. The future it foresaw, however, required a tempering conservatism. This was done by feminizing the modernization process. "New Frontiers" are exciting, but they are also unsettling. Joint efforts to calm public anxiety over the pace of change can be seen in domestic images distributed during Kennedy and Park's diplomatic meeting, notably one photograph of Park Chung Hee's son wearing a cowboy outfit sent to him by Mrs. Kennedy, and another of the Kennedys accepting a gift of Korean *hanbok*, traditional Korean clothing, for their own children.[32] These domestic images are a reminder of the crucial role that both Park's and Kennedy's wives played in their husbands' image making. Looking at Jacqueline Kennedy through a South Korean lens helps to put her into a broader framework of global connections and comparisons, in effect somewhat normalizing her exceptional image (Figures 11.3 and 11.4).

Charles R. Kim's recent study on revolutionary tides in 1950s and 1960s South Korean culture describes the coexistence of forces for radical change and reactionary stability as the result of two interdependent narrative schemas: revolutionary vanguardism and wholesome modernization.[33] If the project of "nationalist modernization" was part of revolutionary vanguardism, then Jacqueline Kennedy and Yuk Young-soo (Park's wife) provided its wholesome modernization counterpart. While their husbands played mavericks, these women gave the public conventionally attractive and attractively conventional assurances of domestic stability.

Jacqueline Kennedy was admired in the Korean press as a perfectly elegant feminine counterpart to her husband's effusive masculinity. Women's journals in particular upheld her as an ideal model of modern womanhood balanced with conventional domestic attributes. For example, the monthly woman's magazine *Yŏwŏn* ran an extended profile of Jacqueline Kennedy the month prior to the presidential election, exploring the theme of "the great woman behind every great man." The profile lauded her for her own accomplishments—her education, her beauty, her wit—but most

Figure 11.3 "A Real Hi Man: Hi Man Park [*sic*], 3, goes western in the Far East as he draws his shooting iron in front of his home in Seoul, South Korea. The youngster is the son of Sen. Chung Hee Park, chairman of South Korea's supreme council. The cowboy outfit was a gift from Mrs. Jacqueline Kennedy during the general's recent visit to President Kennedy in Washington"—AP Wirephoto. December 21, 1961, 4, Lowell Sun Newspaper Archives.

Figure 11.4 Park Chung Hee and John and Jacqueline Kennedy with children's *hanbok* gifted to the Kennedys by Park. Accession Number ST-207-1-62, November 14, 1961, Folder AR13, ST06, Collection "White House Photographs," JFKL.

of all praised her for wielding these assets "unselfishly" on behalf of her husband's advancement. *Yŏwŏn* stressed that her education made her a suitable partner for her "intellectual" husband, her beauty qualified her to complement and amplify his good looks, and her wit was put to best use by deflecting journalists trying to goad her into revealing her own political opinions and instead cleverly deferring to her husband's viewpoints.[34] Some years later, widowhood only underscored this perfect wife persona.

The initial beatification of Jacqueline Kennedy in the wake of her husband's assassination was as much of an international phenomenon as President Kennedy's personalized brand of liberalism. In Korea, where ideals ascribed to Kennedy elevated him to a cult of personality figure, mourning for his passing demanded an equally potent symbol through which the public could channel its grief. Draped in elegant black and flanked by her children, Jacqueline Kennedy provided the ideal mourning surrogate. Venues like newsstands, corner stores, and cinema distributed *ppira* (billets), pamphlets stamped with photographs of a Madonna-esque Jacqueline and her children in attendance at the president's state funeral.[35]

Yuk Young-soo was likewise famously beloved for humanizing her inscrutable husband, illustrating how crucial a "wholesome" anchor was to the public's acceptance of "vanguardism." While Jacqueline Kennedy's image in Korea was of an American wife who paired modern style with domestic behavior, Yuk represented the model Korean wife, proudly wearing traditional Korean dress and standing a step behind her husband at all times. While Park purveyed strict military style and relentless pursuit

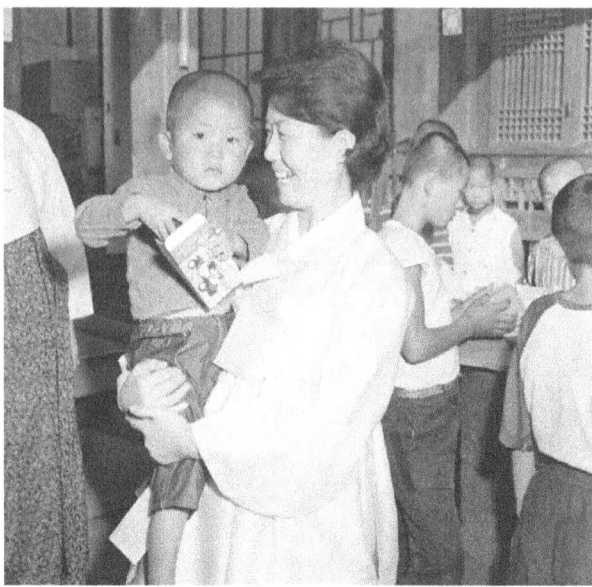

Figure 11.5 Park Chung Hee's wife, Mrs. Yuk Young-soo, visiting a city orphanage. CET0019800, 1961, Ministry of Public Information Collection "Office of Promotional Photographs," National Archives of Korea (NAK).

of development, Yuk provided a human face for the public to relate to—one tied to tradition in attire and engaged in sympathetic humanitarian endeavors, often with children. Even opposition politicians like Kim Dae-Jung spoke fondly of Yuk, beloved as "the opposition party in the Blue House."³⁶ After a bullet meant for him killed her, Park was perceived as increasingly unstable and untethered from humanity. For many Koreans, Yuk's death marked the turning point in Park's descent into increasingly draconian governance, personal volatility, and finally his own assassination in 1979. A *Kyŏnghyang Sinmun* obituary expressed this emotional investment with an epigraph by the prominent poet Pak Mok-wŏl:

> A gnawing pain in the breast, more than sorrow,
> Attends the passing of Mrs. Yuk Yŏng-su.
> Hearts devastated at the felling of our moral pillar,
> Symbol of faith, benevolence, and elegance.
> Her warm faith and wisdom will endure eternally.³⁷

Undermining legitimacy: Political cartoons in the opposition reclamation of Kennedy's image

The selfsame contradiction that Park's administration had to manage—that between Kennedy's personification of the American ideal of championing liberal ideals abroad, and the reality of the United States' imperialist international entanglements—was also seized by Korean intellectuals and students. They did so to advance their own demands for a reformulation of the terms of the US-ROK alliance. But while Park's military regime sought to collapse Kennedy's cultural capital with American military capital and use both to shore up their legitimacy, South Korean opposition forces sought to highlight the contradiction between the two for their own ends. Liberal populists were newly resurgent, thanks to the brief interlude from authoritarian rule between April 1960 and May 1961. Like the junta administration, political opposition forces drew on the power of representation to advocate for their cause. Leftist journals like *Sasanggye* were consistent with the military authorities insofar as they generally featured respectful photographs and coverage of Kennedy himself, but differed by also featuring editorial critiques of US military installations and the behavior of US military personnel in South Korea. The anti-military, pro-SOFA (Status of Forces Agreement) demonstrations of 1962 highlight how populist agitators drew on a shared rhetoric of American cultural and material capital for alternative ends. This movement demonstrates the Korean left's savvy navigation of Cold War ideologies and realities to force concessions from Park's fledgling military regime and Kennedy's conflicted administration.

The short-lived parliamentary democratic government fostered a rise in demonstration culture that lingered into the early Park era.[38] Among the more fraught issues raised by demonstrators was the lack of a SOFA delimiting the rights and responsibilities of US forces in Korea. Although the US military presence in Korea had become permanent after 1953, US officials had consistently refused to negotiate a SOFA. For South Korean liberals, this refusal undermined claims that the United States respected and championed Korean sovereignty. The disjuncture between the promise of independent development represented by Kennedy and the reality of military entitlement was encapsulated in extraterritorial privileges and the contrast between the living conditions in military compounds—slices of suburban Americana which Koreans could not enter without a pass—and the persistent postwar poverty suffered by the majority of the South Korean population.[39]

The sting of this contradiction was inflamed by a string of highly publicized violent encounters between American GIs and Korean civilians in the early 1960s. Cases of US military abuse of Korean civilians without consequence were so well known that they earned their own shorthand "lynchings." High-profile cases included the "Imjin River Incident" fatal shooting of two civilian Korean woodcutters in the DMZ by American soldiers,[40] the beating-induced miscarriage suffered by a pregnant Korean prostitute at the hands of an American GI,[41] and the seizure of a Korean houseboy employed in a military compound by two soldiers who beat him, stripped, him, and hung him from a telegraph pole.[42]

The Korean press was instrumental in connecting this string of violent incidents to a history of fraught US-Korean encounters dating back to the US military's arrival in Korea in 1945. Thus, *Sasanggye* publisher Chang Chun-ha stated that "In our memory the new incidents remain inhumane acts of insult like those preceding them."[43] Other journalists, too, described the 1960 beating of a Korean youth suspected of theft by eight American soldiers, the 1958 forcible shaving of a prostitute's head in penalty for entrance into an American military base, and the infamous 1957 capture, confinement in a crate, and air-shipment to Pusan of a Korean boy caught on a base, among many other unforgotten examples, as a pattern of "human rights violations such as shootings, beatings, lynchings, and insults."[44] The logical solution, Chang argued—and many agreed—was not the customary proffering of words and coins but the legal protection of Korean citizens' human rights in the form of a SOFA.[45]

Newspaper cartoonists, too, addressed GI-civilian conflicts. In Figure 11.6, a US soldier is represented as a nameless and faceless symbol of violence hidden behind an American uniform. Titled "Yet Another GI Lynching Incident," the panel depicts a Korean civilian in *hanbok* quaking before a figure in American military dress sporting a massive fist in place of its head. Dwarfed by the threatening figure, the Korean exclaims, "Its face appears only as a fist"[46] (Figure 11.6).

Despite these critiques of the US military, leftist intellectual journals continued to celebrate Kennedy as a symbol of American liberal internationalism.[47] Like the Park administration, *Sasanggye* confined its images of him to respectful photographs that mirrored written celebrations of his looks, energy, and ideology. Comic strips, while excoriating abuses of authority by the US military, took care not to attack him and the promising ideology he represented and never caricatured him. This allowed the political opposition to cash in on the cultural capital of his image by claiming that they shared in his liberal ideology, and levy this to call for reforms in the material military configuration, for example through a SOFA.

Pro-SOFA demonstrations were ramped up in the first year of military government, and finally came to a head in June 1962. Korean college students led a series of coordinated protests across the nation that turned the incisive critique outlined by South Korea's political left into a potent threat against American ideological leadership on the one hand and the Park regime's domestic stability on the other. As negotiations between the Park and Kennedy administrations stalled in June, Korean college students

Figure 11.6 "Yet Another GI Lynching Incident." *Chosŏn Ilbo*, June 6, 1962.

surged into the streets in a nationwide political protest that lasted for several days over multiple cities.[48]

Ultimately, the protests succeeded in wringing a guarantee of SOFA negotiations from both the Korean and US governments. On the ROK side, Park found himself caught between the need to maintain order and placate a dangerously unsettled public. The specter of the April revolution loomed large in the junta's "obvious fear" that "this kind of spontaneous reaction could provide the spark for a major demonstration."[49] Meanwhile, US personnel in Korea found themselves in a markedly different position vis-à-vis the student demonstrators of 1962 than they had two years prior during the uprising of April 1960. In 1960 American influence had played an instrumental and widely recognized role in convincing Rhee to bow to public demand for his resignation.[50] Initially, Kennedy's election had had the potential to ride this wave to a new crest of public approval in the short-lived Second Republic.

The opposition's successful campaign to divide American ideals (symbolized in the JFK brand) from American actions (enacted in Kennedy administration policy) effectively undermined that earlier possibility. The tenor of public feeling in June 1962 was decidedly unfriendly toward Americans, recast as violent assailants against Korean persons and the collective nation. Kennedy officials were acutely aware that the ramifications of mishandling or avoiding the rapidly escalating situation were potentially significant not only for the Park administration and US interests in the stability of that body but more urgently for the prospects of a continued US military presence in Korea and influential sway in Korean affairs.[51] It rapidly became apparent among American policymakers that if they wished to avoid yet another massive upheaval in Korean politics, perhaps even the third turnover of power in as many years, some sort of concession was necessary.

Figure 11.7 "Kennedy's sudden death—the tragedy of our generation." *Tonga Ilbo*, November 25, 1963.

Conclusion: Negotiating authority, maintaining legitimacy

For Kennedy, this calculated concession proved to be very effective. Critiques of American power certainly did not completely disappear just because a SOFA had appeared. But the Kennedy brand—which Korean militarists and populists had fought to claim as their own—survived surprisingly unscathed. Upon Kennedy's assassination, the US embassy in South Korea was overwhelmed by expressions of condolence from representatives of the political right, left, and the general population. Ambassador Berger's office collected letters from government offices like the Ministry of Defense and the Chamber of Commerce and opposition activists like *Sasanggye* editor Chang Chun-ha, who wrote "Koreans ... mourn this not simply as the loss of a great president of a great nation but feel that they, too, have lost a leader."[52] Even more striking are the touching assortment of personal letters by South Korean citizens who were personally invested in Kennedy's world vision and mourned the passing of its representative. Mr. Hyunjin Rhee, for example, sent the embassy his poem "The Hero Gone," which reads in part:

> The hero gone, Kennedy gone,
> Leaving every thought noble,
> Even dreams for the world ...[53]

Publicly, the *Tonga Ilbo* memorialized Kennedy with a final cartoon. Even here, he remained too sacrosanct for so lowbrow a medium, but that did not stop the cartoon world from mourning him with the rest of the Korean public (Figure 11.7). Despite South Korea's infamously factional politics, Kennedy, in death as in life, remained among its few universally revered symbols.

Kennedy enjoyed a nearly universal approbation in Korea that continues to this day. Despite assuming office at a moment when Korean perceptions of the United States were in flux, and when US policy toward Korea was being recalibrated, he was respected and invoked by both Korean militarists advocating centralized development and Korean reformers in pursuit of social reform and democratization. Despite their differences, both parties invested him with the ideals of American liberalism. For the militarists, forging a relationship between Park and Kennedy allowed them to claim that Park enjoyed the backing of the popular US president and the ideals and material resources that he stood for. Meanwhile, the political opposition upheld Kennedy as the model that the United States, particularly its military, should be striving for, and used the discrepancy between the Kennedy ideal and US imperialism to advocate for causes like a US-ROK SOFA. More enduring than these political maneuverings, however, was the effect of this uniformly positive coverage of Kennedy on the perception of the South Korean public, who remain enamored of his image to this day.

Notes

1 Kennedy served with distinction in the US Navy during the Second World War, and Park was a lifelong officer, under Japanese colonialism and after the war. See Robert

Dallek, *An Unfinished Life: John F. Kennedy, 1917-1963* (Boston, MA: Little, Brown and Co., 2003); Carter Eckert, *Park Chung Hee and Modern Korea: The Roots of Militarism, 1866-1945* (Cambridge: The Belknap Press of Harvard University Press, 2016); and Se-jin Kim, *The Politics of Military Revolution in Korea* (Chapel Hill: University of North Carolina Press, 1971).

2 Park's leadership of the military coup and the following Junta administration was soon formalized. The initial chairman, Lieutenant General Chang To-yŏng, was rapidly relegated to a figurehead position, with vice chairman Park making most key appointments in both the Supreme Council for National Reconstruction (SCNR) and the Korean Central Intelligence Agency. On July 3, 1961, Chang became the first in a string of purges and Park assumed the position of chairman in name as well as fact. See Yong-Sup Han, "The May Sixteenth Military Coup," in *The Park Chung Hee Era: The Transformation of South Korea*, eds. Byung-Kook Kim and Ezra Vogel (Cambridge: Harvard University Press, 2011), 53–55; and Hyung-A Kim, "State Building: The Military Junta's Path to Modernity through Administrative Reforms," in *Park Chung Hee Era*, 89.

3 Jung-en Woo, *Race to the Swift: State and Finance in Korean Industrialization* (New York: Columbia University Press, 1991).

4 Bruce Cumings, *Origins of the Korean War*, vols. 1–2 (Princeton: Princeton University Press, 1981–1990).

5 Contemplating events in Turkey, Korea, Japan, and "all around the fringes," an editorial in *The Nation* asked why it was pro-American, not "neutralist," regimes, that were so often threatened or toppled by insurrection. "Coming Apart at the Seams," *The Nation*, June 18, 1960, 522.

6 Christina Klein, *Cold War Orientalism: Asia in the Middlebrow Imagination, 1945-1961* (Berkeley: University of California Press, 2003), 59.

7 In the 1940s and 1950s, a host of programs addressed American ignorance of foreign affairs, which was increasingly seen as a dangerous liability. Among other measures, government legislation promoted graduate studies in international affairs (the 1948 Smith-Mundt Act, 1949 Point Four program, 1949 Fulbright Act, 1951 Mutual Security Act, and 1958 Higher Education Defense Act) and the rise of area studies in 1945-52, considerably funded by big foundations like Ford and Rockefeller, too.

8 "Memorandum from the President's Deputy Special Assistant for National Security Affairs (Rostow) to President Kennedy," March 15, 1961, *FRUS*, 1961–63, vol. XXII, doc. 428.

9 "Memorandum from Robert Johnson of the National Security Council Staff to the President's Deputy Special Assistant for National Security Affairs (Rostow)," April 3, 1961, *FRUS*, 1961–63, vol. XXII, doc. 439.

10 "Report by Hugh Farley of the International Cooperation Administration to the President's Deputy Special Assistant for National Security Affairs (Rostow)," March 6, 1961, *FRUS*, 1961–63, vol. XXII, doc. 424–5. Farley resigned on February 24, shortly after submitting his report, in order to emphasize the severity of corruption in Korea and his criticism of USOM operations. Ibid., 425; and Donald Macdonald, *U.S.-Korean Relations from Liberation to Self-Reliance, The Twenty-Year Record: An Interpretative Summary of the Archives of the U.S. Department of State for the Period 1945 to 1965* (Boulder: Westview Press, 1992), 29.

11 "Memorandum from Robert Komer of the National Security Council Staff to the President's Deputy Special Assistant for National Security Affairs (Rostow)," March 15, 1961, *FRUS*, 1961–63, vol. XXII, doc. 426.

12 "Short-Range Outlook in the Republic of Korea," Special National Intelligence Estimate (SNIE) 42–61, March 21, 1961, *FRUS*, 1961–63, vol. XXII, doc. 435.
13 See Charles Kim, "Unlikely Revolutionaries: South Korea's First Generation and the Student Protests of 1960" (PhD diss., Columbia University, 2007).
14 "K'enedi taet'ongnyŏng ŭi ch'oech'o ŭi kija hoegyŏn ina kŭhu'e kaech'oe toenŭn kija hoegyŏn esŏ sigan mujehan miguk paekakkwansŏ palp'yo" [White House Record of Kennedy's First Presidential Press Conference and the Opening Session of Congress] *Chosŏn ilbo*, January 24, 1961, 2; Choe Ki-il, "K'enedi haengjŏngbu wa uri ŭi kako" [The Kennedy Administration and Our Resolve], *Sasanggye*, Feburary 1, 1961, 94–100; Yi Kyu-t'ae, "Taet'ongnyŏng hubo rŭl twitpatch'im hanŭn him" [The Power behind the Presidential Candidates], *Yŏwŏn*, December 30, 1960, 11–17.
15 James MacGregor Burns, *John Kennedy: A Political Profile* (New York: Harcourt, Brace, 1960); *Kyŏnghyang Sinmun*, January 7, 1961, 1.
16 Yŏm Ki-hyŏng, "K'enedi-ron" [Kennedy's Theory], *Saebyŏk*, December 15, 1960, 109–15.
17 Ch'oe Ki-il, "K'enedi haengjŏngbu," 94–100.
18 Ki-hyŏng, "K'enedi-ron," 109–15.
19 Yi Po-hyŏng, Cho Sun-sŭng, and Ham Pyŏng-chun, "K'enedi haengjŏngbu rŭl iggŭnŭn pŭrein t'ŭrŏsŭt'ŭ" [The Kennedy Administration's "Brain Trust"], *Sasanggye*, September 1, 1961, 101–23.
20 Ki-il, "K'enedi haengjŏngbu," 96–97.
21 *Kyŏnghyang Sinmun*, January 19, 1961, 3.
22 Ki-hyŏng, "K'enedi-ron," 111.
23 Michael Edison Robinson, *Cultural Nationalism in Colonial Korea, 1920-1925* (Seattle: University of Washington Press, 1988), 145.
24 A. M. Rosenthal, "Korea a Trial for U.S.: Washington Is Hopeful Its Support of the Junta Will Create a Basis for Better Government," *NYT*, July 23, 1961, E4. In an earlier article, he wrote that the "junta members and the officers and civilians around them are concerned and annoyed that the rest of the world . . . particularly [in] the United States . . . does not seem willing to accept their word that they are democrats at heart." Rosenthal, "Bribery Charges Levied at Seoul," *NYT*, July 13, 1961, 2.
25 "Record of National Security Council Action No. 2430," June 13, 1961, *FRUS*, 1961–63, vol. XXII, doc. 483.
26 Under the imposition of martial law thousands of arrests funneled political and social undesirables through a Revolutionary Court and Prosecution. The regime also dissolved the National Assembly and forbade all forms of political activity. The Political Purification Law of March 1962 banned several thousand politicians from political participation for the next six years and shut down over 75 percent of Seoul daily newspapers. See Robert Scalapino, "Which Route for Korea?," *Asian Survey* 2, no. 7 (1962): 1–13 at 3; Carter Eckert et al., *Korea, Old and New* (Cambridge: Harvard University Press, 1990), 360–61; Bruce Cumings, *Korea's Place in the Sun: A Modern History* (New York: W.W. Norton, 2005), 351.
27 Son Sang-ik, "Han'guk Sinmun sisa manhwa-sa yŏn'gu: p'ungjasŏng kwa sahoe pip'anjŏk yŏkhal ŭl chungsim ŭro" [A Study of Korean Newspaper Cartoon History: Viewed from a Satirical and Journalistic Perspective] (PhD diss., Chungang University, 2004), 218–20.
28 Ki-il, "K'enedi haengjŏngbu," 94–100.
29 *Tongailbo*, November 30, 1961, 1.

30 In response to the Kennedy administration's contingent offer of support, Park issued a public pledge in July to restore power to a civilian government. Earlier, on May 19, the Military Revolutionary Committee had rebranded itself as the SCNR to underscore its commitment to Korea's economic development.
31 "Letter from the Ambassador to Korea (Berger) to Secretary of State Rusk," December 15, 1961, *FRUS*, 1961–1963, vol. XXII, doc. 542–44.
32 For cultures of masculinity affecting foreign policy, see Robert Dean, *Imperial Brotherhood: Gender and the Making of Cold War Foreign Policy* (Amherst: University of Massachusetts Press, 2001).
33 Charles Kim, *Youth for Nation: Culture and Protest in Cold War South Korea* (Honolulu: University of Hawai'i Press, 2017).
34 *Yŏwŏn* illustrated Jacqueline Kennedy's intelligence by marveling that Kennedy had courted her with books instead of flowers, rapturously described her beauty as "uncommon and uniquely American," and delighted in stories of her "political a-politicism": her diplomatic skill to redirect pressure from the press. Yi Kyu-t'ae, "Taet'ongnyŏng hubo rŭl twitpatch'im hanŭn him" [The Strength behind the Presidential Candidates] *Yŏwŏn*, December 30, 1960, 164–69.
35 Author interview with Hye Myoung Kim, Woodside, California, December 27, 2017.
36 Kim Dae-Jung, Chŏn Sŭng-hŭi, and Yi Hŭi-ho, *Conscience in Action: The Autobiography of Kim Dae-jung* (Singapore: Palgrave Macmillan, 2019), 208.
37 *Kyŏnghyang sinmun*, August 16, 1974, 3.
38 The reemergence of leftist and unification movements following the April Revolution and Chang Myŏn's moderate amendments to the infamous National Security Law (NSL) alarmed observers at the US embassy and factored significantly into the Kennedy administration's decision to back Park. Within months of the coup, the Park administration brought these radical political impulses to heel, expanding the NSL's already significant writ. Also, the Anti-Communist Act of 1961 doubled down on the Park administration's agenda and helped suppress leftists, too. Kuk Cho, "Tension Between the National Security Law and Constitutionalism in South Korea," *Boston University International Law Journal* 15, no. 125 (1997): 125–74.
39 Within these enclosures, lower-middle-class Americans reaped the fruits of the upward mobility they enjoyed in Korea, where "One could be raised on an Arkansas farm and at eighteen rule a roost just outside the military gates, where a Felliniesque collection of shantytowns, bars, whorehouses, and small tradesmen catered to the American taste." Bruce Cumings, "Silent But Deadly," in *Let the Good Times Roll: Prostitution and the U.S. Military in Asia*, eds. Saundra Pollock Sturdevant and Brenda Stoltzfus (New York: The New Press, 1992), 170.
40 "Hanmiyanggukŭi uŭirul uihayŏ imjingangsagŏnul kaet'anhanda" [The Deplorable Impact of the Imjin River Incident on Fraternal Relations between Korea and the United States], *Chosŏn Ilbo*, February 9, 1962, 3.
41 "Tto migunp'okhaengsagŏn. P'ajusŏ uianburul kut'a nakt'aek'e" [Another Incident of American GI Violence: In Paju a Prostitute Beaten and Miscarries], *Chosŏn Ilbo*, February 25, 1962, 3.
42 *Chosŏn Ilbo*, June 9, 1962, 3, and June 14, 1962, 2.
43 "Urinŭn migukgukminege mutkoja handa" [What We Want from Americans], *Sasangye*, March 1, 1962, 20–21.
44 *Chosŏn ilbo*, February 13, 1962, 2.
45 *Sasangye*, March 1, 1962, 21. While critical of the entitled behavior of US military personnel in Korea, Chang nonetheless acknowledges a history of US military and

developmental support to South Korea, and therefore argues that Koreans and Americans alike should support a SOFA so as to continue the "special relationship."

46 *Chosŏn Ilbo*, June 4, 1962, 2.
47 For background on *Sasanggye*, the preeminent South Korean leftist intellectual journal from 1953 through 1970, see Chang Kyu-sik, "The 'Sasanggye' Intellectuals' Nationalism and Thoughts on the Division of the Korean Peninsula during the 1950s-1970s" [1950~1970 nyŏndae "Sasanggye" chisik'in ŭi pundan insik kwa minjokjuŭiron ŭi kwejŏk], *The Journal of Korean History [Han'guksa yŏn'gu]* 167 (2014): 289–339.
48 "Beating of Korean By G.I.'s Protested," *NYT*, June 7, 1962, 3; "Seoul Releases Students Held in Anti-U.S. Protest," *NYT*, June 8, 1962, 8; "Korean Troops Block a March By Students on U.S. Embassy," *NYT*, June 9, 1962, 10; "Taegu Students Defiant," *NYT*, June 9, 1962, 10.
49 "Embassy Telegram No. 1235, from Ambassador to Korea (Berger) to Secretary of State (Rusk)," June 7, 1962, Cable, Department of State, Issue Date: June 6, 1962, Date Declassified, August 1, 1988, Sanitized, Complete, *Declassified Documents Reference System, the United States, 1946-1979*.
50 In the destruction of government property following Rhee's resignation, American icons were not only spared but often celebrated. For example, the statue of MacArthur by the Anti-Communism Hall was adorned with a garland laurel by appreciative crowds in contrast to the statue of Rhee in Independence Park, which was demolished. See Kang Chun-man, *Han'guk hyŏndaesa sanch'aek: 1960-yŏndae p'yŏn— 4.19 hyŏngmyŏng esŏ 3 sŏn kaehŏn kkaji* [A Walk through Modern Korean History: The 1960s—From the April 19 Revolution to the Third Constitution] (Sŏul-si: Inmul kwa sasangsa, 2004), 37; Lee Chae-bong, "Mi, minjuhyŏngmyŏng makŭl kunsatokjae kusang: Mi, CIA-kukmubu 4.19 kwallyŏn pimilmunsŏ ch'oech'okonggae" [US, Obstruction of the Democratic Revolution Concretization of Military Dictatorship: The First Public Release of Confidential Documents of the American CIA and State Department Regarding the April Revolution], *Sindonga*, September 1, 1995, 574; Lee Chong-o, "4-wŏl hyŏngmyŏng ŭi simhwapaljŏn kwa haksaeng undong ŭi chŏngae" [The Intensification of the April Revolution and the Development of the Student Movement], in *1950-yŏndae Han'guk sahoe wa 4.19 hyŏngmyŏng* [1950s Korean Society and the April 19 Revolution] (Sŏul: T'aeam, 1991), 212.
51 "Taegu Students Defiant."
52 American Embassy in Seoul, "Political Affairs and Relations: Prominent Persons, 1963," KRDB20010482, Confidential U.S. State Department Central Foreign Policy Files: Korea, 1962-1963 (RG 84), National Assembly Library of the Republic of Korea.
53 Ibid.

12

John F. Kennedy through the Lens of a Divided Vietnam

Aaron Lillie and Diu-Huong Nguyen

It was one of the most unforgettable highlights of her study in the United States in the early 1960s when as a young woman Duong Van Mai was invited to a garden party hosted by the White House for foreign students. For this rare occasion at the presidential mansion in 1961, Mai and two other girlfriends dressed in their best *ao dai*, the traditional long dress of Vietnam. As they crowded together on Camelot's hallowed ground, the news spread quickly that President John F. Kennedy would be arriving soon to share a few words of greeting. Vividly describing the details of this social event in her memoir some fifty years later, Mai writes as if it had all just happened yesterday:

> Then Kennedy appeared, as handsome as he had looked in the countless pictures we had seen of him. He had just returned from a vacation. His face was tanned and his hair had turned sandy red from the sun. He walked briskly down the path, spotted My Luong [Mai's friend] and stopped to shake her hand and ask her where she was from. My Luong was so awed she could hardly speak. Then Kennedy moved on. When My Luong showed me her hand—the one that Kennedy had touched—I was green with envy.[1]

Many Vietnamese students at the time would likely have shared that feeling. Mai and her two friends belonged to a very privileged group from a new generation of Vietnamese growing up in a time of rapid change. They were part of a very small number of ordinary Vietnamese citizens (not military or political leaders) to have been able to meet with the American president in person. The overwhelming majority of Vietnamese would only ever know of the charismatic young president from afar through very limited and often very biased sources of information.

Having endured more than half a century of French colonial rule followed by four years of brutal Japanese-Vichy wartime occupation, Vietnam declared its independence in September 1945. Less than a year later, the communist led Viet Minh, a broad-based nationalist coalition headed by Ho Chi Minh, found itself embroiled in a bloody war of decolonization with the French that would last for almost eight years. This war soon was linked with US-Chinese tensions, the Korea War, and the US-Soviet standoff in

Europe, becoming a flashpoint in a growing global Cold War conflict over political ideology. In the early 1950s, following their defeat of the nationalist Guomindang, the Chinese Communist Party began sending large amounts of men and material to support the Viet Minh.[2]

Greatly weakened by its catastrophic defeat and subsequent occupation by Germany during the Second World War, France was unable to afford the financial burden of reconquering its Indo-Chinese colonies and increasingly relied on US support. By the time of the French defeat in 1954 at Dien Bien Phu, Washington was bankrolling around 80 percent of the war's cost.[3] By the early 1950s, the Democratic Republic of Vietnam (DRVN, aka North Vietnam) leadership understood that many in the US foreign policy establishment had come to consider Vietnam a front line in a global conflict to prevent further communist expansion. Washington now posed a looming threat to their dream of a united and independent Vietnam.[4]

In the south of Vietnam, deep religious, political, and philosophical dividing lines reflected the area's history as the younger and more outward looking half of an ancient kingdom. Vietnamese pioneers from the north who settled the sparsely populated Mekong Delta and other areas of the south from the eighteenth through the twentieth centuries were often exposed to broader horizons than their more insular brothers and sisters to the north. Southern Vietnam's distance from the more rigidly traditional religious and political centers in Hue and Hanoi, its greater ethnic and religious diversity, and its exposure to international trade, together with direct French colonial rule in Cochinchina, fostered the development of a distinct southern Vietnamese culture which was more cosmopolitan in outlook. This led to the creation and adoption of many new political, religious, and cultural traditions.

While in North Vietnam most citizens of the DRVN shared the Communist Party's view of the American imperialists, south of the 17th parallel and abroad a much greater diversity of political and religious views resulted in the formation of similarly diverse views of American politics, Kennedy, and the US intervention in Vietnam. This complex local, national, and international background decisively shaped the political imaginaries of southern and northern Vietnamese during this formative time.

During the Geneva conference of 1954, it was agreed that Vietnam would be temporarily divided at the 17th parallel until nationwide elections in 1956. While hoping to avoid another war, the DRVN leadership remained determined to fight to unite the country if necessary. In the South, in the mid-1950s a new government was being installed under the American-backed Catholic leader Ngo Dinh Diem. Diem was seeking to forge a new nation out of a dizzying array of religious sects, political ideologies, armed gangs, and philosophical and intellectual traditions. Working closely with US advisors and building a government almost entirely dependent on steadily increasing American financial and military aid, it seemed at first as if he might be successful. However, by the 1960s, his ironfisted suppression, first of religious sects, the Cao Dai and Hoa Hao, then of the communists, and finally of the Buddhists, eroded his political legitimacy to the point where his government and much of his military turned against him. The task of unifying this diverse group of political and religious factions proved much more complex and difficult than it had initially appeared.

Drawing on newspapers and radio coverage, interviews with Vietnamese intellectuals and academics, now mostly in their eighties, transcripts of political speeches and personal accounts, and Vietnamese and US scholarly works, this chapter reflects the complexity, diversity, and indeed division of Vietnamese public opinion and political culture regarding Kennedy, as it was shaped by the different political, cultural, and religious communities in contemporary Vietnam.

Context and historiography

Reconstructing Vietnamese perceptions of individuals and developments in American politics in the 1950s and 1960s is challenging. While many Vietnamese were engaged in and knowledgeable about political struggles in Southeast Asia, a majority was barely literate or illiterate farmers who knew next to nothing about all but the most momentous political developments in the world. Very few Vietnamese farmers knew anything substantive about American politics, much less individual politicians. Consequently, any attempt to depict contemporary Vietnamese public opinion Kennedy can by default only be a reflection of the perceptions and political views of more privileged and better educated Vietnamese.

Even among the most educated intellectuals in Vietnam, very few followed American politics closely enough to form coherent and lasting memories or to gain a detailed understanding. For many Vietnamese, knowledge and understanding of American history was often simplified and romanticized famous events and individuals. This was true even among many of the most educated and cosmopolitan members of Vietnamese society. Thus, Ho Chi Minh evoked an idealized depiction of the American Revolutionary War in the Vietnamese Declaration of Independence, which he portrayed as a revolution led by a deeply oppressed nation of colonial subjects, living in poverty, working as virtual servants to the British Crown, whose primary role was to produce raw materials to supply the production lines of British factories in England.[5]

Similarly, Ngo Vinh Long, a historian and professor at the University of Maine born in 1944 in the Mekong Delta, remembers that when he was a child, his father used to talk to him about the United States. As a young boy, he learned two names for the United States: *My Quoc* (beautiful country) and *Hiep Chung Quoc Hoa Ky* (racially harmonious country). Long recalls being raised to believe that America was an "ideal place," which his father described as "a beautiful, wonderful country where there is racial harmony."[6] Even today, this sort of romanticized perspective is common among Vietnamese intellectuals. In many cases, revolutionaries who spent most of their lives fighting for the nation's independence and freedom passed these views down to their children. This is because generally speaking, educated Vietnamese, particularly those living south of the 17th parallel, held what they perceived as the American ideals of democracy and freedom of expression in high regard.

Vietnam does not have a long tradition of frank and open public discussions about politics. This is in large part due to the uncertainty fostered by many years of political upheaval during the French colonial period and war of decolonization.

Many Vietnamese learned to self-censor, particularly regarding politics. Hotly debated political issues were usually discussed strictly among close friends and family, if at all. Even today the remnants of the old dividing religious and political lines within Vietnamese society remain a barrier to frank and open discussion of controversial historical figures, politicizing even the most seemingly innocuous of historical inquiries. Public dialogues on Communism, Buddhism, and Catholicism—and Kennedy's name can invoke discussion on all three of these sensitive areas—remain tightly monitored. This discourages many people, particularly those who feel they may have something to lose, such as public figures including academics, government officials, and successful entrepreneurs, from discussing their views openly and honestly.

Publications by historians of the DRVN published inside Vietnam and those written by Vietnamese Americans abroad have generally reflected the long-held views of each side.[7] Today, while some Vietnamese scholars have changed their views of the war and the American presidents, thanks to more recently accessible materials, the official government narrative of the war has not changed substantially. Many authors in Vietnam still write from basically the same point of view regarding "the American imperialist invaders," when analyzing the war with the United States.[8] With regard to Kennedy, they focus primarily on Vietnam and the Vietnam War, and are typically basing their views on American accounts, without reflecting Vietnamese views of American presidents.

During the 1960s, however, most ordinary Vietnamese did not pay much attention to international affairs. US politics and American presidents were not subjects of daily conversation, and Kennedy did not visit Vietnam while he was president, giving people something tangible to talk about. These obstacles to a better understanding of Vietnamese public perceptions of Kennedy are compounded by the fact that scholarly works in English regarding Vietnamese political leanings and opinions on just about any subject are hard to come by. Vietnamese voices and opinions continue to be largely absent from American scholarship on the period, particularly when compared to the innumerable publications on American perspectives of the war.[9]

In Vietnam, primary sources on the 1960s are much more luminous. Almost a century after the publication of the first newspapers, following the Second World War the popularization of vernacular press and radio had brought new habits into the daily lives of almost every Vietnamese family and work place in cities and towns in both the North and the South. As literacy rapidly increased and radios became more widely available, many ordinary Vietnamese became media consumers. With improvements in transportation infrastructure, dailies and journals from Hanoi, Saigon, and other cities could now be more easily distributed to Vietnam's most remote areas.[10]

In the DRVN, many read the daily *Nhan Dan (The People)*, the Vietnamese Labor (i.e., Communist) Party's official central organ launched in March 1951 in Hanoi, and listened to Liberation (Hanoi) Radio for news about the world, the activities of the Communist Party leaders, and the national economy, society and culture, including reports on the difficulties and terrible injustices that their revolutionary comrades in the South were facing. Other contemporary news publications, such as *Quan Doi Nhan Dan (The People's Army Daily)*, *Cuu Quoc (National Salvation)*, *Thong Nhat (Unification)*, or Voice of Vietnam radio broadcasts all followed the Vietnamese

Communist Party's line, either borrowing stories from the Vietnam News Agency or quoting statements directly from *Nhan Dan*, which for many in the north was the primary source of political news.

In the Republic of Vietnam (RVN), the late 1950s and early 1960s saw a rapid surge in the publication of newspapers, serials, and research journals. Dailies like *Tu Do (Freedom)* and *Ngon Luan (Speech)* were widely read. Simultaneously, the BBC, Voice of America, Saigon Radio, and many other local radio stations expanded their broadcasts. Southern audiences enjoyed a wide range of different perspectives in local and world news, although as in the north this was often intermingled with state propaganda focusing, in this case, on the appalling conditions in which their Vietnamese brothers were living under the Communist yoke in the north.[11] While both the DRVN and RVN regimes heavily censored virtually all publications, providing or refusing permission to print and removing the most sensitive anti-government stories and information, overall, broadcasters and publishers in the north were allowed less freedom of expression.[12]

Toward the end of the conflict, *Quan Doi Nhan Dan* analyzed the invasion and failure of the American imperialist invaders. From this perspective, Kennedy should be considered among the most influential US presidents whose decisions determined the fate of the war. Following the Communist Party line, it concluded that the "Kennedy administration did not make any major decision to escalate the war because the death of its chief turned the inherited 'game of containment' into a big commitment [in Vietnam]."[13]

Kennedy's initial contacts with Vietnam

Kennedy's involvement in the conflict in Vietnam began with his first, and only, visit, in 1951. During a tour across the Middle East and Asia as a young congressman, he decided to spend some time in French Indochina. In Vietnam, Kennedy and his brother Robert took it upon themselves to investigate how the French war was being conducted and against what sort of enemy. Not wanting to be bamboozled by the overly optimistic assessments of his French diplomatic handlers, Kennedy sought to find out how the conflict was likely to evolve by consulting at length with reporters, local French officials, and Vietnamese political leaders. During his short visit, he formed a clear enough understanding of the war to accurately predict its outcome.[14]

As Robert Kennedy would later report, the trip made a "very major impression" on his brother.[15] With the exception of General Jean de Lattre de Tassigny, who guided the visitors, Kennedy was unimpressed with the French leadership and left Vietnam with the feeling that the French were completely out of touch with the realities of Vietnamese political life. A third political force, controlled by neither the Viet Minh nor the French, would be necessary to prevent Vietnam from falling into communist hands.[16]

In a radio address delivered soon after his return stateside, Kennedy ferociously attacked the policies of European colonial regimes in Asia, which, he declared, had "no eagerness to understand the real hopes and desires of the people to which they are accredited."[17] Washington, he argued, should not have supported Paris without exacting a promise of political reform aimed at building an indigenous force with sufficient political legitimacy to overcome the Viet Minh's advantage. At the same time, he also made some prophetic statements about the war's likely outcome:

> In Indochina we have allied ourselves to the desperate effort of a French regime to hang on to the remnants of empire. There is no broad, general support of the native Vietnam Government among the people of that area. To check the southern drive of communism makes sense but not only through reliance on the force of arms. The task is rather to build strong native non-Communist sentiment within these areas and rely on that as a spearhead of defense rather than upon the legions of General de Lattre. To do this apart from and in defiance of innately nationalistic aims spells foredoomed failure.[18]

Yet, like most other American officials concerned with Vietnam's future, Kennedy believed that the United States must play a critical role in shaping Vietnamese politics. While considering himself anti-colonial and therefore a strong supporter of decolonization, Kennedy in fact accepted and perpetuated the United States' own peculiar brand of colonial mentality, utilizing many of the same tropes and underlying assumptions as his less idealistic predecessors and colleagues.

In a 1956 speech given to the American Friends of Vietnam committee, Kennedy likened the US role in Vietnam to that of a parent that had given birth to a new nation in Southeast Asia. A parent need not consult a newborn about its future; a direct dialogue with the Vietnamese public was unnecessary. At the same time, however, Kennedy argued that a US-sponsored government in the South could not be successful if the Vietnamese people suffered under foreign domination. Kennedy's paternalistic rhetoric conformed to well-established themes familiar to Americans advocating a distinctly US brand of colonial (or perhaps neocolonial) domination in Asia. He apparently saw no contradiction between advocating self-determination for colonized nations and simultaneously arguing that the United States must play a key role in determining Vietnam's political future.[19]

Attempting to disassociate American involvement in Vietnam from French economic and political imperialism in Indochina, Kennedy frequently linked the conflict in Vietnam to Cold War conflicts around the world. Tailoring his language to appeal to American anti-imperialist and anti-communist sentiments, he argued that "in Indochina, as in Korea, the battle against communism should be a battle, not for economic or political gain, but for the security of the free world, and for the values and institutions which are held dear in France and throughout the non-Communist world, as well as in the United States."[20]

In southern Vietnam many city dwellers, particularly Catholics and those who had done well under French colonial rule, welcomed the prospect of American intervention. Kennedy's rhetoric reassured them that southern Vietnam would be granted some measure of political independence and that RVN supporters would not be abandoned to face whatever terrible fate they feared might await them under communist rule.

In contrast, for northerners and for hundreds of thousands of Vietnamese in the South who supported the National Liberation Front (NLF) after its formation in

December 1960, the signs were more ominous. Immediately following Kennedy's election, it became apparent to the DRVN leadership and to politically well-informed Vietnamese intellectuals that the Cold War and communist expansion in Asia had become a key issue in American politics. Kennedy's bellicose rhetoric had clearly tied Washington's determination to resist communist expansion to America's destiny and to the fate of the free world, placing himself firmly on the side of continued US intervention in Vietnam.

Kennedy in the DRVN

Given the limited number of sources and the high degree of censorship of the media in the DRVN at this time, public opinion and public perceptions of Kennedy in northern Vietnam was, generally speaking, linear and often lacked nuance. To the communists and their supporters—many who supported the revolution were not communists— the creation of the NLF, which had been approved in the north by Decree 15 of the Vietnamese Labor Party in July 1959, confirmed the DRVN's determination to liberate the South and unify Vietnam in their resistance against American invasion.[21]

A commonly held and oft-repeated understanding in the north held that the DRVN would stand firm in its resolve that all of Vietnam should be united, independent, and free from foreign aggression. Among northerners, unquestioning belief in state propaganda about their enemies was widespread. Most saw the United States was an aggressive empire, conspiring to keep Vietnam divided and occupy the South. Despite Washington's enormous military capabilities, it was an article of faith that this US endeavor must eventually fail. The tide of history and Vietnamese nationalism would prevail. In this view, the Americans' RVN ally was merely a puppet government, led by lackey traitors. From the moment Kennedy became president, most northern Vietnamese assumed that the US imperialists were pursuing every way possible to military expand into, and ultimately directly invade, Vietnam, south of the 17th parallel.

The daily *Nhan Dan*, a leading mouthpiece of the Communist Party in the DRVN and a powerful motivational and unifying force throughout the war, reflected this official political narrative permitted and propagated by the DRVN leadership and its censors. It updated northerners on national and international news, focusing primarily on the great achievements and victories of the communist bloc and the conspiracies and failures of the capitalists. It was distributed to all DRVN government offices and virtually all party members. Many ordinary people read it regularly as well. *Nhan Dan* drew a highly propagandistic portrait of Kennedy, from his presidential candidacy until his assassination. It also followed the political machinations of his administration and the various US officers and officials working in the Republic of Vietnam. Occasionally, it would cite the Soviet News Agency TASS, AP, VOA, and American newspapers and follow Kennedy's political and diplomatic activities, often focusing on failed US policies, political crises, economic problems such as inflation, strikes, labor issues, the high price of agricultural products, and other topics like substandard education and racism in the United States.[22]

During the early 1960s, many *Nhan Dan* columns conveyed the party line regarding the dire situation faced by their comrades in the South, who were facing intensified American intervention and the brutally of the Saigon regime. Reports of the dangerous conspiracies of the American imperialist invader often singled out Kennedy as the chief US foreign policymaker, portraying him as a powerful political operator and war baron who had made the decision to divide and destroy Vietnam.[23]

After the US presidential election, in November 1960, a regular *Nhan Dan* column, "Do you know?," introduced northern Vietnamese readers to Kennedy. Asking "What kind of person is Kennedy?," it provided details regarding the character, political ideology, and family background of the newly elected president and future adversary of the DRVN. The article began with Kennedy's background as a scion of one of the twelve richest families in the United States and leading Boston bankers. It then described Kennedy's "special talents," including his "ability to deliver thousands of lengthy speeches without expressing clear positions on important and challenging matters." The article then attacked Kennedy's for insincerity and deceitfulness, writing that "Kennedy could support the far right reactionaries, and [at the same time claim to] protect [labor] union's interests [on the left]." It also addressed African Americans' human rights: "Kennedy sometimes supports the northern representatives, and sometimes he's on the same side with the southern racists." The article's author further pointed out the striking contrast in Kennedy's defense policies: "Kennedy stated there would be an effort to solve the stalemate through disarmament and prohibition of nuclear weapon test. On the other hand, he called for increases to the defense budget, continued the arms race, and supported the testing of nuclear weapons." He also "advocated implementation of sabotage operations to oppose socialist countries, [and] continued policies hostile to China and [supported the] creation of 'two Chinese nations.'" Additionally, Kennedy publicly supported the violent overthrow of the revolutionary government of Cuba. Kennedy and the United States represented a looming threat to world peace and Vietnamese national sovereignty and unification. Generally speaking, in this view, Kennedy retained the imperialist US policies originating from previous administrations. "At the White House, a new president is replacing the old one. But there are no new policies to replace the old ones."[24]

A central topic that *Nhan Dan* broached time and again in the early 1960s was the US invasion of the South and Kennedy's growing financial and military aid to Diem's "puppet" government. In a speech at a meeting in Hanoi to support the American Communist Party, Hoang Quoc Viet, director of the Supreme People's Procuracy of Vietnam and later a member of the Communist Party Politburo, observed that Kennedy's military policies around the world were more aggressive than those of his predecessor, Dwight D. Eisenhower. Kennedy was increasing the military budget at an unforeseen rate and scale and was empowering US military alliances through NATO and SEATO. Hoang Quoc Viet then listed a number of other countries whose national interests Washington had undercut, undermining world peace. He concluded that "in southern Vietnam, the US sabotaged the Geneva accord, intentionally dividing Vietnam [into two parts] forever, and turned South Vietnam into a US military base and new colony. Under the label of anti-communism, the US sent tens of thousands of tons of weapons, and thousands of soldiers to invade South Vietnam."[25]

Another issue of *Nhan Dan* cited an article in I. F. Stone's weekly newspaper called "An Arms Budget Designed to Terrify." Like the afore-cited article, it observed that Kennedy's massive defense budget increases demonstrate that his policies were even more aggressive than Eisenhower's.[26] According to the reporter, Vu Dzung, in a letter to Diem in December 1961 Kennedy had affirmed that "the United States would rapidly increase their financial aid," adding that the "Kennedy administration decided to increase military intervention into southern Vietnam by sending high-ranking officers to serve as military commanders in the ARVN."[27] Similar themes persisted throughout Kennedy's presidency in the pages of *Nhan Dan*, which regularly reported that the US president was promoting a policy of invasion as he continuously increased the US arms budget and sent more and more military advisors to southern Vietnam.[28]

Nhan Dan occasionally also reported on Americans who were politically opposed to Washington's Vietnam policy, though. For example, on January 9, 1962, it cited one American author who insisted that "like it or not, accept it or not, we're directly participating in a hot war in Vietnam," and criticized the ARVN's failure to achieve victory and Kennedy's plans to expand the military intervention in the South.[29]

Periodically, *Nhan Dan* published personal opinions and perspectives of DRVN citizens, too. On February 2, 1961, an author named T. L. wrote a letter to Kennedy unequivocally blaming American foreign policy for the political situation in Vietnam: "It was the United States who divided our country and was behind every conspiracy to create a dictatorship and a puppet government in the South; who made Vietnamese lives in the South more and more miserable; who created fascist courts, arrested, tortured, and killed people in the urban and rural areas; and who destroyed homes and villages." The author then sent a clear message addressed directly to Kennedy: "If you want your statements to be valuable, you should immediately cease your intervention in the south of Vietnam, immediately recall the military advisors back to their home country, and let the people in the south of Vietnam solve their problems on their own."[30]

On January 16, 1963, *Nhan Dan* reprinted a TASS story emphasizing that the United States aimed to serve as a world leader. The story reported that in his address to Congress two days earlier, "Kennedy, with a thoroughly aggressive tone, praised the policy of invasion of South Vietnam . . . [and] insisted that the American goal is a victory on the global level, and the US would never quit its leading role in the world."[31] This view reflected what most people in northern Vietnam believed at the time: that it was the United States who was breathing new life into the Cold War, and that Kennedy was leading this effort.

Kennedy in the RVN

After the hasty departure of the French in 1954, a coalition of anti-communist, anti-Viet Minh southerners formed in the former French colony of Cochinchina. This happened first under the flag of a French-controlled puppet state, the Associated State of Vietnam, and by 1955 around the newly created Republic of Vietnam under the authority of the American-backed dictator Diem.

During the mid-1950s, the number, complexity, and constantly evolving nature of the factions and ideologies competing for a place in this newly minted southern Vietnamese state were stupefying. For Diem and his American advisors, trying to coalesce a nation-state from this simmering cauldron of religious sects, philosophies, parties, and intellectual communities was extremely challenging. To many outsider observers it appeared at first as if he was remarkably successful.[32]

However, unlike in the north, where communist thinking and ideology was overwhelmingly dominant, omnipresent, and extremely conspicuous, in the RVN ideologies and political opinions were often unpredictably shifting and hazardous. A number of southerners who would later support the revolution early on adopted a wait and see attitude toward the Diem regime and his American patron. For many Vietnamese, the path they would eventually follow and the political ideologies that would explain and validate their decisions along the way had not yet fully developed by 1954. As a result, among those cosmopolitan enough to follow world events, perceptions of a public figure like Kennedy was a constantly evolving and diverse reflection of the South's political, economic, and cultural complexity at the time.

As Washington's military and political involvement in Vietnam steadily grew in the early 1960s, some southern communities felt the need to begin a dialogue with the Kennedy administration. Both the Buddhists, during the Buddhist crisis in 1963, and the Catholics, who urged him to support their struggle against communism, entreated Kennedy to pressure Diem to change his policies. For example, in August 1963, during the height of the Buddhist crisis, a monk, Nguyen Bao Xuan, hoping to obtain Kennedy's support in the Buddhist struggle against persecution by the Diem government, wrote a letter requesting a meeting with the president and urging him to intervene on behalf of the protestors.[33]

At the same time, many other Vietnamese, particularly Communist Party members supporting the National Liberation Front, viewed Kennedy and his administration as the latest representatives of an interventionist American foreign policy.[34] This, however, did not necessarily preclude some of them from feeling a certain personal admiration for Kennedy. As Trinh Tuc, a former NLF newspaper editor active in the protests in Hue from 1962 until his arrest in 1964 put it:

> The student protesters only spoke about resisting America in a general sense. They spoke and demonstrated about the American policy of invading Vietnam, they spoke about resisting the American soldiers [stationed in Hue and still called advisors at this point], and about the oppression of the Buddhists and the high school and college students, they did not speak about Kennedy directly, they only spoke in generalities.[35]

To a large extent, among this political segment of southern Vietnamese society, Kennedy was viewed as an individual, insulated from the animosities aimed at his administration as a whole. From Tuc's perspective as a young revolutionary activist, Kennedy was a talented, youthful, strong, creative, open-minded, and politically adroit president who never really had the opportunity to fully implement his policies because of his assassination in 1963.[36] This point of view reflected the diversity of news sources available in Hue during that time.

Others, who were more sympathetic to the RVN and did not share Tuc's enthusiasm for revolution, had an even more favorable view of Kennedy. Thus, a scion of an elite family that had done well under the French and a former South Vietnamese ambassador to the United States under Nguyen Van Thieu, Bui Diem, was a young man at the time of Kennedy's inauguration. Years later, he wrote an insider's account of the war, *In the Jaws of History*, in which he described the impact of Kennedy's inaugural speech on him.[37]

> The United States and what it stood for had long ago invaded my imagination. As a schoolboy, I had read avidly about Franklin Delano Roosevelt and the way he had kept the Allies alive during World War II. John F. Kennedy, too, had been an inspirational figure. I was so attracted by the idealism he projected. I had followed his election closely and had been taken by his inaugural address, with its vision of an America that would "bear any burden, pay any price" [in order to protect freedom and democracy]. To my mind that had been a model speech, articulating a sense of what the United States represented in the world and of the energetic, confident role it had carved out for itself. For a young nationalist from an underdeveloped and threatened land, Kennedy's sentiments reinforce hopes of what might be and perhaps would be.[38]

Other Vietnamese observers of the Kennedy administration were similarly taken with the young president. Consider again Duong Van Mai Elliot. Born in 1941 as the daughter of a highly educated French colonial Vietnamese official, as a young woman she remembered vividly the lasting impression that the handsome and charismatic Kennedy left on her as he assumed office:

> The young President Kennedy overcame all my resistance to him on the day he took the oath of office. Standing hatless in the cold, his breath turning into white vapor as he spoke, he issued his ringing pledge that America would "pay any price, bear any burden, meet any hardship, support any friend, oppose any foe, to assure the survival and the success of liberty." I felt relieved; South Vietnam would surely be included in this worldwide embrace. At the moment, when Kennedy promised to set America on a new heroic course of defending freedom and helping "peoples in the huts and villages of half the globe" to "break the bonds of mass misery," the United States appeared noble to me. His was the rhetoric of an innocent, idealistic, but also arrogant era, when America believed that, with its immense resources, it could defend and nurture the whole world. Vietnam, of course, would shatter that illusion.[39]

As is evident from the impact it had on members of the educated elite like her and Bui Diem, Kennedy's pledge was exactly what many of Vietnam's most well-heeled citizens wanted to hear. Even those families that had acquired positions of wealth and privilege in the French colonial system still yearned for greater independence and an end to French colonial domination. However, this yearning was balanced by a vivid fear and distaste for North Vietnam's Viet Minh government—and Kennedy appeared to be firmly committed to helping prevent a communist victory in the South.

Members of Vietnam's economic, intellectual, and political elite who had refused to support the Viet Minh against the French had a particularly good reason to fear communist oppression and reprisal. Many who were considered important collaborators were targeted for assassination during the war. Others, who had done well under the French colonial system, faced public humiliation and were often dispossessed of their properties in the north as part of the 1954–56 land reforms. During this time, tens of thousands faced public show trials that frequently ended in executions.[40] Catholics felt particularly vulnerable because as a community they were assumed to oppose communism on religious and philosophical grounds and, thus, were frequently the object of intense suspicion by the Viet Minh.

Kennedy's eloquent blend of anti-colonial and anti-communist rhetoric inspired this group with the hope that the United States would sponsor and support the creation of an American-style republic while simultaneously preventing a communist takeover. Kennedy's persona buttressed this hope. As Mai Elliot put it:

> Now that I was persuaded of Kennedy's resolve to stand up to communism, I gave in to the charm and intellect of the new young and handsome president. Like most Americans, I was entirely caught up in the general adulation, and in the public relations and media frenzy over him and his beautiful wife. I became a big fan of the First Family, and in particular of Jacqueline Kennedy, whose bouffant hairdo I copied. The advisors that the president had assembled—the best and the brightest—impressed me to no end.[41]

Southern Vietnamese who consciously adopted a more neutral stance to the conflict in their country often developed a similar stance toward Kennedy. For example, in a vibrant community of academics, poets, artists, and musicians that had taken shape in the late 1950s and early 1960s in Hue around the newly built university and two elite high schools, Quoc Hoc and Dong Khanh, a number of prominent cultural and intellectual leaders resolutely refused to take sides in the war with either the Republic or the NLF. They included such luminaries as the famous folk singer Trinh Cong Son as well as popular writers and professors like Ngo Kha and Buu Y. Today Buu Y is still alive and living in Hue. Fluent in French, in the 1960s, he often obtained his news from French and other international sources like VOA and BBC. During an interview in May 2018, Buu Y shared his recollections of Kennedy:

> Kennedy was famous among young Vietnamese as a unique, special politician; a young and good looking president with a beautiful wife. His policies were strong, especially in relation to the USSR. In particular, what made Kennedy well known back then was that he was able to stop the USSR's actions when the USSR prepared to install their missiles in Cuba. He was known at the time to be considering whether the US should intervene [in Vietnam with ground troops] or not, and how to help Vietnam. He also didn't agree to the assassination of Ngo Dinh Diem.[42]

Buu Y, like a number of other prominent intellectuals from Hue at this time, never took sides in the war. Instead, he hid out during its height to avoid forced conscription by the RVN, and refused all entreaties by his friends in the NLF to join the revolution. As a result, his interpretation of the available local and international news sources reflected a relatively unbiased perspective, derived largely unfiltered from what he had read and heard at the time.

In the early 1960s, supporters of the RVN in Vietnam were deeply divided on the issue of Buddhism. Many leaders, primarily Catholics, remained fiercely loyal to the Diem regime, while a significant number of Buddhists and people sympathetic to the Buddhist community had either never supported Diem or had lost faith in him and began to search for alternatives. When Diem's blatantly pro-Catholic policies began to arouse public indignation among the Buddhists, causing thousands of them to flood the streets of Hue in protest, it became evident that Diem's policies were becoming a major source of political instability, which were further undermining the popularity of an already tottering political regime.

In the summer of 1963, opposition to Diem and his family reached a boiling point. The Kennedy administration found itself torn between two factions in the White House. Should it remain loyal to its longtime ally Diem, or begin supporting a popular movement that reflected the religious, spiritual, and political ideas of a large and highly respected segment of Vietnamese society? After a long and heated debate, Kennedy opted to remain true to his rhetoric regarding the paramount importance of broad-based popular support for the RVN government, feeling that at this point that he had no alternative but to begin to speak publicly about the limits of American support for Diem.[43]

By October of 1963, having been given no sign from Diem that significant policy changes were on the horizon, Kennedy came down firmly on the side of the Buddhists and began putting pressure on Diem to institute major political reforms and stop relying heavily on his cunning but extremely unpopular younger brother Ngo Dinh Nhu for political advice. "At the urging of the McNamara-Taylor mission in Saigon, [Kennedy] authorized the suspension of economic subsidies for South Vietnam's commercial imports and a cut-off of financial aid to the Vietnamese Special Forces, which were under the direct control of Ngo Dinh Nhu."[44] On November 2, a military junta led by Duong Van Minh overthrew and brutally murdered both Diem and his brother Nhu.

While many Vietnamese supporters of the Republic adopted a stance of pragmatic acceptance toward these events, understanding that the military coup could not have taken place without at least the tacit approval of the United States, a number of Diem supporters were enraged by Kennedy's decision to withdraw his support which they considered the ultimate betrayal of a close friend and ally of the United States. Among this group, a few even speculated that the sudden and violent deaths of both Diem and Kennedy might somehow be connected, perhaps by karma: "In November 1963, I witnessed on TV the tragic death of President Kennedy in Dallas. Years later, some Vietnamese people believed that the death of Pres. Kennedy, who approved the coup, and the assassination of his brother Robert K. in 1968, was the result of a curse by the Ngo family, who had also lost two brothers in the November coup d'etat."[45] Mai Elliott reported that this feeling was especially common among Catholics who had fled the north and resettled in the South after the DRVN's victory in 1954. "Diem's hard-core supporters, especially Catholic refugees, never forgave . . . Kennedy for Diem's death. At the time of Kennedy's assassination, many expressed satisfaction that Diem had reached beyond the grave to exact his revenge."[46] These were a minority, however. Diem's unpopularity was so pervasive, even among members of his own government that after his assassination the newly installed US-backed military dictatorship declared the date of his fall a national holiday.[47]

Conclusion

As in the United States, so in Vietnam, perceptions, ideas, and imaginings about Kennedy and his administration have evolved over the years as more information and time to reflect has become available. Today, although the Vietnamese government has changed relatively little about its official narrative of the war, even some of the United States' most prominent adversaries among DRVN leadership during the war have come to see Kennedy in a very different light. For example, in an interview in 1998, former minister of defense of the Democratic Republic of Vietnam, Vo Nguyen Giap, who is widely considered the greatest Vietnamese general in modern history, told John Kennedy Jr. that

> when your father was president . . . [I] had to very carefully research [Kennedy's] thoughts and policies. . . . I originally believed that his plan was to use military strength to help the Saigon government to stop the communist movement, but now, by way of [previously unavailable] historical documents, I have learned some time later that President Kennedy had rethought this and didn't want to support the Ngo Dinh Diem regime in Saigon. He wanted the US to be involved in the Vietnam War only to a certain extent. If that unfortunate event—the death of your father—had not taken place, things would have been somewhat different, not as they were under Johnson and Nixon.[48]

As is evident from the multitude of different perspectives touched on in this article, Vietnamese perceptions of Kennedy depended greatly on the particular community, political ideology, and time period. These differences reveal the complexity and challenges of reconstructing Kennedy from the ground up in a divided Vietnam in the mid-twentieth century.

Notes

1. Duong Van Mai Elliott, *The Sacred Willow: Four Generations in a Life of a Vietnamese Family* (New York: Oxford University Press, 1999), 285.
2. Christopher Goscha, *Vietnam: A New History* (New York: Basic Books, 2016), 252.
3. Ibid.
4. During the Second World War the Viet Minh worked together with the OSS to rescue American pilots shot down in China. After declaring independence in 1945,

DRVN President Ho Chi Minh wrote a letter to President Truman in 1946 requesting increased cooperation between the United States and the DRVN. Truman never responded. The letter is available online: https://www.archives.gov/historical-docs/todays-doc/?dod-date=228 (accessed December 17, 2018).
5   Official English translation of the Declaration of Independence of the DRVN, September 2, 1945, available online: http://chinhphu.vn/portal/page/portal/English/TheSocialistRepublicOfVietnam/AboutVietnam/AboutVietnamDetail?categoryId=10000103&articleId=10002648.
6   Christian Appy, *Patriots: The Vietnam War Remembered from All Sides* (New York: Penguin Books, 2003), 151.
7   This can also be observed in recent publications. See Institute of Military History, *Lich su Khang chien Chong My Cuu Nuoc, 1954-1975 [History of the Resistance against America to Save the Nation, 1954-1975]*, 9 vols. (Hanoi: Chinh Tri Quoc Gia Press, 2015); Institute of History Studies, *Lich su Viet Nam [History of Vietnam]*, 15 vols. (Hanoi: Khoa hoc Xa Hoi, 2017); Tran Gia Phung, *Viet Su Dai Cuong [Basic Vietnamese History]*, 7 vols. (Toronto: Non Nuoc Press, 2000s); Le Manh Hung, *Nhin lai Su Viet [Looking Back at Vietnamese History]*, 5 vols. (Arlington: To hop Xuat ban Mien Dong Hoa Ky Publishing House, 2016).
8   Tran Trong Trung, *Cuoc Chien tranh Sau Doi Tong Thong [The War of Six Presidents]*, (Ho Chi Minh City: Van Nghe Press, 1986); Nguyen Phuong Nam, *Tham bai cua Bay Dieu Hau: Ve cac Tong Thong My trong Chien tranh Viet Nam [Disasters of the Hawks: The American Presidents in the Viet Nam War]*, (Hanoi: Chinh Tri Quoc Gia Press, 2010); Bui Hanh Can, *Nam doi Tong Thong My trong Chien tranh Xam luoc Viet Nam [Five American Presidents in the War of Invasion in Vietnam]*, (Hanoi: Quan Doi Nhan Dan Press, 2015); Maud Guilaumin, *Ban linh Jackie Kennedy - Cuoc doi mot Huyen Thoai soi chieu qua nhung Bien co Chan dong [Boldness of Jackie Kennedy—The Legendary Life through Challenges]*, trans. by Hieu Constant, with an introduction by Nguyen Bui Quoc Dung (Hanoi: Stylory and The Gioi Press, 2017); Phan Van Ca, "Nhung Quyet dinh cua Chinh quyen John F. Kennedy ve Viet Nam nam 1961" [Decisions on Vietnam of John F. Kennedy Administration in 1961], *Tap chi Phat Trien Khoa hoc va Cong Nghe [Journal of Science and Technology Development]* 18, no. 5 (2015): 37–50.
9   Aaron Lillie, "Vietnam's Forgotten Revolutionaries: Student Voices from inside the Vietnamese Revolution" (M.A. thesis, University of Washington, Seattle, 2014), 8.
10 David Marr, "Introduction," in *Mass Media in Vietnam*, ed. David Marr (Canberra: Panther Publishing and Press, 1998), 2.
11 Huong Nguyen, "Eve of Destruction: A Social History of Vietnam's Royal City, 1957-1967" (PhD diss., University of Washington, Seattle, 2017), 121.
12 Marr, "Introduction," 3. See also Nguyen, "Eve of Destruction," 122–24.
13 "Conclusion of the Invasions and Failures of the American Imperialists," *Quan Doi Nhan Dan*, March 3, 1975, 2.
14 For Kennedy's speeches, see "Remarks of Senator John F. Kennedy on Indochina before the Senate," Washington, April 6, 1954. Available online: www.jfklibrary.org/Research/Research-Aids/JFK-Speeches/United-States-Senate-Indochina_19540406.aspx (accessed July 19, 2018).
15 Thurston Clarke, "Ask How," *NYT*, January 15, 2005, 1.
16 Richard Mahoney, *Sons and Brothers: The Days of Jack and Bobby Kennedy* (New York: Arcade, 1999), 13. See also "Kennedy on Indochina."
17 Mahoney, *Sons and Brothers*, 13.

18 "Kennedy on Indochina."
19 Lillie, "Revolutionaries," 18.
20 "Kennedy on Indochina."
21 The Communist Party of Vietnam, *Van Kien Dang toan tap [The Vietnamese Communist Party Documentations]*, vol. 20 (Hanoi: Chinh Tri Quoc Gia, 2002), 57, 70, 81–89.
22 "America Is Facing a Dilemma," *Nhan Dan*, February 1, 1961, 2; "American Economy Stagnates in All Aspects," *Nhan Dan*, February 5, 1961, 2; "American Agriculture Is in Serious Crisis," *Nhan Dan*, March 21, 1961, 2.
23 Numerous *Nhan Dan* columns, articles, and op-eds between 1960 and 1963 made this point. See "We Requested America Goes Home," *Nhan Dan*, January 23, 1961, 2; "Letter of the Ministry of Foreign Affairs of the DRVN about the American Government's Military Intervention in South Vietnam," *Nhan Dan*, March 1, 1962, 3–4.
24 "What Kind of Person Is Kennedy?" *Nhan Dan*, November 12, 1960, 4.
25 "The Strong Resistance of the American Communist Party and the Peace, Democratic Forces in the US Will Definitely Defeat the Crazy Attack of the American Government," *Nhan Dan*, January 21, 1962, 3.
26 For the original article, see http://www.ifstone.org/weekly/IFStonesWeekly-1962feb12.pdf (accessed August 1, 2018).
27 "America–Diem Communiqué Discloses American Plot to Escalate Invasion in South Vietnam," *Nhan Dan*, January 7, 1962, 4.
28 "The US Is Urgently Expanding the Invasion of South Vietnam," *Nhan Dan*, February 11, 1962, 4.
29 "An American Admitted the US Directly Intervened in South Vietnam, *Nhan Dan*, January 9, 1962, 4.
30 "Letter for Mr. Kennedy, the New President of the US," *Nhan Dan*, February 2, 1961, 2.
31 "Kennedy again Advocates War," *Nhan Dan*, January 16, 1963, 4.
32 See Jessica Chapman, *Cauldron of Resistance: Ngo Dinh Diem, The United States and 1950s Southern Vietnam* (Ithaca: Cornell University Press, 2013); Frederik Logevall, *Embers of War: The Fall of an Empire and the Making of America's Vietnam* (New York: Random House, 2012).
33 Reverend Nguyen Xuan Bao to Kennedy, September 5, 1963, re: "Sufferings of Vietnamese Buddhists," Vietnam Working Group, Bureau of Far Eastern Affairs, Vietnam Center and Archive, F038300030014, Box 0003, Folder 0014, The Vietnam Center and Archive, Texas Tech University, Lubbock.
34 Lillie, "Revolutionaries," 44. A substantial number of southerners, particularly communists, got their news from underground newspapers that frequently reprinted articles written by prominent communists from the north, and thus, shared many of the same political views with their northern comrades. Also, Communist Party members in the South were indoctrinated in Vietnamese communism through training courses usually taught at small military bases in the jungle. Instructors were generally long time party members who supported the DRVN and shared the same views as the communists in the north.
35 Aaron Lillie, interview with Trinh Tuc, Hue, August 8, 2018.
36 Ibid.
37 Bui Diem's uncle had served as prime minister of the French-controlled Vietnamese puppet state nominally under the control of emperor Bao Dai in the French protectorate of Annam, the central part of Vietnam today.

38 Bui Diem, *In the Jaws of History* (Bloomington: Indiana University Press, 1999), 117.
39 Elliott, *Sacred Willow*, 280.
40 Alex-Thai Vo, "Nguyễn Thị Năm and the Land Reform in North Vietnam, 1953," *Journal of Vietnamese Studies* 10, no. 1 (2015): 1–62.
41 Elliott, *Sacred Willow*, 280.
42 Diu-Huong Nguyen, interview with Buu Y, Hue, May 2, 2018.
43 Walter Cronkite, interview with Kennedy, September 2, 1963. Available online: http://www.presidency.ucsb.edu/ws/?pid=9388 (accessed July 19, 2018).
44 Lam Quang Thi, *The Twenty-Five Year Century: A South Vietnamese General Remembers the Indochina War to the Fall of Saigon* (Denton: University of North Texas Press, 2002), 107.
45 Ibid., 110.
46 Elliott, *Sacred Willow*, 299.
47 Charles Keyes, *The Golden Peninsula: Culture and Adaptation in Mainland Southeast Asia* (Honolulu: University of Hawaii Press, 1995), 289.
48 John Kennedy Jr., "The George Interview: Vietnam's Ruthless Warrior General Vo Nguyen Giap," *George*, November 1998. Available online: http://sangam.org/wp-content/uploads/2013/10/Giap-Interview-by-John-Kennedy-George-magazine-Nov-1998.pdf (accessed July 19, 2018).

Part IV

Intermediaries and Afterlives

13

The President's Messenger: American Visions, Indian Citizens, and National Development in the Kennedy Years

Benjamin Siegel

In the summer of 1963, the United States Information Service retained the services of a research firm in Bombay, tasking it with a survey of the social and political attitudes of the city's "middle and upper classes."[1] The firm's report detailed Indian opinion on technical aid and the European common market; on the relevance of Gandhian thought and the specter of nuclear arms in Asia; on preferred genres of film and the desirability of "free" versus arranged marriages. Yet most striking to the newly appointed US ambassador to India Chester Bowles was the fact that a third of those surveyed had named John F. Kennedy the world figure they would most like to meet. Bowles marveled that the young American president had tied evenly with the aging Indian premier, Jawaharlal Nehru. "There is every evidence," he wrote to Kennedy, "that you could carry Bombay as easily as you carry Boston."[2]

Indians' ardor for the American president seemed to only grow in the wake of his assassination in November 1963. Tributes would pour in from across the Republic, lauding the late president whom Indian papers had extolled, at his election, as a leader ready to "abandon the cold war strategy and work in cooperation with other countries for peace and freedom."[3] Indian publishers, in the wake of Kennedy's death, would scramble to meet popular demand for accounts of his life.[4] And the site of his assassination would become a requisite pilgrimage for Indian politicians traveling to the United States in subsequent years.

Well before he assumed the office of the presidency, Indian citizens perceived Kennedy as an intimately knowable figure—a statesman whose luster was similar to that enjoyed by a cadre of Indian politicians whose likenesses were emblazoned on posters, calendars, and murals. Kennedy's presidency coincided with a radical transformation in the Indian public's perception of the United States, as well. In the wake of the Sino-Indian War of October 1962, nearly 62 percent of Indians surveyed professed a "very good" opinion of the United States, as compared with 7.5 percent who had declared the same a month earlier.[5] In their transformative affection for the US president, Indians joined a global sodality of Asians, Africans, and Latin Americans who saw in his administration a wholly unprecedented consideration for the aspirations of nations far away from the American heartland.

Yet Indians' sense of intimacy with the American president was bolstered by a dynamic unique to the context of a changing nation in its second decade of independence, as well as the particulars of an ambassadorial appointment whose background in administration and economics offered a strategic tonic to a country roiled by those changes. If Kennedy's presidency might reasonably be seen as the first to lay plausible claim to the title of "leader of the free world," it found unusual traction in an Indian context. This was, as the present chapter argues, in large measure thanks to the administration's use of strategic intermediaries—Ambassador John Kenneth Galbraith, and to a lesser extent First Lady Jacqueline Kennedy and Vice President Lyndon B. Johnson—who could tap into a mounting hunger for new sources of authority.

This dynamic was an inadvertent one. "No post," Galbraith had declared upon his arrival in New Delhi in April 1961, "ever seemed to me so important as that of Ambassador from the United States to India."[6] Yet Kennedy's designation of Galbraith was in fact a consolation prize to the prolix and towering Harvard professor, who had declined an offer to chair the Council of Economic Advisors and had lobbied unsuccessfully to be named the president-elect's Congressional replacement. But whereas Galbraith's first encounters with India, as an economic advisor in 1956 and 1959, had come at the high noon of planning ideologies in the country, his ambassadorial career came at a moment when the confidence of an earlier moment was yielding to the uncertainties of the next.

In the middle of the 1950s, even as a Fabian socialism reigned supreme, New Delhi had emerged as a central site for pivotal negotiations over economic development and national planning. "[At] no other place in the world at the time," Galbraith himself would recall, was there such easy and intense exchange between people of the socialist and the nonsocialist worlds and of the rich countries and the poor."[7] By the time Galbraith had returned, however, the Planning Commission had ceded much of its authority over national development to the Finance Ministry. P. C. Mahalanobis—the head of the Indian Statistical Institute who had first introduced Galbraith to India—who had fallen out with the aging prime minister.[8] And the authority of Nehru himself had begun to ebb, with Indian politicians and citizens unsure as to who might rightly claim his mantle upon his death.

It was in this crucible that the United States could maneuver for new authority in India. Kennedy's youth and charisma, alongside the promise of a changed geopolitical configuration, allowed Indians to look overseas and see an American in the familiar, "saintly idiom" of Indian politics.[9] A brief charm offensive by gruff vice president in May 1961 and a highly public visit from the First Lady in March 1962 helped cement the image of a beneficent imperium willing to midwife the aspirations of a Third World public. But Galbraith, Kennedy's single most visible interlocutor in India, was a sober-minded student of Indian economics, politics, and administration, who had long insisted that Indians look beyond dogma in formulating national policy—a position that resonated loudly against the backdrop of planning's decline.

In their assessments of the Kennedy administration's efforts in South Asia, historians of American foreign relations and the Cold War have foregrounded the critical role of the Kashmir crisis, the Sino-Indian War of 1962, and the military and fiscal support of the United States of Pakistan against the objections of Indian policymakers.[10] The Kennedy administration is rightly cast, in most recent accounts, as a watershed moment in American policymaking in South Asia. The ascent of a president who had long argued a case for Indian aid in the Senate and the subsequent appointment of a cadre of liberal thinkers in the State Department and in New Delhi spoke to India's centrality to a new, flexible approach to nonalignment and developmental aid.[11] If this posture alienated Pakistan, the longtime ally of the United States, and was dampened by the personal antipathy between the American president and the Indian premier, it nonetheless ushered in a new detente between Washington and New Delhi. Yet in giving primacy to the debates in Foggy Bottom, these accounts fail to account for the changes which were transforming Indian politics in the same moment, and the different visions of the future which were available to Indian actors in the years surrounding Nehru's death. If Kennedy's allure in India—the notion that he could easily "carry Bombay"—owed much to the charisma of a young president, it owed a similar debt to US interlocutors who could suggest new futures for Indian economic planning, and who enjoyed particular visibility in India. Among them was an ambassador as ready to walk barefoot alongside farmers as he was debating policy futures with planners and university professors.[12]

Long before his administration would place India as the center of its new strategy for the nonaligned world, Senator Kennedy had found favor among Indian observers for his dogged support of aid for India and his insistence that a failure to support Asia's largest democracy risked ceding economic dominance of the continent to Communist China.[13] India was central to the young senator's efforts to shore up his foreign policy *bona fides* and build alliances with the liberal wing of the Democratic Party. In October 1957, Kennedy had declared India to be the "broker" between, and the "centerpiece" of, "uncommitted nations" in a long *Foreign Policy* article; early the following year, Kennedy would declare in the *Progressive* that India was the greatest example of democratically minded economic development.[14]

In the summer of 1958, Kennedy would enlist former ambassador John Sherman Cooper, a Republican congressman from Kentucky, to introduce a bipartisan bill calling for a major increase in aid to India.[15] India, Kennedy declared, "represents as great a hope, as commanding a challenge as Western Europe did in 1947."[16] If its position of nonalignment vexed certain American politicians, Kennedy urged them to remember the United States' own "policy of non-involvement in the great international controversies of the nineteenth century." So, too, did Kennedy suggest that India's Five-Year plans were the necessary precondition for "future private investment in India," citing the support of industrialists like G. D. Birla and J. R. D. Tata for government investment in essential sectors.[17] The Kennedy-Cooper resolution failed, only to be reintroduced successfully a year later with "South Asia" substituted for "India," and redrafted with help of liberal economists at the MIT Center for International Studies and Indian diplomats and economists. Yet even in its first iteration, it had established Kennedy, in India, as a promising advocate for American assistance at a moment when India's ambitious second-year plan was being dramatically scaled back on account of depleted coffers.[18]

Indian adulation for the US senator was tempered by a sense that Kennedy's interest was overly instrumental. Bombay's *Economic Weekly* noted with some surprise that in a Committee for International Economic Growth meeting in May 1959 attended by Kennedy and his fellow presidential aspirant Richard Nixon, it was the latter who had emphasized aid in the interest of "plenty over want, of health over disease, of freedom over tyranny" on their own grounds, as opposed to baldly geopolitical ones.[19] Yet Kennedy had, in developing his own case for India, relied upon the support of a team of liberal economists and modernization theorists, Max F. Millikan and Walt Rostow chief among them. Yet since 1957, he had increasingly and frequently met with Galbraith—whom he had first met as an undergraduate in Harvard's Winthrop House. Kennedy had first sought out Galbraith's advice on agricultural policy, but he had become increasingly eager for the economist's reports on India, where Galbraith had dived into the deep end of vital policy debates.[20]

Galbraith himself had "discovered" India quite by accident, spending a sabbatical year in Geneva. In summer 1955, a dinner guest had brought P. C. Mahalanobis, the doyen of Indian planning and the head of the Indian Statistical Institute, to Galbraith's house, and by the statistician's account of the work being done in New Delhi, Galbraith began planning his visit.[21] He pored over copies of the draft Second Five-Year Plan that Mahalanobis had sent, while his secretary reached out to former students now working in India—among them, a researcher at the Reserve Bank of India in New Delhi, a manager at the Swadeshi Cotton Mills in Kanpur, and an economist at Benares Hindu University.[22]

Mahalanobis's invitation to Galbraith came at a time when the statistician's own authority in New Delhi owed much to his contacts with overseas economists. A coterie of foreign economists from the first and second worlds had congregated at the Indian Statistical Institute; their lively debates there had provided cover for Mahalanobis as he put forth his own ambitious program for the Second Five-Year Plan.[23] That program, which appeared in *Sankhya: the Indian Journal of Statistics* as "The Operational Research Approach to Planning in India," had called for major investment in heavy industry, investment in capital goods for long-term growth, a large public sector, and a massive push for Indian economic self-reliance. The plan had the support of Nehru and the left wing of the Congress party but vexed the more conservative members on the Indian Planning Commission.

Galbraith had treaded cautiously into these debates, thinking through the draft plan alongside Indian and foreign colleagues. In three papers he drafted for the Institute, he urged Indian planners to eschew doctrinaire thinking and to pay attention to the particular contexts and circumstances of Indian development.[24] The country's reflexive socialist impulse, he declared, was an impediment to a careful consideration of the merits and drawbacks of the free market; most prominently, it was in their approach to public industries "that Indian leaders are being least guided by experience and reflecting least deeply in their course."[25] Indians did not recoil from the gentle criticism of an American interlocutor who trespassed carefully into thorny internecine debates. Audiences in Madras came to hear Galbraith praise a "highly competent government" that could profitably reduce its involvement in certain tasks to increase its success in others.[26] Galbraith garnered an increasingly certain reputation as a freethinking interlocutor keenly aware of Indian public opinion.[27]

Galbraith's was a confident message delivered inopportunely. The economist's departure from India in 1956 came as the country plunged into a massive foreign exchange crisis, with the country's sterling balances depleted and its export of raw materials quickly declining.[28] The confidence that had accompanied the introduction of the Second Five-Year Plan crumbled quickly and with it many Indians' faith in the wisdom of planning itself. Galbraith kept tabs on these developments in his continued correspondence with Indian economists and planners.[29] If publicly, the economist would pithily describe India's "smallish socialized sector atop what, no doubt, is the world's greatest example of functioning anarchy" in *Foreign Affairs*, he would declare in the same breath that there was no one model, capitalist or communist, that applied wholly to India—a pliability that would make him an ideal representative for an administration eager to distance itself from earlier dogmatism.[30] Galbraith returned to India in 1959 to consult on public ownership of the country's steel industry, visiting the new steel plants in Jamshedpur, Rourkela, and Bilhai.[31] Galbraith would speak with barefooted workers at Bilhai and listen to Russian shortwave music with Pitamber Pant—Mahalanobis' protégé and a close confidant of Nehru—before meeting with the prime minister himself to discuss the economist's recently published *The Affluent Society*.[32] Nehru was at a political nadir after the rejection of his call for collective farming at Nagpur in January 1959. But the prime minister and the Harvard economist enjoyed an easy rapport, unaware that they would meet again in two years' time under drastically changed circumstances.

In the wake of Kennedy's electoral success in November 1960, Indian luminaries rushed to congratulate the young senator. Sarvepalli Radhakrishnan, Rajendra Prasad, and the Dalai Lama sent their congratulations to the new president, and Ambassador M. C. Chagla invited the president-elect to a premiere of Satyajit Ray's *World of Apu*.[33] At the heart of the exhilaration that marked Indians' response to Kennedy's election was the sense that it represented, as Patna's *Indian Nation* declared, the "triumph of liberal elements in the USA."[34] The appointments of Dean Rusk and Chester Bowles to the State Department, and the rumor that Galbraith was under consideration, all spoke to an Indian hope that Kennedy would "love to abandon the cold war strategy and work in cooperation with other countries for peace and freedom." The *Times of India* was bullish in its hopes for a new chapter in Indo-American relations. "The President-elect himself," it suggested, "has shown a keen awareness of India's key position in the non-Communist world."[35] Nehru had admired the Kennedy campaign from a distance and had cheered on his victory over Nixon.[36] Upon his election, he reached out to the new president to laud his "continuing efforts to create a peaceful world community," and Kennedy had responded with praise for India's Five-Year Plans, which boded well "not only for the future of India but is an example for the whole world of the achievements possible to a free society."[37]

As a senator, Kennedy had appropriated the plan for a "Point Four Youth Corps" first made by Wisconsin representative Henry Reuss in the wake of his Asian tour in 1957; he echoed this call in his October 1960 speech presaging the creation of the Peace Corps.[38] He also mined American university departments in search of foreign policy expertise, bringing in Walt Rostow, Lincoln Gordon, Edward Mason, Eugene Staley, Samuel Hayes, Max Millikan, and Lucien Pye to give grist to the promise of new policies for the developing world. Indian observers watched these appointments with interest: as early as July 1960, the *Economic Weekly* had allowed itself to speculate on whether or not Adlai Stevenson and Chester Bowles would be elevated to positions of importance in a Kennedy administration, and what sorts of "urbane and humanistic approach to policy" Indians might expect.[39]

Most exciting for Indian observers, however, was the revelation at the end of 1960 that Galbraith was to be tapped as ambassador. Galbraith, the *Times of India* suggested, like Kennedy himself, wanted to see India "built as a show place of free planning"—a goal that electrified Indian bureaucrats.[40] Despite Indians' belief that Galbraith had lobbied for the India posting, Galbraith had in fact been a reluctant appointee.[41] Declining the president-elect's offer to serve as chair of the Council of Economic Advisors, Galbraith had quietly lobbied to be named Kennedy's replacement in the Senate, before it was clear that the president had his brother, Edward, in mind. Galbraith accepted the posting to India with some reluctance—his antipathy toward the new secretary of state, Dean Rusk, was such that he had to be talked out of resigning his post by National Security Advisor McGeorge Bundy prior to even going through his confirmation hearings. Yet Galbraith's excitement for the posting grew alongside the centrality of India to US bureaucrats and politicians themselves.

The Harvard economist was wading again into a thorny political morass. As he arrived in India in April 1961, New Delhi's depleted coffers were suggesting the necessity of another PL480 agreement to stave off hunger. A new draft outline for the Third Five-Year Plan was suggesting the need for a large outlay from the center and an increased commitment to public sector enterprises. And the socialist principles which had animated state policy since independence were in recession after Nehru's decisive failure at Nagpur. Meanwhile, in the wake of big talk, Kennedy's policy team was itself debating the material extent of aid which it was prepared to extend to India. New Delhi had formally requested $2.5 billion to support the execution of the Third Five-Year Plan, a loosening of the restrictions on the US Development Loan Fund which would allow it to issue loans on a general, and not per-project basis, and the appointment of a full-time high-ranking government officer to be an advocate for India's plans and its requirements.[42] Galbraith, Rostow, Bowles, and others debated this proposal, and a memorandum sent by B. K. Nehru made a similar case for greater Indian autonomy in what they did with American aid, and for India receiving a greater proportion of America's total international assistance budget.[43] One of the most astute analyses came from the outgoing labor attaché at the American Embassy in New Delhi, David S. Burgess, who declared that Kennedy's election would give succor to the growing number of Indians who had come to believe, since the inception of the Technical Cooperation Mission in 1952, "that we are primarily interested in their nation's welfare for its own sake and are not attempting by subterfuge to cajole India into allying herself militarily with us."[44] Yet he urged Galbraith and his incoming staff to double down on the efforts of the United States in agriculture; overcome a weariness of supporting public sector industries to compete more effectively with the Soviets; expand American business connections with firms other than the "big four" of the Tatas, Birlas, Dalmias, and Jains; and deepen networks with "business associations, labor unions, independent cooperatives, charitable organizations, writers' societies, professional clubs, educational associations, youth organizations"—in the interest of further influence.

Debates over the future of US assistance in India swirled as Galbraith arrived at New Delhi's Palam airport on April 8. Stepping off the plane, the ambassador averred that President Kennedy was ushering in an era characterized by a "more effective organization of our assistance to the less developed lands." If earlier assistance had been dogmatic, Galbraith declared that the Kennedy administration's program "will recognize that different countries have different needs and preferences in economic organization. If it demonstrates any such preference it will be strictly on behalf of what gets results."[45] The ambassador conveyed the same to his staff at the sprawling embassy—the United States' largest in Asia—asking for their help in assuring the Indian public that, before ideology, "we are for liberty, social justice, and improved material wellbeing."[46]

Indian papers buzzed with breathless reports of what this new message might practically mean, and what significance Indian citizens could attribute to the appointment of a liberal economist with a long engagement with the country as the new representative of the United States.[47] Even in the absence of any real policy announcements, Bombay's *Jyothi* contrasted Galbraith favorably with his predecessors—particularly Henry Grady, who, if also an economist, had treated Indian leaders "as if they were a class of juniors trying to understand the principles of 'marginal utility' and 'supply and demand.'"[48] Galbraith was, by contrast, the learned representative of a president with "full respect for Indian leadership and a full comprehension of what Indo-American cooperation can do for the free world and for world peace." The *Free Press Journal*'s report of a new "economic cell" at the US embassy and an upcoming national tour that Galbraith would undertake—both designed to make the case for greater aid—was unfounded.[49] Yet it underscored the weight behind more sober reports on Galbraith and Kennedy, and their concurrence that "new thinking" was needed on the question of Indian aid.[50]

Indian observers who put their stock in the new ambassador were not disappointed. Galbraith defended India's position of nonalignment vociferously to Dean Rusk and continued to press forth the case for greater aid to India.[51] Within three weeks of his arrival, the United States had proposed a billion dollars of assistance to India at the meeting of the "Aid India Club" in Paris, exhorting other member states to follow suit. The stance flummoxed other members of the creditors' consortium and heartened observers in India.[52] "The stand taken by the United States," *Economic Weekly* opined, "reflects the radical change that has taken place." Nehru wrote to Kennedy with gratitude, while continuing to press for "maximum flexibility" in the conditions attached to aid. Galbraith, for his part, took the State Department by surprise with an off-the-cuff statement that the proposed fourth steel plant that Indian authorities had planned in the city of Bokaro was "within the range" of American aid.

Galbraith was not the only American winning plaudits for the United States: Indians looking for signs of further detente had reason to cheer Vice President Johnson's May 1961 visit to India. The garrulous Texan kept the Indian prime minister up late into the night—even if Nehru responded coolly to Johnson's suggestion that India play a greater part in containing communism in Asia.[53] More significant was Johnson's impromptu, open-air tour of Old Delhi, which spoke of a new openness in American attitudes.⁵⁴ In Agra, Johnson underscored the point further by riding in a bullock cart in sweltering heat, taking time for a "great amount of friendly hand-shaking." Johnson, Galbraith quipped, "would run well nationwide," and his visit had "markedly strengthened [the] Indian picture of new administration as liberal and compassionate and much interested in Indian problems."⁵⁵

If the Indian popular press made good capital on Johnson's visit, it was still the American ambassador whose proclamations were meticulously parsed by an educated Indian public. Galbraith had returned home from a June 1961 visit to the United States with a flurry of announcements concerning aid, including a $60 million dollar, interest-free loan to build 860 miles of highways and nineteen bridges in India, and the favorable prospects of the United States assisting India's proposed Bokaro steel plant.⁵⁶ If constrained from speaking too directly about American policy, Galbraith took it upon himself in the summer of 1961 to draft four major addresses on economic policy and administration in India.⁵⁷ Galbraith delivered these speeches at universities in Madras, Calcutta, Bombay, and New Delhi, usually before or after inaugurating a new, American-funded project near each city—a mid-day meal scheme, a dairy plant, and other ventures designed to show American largess at the ground level. In Madras, he decried the "standard prescription" for economic development which had guided planners since the Second World War, suggesting that an emphasis on technical knowledge, capital, manpower, and planning had too often overlooked social context.⁵⁸ In Calcutta, Galbraith once more skewered the notion of a "common formula" for economic development, arguing that a proliferation of foreign aid subsidizing Indian planning had let Indian planners avoid thorny questions about which goals to prioritize.⁵⁹ In Bombay, Galbraith continued to urge Indian planners to differentiate between what was necessary in a plan and what was merely desirable.⁶⁰ And at the Indian Institute of Public Administration in New Delhi, Galbraith delved into the question which had captivated him since 1956, that of public enterprise in India. He urged Indians to balance "control with freedom," implicitly pushing planners to support the latter.⁶¹

The *Indian Express* lauded an economist cum ambassador willing to "jolt current thinking on economic development out of the grooves in which it has settled," and the *Hindustan Standard* praised the "veiled warning[s] which the planners should not miss."⁶² Vernacular papers in Telugu, Tamil, Hindi, Urdu, and Bengali reported extensively on each speech, taking pride where the ambassador had gone to lengths to highlight India's progress in place of its defects. The Telugu-language *Andhra Jyothi* in Vijayawada foregrounded Galbraith's promise that India would not need technical aid in the future.⁶³ Calcutta's Hindi-language *Vishavmitra* beamed at the ambassador's declaration that India's own experiences would soon prove useful to lesser-developed countries.⁶⁴ And the popular Hindi daily *Jagran* lauded the American's declaration that "modern" equipment was not the only road to development.⁶⁵ If the prolix Galbraith might have objected to his disquisitions being reduced to these quick talking points, they nonetheless increased his—and the Kennedy administration's—public prominence.

In the wake of these addresses, Galbraith traveled to Calcutta to announce American support for the city's Master Plan, a five-to-seven-year urban redevelopment scheme undertaken with Ford Foundation support, gaining applause from all but the most diehard Bengali communists.[66] The ambassador then traveled to Trivandrum, Kerala, to inaugurate a school lunch program operating with American grains.[67] Rosy accounts of Galbraith's check-cutting helped mask the frosty pallor which characterized Nehru's trip to the United States in November 1961. Kennedy had expected that he would have the same quick rapport with the Indian premier as he had had with other nonaligned leaders like Kwame Nkrumah, Julius Nyerere, Sukarno, and others.[68] Yet the Oval Office meeting between Nehru and Kennedy emerged as a nadir of the American president's diplomatic career: Kennedy found the aging Nehru to be irritable and withdrawn, offering only grunted, monosyllabic replies to his probing questions, declaring it "the worst head-of-state visit I have had." On *Meet the Press*, Galbraith assured his American viewers that the two men were merely in a "process of getting acquainted."[69]

Yet if Galbraith had to run defense in the United States, these dynamics were less visible in India, where papers had run panegyrical reports before and after Galbraith and Nehru's trip. A profile in Bombay's *Sunday Standard* lauded Galbraith's "love of harmony and justice, and sympathy for pain and suffering," casting him—and by extension, the United States—as consumed by the problem of India's poverty.[70] Even a more sober-minded assessment in the *Financial Express* credited the ambassador with having "gone to some length to interpret the US assessment of Indian planning and to suggest, albeit mildly, correctives to imbalances which he detected."[71] At a birthday party for the seventy-two-year-old Nehru at the Waldorf-Astoria hotel, Galbraith had delivered a "present" in the form of a grant to underwrite an educational consortium of nine engineering colleges and institutes which would support the development of the two-year-old Indian Institute of Technology at Kanpur into one of the world's leading technological institutions. Galbraith returned to India to tout this investment at an address on education and development.[72] "A dollar or a rupee invested in the intellectual improvement of human beings," he declared, "will often bring a greater increase in national income than a dollar or a rupee devoted to railways, dams, machine tools or other tangible capital goods."

Less than a year after Johnson's flying visit had given Indian audiences a taste of Texan swagger, Jacqueline Kennedy's eleven-day tour of India, in February 1962, put American opulence and glamour on display.[73] Indian audiences flocked to see the *Amriki Rani* floating on a launch down the Ganges, taking in a Buddhist ceremony at Sarnath, and accepting tiger cubs on behalf of the Washington, D. C. zoo. If Galbraith tried to shield the Indian public from the 200 dollars that the First Lady spent on Benares silks, and the trunks of Oleg Cassini gowns she ferried on her South Asian tour, he nonetheless welcomed the opportunity to showcase American splendor through Mrs. Kennedy's personal allure, which reflected as positively on the president as earlier joint visits by the couple—to Paris, for instance, in June 1961.

As for Galbraith, throughout 1962 academic audiences heard him work through the themes which had animated his earlier public addresses in India: the question of poverty and development and the need to eschew dogmatic approaches to each. At Gujarat University, the offered his remedy to the "prophets of the commonplace," who cast poverty a disease but refused to offer a proper diagnosis. Each of the standard explanations of India's poverty—character, colonial impoverishment, ignorance, poor governance, or diminished resources—was inadequate in and of itself. Poverty, he declared, needed to be assessed only in its full social context, and cited the work of journalist Kusum Nair as the sort of investigation that planners should heed.[74]

Returning to the United States to convalesce after an illness, Galbraith developed these themes further at a commencement address at Lewis and Clark College, and a second speech at San Francisco's Commonwealth Club.[75] Even from this distance, Indian papers took keen note of Galbraith's declamations, for instance in Portland, that technical aid stripped of strong social awareness was meaningless. "Technical assistance," he contended "is easier to provide to farmers than land reform. A hydroelectric power project is easier to launch than a sound system of elementary education." In San Francisco, Galbraith urged the United States to "meet the Marxian promise of reform of restarting institutions" in its developmental promises overseas. This institutional approach—not dissimilar from that which Gunnar Myrdal was, at the same time, urging for India—was in evidence in his next address, back in Calcutta, where he declared that India, for its work on popular education, village development, family planning, and land consolidation, would in time become a model for the other developing countries of Asia and Africa.[76]

Galbraith's extended disquisition on the ends and means of development was interrupted, on October 16, by the outbreak of the Cuban Missile Crisis. Scrambling to defend American actions to the skeptical Indian authorities, he watched with worry as Indo-Chinese tensions continued to mount, culminating in a massive Chinese offensive on October 23. In two weeks' time, Galbraith was summoned to the prime minister's office, where Nehru—"deathly tired and a little beaten"—reached out to request American "support." A million rounds, 40,000 land mines, and 100,000 mortar rounds streamed into India over the objections of American conservatives—and the sad resignation of the prime minister, crestfallen over the betrayal of the principles of the Panchsheel Treaty and nonalignment alike. Policymakers within the administration had argued that the Sino-Indian War was the lever needed to bend India into alignment with the United States—a culmination of the policy objectives that Kennedy had espoused since his campaigning days.

It has been tempting for historians to see in the Sino-Indian War the most sustained effort by the Kennedy administration to yoke Indians into alignment with the West. Historians of the Cold War, echoing the disappointment of policymakers themselves, suggest that India's subsequent failure to move more thoroughly into the orbit of the United States—alongside the diminished influence of the United States in Pakistan in the wake of Indian support—represents a failure of American diplomacy in South Asia. Yet this gloss moves too quickly past the fundamental shift in Indian perceptions of the United States in the wake of the Kennedy administration's skilled use of intermediaries—principally Ambassador Galbraith, but also Vice President Johnson and the First Lady Jacqueline Kennedy—to mold those perceptions and the capacious approach to economics and administration advanced by its ambassadorial representative.

Kennedy's assassination in November 1963 would stun the Indian populace. Prime Minister Nehru would decry the murder of "a man of ideals, vision and courage, who sought to serve his own people as well as the larger causes of the world."[77] Yet even as he spoke, Nehru's own ability to convey the strength and clarity of his Fabian vision was fading. His health in decline, the prime minister watched as the Congress Party's fissures deepened into cleaves: a dominant, moderate faction headed by the diminutive Lal Bahadur Shastri, and the hard-line Hindu nationalist camp led by Morarji Desai.[78] More importantly, however, by the time of Kennedy's assassination, it was clear that the heyday of planning itself had passed: the Finance Ministry had wrested a great deal of control over the planning process itself from the once largely autonomous Planning Commission, and even as American representatives like Galbraith paid lip service to them, the allure of Five-Year Plans had wholly faded.[79] What the United States did offer, in this period, was a sense that in the place of a planning, a more contextual and rooted approach to economics, administration, and politics might emerge—one embodied in the person of the president and transmitted with clarity and acumen by his economically minded ambassador.

Notes

1 "Middle and Upper Class Bombay Opinion on Political and Social Issues," September 5, 1963, Box 118A, President's Office Files (POF) (#3), Presidential Papers (PP), John F. Kennedy Presidential Library, Boston (JFKL).
2 Bowles to Kennedy, September 9, 1963, Box 118A, POF (#3), PP, JFKL.
3 "Odds & Ends," *Indian Nation*, December 15, 1960.
4 In Hindi, see Shyam Bihar Lal Dikshit, *Amerika ke Pentisavem Rashtrapati: Jaun Phitsajerada Kainedi [America's Thirty-Fifth President, John Fitzgerald Kennedy]* (Delhi: Dharmabhoomi Prakashan, 1964); and Narasimha Ram Shukla, *Amariki Rashtrapati Kenedi* (unknown publisher, 1964). In Marathi, see Damodar Narhar Shikhare, *Dhirodatta Kenedi* (unknown publisher, 1964). In Tamil, see Jan Tapilyu Kartnar and En Ramaratnam, *Kalappokkai marrutal: Janatipati Kennati patavi erra mutal varusattil ceyta piracankankal* (Cennai: Palaniyappa, 1963); Naki, *Manitarul manikkam Kennati* (Cennai: Vanati Patippakam, 1964); and Murukucuntaram, *Kennati: vira varalaru* (Irotu: Vela, 1965). In Telugu, see Potluri Venkateswararao, *Kennedihatya kesu: yadardhagadha* (Madras: Balaji Publications, 1964). One enterprising Punjabi publisher issued an improbable three-figure biography of Kennedy, Churchill, and Nehru: Aisa Amol, *Tinna maham purasha* (Jalandhar: Dhanapata Rae, 1964).
5 John Kenneth Galbraith, *Letters to Kennedy*, ed. James Goodman (Cambridge: Harvard University Press, 1998), 118–20.
6 Galbraith, "Statement on Arrival in New Delhi, April 8, 1961," Box 545, John Kenneth Galbraith Papers (JKGP), JFKL.
7 George Rosen, *Western Economists and Eastern Societies: Agents of Change in South Asia, 1950-1970* (Baltimore: Johns Hopkins University Press, 1985), 59.
8 Medha Kudaisya, "'A Mighty Adventure': Institutionalising the Idea of Planning in Postcolonial India, 1947–60," *MAS* 43, no. 4 (2008): 939–78.
9 W. H. Morris-Jones, "India's Political Idioms," in *Modern India: An Interpretive Anthology*, ed. Thomas R. Metcalf (London: Macmillan, 1971), 273–91.
10 Mostly recently, and skillfully, see Rudra Chaudhuri, *Forged in Crisis: India and the United States Since 1947* (New York: Oxford University Press, 2014).

11 See Dennis Merrill, *Bread and the Ballot: The United States and India's Economic Development, 1947-1963* (Chapel Hill: University of North Carolina Press, 1990); Robert McMahon, "Choosing Sides in South Asia," in *Kennedy's Quest for Victory: American Foreign Policy, 1961-1963*, ed. Thomas Paterson (Oxford: Oxford University Press, 1992), 198–222; Paul McGarr, *The Cold War in South Asia* (Cambridge: Cambridge University Press, 2013); and Robert Rakove, *Kennedy, Johnson, and the Nonaligned World* (New York: Cambridge University Press, 2014).
12 "Ambassador Galbraith Meets Farmer," *Nav Bharat*, May 29, 1962.
13 McGarr, *Cold War*, 73.
14 McMahon, "Choosing Sides," 200.
15 John F. Kennedy, "A Democrat Looks at Foreign Policy," *Foreign Affairs* 36, no. 1 (1957): 44–59.
16 Dennis Kux, *India and the United States Estranged Democracies, 1941-1991* (Collingdale, PA: DIANE Publishing, 1992), 148.
17 Zaheer Baber, "Social Scientific Knowledge and American Interests," in *Handbook of Development Policy Studies*, eds. Gedeon Mudacumura and M. Shamsul Haque (New York: Marcel Dekker, 2004), 117–18.
18 See "Resolution Moved by Senator Kennedy and Senator Cooper in the U.S. Senate Proposing That a Mission from the U.S.A. and Other Western Countries Should Visit India to Assess Indian Needs for Fulfillment of Her Five Year Plans," 1959, External Affairs, America, Progs., Nos. 49(1)-AMS, 1959 (Secret), National Archives of India. On the 1956-7 budget crisis, see Francine Frankel, *India's Political Economy, 1947-2004* (New Delhi: Oxford University Press, 2005), 148–49.
19 "A Promising Start," *Economic Weekly* XI, no. 19 (1959): 1–2.
20 Richard Parker, *John Kenneth Galbraith* (New York: Farrar, Straus and Giroux, 2015), 326–27.
21 Ibid., 275–76.
22 P. C. Mahalanobis, "Draft Plan Frame for the Second Five Year Plan, 1956-1961," October 10, 1955; Galbraith to November 20, 1955, Box 38, General Correspondence, JKGP, JFKL.
23 Kudaisya, "A Mighty Adventure," 961–63.
24 Galbraith, "The New Indian Five Year Plan: A Survey of the Central Issues," "The Setting," "The First Plan," Box 38, General Correspondence, JKGP, JFKL.
25 John Kenneth Galbraith, *Economic Planning in India* (Calcutta: Indian Statistical Institute, 1956).
26 Galbraith, "Lecture Notes, Madras Chamber of Commerce," April 9, 1956, Box 38, General Correspondence, JKGP, JFKL.
27 "Discouraging Travel," *The Statesman*, April 30, 1956, 2.
28 The Eisenhower administration would make significant overtures to India in the wake of this crisis; see McMahon, "Choosing Sides," 201.
29 See Galbraith's extensive correspondence with Sachin Chaudhuri, Pitamber Pant, P. C. Mahalanobis, and others in Box 38, General Correspondence, JKGP, JFKL.
30 John Kenneth Galbraith, "Rival Economic Theories in India," *Foreign Affairs* 36 (1958): 587–96.
31 Galbraith, "Notes on India, 1959," Box 768, Book Manuscripts, JKGP, JFKL.
32 Parker, *Galbraith*, 326.
33 Dalai Lama to Kennedy, December 29, 1960, Box 118A, POF (#3), PP, JFKL; Kennedy to Radhakrishnan, January 30, 1961; and Kennedy to Prasad, January 1961, Box 106,

National Security Files (NSF), PP, JFKL; M. G. Chagla, "Letter to John F. Kennedy," December 23, 1960, Box 118A, POF (#3), PP, JFKL.
34 "Odds & Ends," *Indian Nation*, December 15, 1960.
35 "Next Ambassador of U.S. to India," *Times of India*, December 14, 1960, 6.
36 McGarr, *Cold War*, 93.
37 McMahon, "Choosing Sides," 205.
38 David Ekbladh, *The Great American Mission: Modernization and the Construction of an American World Order* (Princeton: Princeton University Press, 2010), 192–93; Michael Latham, *The Right Kind of Revolution* (Ithaca: Cornell University Press, 2011); see also Daniel Immerwahr, *Thinking Small: The United States and the Lure of Community Development* (Cambridge: Harvard University Press, 2015), 61–64.
39 "Kennedy's Triumph," *Economic Weekly*, July 23, 1960, 1136.
40 "Next Ambassador of U.S. to India: Professor J.K. Galbraith Tipped for Post," *Times of India*, December 14, 1960, 6. On planning, see Nikhil Menon, "Planned Democracy: Development, Citizenship, and the Practices of Planning in Independent India, c. 1947-1966" (PhD diss., Princeton University, 2017).
41 Parker, *Galbraith*, 347–48.
42 "What the Indians Want," February 1961, Box 106, NSF, PP, JFKL.
43 Landon to Rostow, February 10, 1961, Box 106, NSF, PP, JFKL.
44 Burgess to Rostow, March 13, 1961, Box 106, NSF, PP, JFKL.
45 Galbraith, "Statement on Arrival in New Delhi, April 8, 1961," Box 545, Ambassador to India File, JKGP, JFKL.
46 Galbraith, "Notes," April 1961, Box 545, Ambassador to India File, JKGP, JFKL.
47 See "Profile of Mr. Galbraith," *Nav Saurashtra*, April 10, 1961; "Profile of Mr. Galbraith," *Lokvani*, April 11, 1961; "John Kenneth Galbraith: American Ambassador to India," *Deenabandhu*, April 14, 1961; "American Ambassador John K. Galbraith," *Garjana*, April 14, 1961; and "The New US Ambassador, Prof. Galbraith," *Nai Dunia*, April 23, 1961.
48 J. N. Sahni, "From the Qutab Minar," *Bharati Jyoti*, April 16, 1961.
49 "Galbraith Will Usher in New Indo-U.S. Ties," *Free Press Journal*, April 18, 1961.
50 "Mr. Galbraith Explains New Thinking Adopted in U.S. in Giving Aid to India," *Gujrat Mitra*, April 25, 1961.
51 Merrill, *Bread and Ballot*, 175.
52 Lucius Battle, "Memorandum for Ralph Dungan," May 1, 1961, Box 106, NSF, PP, JFKL; see also Merrill, *Bread and Ballot*, 175. West Germany, France, the United Kingdom, and Canada eventually pledged $780 million to India, and the World Bank contributed another $400 million.
53 McGarr, *Cold War*, 97.
54 Galbraith to Rusk, May 19, 1961, Box 201, General Correspondence, JKGP, JFKL.
55 Galbraith to Rusk, May 20, 1961, Box 201, General Correspondence, JKGP, JFKL.
56 "$60 Million IDA Loan for Indian Roads Approved," *Economic Times*, June 24, 1961.
57 Galbraith would later rewrite these speeches into a short treatise on economic development more broadly; see Galbraith, *Economic Development in Perspective* (Cambridge: Harvard University Press, 1964).
58 Galbraith, "Economic Development in Perspective: Address at the University of Madras," July 19, 1961, Box 545, Ambassador to India File, JKGP, JFKL.
59 "Galbraith Urges Sparing Use of Foreign Loans, Know-How," *Hindustan Times*, July 22, 1961, Box 545, Ambassador to India File, JKGP, JFKL.

60 "Ambassador Galbraith's Address at Bombay University," July 31, 1961, Box 545, Ambassador to India File, JKGP, JFKL.
61 "Parliamentary Control Over Public Corporations," *Commerce*, September 2, 1961, 1.
62 "Plan Perspectives," *Indian Express*, July 21, 1961; "Galbraith's Visit to Milk Plants," *Hindustan Standard*, July 23, 1961.
63 "India Will Not Need Technical Aid in Future: Ambassador Galbraith," *Andhra Jyothi*, July 21, 1961, 4.
64 "Ambassador Galbraith Says India Is a Much Developed Country in Comparison to Other Underdeveloped Countries of the World," *Vishavmitra*, July 22, 1961.
65 "Ambassador Galbraith Says That Modern Means and Equipment Should Be Used With Great Caution," *Jagran*, July 22, 1961.
66 "Message of Hope," *Hindusthan Standard*, October 11, 1961, 2.
67 "Ambassador Galbraith Inaugurates Kerala School Lunch Programme," October 14, 1961, JKGP, Box 545, JFKL.
68 Rakove, *Kennedy*, 85–86; Chaudhuri, *Forged in Crisis*, 123; "Kennedy Meeting Issue etc.," 1961, External Affairs, America, Progs., nos. 73(56)-AMS, 1961, National Archives of India.
69 "John Kenneth Galbraith," *Meet the Press* (NBC, November 12, 1961), Box 545, Ambassador to India File, JKGP, JFKL.
70 Leo Fredericks, "Galbraith Prefers Writing to Anything Else," *Sunday Standard*, October 29, 1961.
71 "Mr. Nehru's Visit," *Financial Express*, November 11, 1961.
72 Galbraith, "Education and Economic Development: An Economist's View," December 9, 1961, Box 545, Ambassador to India File, JKGP, JFKL.
73 Deborah Baker, *A Blue Hand: The Beats in India* (London: Penguin, 2008), 118–19; "Schedule for Mrs. Kennedy in India and Pakistan," February 13, 1962, Box 118A, POF (#3), PP, JFKL.
74 "The Causes of Poverty: A Clinical View," March 23, 1962, Box 545, Ambassador to India File, JKGP, JFKL.
75 "The Approach to Poverty," June 1, 1962, JKGP, Box 545, JFKL; "Western Pattern Is Best Suited to Developing Nations, Says Galbraith," *Economic Times*, June 5, 1962, 6; "Two Ways of Economic Development," *Ajintha*, June 8, 1962, 3.
76 "The Developing and the Developed: A Revised View," July 21, 1962, Box 545, Ambassador to India File, JKGP, JFKL. On Myrdal, see Benjamin Siegel, "Asian Drama Revisited," *Humanity* 8, no. 1 (2017): 195–205.
77 Rakove, *Kennedy*, xvii–xviii.
78 "Lal Bahadur Shastri: Nehru's Successor," June 9, 1964, Lal Bahadur Shastri, Box 5, RG 59/5254, National Archives, College Park.
79 Kudaisya, "A Mighty Adventure," 974.

14

Mediating the Kennedy Presidency: James Baldwin's Decade in Turkey

Begüm Adalet

In May 1970, American author James Baldwin videotaped a lengthy interview with Turkish filmmaker Sedat Pakay over the course of two days in Istanbul. Among the topics covered in their conversation were racism and empire, which Baldwin related to what he called "American ignorance," that is, the ignorance of people who "think they know something about the rest of the world because they think they are better than the rest of the world."[1] When Pakay asked him about Vietnam, Baldwin criticized the presumption that one could "bomb a people into freedom," and situated the war in a longer history of American imperialism, which was informed by "a really weird determination to protect something called Manifest Destiny" and had entailed the subjugation of "the lesser races of the world, the Philippines, the Indians, the Mexicans."[2] The "American way of life" now surfaced as a "new kind of totalitarianism which doesn't call itself that," Baldwin continued: "It calls itself foreign aid; it calls itself black capitalism; it calls itself the Peace Corp[s]."[3] Although the interview took place when Richard Nixon was the president, Baldwin's evocation of foreign aid and the Peace Corps signaled a retroactive summoning of President John F. Kennedy's administration. It is the contention of this chapter that Baldwin acted as an interpreter and mediator of the Kennedy presidency in Turkey, where he lived intermittently between 1961 and 1972.

While transnational histories chronicle the ways in which the American presidency has been experienced as a global presidency, it is also important to note the ways in which Third World perceptions of the United States could be mediated, sometimes retrospectively, by third parties like Baldwin. To be sure, Baldwin had not always been outspoken against American imperialism, and throughout the 1950s his nonfictional essays in fact rested on tropes of American exceptionalism.[4] But from the early 1960s, in his role as a commentator on racism and empire, Baldwin—and others like him in other countries in the Third World—challenged the efforts of American diplomacy, and especially of institutions like the United States Information Agency (USIA), the CIA, and the FBI, to manage the terms in which the United States was envisioned and understood during the Cold War.[5] Baldwin offered an alternative to bilateral foreign policy frameworks, and he offered the people of Turkey a different account of the

Kennedy years and of the United States itself, refracting its diplomatic self-portrayal and image management through the prism of his own experiences, critiques, and aspirations.

James Baldwin was born in Harlem in 1924 and was the author of celebrated novels and plays, including *Go Tell It on the Mountain*, *The Amen Corner*, and *Giovanni's Room*, as well as collections of essays, such as *Notes of a Native Son*, *Nobody Knows My Name*, and *The Fire Next Time*. An incisive commentator on racism in the United States, James Baldwin was also a self-designated "transatlantic commuter" who lived in France and Turkey, intermittently, over several decades.[6] Baldwin first moved to Paris in 1948 and died at his home in St. Paul-de-Vence in 1987, although he frequently returned to the United States for extended periods in the intervening years. During these visits, Baldwin became an active member of the civil rights movement: In 1960, he covered the sit-in movement and met members of the Congress of Racial Equality (CORE) in Tallahassee, Florida; in 1963, he accompanied Medgar Evers of the National Association for the Advancement of Colored People (NAACP) on an investigation of a reported lynching in Jackson, Mississippi, and assisted James Forman and the Student Non-Violent Coordinating Committee (SNCC) in the drive to register black voters in Selma, Alabama; and in 1965, he joined Martin Luther King Jr's civil rights march from Selma to Montgomery.[7] Baldwin's years abroad were also interspersed with visits to Switzerland (1951–52), Israel (1961), Senegal, Guinea, and Sierra Leone (1962), as well as the Soviet Union (1985–86), among others.

Baldwin's first trip to Turkey took place in 1961, at the invitation of a friend, Engin Cezzar, whom he met in New York and cast as Giovanni in the Actors Studio production of *Giovanni's Room* in 1957. Over the next decade, Baldwin repeatedly returned, sometimes spending months at a time in the country.[8] He completed or worked on a number of his books during these visits, including *Another Country*, *The Fire Next Time*, *Blues for Mister Charlie*, *Tell Me How Long the Train's Been Gone*, and *No Name in the Streets*. He was also featured prominently in the Turkish press, gave interviews to newspapers and magazines, and was the subject of the aforementioned short film by Pakay.

Yet the author never learned more than a few words of Turkish and the people he was in contact with the most were English-speaking students of elite institutions, such as Robert College, as well as novelists, journalists, and actors. The closest impact that Baldwin came to having outside of elite circles of Istanbul was when Cezzar persuaded him to direct the Turkish production of Canadian playwright John Herbert's *Fortune and Men's Eyes*. The play ran for 103 performances from 1969 to 1970, despite its "controversial" themes such as violence and homosexuality in a juvenile detention center, and went on a national tour.[9] According to Magdalena Zaborowska's conversation with the lead actor, the play's "success in 'proletarian locations, very leftist, and working-class,' such as Zonguldak, as [Ali] Poyrazoglu classified them, was a particularly significant achievement."[10] Baldwin's message, which Poyrazoglu interpreted as "the prison could be anywhere," gained in popularity as the author and Turkish students and workers became increasingly disillusioned with US foreign policies and as official Turkish-American relations worsened throughout the 1960s.[11]

Turkey and the United States during the Global Sixties

Turkey had positioned itself as a steadfast US ally during the previous decade, sending troops to Korea and eagerly joining NATO as well as Western bloc-sponsored regional arrangements such as the Baghdad Pact (renamed CENTO in 1959). Such gestures had guaranteed the receipt of Truman Doctrine and Marshall Plan funds, which contributed to the construction of an extensive highway network and jumpstarted the tourism industry in Turkey. But the latter parts of the 1950s saw an economic downturn and disagreements between Prime Minister Adnan Menderes and American advisors who criticized his populist policies.[12] After Menderes was ousted by a military coup in 1960, Turkish-American relations continued to degenerate, with episodes such as the 1960 crash of a US military reconnaissance plane flying over the Soviet Union that had taken off from a US airbase in Turkey, and the resolution of the 1962 Cuban Missile Crisis with "the USSR and the United States bargain[ing] behind closed doors over missiles in Turkey and Cuba," each of "which were reduced to voiceless client states risking nuclear war on their soil."[13]

Although Kennedy's assassination was mourned widely and his name was given to a major boulevard in Istanbul, widespread coverage of President Lyndon Johnson's 1964 letter to Prime Minister Inonu, which included a harsh ultimatum against an intervention in Cyprus, contributed to the growing anti-American sentiment in Turkey. On the same day that a reported 20,000 students marched to the American embassy in Ankara in order to protest the Johnson letter, the daily *Cumhuriyet* ran its story of the demonstration on the cover page, alongside an interview with James Baldwin, titled "America does not only belong to whites!"[14]

By 1968, student protests of the American Sixth Fleet and the Peace Corps, along with university occupations and anti-NATO demonstrations were reaching a climax in Turkey.[15] In 1969 followed the burning of Robert Komer's car on a university campus during his brief but highly contested post as US ambassador to Turkey, right after he had served as the head of Civil Operation and Revolutionary Development Support program in South Vietnam; and in 1971 young leftist activists kidnapped four American soldiers. Under the country's relatively liberal constitution of 1961, which had paved the way for unionization, collective bargaining, and free speech, there was a wave of massive strikes, factory occupations, and the election of Workers' Party (TIP) representatives to parliament. The leader of the party, Mehmet Ali Aybar, visited North Vietnam in 1967 and participated in Bertrand Russell and Jean-Paul Sartre's International War Crimes Tribunal; both actions were highly publicized in the Turkish press.[16]

In the late 1960s, a growing number of people in Turkey were following Baldwin's increasingly critical reappraisal of American foreign policy and of the Kennedy presidency. A prominent example was a serialized conversation between journalist Metin Toker and Ismet Inonu, leader of the Republican Party and the prime minister between 1961 and 1965.[17] Inonu, who when in office had continued to position Turkey as a vital ally of the United States, now insisted that Johnson's controversial Cyprus letter had been made possible by the earlier "betrayal" by Kennedy during the Cuban Missile Crisis. The "betrayal of friends," Inonu proclaimed, "wounded more than anything else." Throughout the interviews, Inonu revealed how the crisis had positioned

Istanbul or Ankara to become the "new Hiroshimas of a nuclear war." While he had made clear to the Kennedy administration his government's unwavering support during the tense standoff of the United States with the Soviet Union, the favor had not been returned during Turkey's escalating crisis with Greece, with the consequence that we were "shook [by the Americans' response] in a very deep, irreparable manner." For political leaders such as Inonu, it seems, the shine was fading from Camelot, and American hegemonic guidance was increasingly the source of tension, irritation, and even open defiance.[18]

It is impossible to exactly measure the impact Baldwin's activities in Turkey had on the growing radicalism among Turkish students or, more broadly, on the slow yet clear shift against the memory of the Kennedy presidency in Turkish public opinion. But the country's brief but popular reckoning with the imperial US presidency throughout the 1960s and 1970s can be assessed alongside the author's appearances in the Turkish mainstream media during that period.

Baldwin in the news

Baldwin's interviews in Turkey covered a wide range of topics pertaining to American politics. His commentary on the American presidency, and especially the Kennedy administration, became more critical in tone toward the end of the decade. He for instance told renowned journalist Mehmet Ali Birand in 1964 that the most progress on civil rights had been made during the Kennedy Presidency, although he was quick to add that the "justice loving (!) white oppresses me, kills me, won't let me in his restaurant, kicks me out of his neighborhood, spits in my face, even though it was me who made him rich in the first place."[19] In 1967, by contrast, he told a journalist who asked him if the civil rights movement would lead to a black revolution that he did not foresee such a possibility because "nobody, including Kennedy, has taken the issue seriously. Had they done so, it would not be necessary to talk about the white-black issue today."[20]

Baldwin was repeatedly asked to rank various US administrations in terms of the progress they made on racial equality. In one case, when a representative of the daily *Milliyet* asked which president did the greatest service for equal rights among Roosevelt, Truman, Eisenhower, Kennedy, and Johnson, Baldwin responded, Roosevelt. Asked what he thought of President Johnson, Baldwin replied that "Johnson and I do not represent the same people," and that his choice for the Democratic nomination in 1968 was Abraham Lincoln, "so that he can complete the American Revolution!" During the same conversation, Baldwin informed his interviewer: "Three years ago I went to the Attorney General with my friends and told him that bloody events were likely to erupt. Unfortunately nothing has been done since. You see where things are at now."[21]

This particular interview captures Baldwin reflecting on a famously heated meeting he had with Robert Kennedy in Manhattan in 1963. The meeting was occasioned by a wire that Baldwin had sent Kennedy on May 12, protesting "police assaults on peaceful civil rights demonstrators in Birmingham, Alabama, and blam[ing] the violence in part on inaction by President John F. Kennedy."[22] Baldwin was accompanied by a group of intellectuals and artists, including lawyer Clarence Jones, singer Lena Horne, playwright Lorraine Hansberry, actor Harry Belafonte, psychology professor Kenneth Clark, and a CORE Freedom Rider named Jerome Smith, who had been severely beaten by a white mob in Mississippi in 1961. According to the *NYT*, the group told Kennedy that an "'explosive situation' had developed in race relations in the North that, potentially, was at least equal to the growing racial strife in the South."[23] Although the exact contents of the meeting have been disputed, there is a consensus that Kennedy was greatly dismayed when Hansberry abruptly left the meeting and that he was angered about Smith's suggestion that he would never fight for the United States in a war against Cuba.[24] Baldwin, in turn, was exasperated at Kennedy's suggestion that "it was conceivable that in 40 years in America we might have a Negro President." Baldwin later wrote in the *NYT Magazine* that the comment rested on a dubious comparison: "From the point of view of the man in the Harlem barber shop, Bobby Kennedy only got here yesterday and now he is already on his way to the presidency. We were here for 400 years and now he tells us that maybe in 40 years, if you are good, we may let you become President."[25] For Baldwin, Kennedy's condescension overlooked a key discrepancy in the historical experiences of the Irish and African Americans: "the Irish, too, had a foul and dishonorable Middle Passage," he would write in 1985, "[but] they became white when they got here and began rising in the world, whereas I became black and began sinking."[26]

After Baldwin left the meeting, he taped an interview with Kenneth Clark for WGBH-TV, and repeated his sentiment that he was shocked "that the Attorney General did not know . . . that I would have trouble convincing my nephew to go to Cuba, for example, to liberate the Cubans in the name of a government which now says it is doing everything it can do but cannot liberate me."[27] Baldwin's critique of the parameters of citizenship, and especially the contrast between the requirements of belonging in the nation and its persistent exclusionary nature, would be reprised by Kennedy in his June 11 speech in which he identified civil rights as a "moral issue" of vital importance to the geostrategic posture of the United States. A number of authors have speculated that Baldwin's meeting with the attorney general had a direct influence on the content of the president's speech a few weeks later, especially Kennedy's statement that the participation of African Americans in US interventions abroad required the extension of political and civil rights at home.[28] Still, Baldwin's insistence to the Turkish reporter that "nothing had been done since" the meeting suggests that he did not believe that the Kennedy administration had sufficiently heeded his words.

An additional outcome of the May 1963 meeting with the attorney general, according to William Maxwell, was intensified surveillance of Baldwin: Robert Kennedy, who was "humiliated by Baldwin's sharpness at the meeting," may have decided to "order a sweep of FBI records on the author."[29] Although there is no written record to attest to this speculation, there was an upsurge of material collected on the author after this date, and parts of the massive FBI files on Baldwin were in fact shared directly with the White House, as in the example of a report that Edgar Hoover also forwarded to the attorney general.[30] Baldwin, however, was aware of both the intense surveillance he was under and the attorney general's complicity with it: "In 'Re/member this house,' an unfinished memoir written in the 1980s, Baldwin lashed back at the Kennedy-

FBI nexus with a colorful image of an intimidating, cigar-chomping Bobby Kennedy carrying 'an FBI file cabinet in his brain.'"[31]

Baldwin's unfavorable assessment of Robert Kennedy also appeared in his Turkey interviews. In 1967, he told a reporter who asked about the prospects for another Kennedy presidency that "Robert Kennedy has made enormous progress along those lines he deems most desirable, and will almost certainly—especially considering the enormous proportion of women in the United States who have almost nothing to do *but* vote—be our President one day. I am curious indeed to know if he will then find it expedient to visit any American state and inform them that 'apartheid is evil.'"[32] When asked to assess the possibility of the potential repetition of a Kennedy presidency, Baldwin thus presented his Turkish audience with dim prospects, not hesitating to ridicule the popularity of his old acquaintance and highlighting what he perceived to be the attorney general's hypocrisy in his uneven treatment of racism at home and abroad.

Baldwin also used these interviews as an opportunity to assess specific Kennedy administration initiatives. The premier example here was the Peace Corps, an important legacy of the Kennedy administration in Turkey (as elsewhere). While received with much fanfare when announced by Kennedy, that program did not attract much attention beyond a handful of sympathetic accounts when it was implemented in Turkey in 1962.[33] Moreover, by 1966, when more than 500 American teachers were posted across the country, newspapers started calling them missionaries, cult members or CIA agents. Particularly suspect were the volunteers who took posts in Turkey's Kurdish and Arab-populated east.[34] The insinuation that Americans sought to foster "separatism" in these areas was popular even in leftist circles, during a time when an otherwise splintering socialist politics was united under an overtly nationalistic outlook.[35] As the lines between anti-imperialism and xenophobia became blurry and as criticism by Members of Parliament, high-school teachers, and university students multiplied, the Peace Corps in Turkey ended when the last members of the personnel were asked to leave the country in 1971.[36]

In his interviews in Turkey, Baldwin interpreted the Peace Corps and other aid programs as the new face of American imperialism.[37] These projects were framed in terms of American "freedom," but this was a "freedom which ultimately reduces itself to the freedom to make money, and the freedom to inflict one's will on other people."[38] Baldwin insisted that Americans who approved of these initiatives and thought that they understood the rest of the world were in fact oblivious to the workings of global capitalism: "They don't know the price paid by millions of peasants all over the world for the tin, the [inaudible], the minerals, the diamonds, whatever, which go into [the] making of a Western society."[39] Writing two years later, Baldwin also pointed out the "similarities between the 'anti-poverty' programs in the American ghetto" and "'foreign aid' in the 'underdeveloped' nations." "What America is doing within her borders," he continued, "she is doing around the world."[40]

While Baldwin and critics in Turkey interpreted the Peace Corps as an episode in the United States' conjoined domestic and global operations, the initiative was also consistent with cultural diplomacy efforts to shape perceptions of so-called American "race relations" across the world.[41] Kennedy, who had campaigned on

African independence and domestic civil rights, appointed his brother-in-law, Sargent Shriver as the first director of the Peace Corps.[42] While Shriver sent the first group of volunteers to Ghana and Nigeria, boycotted segregated institutions in the south, and made an effort to recruit from black colleges, such efforts amounted to little more than international propaganda and they were certainly not concrete steps toward dismantling Jim Crow institutions.[43]

State Department and USIA efforts to manage the American image abroad continued throughout the 1960s, as white supremacy made international headlines. An important example of the USIA's careful packaging of the civil rights struggle was its reporting on the March on Washington for foreign audiences, including a film that the agency produced about the March in which Baldwin appeared alongside celebrities Harry Belafonte, Sidney Poitier, Marlon Brando, and Charlton Heston.[44] While Baldwin can be heard adopting an optimistic tone on the tape, saying that "No matter how bitter I become, I always believed in the potential of this country," his insistence that "it will be a matter of attacking really, J. Edgar Hoover, and asking very rude questions such as why the FBI can find a 'junkie' but cannot find a man who bombs the homes of Negro leaders in the deep south" were actually censored when the program aired on television.[45] In other words, among the forms that American efforts to manage the international portrayal of "race relations" took was censorship of vocal activists like Baldwin, whose criticism continued to target the Kennedy administration, as well as the Federal Bureau over the years.[46]

Despite many other examples of censorship, Baldwin continuously challenged the projected image of American democracy abroad and used his years of overseas residency as an opportunity to call international attention to the civil rights struggle. During one trip to Paris in August 1963, he placed an advertisement in the *Herald Tribune*, "calling a meeting about civil rights in the United States, to be held on August 17 at the Living Room, a Paris nightclub." As many as one hundred people attended the meeting, which discussed the possibility of a sympathy march on the American embassy in Paris, as well as a sit-down strike. While a formal march did not materialize, the group drafted a petition which they paid to run in the international editions of the *NYT* and the *Herald Tribune*. Readers across Europe received the newspapers, "clipped out and signed the petitions and delivered them to US diplomatic posts in many countries. Forty-seven were delivered in London, thirty-five in Rome, and eight in Madrid."[47] Thus, Baldwin contributed to turning the March on Washington into a worldwide event, despite the efforts of American agencies to manage its coverage abroad.

Baldwin did not organize a similar event in Turkey, which seems to have been exempt from propaganda efforts to manage and mitigate America's image as a racially oppressive state. According to internal USIA memoranda from as late as 1971, "overplaying the racial issue in the United States" did not help in the country, where the agency found "less real interest here in the subject than in many other countries, particularly European."[48] As Baldwin became an outspoken commentator on American racism to global audiences, however, his ability to undermine cultural diplomacy did not go unnoticed by institutions that were committed to such efforts. It is thus unsurprising that both FBI scrutiny and American censorship followed Baldwin to Turkey over the years.

In 1966, the FBI reconstructed Baldwin's "complicated itinerary to and from Turkey . . . with the aid of passport numbers, ship manifests, and flight schedules," as well as information about his stay with actor Cezzar.[49] The Bureau even shared "the news [of Baldwin's stay in Turkey] with the Secret Service, the branch of federal law enforcement charged with protecting US presidents since 1902."[50] It was during this visit that Edgar Hoover became interested in the author's Turkey interviews, especially those "regarding racial problems in the US" and arranged for a few to be translated into English.[51] One example was an interview where Baldwin told the journalist that he could not settle in Turkey permanently because "in the white-black conflicts in my country I must contribute my share by returning to America."[52] Another FBI-translated and -catalogued article, in which Baldwin is cited as praising Istanbul, where "everyone is friendly and close to another," contains the partially incorrect information: "Before coming here, he stayed for 18 months in Hollywood and prepared a scenario which was taken from a biography which reflects the white-black problem. So much so that, because of this, he was a delegate at the famous meeting between the blacks and Kennedy; he explained all the details of this problem to President Kennedy; and he wanted a remedy to be found for it."[53] But when Baldwin was surveyed by *Newsweek* while living in Istanbul—in a questionnaire that he found "infuriating," dishonest and insulting to black people[54]—the journal declined to publish the results, even as his highly critical discussion of America appeared uncensored in *Milliyet*, hinting at the possibility that he was able to escape certain types of censorship in the relatively open atmosphere of an inter-coup period Turkey.[55]

It was in the context of these overseas trips that Baldwin's writings about racism began to make more explicit connections to imperialism and to relate these to other struggles across the globe. In 1966, he published "Report from Occupied Territories" in the *Nation*, where he drew links between those dying "like flies" in Vietnam and Harlem: "The meek shall inherit the earth, it is said. This presents a very bleak image to those who live in occupied territory. The meek South Asians [*sic*], those who remain, shall have their free elections, and the meek American Negroes—those who survive—shall enter the Great Society."[56] The next year, he gave an interview to *Cep Dergisi* in Istanbul, where he was asked about his opinion on the use of African American soldiers in Vietnam and sociologists' view that "the armed services give opportunity to the poor and underprivileged." Going further than his earlier comments about why it would be unreasonable to expect African Americans to enlist in a project to "liberate the Cubans," Baldwin was unequivocal in his condemnation of the war: "I consider the American adventure in Vietnam a desperate and despicable folly, for which future generations will pay very heavily. I do not think that any American soldier should be fighting there. But to send Negro soldiers there—to ask Negro soldiers to die there, while one is busily destroying their kinsmen at home—is of an impertinence so arrogant, an immorality so flagrant, as to take one's breath away."[57]

In this same interview, Baldwin also reflected on his status in Turkey and spoke of the dangers of "being an expatriate," that is, the possibility that he might not be "responsible for Turkish society," and that this was not a place where his "social obligations could be discharged."[58] But when a *Cumhuriyet* reporter asked him about his dreams for the future of the United States, Baldwin embarked on a history lesson, explaining that the future he imagined already existed in the past of the country, namely in the Reconstruction era: "blacks and whites were side by side even in trade unions in the south. We had black members in Parliament . . . . Unfortunately, northern capitalists and southern landlords [aghas] destroyed this unity and order. The first laws that separated white and black began to appear after 1910." Asked why the northern capitalists and the southern landlords encouraged segregation, he added, "economic pressure . . . the ambition to make more profit."[59] Baldwin's brief excursion into the history of Reconstruction, along with the other interviews discussed in this essay, suggest that he felt a responsibility, perhaps even a "social obligation," to explain American racism and its historical entanglements with capitalism to audiences in Turkey who were also witnessing and participating in local movements of anti-imperialism and anti-capitalism during the same period.

Strategic comparisons

While Baldwin used his interviews in Turkey as a platform to provide commentaries on the Kennedy presidency, the civil rights struggle, and American history more broadly, his years abroad also helped inform and crystallize his own transnational perspective. During his first visit to the country, for instance, Baldwin had informed his editor that in Turkey, "the whole somber question of America's role in the world today stared at me in a new and inescapable way."[60] That his experience in Turkey reshaped his comparative understanding of the United States was a suggestion that he would revisit frequently over the years. In an interview with Ida Lewis in 1970, for instance, he described the country as a "satellite on the Russian border," and continued: "That's something to watch. You learn about the brutality and the power of the Western world. You're living with people whom nobody cares about, who are bounced like a tennis ball between the great powers. Not that I wasn't previously aware of the cynicism of power politics and foreign aid, but it was a revelation to see it functioning every day in that sort of a theatre."[61]

These renewed reflections on imperialism allowed Baldwin to distinguish himself from other Americans in Turkey, and especially the USIA personnel, whom he increasingly suspected of spying on him.[62] He told anthropologist Margaret Mead during their 1970 "rap on race" that he was in fact a "great threat to the American colony there . . . . I was one of the very few black things in Istanbul, except for various soldiers and sailors, and certainly the most famous black American there." While he insisted that he "didn't want to be dragged to any of those ghastly embassy parties," his absence at these events caught the attention of "the Turks," especially one student who asked why he seemed to be on a blacklist.[63] Baldwin complained to Mead of the American colony's inability to comprehend political grievances: "They don't understand the Turks when the Turks hit the streets any more than they understood Birmingham when the blacks there hit the streets. They do not know yet how it is that the Japanese students were able to prevent Eisenhower from landing in Japan. They don't know why, a few months ago, Turkish students lined up on the Bosphorus and forbade the Sixth Fleet to enter, drove them out. The Americans don't know why, but I know why."

Despite his insistence on an exceptional insight into the Turks' grievances, Baldwin told Ida Lewis that his relational perspective was not necessarily reciprocated by "the people of Istanbul," who "know nothing about what the black man has gone through in America," and "still think of America as a promised land."[64] But in his conversations with audiences in Turkey, he would strategically downplay these criticisms in order to connect the experience of Turks and Kurds within the ambit of American empire to that of African Americans living under racial oppression. When Sedat Pakay asked him if it was possible to compare African American and Turkish people, for instance, Baldwin insisted on a shared oppression, noting that "there is something similar about all people who stand in relation to a major cultural power in a disadvantaged way."[65] In another conversation with journalist Zeynep Oral, Baldwin drew parallels between black Americans and the "uneducated, oppressed, exploited" classes in Turkey.[66] It was these similarities, he added, that led him and his friend Yasar Kemal, the Kurdish novelist he met in Istanbul, to embark on similar work of activism. In another example, Baldwin attended the staging of a play by Kemal and told reporters afterward that despite the differences in the problems between America and Anatolia, he found shared "psychological elements" in both places.[67]

In strategically articulating an affinity between the people of Turkey and African Americans, Baldwin would on occasion situate them both within the matrix of America's racial classifications. He told one reporter that Turks would not be accepted as white in the United States, certainly not by the governor of Alabama, and that they would probably read as "Puerto Rican in New York, Mexican in California, and black in the South."[68] It is difficult to assess whether Baldwin actually believed that his audience would be racialized in this particular way; despite his frequent efforts to draw out the affinities between Turkish and African American subjects, he would vehemently deny the existence of such similarities in other contexts. Still, his efforts to invite his interlocutors into a framework of solidarity of the oppressed seem to have opened up possibilities of identification, rather than mere empathy, in discussions about American racism in Turkey.[69]

Conclusion

Baldwin was aware of the ways in which geography and history might complicate solidarity, which does not emerge inevitably but should be forged in concrete political moments.[70] His openness to being interviewed in Turkey and his willingness to answer questions about American society and history were part of his contributions to the construction of a necessarily fragile internationalist politics. His forthright account of racism unfolded alongside his interpretation of the Kennedy administration, with its achievements and shortcomings alike. The author's narrative of Kennedy initiatives like the Peace Corps and his recollections about his personal experiences with the attorney general and the FBI were also formative of his increasingly critical attitude toward empire. It was as a retroactive mediator of the Kennedy presidency that Baldwin left one of his indelible marks in Turkey, during a time when the country was experiencing its own moment of anti-imperialist and anti-capitalist mobilization.

Notes

1. Kim Fortuny, "James Baldwin's 1970 Turkish Interview: 'The American Way of Life' and the Rhetoric of War from Vietnam to the near and Middle East," *Texas Studies in Literature and Language* 55, no. 4 (2013): 434–51, 438.
2. Fortuny, "James Baldwin's 1970 Turkish Interview," 436, 446.
3. Ibid., 447.
4. For examples of Baldwin's early American exceptionalism, see "Princes and Powers," reprinted in James Baldwin, *Collected Essays*, ed. Toni Morrison (New York: The Library of America, 1998); James Baldwin and Sol Stein, *Native Sons* (New York: One World Ballantine Books, 2004). For discussions of his gradual shift from an exceptionalist framework toward a transnational one, see Nikhil Singh, *Black Is a Country: Race and the Unfinished Struggle for Democracy* (Cambridge: Harvard University Press, 2004); Cheryl Wall, "Stranger at Home: James Baldwin on What It Means to Be an American," in *James Baldwin: America and Beyond*, eds. Cora Kaplan and Bill Schwarz (Ann Arbor: University of Michigan Press, 2011); Begüm Adalet, "Tensions, Terrors, Tenderness: James Baldwin's Politics of Comparison," *Comparative Studies in South Asia, Africa, and the Middle East* 38, no. 3 (2018): 508–23.
5. See Kevin Gaines, "African American Expatriates in Ghana and the Black Radical Tradition," in *Transnational Blackness: Navigating the Global Color Line*, eds. Manning Marable and Vanessa Agard-Jones (New York: Palgrave Macmillan, 2008), 293–300; Alex Lubin, *Geographies of Liberation: The Making of an Afro-Arab Political Imaginary* (Chapel Hill: University of North Carolina Press, 2014); Sohail Daulatzai, *Black Star, Crescent Moon: The Muslim International and Black Freedom beyond America* (Minneapolis: University of Minnesota Press, 2012). For examples of how the American propaganda infrastructure continued to place limits on transnational dialogue, see Penny von Eschen, *Race Against Empire: Black Americans and Anticolonialism, 1937-1957* (Ithaca: Cornell University Press, 1997); Singh, *Black Is a Country*; Brian Russell Roberts and Keith Foulcher, eds., *Indonesian Notebook: A Sourcebook on Richard Wright and the Bandung Conference* (Durham: Duke University Press, 2016).
6. The phrase "transatlantic commuter" appears in "Exclusive Interview with James Baldwin, Joe Walker/1972," *Muhammad Speaks* 11–12 (1972), reprinted *Conversations with James Baldwin*, eds. Fred Stanley and Louis Pratt (Jackson: University Press of Mississippi, 1989), 127–42.
7. Baldwin, "Chronology," in Baldwin, *Collected Essays*, 845–55.
8. For the most comprehensive account of Baldwin's time in Turkey, see Magdalena Zaborowska, *James Baldwin's Turkish Decade: Erotics of Exile* (Durham: Duke University Press, 2009).
9. Çiğdem Üşekes, "In Another Country: James Baldwin and the Turkish Theatre Scene," *New England Theatre Journal* 21 (2010): 106.
10. Zaborowska, *James Baldwin's Turkish Decade*, 181.
11. Ibid.
12. Begüm Adalet, *Hotels and Highways: The Construction of Modernization Theory in Cold War Turkey* (Stanford: Stanford University Press, 2018).
13. Perin Gürel, *The Limits of Westernization: A Cultural History of America in Turkey* (New York: Columbia University Press, 2017), 84–85. Also see Baskin Oran, *Turkish Foreign Policy, 1919-2006: Facts and Analyses with Documents* (Salt Lake City: University of Utah Press, 2010).

14 "Amerika yalnız beyazların değil" [America Does Not Only Belong to Whites!], *Cumhuriyet*, August 29, 1964, 1.
15 "Amerikan bayrağını yaktılar" [They Burned the American Flag], *Milliyet*, February 27, 1969, 3; "Barış gönüllüsünü protesto etmek için kürsüye pislediler" [They Pissed on the Lectern in Protest of the Peace Corps], *Milliyet*, December 6, 1970, 3.
16 *Sosyalizm ve Toplumsal Mücadeleler Ansiklopedisi, 7. Cilt* [The Encyclopedia of Socialism and Social Struggles, Volume 7] (Istanbul: Iletişim, 1988). See also Kenan Behzat Sharpe, "A Mediterranean Sixties: Cultural Politics in Turkey, Greece, and Beyond," in *The Routledge Handbook of the Global Sixties*, eds. Chen Jian, Martin Klimke, Masha Kirasirova, Mary Nolan, Marilyn Young, and Joanna Waley-Cohen (New York: Routledge, 2018), 168–80.
17 "İnönü Küba krizinde tereddüt göstermeden Amerika'nın yanında yer aldı" [Inonu Stood by the Americans without Hesitation during the Cuba Crisis], *Milliyet*, February 4, 1969, 5; "Nükleer bir savaşın Hiroşiması Ankara veya İstanbul olacaktı" [Ankara or Istanbul Were Going to Become the Hiroshima of a Nuclear War], *Milliyet*, February 5, 1969, 5; "Kıbrıs olaylarının perde arkasında Amerika vardı" [America Was Behind the Scenes of the Cyprus Events], *Milliyet*, February 6, 1969, 5.
18 In 1974, Prime Minister Bulent Ecevit would ignore American warnings and launch a brutal invasion of Cyprus, while also refusing to halt poppy seed production despite threats of an American embargo and a freeze of all loans. Turkish-American relations would remain contentious until the 1980 coup, which saw the installation of a neoliberal technocrat who had worked for the World Bank and promised the liberalization of the Turkish economy and its further opening to foreign capital.
19 Mehmed Ali Birand, "Amerika'daki renk mücadelesinin en popüler siması zenci yazar James Baldwin Istanbul'da" [James Baldwin, the Most Popular Face of America's Color Struggle, Is in Istanbul], *Milliyet*, August 21, 1964, 6.
20 "Cezzarlar zenci yazar Baldwin'in eserini oynayacak" [The Cezzars Are to Perform Black Author Baldwin's Play], *Cumhuriyet*, April 5, 1967, 4.
21 Sami Kohen, "Ikaz Ediyorum!" [I caution!], *Milliyet*, July 25, 1966, 5.
22 Baldwin, "Chronology," 851.
23 "Robert Kennedy Consults Negroes Here about North," *NYT*, May 25, 1963, 1.
24 Baldwin later wrote that Bobby Kennedy was the "one person Lorraine couldn't get through to": "Sweet Lorraine," *Esquire*, November 1969, reprinted in *Collected Essays*, 760. For a reconstruction of the meeting that brings together accounts by Arthur Schlesinger, *Newsweek* and *NYT*, see Todd Saucedo, "The Fire Within: The Baldwin Meeting and the Evolution of the Kennedy Administration's Approach to Civil Rights" (MA thesis, University of Central Florida, 2007).
25 "American Dream and American Negro," *NYT Magazine*, March 7, 1965, reprinted in Baldwin, *Collected Essays*, 718. Baldwin also references Kennedy's comment in *The Fire Next Time*.
26 Baldwin, "The Price of the Ticket," reprinted in Baldwin, *Collected Essays*, 842.
27 "A conversation with James Baldwin: Kenneth Clark/1963," Reprinted from *Freedomways* 3 (1963): 361–68, reprinted in Fred Stanley and Louis Pratt, eds., *Conversations with James Baldwin* (Jackson: University Press of Mississippi, 1989), 41.
28 Kennedy declared: "Today we are committed to a worldwide struggle to promote and protect the rights of all who wish to be free. And when Americans are sent to Vietnam or West Berlin, we do not ask for whites only. It ought to be possible, therefore, for American students of any color to attend any public institution they select without having to be backed up by troops. It ought to be possible for American consumers

of any color to receive equal service in places of public accommodation, such as hotels and restaurants and theaters and retail stores, without being forced to resort to demonstrations in the street, and it ought to be possible for American citizens of any color to register to vote in a free election without interference or fear of reprisal." Radio and Television Report to the American People on Civil Rights, June 11, 1963. Available online: https://www.jfklibrary.org/Research/Research-Aids/JFK-Speeches/Civil-Rights-Radio-and-Television-Report_19630611.aspx. See Saucedo, "The Fire Within" for an overview of these theories.

29 *James Baldwin: The FBI File*, ed. William Maxwell (New York: Arcade, 2017), 50. The first set of FBI files on Baldwin dates to 1960 and the entire record runs 1,884 pages in length. The files, which are publicly available under the US Freedom of Information Act, were unearthed during the writing of William Maxwell, *F.B. Eyes: How J. Edgar Hoover's Ghostreaders Framed African American Literature* (Princeton: Princeton University Press, 2015).

30 In his report, Hoover insisted that the allegation that "Agents of our New York office had attempted to enter Mr. Baldwin's apartment on May 27, 1963" was "completely without foundation." Edgar Hoover to Kenneth O'Donnell, Special Assistant to the President, June 6, 1963, 1023–25. Available online: http://omeka.wustl.edu/omeka/e xhibits/show/fbeyes/baldwin.

31 *FBI File*, 51.

32 "James Baldwin Breaks His Silence," Cep Dergisi/1967, translated in *Conversations with James Baldwin*, 62.

33 "İki barış gönüllüsünün ilk dostu bir kedi oldu" [The first friend two peace volunteers make is a cat], *Milliyet,* October 5, 1962, 3; "Diyarbakır'da sevimli bir Amerikalı" [A charming American in Diyarbakir], *Cumhuriyet,* July 22, 1963, 4.

34 "Zararlı tarikatçıların dağıtılması istendi" [It Is Requested That Harmful Cultists Be Disbanded], *Milliyet,* February 2, 1966, 3; "Barış gönüllülerinin telsiz cihazları taşıdığı iddia ediliyor" [It Is Claimed That Peace Volunteers Carry Transmitters], *Milliyet*, October 2, 1966, 7; "Barış gönüllüleri başkanı 'biz casus değiliz' dedi" [The Head of Peace Volunteers Says "We Are No Spies"], *Milliyet*, December 23, 1966, 7; Ilhan Selçuk, "Doğu planı" [The Eastern Scheme], *Cumhuriyet,* March 2, 1967, 4.

35 *Sosyalizm ve Toplumsal Mücadeleler Ansiklopedisi, 7. Cilt.*

36 Murat Soysal, "Barış gönüllüleri ve Türkiye'deki Faaliyetleri," *Ankara Üniversitesi Türk İnkılap Tarihi Enstitüsü Atatürk Yolu Dergisi* 56 (2015): 113–46.

37 Fortuny, "James Baldwin's 1970 Turkish Interview," 447.

38 Ibid.

39 Ibid., 443.

40 Baldwin, "No Name in the Streets," in *Collected Essays,* 405.

41 On the Goodwill Ambassadors with jazz artists such as Louis Armstrong and Dizzy Gillespie, see Penny von Eschen, *Satchmo Blows Up the World: Jazz Ambassadors Play the Cold War* (Cambridge: Harvard University Press, 2006).

42 Thomas Borstelmann, *The Cold War and the Color Line: American Race Relations in the Global Arena* (Cambridge: Harvard University Press, 2001), 59, 136.

43 Julius Amin notes that the number of African Americans who enlisted in the Peace Corps did not exceed 4 percent. "The Peace Corps and the Struggle for African American Equality," *Journal of Black Studies* 29, no. 6 (1999): 809–26. See also Elizabeth Hoffman, *All You Need Is Love: The Peace Corps and the Spirit of the 1960s* (Cambridge: Harvard University Press, 2000).

44 Hollywood Roundtable. Available online: https://unwritten-record.blogs.archives.gov/2012/09/21/hollywood-roundtable/ (accessed October 2, 2016).
45 http://omeka.wustl.edu/omeka/exhibits/show/fbeyes/baldwin, 1048.
46 In May 1963, three months before the March on Washington, for instance, Baldwin made the documentary, *Take this Hammer*, with KQED Television. The film records Baldwin speaking to black youth and community organizers in San Francisco about urban redevelopment and gentrification, which he incisively dubs "Negro removal." Speaking days after the violence of Birmingham, Baldwin insists "that there is no moral distance, no moral distance, which is to say, no distance, between the facts of life in San Francisco and the facts of life in Birmingham and that there is no moral distance, which is to say no distance, between President Kennedy and Bull Connor because the same machine put them both in power." These comments, along with another fifteen minutes of film, were censored by KQED and did not appear in the documentary when it aired. See "Take this hammer" documentary, KQED-TV, channel 9, transcription, Box 2, James Baldwin Letters and Manuscripts, Schomburg Center for Research in Black Culture, Manuscripts, Archives and Rare Books Division, The New York Public Library, New York (Baldwin Letters and Manuscripts). Baldwin's censored comments can be heard on the Director's Cut version which was released in 2013: https://diva.sfsu.edu/collections/sfbatv/bundles/216518. See also Ed Pavlic, "Welcome to the Errordome: Are Editors Still Afraid of James Baldwin?" Available online: https://pen.org/nonfiction/%E2%80%9Cwelcome-errordome%E2%80%9D-are-editors-still-afraid-james-baldwin
47 Mary Dudziak, *Cold War Civil Rights: Race and the Image of American Democracy* (Princeton: Princeton University Press, 2000), 189–91.
48 USIA and Bureau of Educational and Cultural Affairs, Department of State, Country Program Memorandum for Turkey, June 30, 1971, Box 2, Office of Research, Western Europe, 1964-1973, Records of USIA, Record Group 306, National Archives, College Park.
49 *FBI File,* 281–82.
50 As Maxwell extrapolates from the files, "The Bureau knew that Baldwin had not 'threatened bodily harm to any government official or employee,' and had avoided 'conduct or statements indicating a propensity for violence and antipathy toward good order and government . . . . Instead, his undefined 'background' was found to be 'potentially dangerous,' or his ties to the 'communist movement' were thought to be too strong, or he had 'been under active investigation as a member of other groups or organizations inimical to the US." *FBI File*, 266.
51 Director, FBI, "Memorandum: James Baldwin; Security Matter," March 31, 1967, 1374, http://omeka.wustl.edu/omeka/exhibits/show/fbeyes/baldwin.
52 "Looking at New York from Istanbul," 604 http://omeka.wustl.edu/omeka/exhibits/show/fbeyes/baldwin. The article originally appeared in *Yeni Gazete*, November 25, 1966.
53 "Yasar Kemal, Engin Cezzar, and James Baldwin have formed a partnership," 932–34 http://omeka.wustl.edu/omeka/exhibits/show/fbeyes/baldwin. The original article appeared in *Milliyet*, August 18, 1969, 5.
54 Baldwin to David Baldwin, July 26, 1966, Box 4, Baldwin Letters and Manuscripts.
55 See *Newsweek*, August 22, 1966. In fact, one article, pointedly titled "the work that Baldwin wrote in Turkey was banned in America" (falsely) reported that the USIA had banned *Tell Me How Long the Train's Been Gone*. *Milliyet*, December 4, 1969, 8.
56 Baldwin, "Report from Occupied Territories," in *Collected Essays,* 738.

57 "James Baldwin Breaks His Silence," 62.
58 Ibid., 60.
59 "Siyahların isyanı: James Baldwin anlatıyor" [The Revolt of Blacks: James Baldwin Recounts], *Cumhuriyet,* September 8, 1965, 4.
60 James Baldwin to Robert Mills, February 1962, published in "Israel: Letters from a Journey by James Baldwin, with Introductory Note by Robert Mills" *Harper's Magazine,* May 1963, 48–52.
61 "Conversation: Ida Lewis and James Baldwin," *Essence* 16 (1970), reprinted in *Conversations with James Baldwin,* 86.
62 David Leeming, *James Baldwin: A Biography* (New York: Alfred A. Knopf, 1994), 308.
63 Margaret Mead and James Baldwin, *A Rap on Race* (Philadelphia: Lippincott Company, 1971), 84.
64 "Conversation: Ida Lewis and James Baldwin," 87.
65 Fortuny, "James Baldwin's 1970 Turkish Interview," 448.
66 Zeynep Oral, "Istanbul'da tatil yapan Baldwin diyor ki: Amerika'da dehşet saçan zenciler değil beyazlardır" [Baldwin, Vacationing in Istanbul Says: It's White Americans Who Are Terrorizing Everyone, Not Blacks], *Milliyet,* July 29, 1969, 8.
67 "James Baldwin *Teneke*'yi seyretti" [James Baldwin Watched *Teneke*], *Cumhuriyet,* December 17, 1965, 6.
68 "Siyahların isyanı," 4.
69 Refik Erduran, "Biz ne rengiz?" [What Color Are We?] *Milliyet,* May 12, 1966, 2.
70 Adalet, "Tensions, Terrors, Tenderness."

15

"The Kennedys Know Something about That, Too": Law, Lineage, and Martyrdom in US-South Africa Relations

Myra Ann Houser

Introduction

> Because of our history and heritage, the struggle against apartheid is America's struggle too. And the personal ordeal of Nelson Mandela has deeply touched the conscience of our country. . . . Five years ago, Winnie Mandela was gracious enough to meet with me on my visit to South Africa. It was a moment I shall never forget. She took me aside and asked me this question—How do you raise a child without a father? The Kennedys know something about that too, she said. Nelson Mandela's country would not permit him to be a father to his children—but now he is the father of his country.[1]

When Edward M. (Ted) Kennedy secured a long-anticipated South African visa, his visit to Winnie Madikizela-Mandela was warm and professional, as both parties reported. The Massachusetts senator and holder of the state's "Kennedy Seat" spoke about his delegation's official tour, assessing US trade implications upon apartheid policies. He also, however, connected personally with liberation movement leaders, particularly from the United Democratic Front, African National Congress, and Pan-Africanist Congress. Notably, Kennedy met with Madikizela-Mandela, whose husband had been imprisoned for more than two decades. He picketed outside of Pollsmoor Prison, Mandela's then-incarceration site. In their reflections, both Madikizela-Mandela and Kennedy recalled a conversation where the former shared concerns over raising her two daughters alone. "How do you raise a child without a father?" she wondered. "The Kennedys know something about that, too." During his anti-apartheid efforts, Ted Kennedy both contributed to and built upon his older brothers' relationships with liberation movement leaders, extending the family legacy into one of the twentieth century's last decolonization efforts.

Mandela's question reflects the degree to which southern African leaders viewed the privileged American Kennedys as materially connected to anti-apartheid struggles. Following John F. Kennedy's efforts to court African leaders, his assassination, Robert

Kennedy's iconic 1966 South Africa visit, his assassination, and Ted Kennedy's South Africa visit, South African leaders may have viewed the "presidency" or, at least, American leadership, as a structure upon which the family had tried and failed to maintain control—not dissimilar in some ways to how elite, educated Africans had found themselves within sight, yet barred, from colonial society's upper echelons.

In addition to this personal connection, the Southern Africa Project of the Lawyers' Committee for Civil Rights Under Law provided a professional connection between ANC leaders and US Executive Branches. John Kennedy helped found the Lawyers' Committee to work on US domestic issues less than six months before his death, and Robert Kennedy's 1966 South Africa visit forged the transatlantic partnership. The Project worked heavily with both the ANC and PAC and was often closely connected, though not fused with, subsequent US presidential administrations. Thus, and perhaps even especially, following the president's death, South Africans maintained affiliation with this part of American government, even when the two countries had overall troubled relationships. The officials who worked through the Project as private citizens molded both professional and personal relationships throughout the Cold War and apartheid's subsequent fall.

Relational foundations

John Kennedy's campaign interest and subsequent friendships with icons such as Kwame Nkrumah, Julius Nyerere, and Ahmed Ben Bella perhaps led to Robert Kennedy's later interest in southern Africa. Nyerere had, after all, often lounged with Robert around his Northern Virginia swimming pool during official visits to the United States. The two became close personal friends, as well as political colleagues. Youngest brother Ted Kennedy would, as he did in so many cases and causes, eventually adopt and carry the anti-apartheid mantle his brothers had begun to craft. Unlike his predecessors, John Kennedy seemed to recognize the importance of advancing US civil rights as a means of answering questions such as, "What moral right have Americans to condemn apartheid in South Africa when still maintaining it by law?"[2] Thus, domestic race policy became central to efforts to court nonaligned leaders. Despite a Cold War interest in gaining spheres of influence within Africa, however, Kennedy's actual policies did not always differ from those of the status quo. Both he and Robert famously wondered if the push for economic sanctions against South Africa would only push the country farther into poverty and a doubling-down of apartheid. For his part, President Kennedy presided over the Central Intelligence Agency during its formation and early efforts to undermine African leaders—including through provision of intelligence info to the forces who captured Mandela and to those who murdered Patrice Lumumba. The humane public face at times belied a deep mistrust of African leaders, and in some ways the Lawyers' Committee reflected this same tendency to work one way through rhetoric and another through organizational action.

Frustrated with civil rights gridlock (and their own constitutional limits on interfering) in the South, and receiving pressure from potential African Cold War allies, liberal domestic constituents, civil rights activists, and Dixiecrats within their own party ("the liberals who would rather be right than win"[3]), the president, vice president, and attorney general of the United States during the summer of 1963 held meetings with members of professional classes—medical workers, teachers, labor leaders, ministers—asking them to work within their fields to enact change. These became central to Kennedy's civil rights work, much of which unfolded under increasing pressure during the last five months of his life. Subsequently, a group of attorneys formed the Lawyers' Committee for Civil Rights Under Law, with Robert and Ted Kennedy becoming committed members.

Connecting to southern Africa

Following President Kennedy's assassination, the Lawyers' Committee became a useful vehicle for the family and other prominent lawyers interested in continual engagement with nonaligned blocs. In the middle of 1966, Robert F. Kennedy visited South Africa as an invited guest of the National Union of South African Students and Johannesburg Bar Association. NUSAS had initially hoped to attract Martin Luther King Jr. but after the South African government denied him a visa, decided to join the Bar groups in reaching out to Kennedy, thinking him among the most successful of Americans utilizing courts for desegregation—and banking on the fact that the regime would not want to completely fall out with a probable future president of the United States. As Kennedy accepted the invitation, American ears turned to Africa, with many pro-liberation allies attempting to ride the senator's coattails. President Lyndon B. Johnson delivered his "first and last address on Africa" during the week before the visit.[4] US activists toward Africa seized upon the opportunity to gain sympathy from a sympathetic lawyer. In 1966, the American Committee on Africa, which had previously asked Robert F. Kennedy to keynote its 1965 Africa Defense and Aid Fund Fundraiser, raised the issues of sanctions and political prisoner defense—requesting that the senator utilize his attention strategically. Director George Houser[5] wrote:

> There is one thing in particular that I am most anxious to discuss with you before you go to South Africa. It pertains to the problem of legal defense for persons, both black and white, who are facing trial for opposition to the government's apartheid policy. Since the Defence and Aid Fund was banned in March, there has been a difficult problem of getting funds into South Africa to help with legal defense. There are many lawyers in South Africa still, of course, willing to take on cases of this sort; but it is impossible for many of them to do it without being paid at wages enough to cover expenses . . . . We have been in touch with a good number of lawyers here who are vitally concerned about this, and wish to help out in any way they can. I would particularly like to urge you to be in touch with some of the lawyers' organizations in South Africa to have some private discussions on the problems of legal defense, and ways in which those outside can relate to this problem.[6]

The South African visit did not go as the country's government had hoped. Apartheid regime officials banned several NUSAS leaders and refused entry to nearly three dozen

American journalists accompanying Kennedy. During his flight over, Kennedy was asked to register his race, but commented upon arrival that "I didn't fill out the card." After landing near midnight, he was welcomed by an interracial crowd of more than four thousand students, who lifted him onto their shoulders as they marched into the terminal.[7] Along with his wife Ethel, Kennedy ultimately spent five days in 1966 speaking to university students in Cape Town, Johannesburg, and Durban; meeting with liberation leaders such as banned ANC president and recent Nobel Peace Prize winner Albert Luthuli; touring townships; and visiting the homes of African, Asian, and colored South Africans. He does not appear to have held the private meetings Houser called for. At the University of Cape Town, he delivered his famous "Ripple of Hope" speech, drafted in part by anti-apartheid activist Allard Lowenstein, and speaking the words that would eventually be inscribed upon his tombstone. He began by exhorting:

> I came here because of my deep interest and affection for a land settled by the Dutch in the mid-seventeenth century, then taken over by the British, and at last independent; a land in which the native inhabitants were at first subdued, but relations with whom remain a problem to this day; a land which defined itself on a hostile frontier; a land which has tamed rich natural resources through the energetic application of modern technology; a land which once imported slaves, and now must struggle to wipe out the last traces of that former bondage. I refer, of course, to the United States of America.[8]

The audience chuckled upon catching the joke that Kennedy made in referring to his own country and not South Africa. In the crowd, attorney Joel Carlson listened intently. Robert F. Kennedy continued his speech, drawing common cause with South African activists. He spoke four more times, alternately encouraging black South Africans and their allies and gently chiding those who he viewed as upholders of the status quo. Despite government efforts to keep the visit off of international press radars, Kennedy was received with great warmth—and, of course, great scorn—inside the country. According to one of his biographers, a New York outlet noted that "neither Kennedy nor any other politician like him will ever be welcome again in their apartheid state. Once is more than enough."[9]

Following a brief visit to Nyerere in Tanzania, the senator returned home. While some aides later insisted that Kennedy became more sympathetic to the plight of South Africans following his visit, it is clear that he did not shift his ideas about strategy. In a letter to ACOA Co-Chair Donald S. Harrington, Kennedy wrote that he could not support a boycott, consistent with his view that South Africa did not threaten US national security in the way Cuba did, and expressed concern for the procedural elements of involvement. He wrote:

> I agree with your opposition to the policy of apartheid as practiced in that country. However, as you know, the government has sovereignty over practices in that country and influences over that policy can only be exercised indirectly. It was my hope to provoke a full and free debate about this controversial issue as

open discussion of a problem is a necessity if any solutions are to be reached. . . . Responding to a question during my spot in Tanzania concerning the situation in South Africa as a threat to world peace, I replied that I would not use that expression to describe South Africa now, but unless there are changes—if the situation is allowed to continue—it would certainly be explosive. I have no doubt that this is a most difficult problem and I will give careful consideration to any suggestion that may ease the tensions which exist in South Africa.[10]

Harrington continued to disagree, arguing that apartheid did threaten civil procedure within established international legal norms. Joel Carlson, the white South African attorney in attendance at the Cape Town speech, along with US ambassador to the UN Arthur J. Goldberg and Lawyers' Committee founder Morris B. Abram, soon became Harrington's allies, building off of the Kennedy brothers' own pet project.

Goldberg had been appointed to his post in 1965 following Adlai Stevenson's sudden death. In Goldberg's mind, apartheid and its erosion of rule of law threatened not only South Africa but also any world power that supported it. Shortly after his appointment, he told the Overseas Press Club that "there is simply no alternative in a nuclear age to world peace through the rule of law" and that, had the UN existed prior to the Second World War, its utilization of basic civil procedure could have averted Nazi-driven conflict.[11] He urged the world community to take harsher action against two countries—South Africa and the new Southern Rhodesia—both of which practiced laws that should bring "deepest shock and revulsion" and established his intent to push for UN sanctions against both.[12]

Yet Americans remained deeply mistrustful of the UN, and Goldberg remained equally reluctant to take dramatic action without widespread approval. One of these Americans, former president and elder statesman Dwight D. Eisenhower, expressed his puzzlement with the "Dark Continent" and asked, "Didn't Somalia consist of wild jungle? . . . people (who) were primitive and aborigines."[13] In response, Goldberg reiterated his now-entrenched thoughts:

> Because of the violence, hatred, and deprivation of what we consider to be human rights inherent in the question of Apartheid, I firmly believe we must make every effort to resolve the problem. The international implications of South Africa grow deeper every day, and I feel that the UN does have a right to consider certain aspects of these policies.[14]

ABA members, now often at odds with the Lawyers' Committee, vehemently critiqued and effectively halted US debate and ratification of three UN treaties governing slavery, forced labor, and women's rights. A large contingent of the group's Section on International Comparative Law argued that the documents were "not proper subjects for the exercise of treaty-making power."[15] Additionally, the section found, ratifying the treaties would indeed make the United States subject to them—a constraint it opposed.[16] With the ABA deadlocked, Goldberg and a minority of prominent lawyers expressed embarrassment at their home country's intransigence.[17] To top it off, by 1967, the International Commission of Jurists channel through which liberal lawyers had often worked was in a state of crisis following public discovery of the covert CIA funding; the latter quickly announced a cessation of funding to NGOs, Johnson's Justice Department launched an investigation, and the UN General Assembly—egged on by a gleeful Soviet Union—debated whether to revoke NGO consultative status all together.[18]

Naturally, apartheid opponents also hoped to see South Africa's trusteeship of Namibia terminated.[19] John F. Kennedy had led efforts to this effect during his presidency, and the US largely lent its support to General Resolution 2145, which would have stripped South Africa's mandate. Despite their concerns, however, they remained confused as to which liberation movement to support. The South-West African People's Organization (SWAPO), which held much hegemony within Namibia's liberation terrain, operated as a government in exile, with Sam Nujoma often being accorded state visits; the group participated in the Non-Aligned Movement's 1961 Belgrade founding. Since 1962, it had established provisional headquarters in Dar es Salaam and diplomatic missions across the continent. With the organization's official UN representation pending (it would be the first southern African liberation movement to gain Permanent Observer status), Goldberg and allies worried that meeting with Nujoma or his colleagues would show a partisan favoritism to a group that had not yet, in their opinions, proven itself worth of such public endorsement.[20]

South African officials' propensity to move around laws heightened this. In early 1963, as American desegregation conflicts spiraled out of control, the UN had celebrated the Universal Declaration of Human Rights' fifteenth anniversary. Part of this included requesting South Africa's delegation to fulfill its obligations in submitting an annual report. The country's UN representative balked at this, just as he had the year before when Somalia's and Ethiopia's delegations sent Secretary General U Thant communications registering opposition to the arrest of Nelson Mandela. Arguing that domestic legal affairs did not concern Human Rights and that the phenomenon could be explained by the fact that "Oliver Tambo and other members of the former African National Congress who now find themselves overseas, are of course very active in Afro-Asian circles."[21]

Discouraged and yet desirous of a route forward, the Lawyers' Committee tasked Abram with exploring options for this type of work.[22] In the middle of his research, Carlson appeared. He had managed to leave South Africa during the 1967 Trial of the Namibians' recess, visiting Washington, DC, and New York City, seeking financial assistance and international pressure from both the United States and United Nations. During his long weekend, Jennifer Davis and husband Michael—an exiled former advocate instructed by Mandela and Tambo—hosted him. On Capitol Hill, he gained audiences with several US Congressmen—including senators Robert and Ted Kennedy—to discuss the new Terrorism Act and the necessity of bringing economic sanctions to bear upon the country.[23] He recalled Robert acting "shocked" at the new provisions, despite his own recent South African journey.[24] In New York City, he made contact with a sympathetic ES Reddy, director of the UN Trust Fund for South Africa, who encouraged him to contact Sverker Astrom, Sweden's UN ambassador, along with Lawyers' Committee members.

Abram viewed Carlson's request as an opportunity for procedurally minded lawyers to provide "international exposure to the farce which these trials are."[25] He recognized the value of his colleague's request, writing that

> I see now an opening to get legal representation for South Africans . . . I am very impressed with (Carlson), particularly as he is doing his duty with the foreknowledge that he has placed himself in great danger . . . Carlson advises what I think you know already, that the South African Bar will not touch cases such as this. On the other hand, Carlson and a small coterie he can gather around him will take such cases. I have discussed this with Burke Marshall who is meeting with Carlson today prepatory to a meeting with the Lawyers' Committee for Civil Rights Under Law. Hopefully Burke can persuade that Committee to become the vehicle for support on this side of the Atlantic.[26]

At the meeting, Carlson expressed hesitation at the Lawyers' Committee's proposed support, telling his American colleagues that "the South African government was proud of its granite inflexibility in the face of the world."[27] In response, the lawyers promised to assist in arranging funds both for Carlson's clients—and himself, should he be detained upon his return home.

After Carlson arrived back in Johannesburg, the Lawyers' Committee sent its first monetary assistance, and Abram contacted him to voice support on behalf of the Kennedy brothers and other group members. The organization instructed Carlson to continue instructing his clients' defense team and pledged to provide the remainder of the case's funds. Carlson described the group as providing invaluable support in both monetary and emotional arenas. "It was a link with professional colleagues dedicated to upholding civil rights in America, who fully understood what was necessary for lawyers working in a polices state," he wrote. "Of the many worthwhile results coming from my trip, this was of inestimable value."[28]

The strategic counsel that Committee members offered in the matter of the SWAPO leaders tried in what has been colloquially referred to as "the Namibian Rivonia Trial" proved useful as well. Carlson argued that officials had illegally applied the Terrorism Act, though the defendants were not South African citizens and therefore not subject to its jurisdiction. At trial's end, none of the men received the death penalty. As in the Rivonia Trial, onlookers viewed the consequent life sentences as a result of international pressure.[29] Ya Toivo, who served nearly three decades on Robben Island before becoming Minister of Labor in independent Namibia noted that "his actions embarrassed the authorities. That's why they had to sentence us to prison, not death."[30] In 1968, the state settled with one defendant, paying 3,000 South African Rand in response to his suit alleging that he had been tortured by security police.[31] All other defendants endured the conditions of detention and torture, considered a victory in the harsh terrain of political repression. In the long term, this case also established, in the minds of Goldberg, Kennedys and others, a certainty that South Africa did illegally occupy Namibia and a growing belief that economic boycotts could succeed in molding South Africa's domestic policies when court work failed.

Lawyers' committees and views of the United States

During the 1970s, the Southern Africa Project evolved into a major Lawyers' Committee initiative—and its only one overseas. In the post-Rivonia era, it litigated anti-discrimination cases against US companies doing business in South Africa, and it launched an ultimately unsuccessful pilot program to advocate on behalf of South African activists seeking travel documentation to leave the country. Additionally, it expanded its range beyond ANC/SWAPO solidarities to engage with Pan-Africanist Congress, Black Consciousness, and fellow activists not recognized by the UN with official representative status. Due to increasing restrictions on dissent within South Africa and a fluctuation of mainstream US Civil Rights movements after the 1968 assassinations of Martin Luther King Jr. and Robert Kennedy, this period did not involve as much outward engagement between South Africans, Namibians, and the dynasty. Yet, at least privately, the connection continued. Ted Kennedy quoted Robert F. Kennedy's Ripple of Hope speech at length as he delivered his brother's eulogy. Writing on the latter's death and his assumption of duties as family figurehead, he commented that "I knew that my role now was to ensure a continuum in this beautiful process, this precious tradition of the Kennedy family, regathering itself, replenishing its young with knowledge and love."[32] While the 1970s were, in many ways, a fraught era for Ted Kennedy, they also saw a shift in US attitudes toward South Africa. The prominence of anti-apartheid activism in international news dissipated as the government cracked down on internal resistance. By the decade's end, however, a resurgence of powerful images emanating from sites such as Soweto—where police opened fire on children protesting their school language structure—and Port Elizabeth—where family and friends of Black Consciousness leader Steve Biko shared photographs of his brutalized corpse—began bringing South Africa back into the international public eye. Thus, for Kennedy, South Africa became a site to overtly build upon the family legacy.

During the 1980s, in the wake of his failed presidential primary campaign, Ted Kennedy turned increasingly toward the South African interest of his brothers, providing us another lens into the decolonization of the US presidency and Senate. Unlike Robert F. Kennedy, he did view apartheid as an American concern, and one that should be addressed through federal trade policy. This began with the 1984–86 Free South Africa Movement protests, where members of the prominent family comprised some of the "designer arrests" of protestors attempting to enter the country's Washington, DC, embassy. Some of the arrests included those of the nieces and nephews who "Uncle Teddy" brought to march, utilizing his role as paterfamilias to lend credibility to the unfolding shift toward anti-apartheid as a cause célèbre. Of course, without a presidency to utilize, much of the rest of the dynasty's South Africa-related story unfolded under congressional activism. Like his brothers' endorsements of civil rights and anti-war platforms, Ted Kennedy's adoption of the mantle contributed to a building of political credibility within anti-apartheid movements. It helped spring a foreign policy issue with which few white Americans connected into a protest movement that would drive the country's largest-ever acts of civil disobedience and prompt conversations about parallel constructions of race within the United States.

The youngest brother takes the mantle

The mantle that Ted Kennedy began to carry did, in many ways, tap into the very friendships and personal connections that he inherited from his brothers. His life's longevity, however, allowed him to see these relationships through in a unique way. And, although he had been the youngest of the lot, he had in many ways previously helped advise and shape presidential and presidential-hopeful policies toward Africa. In his memoirs, Kennedy wrote of his post-Harvard graduation journey across North Africa. Then-senator Kennedy had suggested the itinerary to his brother who wanted to see the world, "and he wanted me to look at the African countries just emerging from European rule."[33] During that tour, nearly three decades before the visit to South African nationalists, a young Ted Kennedy embedded himself with the Algerian army, gaining an education in revolution and noting that "the insurrection was all around. The Algerians had experienced the most brutal kinds of torture from the colonial army, and this enhanced their hatred and bolstered the movement for independence. Nothing could stop it."[34] He then decompressed with John F. Kennedy during a Mediterranean hiatus.

Just four years later, the president-elect again urged his brother to visit the continent, particularly the newly independent Congo and Rhodesia, to assess where Cold War powers might fit in the widening colonial power vacuum; Kennedy ultimately spent four weeks in West Africa. "That's a continent that's going to be extremely important," Kennedy recalled his brother telling him.[35] Robert F. Kennedy, for his part, would speak those words nearly verbatim when justifying his own Africa trip. It seems likely, then, that the youngest and only surviving Kennedy brother may have viewed John F. Kennedy's and Robert F. Kennedy's African efforts not as a precursor to his own but as continuation of his youthful voyages of discovery. Africa ostensibly represented an opportunity to connect with people and enact policies, as well as a space for harkening back to his and his family's own youthful optimism.

During his own South Africa visits, he both built upon the Kennedy Mystique and conveyed his own particular sense of the struggle. When Desmond Tutu, alongside Alan Boesak, visited the United States after receiving his Nobel Peace Prize, he encouraged protestors at the embassy and lunched with Kennedy, telling him that he needed to come to South Africa, because "the world will not pay attention until someone like you comes to South Africa and brings the cameras and the spotlights with you."[36] Though biographer Adam Clymer argues that the youngest brother was initially reluctant and uncertain that he could impact anyone at the level of RFK, Ted Kennedy eventually acquiesced. Before journeying to South Africa, he spent the holidays in Ethiopia and Sudan, taking two of his children to watch and aid in hunger relief efforts.[37]

Kennedy traveled to the country three times during the late 1980s and early 1990s, meeting Winnie Mandela in her banishment post at Brandfort during his first journey. Like his brothers, he had worked to build relationships with African leaders, despite his geographical distance; the family reputation, of course, largely facilitated this. Tutu remembered that "it seems like I've known him forever, you know, and with the kind of name he has, you sometimes think that you've known public figures for a long time when in fact your acquaintance is from the media and things of that kind."[38] Former staffer Nancy Soderberg noted the gravitas that the name seemed to carry, as it opened doors professionally for her:

> He had a huge impact on that, so for me, going to South Africa on behalf of Ted—no one knows who I am, and you just run around the world in Ted Kennedy's name and everybody will see you.... Solidarity people came in Poland, and there's all the ANC people, and you know now they're all presidents. I was up in the Clinton Global Initiative thing a couple of weeks ago in New York, and they have these heads of state reception. I knew them all back when they were activists and in jail and rebels. It's really fun, and it's because of Kennedy, and just the name is still magic around the world.[39]

Ted's first South African visit, in 1985, largely seemed a continuance of Robert F. Kennedy's unfinished work. Tutu remembers Ethel Kennedy saying that "it would be a good thing for a return visit of the Kennedys to South Africa because it was so crucial to keep the apartheid situation on the agenda of the world."[40] Indeed, a host of Kennedys this time joined their patriarch for the January visit.

The visit was certainly not without contention—a lecture from the US ambassador on a need to tow official line, a meeting with Mangosuthu Buthelezi to hear a critique of sanctions bills, and about 100 Azanian Peoples' Organization cadres holding signs saying "Kennedy go home."[41] While it is unclear how meta these signs were intended to be, they echoed those from Robert F. Kennedy's visit nearly two decades earlier, when white nationalist leaders chanted and held signs proclaiming "Yankee Go Home." AZAPO argued that Kennedy's protest visit, like Jesse Jackson's a few years before, "give credibility to the settler regime and the forces of imperialism."[42]

The AZAPO protest led to violent skirmishes after Kennedy refused to sign a renunciation of violence in order to be allowed a visit with Nelson Mandela, then in Pollsmoor Prison. He protested outside the prison instead. After protests at Soweto's iconic Regina Mundi church became heated, he canceled his address there. This physical confrontation seemed to move Kennedy on a personal level, particularly given the context of his brothers' murders and threats against his own personal safety. Tutu's interviewer noted, "He has had many encounters with violence in his life, and his family have. He has been stoned by people who were against his stand on segregation busing in Boston, but I'm sure to have had that last visit, the last part of the visit and have violence break out would have been too bad."[43]

And while violence and skirmishes dominated coverage of Kennedy's visit, he also constructed an itinerary much broader than Robert F. Kennedy's. He visited black worker hostels in Soweto and voiced his opposition to the Bantustan system. Perhaps most strikingly, Ted Kennedy, unlike Robert F. Kennedy, was granted an audience with South African government officials; Foreign Minister Pik Botha visited with him and defended the Bantustan policy, asking him not to support sanctions bills. He met, too, of course, with Winne Mandela. Niece Kathleen Kennedy Townsend accompanied him and bestowed upon her the Robert F. Kennedy Human Rights Award.[44] Later, he traveled to Windhoek, Namibia, to denounce South Africa's occupation of the country, and on to Zambia, where he met with exiled ANC president Oliver Tambo. While

Kennedy's visit did not consist of as many speaking engagements as his brother's, he delivered his most well-received speech at the airport, speaking before he departed not to the predominantly white masses of students as had been the case during much of 1966, but to the masses of people:

> To any who turn their heads, who pretend that they do not see, I reply, "Let them read, as I have, the repressive words of South Africa's statutes. . . . And if anyone doubts that it is wrong, let them come to Soweto. Let them go to Onverwacht; let them go to Crossroads; let them go to Brandfort—let them ask Winnie Mandela . . . . Apartheid in constitutional clothes will never mend the fabric of a society where most of the inhabitants are treated as legal strangers to their own land."[45]

He illegally and pointedly quoted from the banned Mandela, connecting with the South Africans watching him depart. Within the family context, Ted Kennedy seemed to shine more brightly in Tutu's mind than his brothers. This did not result only from his longevity. The brother who saw the end of apartheid had also seemed to the archbishop its most ardent opponent. John Kennedy's early, yet often tepid, support had changed the nature of US relations to the armed struggle in many ways, but in some South African eyes, it was his brothers who transformed it. Tutu noted:

> South Africans committed to democracy have a warm regard for the Kennedy family. We have to say that in practice the US Administration did not give our liberation struggles adequate support in the early 1960s after some of our political movements were banned—which is why they say they were forced to turn to Eastern Europe to help. But the ideals which the Kennedys stood for—and which Bobby and Ted traveled to South Africa to propagate in 1966 and 1985 respectively—have given us inspiration and encouragement.[46]

In the US, the 1986 Comprehensive Anti-Apartheid Act passed shortly after Kennedy's visit. Throughout, he helped drive community organizing and cosponsored the CAA, then garnered support for its override of a Reagan veto. This perhaps stung for some South Africans who had thought his visit contained less star wattage than his brother's, including *Sunday Times* writers who argued that Kennedy was "not even a very important member of the United States Congress."[47]

"That family has such a sense of history"

In 1994, American delegations veritably flooded both South Africa's April elections monitoring and Mandela's May inaugurations. Of the many symbolic moments emerging from the transition to political democracy, several of them centered around Kennedy's continuation of the family legacy. Thurgood Marshall Jr. whose own family name is so iconic to US history, noted that Ethel Kennedy scolded him at a forum commemorating the twenty-fifth anniversary of Robert F. Kennedy's death less than a year before the elections. "I never thought to figure out where all that came from," he said. "That family has such a sense of history and family connection that it could have been any number of things. . . . I was not keeping up the Kennedy tradition and preparing properly."[48] He noted how, on the flight to South Africa, Kennedy stood among the US civil rights icons who seemed to symbolize both struggle and solidarity:

> With so many big and memorable personalities with so much to offer, the Senator had such a connection to that cause. I have to believe that everybody on that trip, if they remember one thing other than Nelson Mandela doing the oath, it was that Ted Kennedy was there—and John Lewis. It's the mantle they carry, not only because of what they've done, but because they carry with them, symbolically, the struggles of so many people.[49]

Conclusion

In the midst of debates over the CAA, Kennedy received a South African visa. While Kennedy did not visit the country, Robert F. Kennedy's 1966 journey had marked the first, and for many years last, time a high-profile US dignitary would pay the country such a symbolic visit. Ted Kennedy's 1985 journey represented more than a decade of unsuccessful visa applications and came in the midst of a moment when working through the "special committee formed at the behest of the President of the United States" presented one of the limited options for a man perhaps still smarting from a lost election to once again lay his family's claim on the White House. His meeting with Madikizela-Mandela reflected the turmoil in which both progressive Americans and most South Africans found themselves in the mid-1980s. Given an almost complete information blockade separating South Africa from the rest of the world, Mandela's question to Kennedy represented a deeply personal memory of the family whose scions she had known of two decades prior. It reflects the enduring connections that wove from Washington to Johannesburg, veering through Dallas and Los Angeles and Robben Island, during one of Africa's most prominent decolonization stories and one of America's most iconic families.

Notes

1 Edward M. Kennedy, "Tribute to Oliver Tambo, President of the African National Congress," June 25, 1990, 1–2, Folder 714, Box 68, "USA: Tambo Correspondence," Oliver Tambo Papers, University of Fort Hare, South Africa.
2 *Nigerian Pilot*, quoted in Philip Muehlenbeck, *Betting on the Africans: John F. Kennedy's Courting of African Nationalist Leaders* (Oxford: Oxford University Press, 2012), 196.
3 Burke Marshall, interview by Larry Hackman, January 19–20, 1970, 32.33, in Robert F. Kennedy Oral History Collection, John F. Kennedy Presidential Museum and Library, Boston.
4 Larry Tye, *Bobby Kennedy* (New York, Random House, 2016), 372.
5 No relation to the author.

6. George Houser to Robert F. Kennedy, May 25, 1966, Box 47, Correspondence Folder, American Committee on Africa Papers (ACAP), Amistad Research Center (ARC), Tulane University, New Orleans.
7. Tye, *Kennedy,* 372.
8. Robert F. Kennedy, "Day of Affirmation Speech," delivered at the National Union of South African Students Meeting, Cape Town South Africa, June 6, 1966.
9. Tye, *Kennedy,* 376.
10. Robert F. Kennedy to Donald Harrington, July 27, 1966, Box 47, Correspondence Folder, ACAP, ARC.
11. Arthur Goldberg, "Freedom under Law," address to the Overseas Press Club, New York City, September 15, 1965, quoted in Daniel Moynihan, ed., *The Defenses of Freedom: The Public Papers of Arthur J. Goldberg* (New York: Harper and Row, 1966), vii.
12. Goldberg, "Freedom under Law," 34.
13. Larry Grubbs, *Secular Missionaries: Americans and African Development in the 1960s* (Amherst: University of Massachusetts Press, 2010), 19.
14. Goldberg to Eisenhower, June 14, 1966, Folder 4, Box 47, Papers of Arthur J. Goldberg (PAG), Library of Congress (LOC).
15. Richard Gardner to Goldberg, April 24, 1967, Box 45, Folder 8, PAG, LOC.
16. Ibid.
17. Ibid.
18. Howard Tolley, *The International Commission of Jurists: Global Advocates for Human Rights* (Philadelphia: University of Pennsylvania Press, 1994), 98.
19. Goldberg to *NYT* editor, May 1967, Folder 4, Box 47, PAG, LOC.
20. Anderson to Goldberg, May 2, 1967, Folder 4, Box 47, PAG, LOC.
21. MI Botha to the Secretary of Foreign Affairs, August 30, 1962, Volumes 7, File 11/4/3, Box 26, "Human Rights Commission," National Archives of South Africa.
22. Baker to Goldberg, June 4, 1966, Folder 4, Box 47, PAG, LOC.
23. Joel Carlson, *No Neutral Ground* (New York; Crowell, 1976), 196–97.
24. Ibid., 198.
25. Abram to Goldberg, November 6, 1967, Folder 4, Box 47, PAG, LOC.
26. Ibid.
27. Carlson, *No Neutral Ground,* 199.
28. Ibid., 202.
29. Author, e-mail correspondence with E. S. Reddy, December 2, 2008.
30. Jim Dwyer, "Joel Carlson, 75, Lawyer Who Fought Apartheid in the '50s,'" *NYT,* December 4, 2001, A19.
31. "Lawyers' Committee for Civil Rights under Law: Ten-Year Report," November 1973, 96; Z. Pallo Jordan, ed., *Oliver Tambo Remembered: His Life in Exile* (New York: Palgrave, 2007), 27.
32. Edward M. Kennedy, *True Compass: A Memoir* (New York: Twelve, 2009), 283.
33. Ibid., 209.
34. Ibid., 111.
35. Ibid., 163.
36. Adam Clymer, *Edward M. Kennedy* (New York: William Morrow, 1999), 363.
37. Ibid., 364.
38. James Sterling Young and Stephen Knott, interview with Desmond Tutu, May 13, 2006, Williamsburg, Edward M. Kennedy Oral History Project, Miller Center, University of Virginia (EKOHP).

39 Janet Heininger, interview with Nancy Soderberg, October 9, 2008, Jacksonville, EKOHP.
40 Young and Knott, interview with Tutu.
41 Ibid.
42 Clymer, *Kennedy,* 365.
43 Young and Knott, interview with Tutu.
44 Clymer, *Kennedy,* 368.
45 Ibid., 369.
46 Tutu to Jacques Lowe, November 8, 1992, Box 12, Desmond Tutu Correspondence, Mayibuye Centre, University of the Western Cape, South Africa.
47 Clymer, *Kennedy,* 370.
48 Janet Heininger, interview with Thurgood Marshall, Jr., July 26, 2007, Washington, EKOHP.
49 Ibid.

Conclusion: "Someone Talking the Same Language with All of Us"

Robert B. Rakove

Zebedeo Omwando, a Kenyan farmer, hoped for a loan. An Iranian woman, Fakhri Garakani, labored thousands of hours, aspiring to cultivate a giver-receiver relationship. Peruvian sculptor Carlos Pazos may well have had similar aspirations. An Ivorian farmer, whose name is lost to history, traveled forty kilometers to Abidjan, so he might properly mourn a friend he had never seen. The object of their correspondence, labors, and sorrow, President John Fitzgerald Kennedy, served out his tragically shortened tenure without discernible awareness of his would-be interlocutors. Does this render their sentiments, entreaties, and agendas naive? What are we to make of the ways by which their lives became intertwined with his?

In a recent essay about the thirty-fifth president, Anders Stephanson writes, "There is a mountain of writing about Kennedy and the Kennedys, the mastering of which would require several scholarly lives."[1] The popular fascination with, and reverence for, Kennedy races substantially ahead of historical assessments of the man. Post-revisionist scholarship on him has often proved more appreciative in its conclusions, yet historians would still—for the most part—hesitate to place him where the public does so readily: in the ranks of great presidents. Yet when cartoonist Barry Blitt drew Kennedy with four other recognizable greats in a February 2016 cover illustration for the *New Yorker*—the five of them expressing various forms of dismay while watching the Republican Party primary—the inclusion was seamless and natural. His lips pursed, Kennedy stands behind Abraham Lincoln, and dips his fingers into a box of antacids. In its own way, the illustration reflects a contemporary understanding of Kennedy, alluding gently to his lifelong health struggles—the extent of which remained well-concealed during and well after his lifetime.[2]

While his popular image has been revised and complicated by such posthumous revelations, and his presidency recedes from living memory, Kennedy still retains an uncommon ability to fascinate, within and outside of the United States. A November 2013 Gallup Poll determined that, of all age cohorts, young Americans, between the ages of eighteen and twenty-nine, held the most positive views of him.[3] Veteran election analyst Larry Sabato perceives Kennedy's image to be, for the most part, "as strong today as it was in the 1960s."[4] These findings, of course, attest at least partly to the extensive efforts of Kennedy's family and friends to enshrine his image, and the public's receptiveness to such campaigns. Yet the Kennedy family, while atypically canny in their pursuit of this endeavor, hardly invented it. Every presidential library

Conclusion: "Someone Talking the Same Language with All of Us" 265

embodies an active effort at hagiography, on the part of loyalists and surviving relatives. Outcomes vary widely, and success is not guaranteed.

One measure of this disparity is the visibility of Kennedy monuments, inside and outside of the United States. He is the namesake for a central park in Lima, Peru, for a bridge connecting the banks of the Niger River in the Nigerien capital, Niamey, and an entire district of the Honduran capital of Tegucigalpa. He seemingly counts more *avenidas*, *avenues*, *boulevards*, *rues*, *ruas*, *vias*, *piazzas*, and *calles* to his name than any other modern American president—even Franklin Delano Roosevelt.[5] Countless individuals around the world, as suggested by one chapter above, received their given name in tribute to him. The commercial appropriation of his name is also intriguing. As of this writing, the Kennedy name appears to grace—among other entities—a chicken restaurant on the island of Java, a São Paulo video store, and a fish farm on the outskirts of the eastern Indian city of Imphal. How did it travel so widely?

In seeking to answer this question, the present volume attempts something new: to detail the reception, interpretation, and at times memory of John F. Kennedy throughout (but not only in) the Global South. It examines a variety of subjects, ranging from the famous—Mao Zedong and James Baldwin—to the aforementioned Omwando, Pazos, and Garakani. It employs media analysis, archival research, and firsthand oral history to uncover the views, aspirations, and memories of individuals who responded in some way to the image Kennedy projected. At times, these chapters inform us about Kennedy, enriching our understanding of a famously elusive man in unexpected ways. More critically, however, they help us to grasp the world that he faced at the dawn of the 1960s: the fleeting but pivotal confluence of separate events and trends that both motivated Kennedy's program of global outreach and rendered at least some segments of its intended audience highly receptive to it. Rather than recounting these chapters one by one, this brief conclusion will attempt a degree of synthesis—highlighting common themes as well as (inevitable) points of contention between them.

One major theme within the collection is immediacy. George Kennan famously observed that his famous "Long Telegram" would have been dismissed as alarmism if it had been sent six months earlier; six months later, it would have been largely redundant.[6] The same may be said of Kennedy, who took office within months of the historic zenith of decolonization, at a fateful moment in the dissemination of mass media, at a perceived (and constructed) moment of intergenerational transition, and *before* Vietnam and the broader disaffection that soured Washington's relations with much of the Global South. The Third World project still balanced between the ultimately conflictual principles of nonalignment and Afro-Asian solidarity. While the abduction and execution of Patrice Lumumba in 1960–61 represented a sharp setback to postcolonial nationalism, Africa had yet to witness the overthrow and murder of a head of state.

These chapters build upon the sense of immediacy and evanescent opportunity present in the early 1960s, elucidating intense but fleeting confluences. Benjamin Siegel explicates the well-known affinity felt for Kennedy in India, paying special attention to the appointment of the economist John Kenneth Galbraith as ambassador in New Delhi. Galbraith's arrival in New Delhi proved well-timed, as the veteran economist was able to provide incisive and surprisingly tactful advice as India shifted away from the orthodox models of state planning prevalent during the 1950s. South Korea, the subject of Inga Kim Diederich's study, had just engaged in its own rite of torch-passing: the April 19 Revolution that ousted the autocratic Syngman Rhee. Irish attitudes toward America, as David Kilroy notes, were comparatively favorable in the early 1960s, unmarred by the Vietnam War, and of course boosted by the exuberant experience of hosting a Catholic president of local ancestry. So, too, did Kennedy's general support for decolonization and high regard for Ireland's historical example dovetail with Dublin's stance toward the Global South and its contribution to the UN mission in the Congo.

Developments in media—regionally and globally—preceded and enabled Kennedy's efforts in the Third World. Kenya, the focus of Kara Moskowitz's chapter, is as revealing a microcosm as any in the explosion of media. In this case, the growing reach of vernacular newspapers and rising levels of transistor radio ownership made Kenyans familiar with Kennedy—even before he took office. In Morocco, the subject of David Stenner's chapter, the Istiqlal party's two newspapers, *al-'Alam* and *al-Istiqlal*, were themselves relatively new.

More than any other chapter in this collection, Sönke Kunkel's contribution speaks to global factors amplifying the Kennedy effect. He moves beyond a prevailing stress on the promulgation of television—inevitably the first medium one conjures to mind in association with Kennedy—to note the increased reach, also, of radio, newspapers, and glossy picture magazines across the Global South. So, too, he notes the increased convergence between political reporting and narrative-based entertainment: "Unlike Khrushchev or Adenauer, Kennedy fit the bill." (The 1995 founding of *George,* a briefly published "politics-as-lifestyle" magazine helmed by John F. Kennedy Jr. was perhaps too fitting an epilogue.) Kennedy's success emerges here as a function of the adaptability of his image: as family man, compassionate reformer, or striver for justice. It also stemmed from the experientially informed choices of Edward R. Murrow's United States Information Agency.[7] Kunkel strikes an adroit balance: noting both Kennedy's "great talent" in responding to the specific concerns and aspirations of his global audience, but also the efforts of that same audience, which "evaluated Kennedy's actions in terms of their own concerns, formulated expectations, and thereby created the pressures which led Kennedy to act in the first place."

But were such successes sustainable? In a number of cases, the affinity felt for Kennedy appears to be fleeting or tragic. Kennedy dealt with the democratic government in Seoul for only a few months, before its overthrow by General Park Chung Hee, who would rule South Korea until his assassination in 1979. Kennedy and his administration adapted to and embraced the new authoritarian regime. Conservative Moroccan nationalists, the subjects of Stenner's chapter, appear to have experienced—at most—a brief moment of optimism toward JFK. While his chapter is a story of the outsized, ultimately forlorn, expectations attendant on the author of the 1957 Algeria speech, it also describes their growing disaffection from Kennedy's counterpart in Rabat, the young King Hassan II. Considering Siegel's chapter, the US window of opportunity to prevail in what David Engerman has separately termed India's "Economic Cold War" proved fleeting. Congress, during its 1963 consideration of the president's foreign aid bill, rebuked promises made by Kennedy and Galbraith, and the succeeding Johnson administration proved distressingly willing to seek various political and economic concessions in response for its aid.[8]

Similarly, while Kennedy's late embrace of civil rights bolstered his support among African Americans and impressed African elites, some degree of rupture and disaffection was inevitable. The conceptual linkage between American racism and colonialism, as depicted by Sam Klug, and the corresponding sense of solidarity between African American activists and African nationalists emerged by the middle of the decade—posing challenges both to the pace of domestic civil rights reform and to Washington's equivocal position toward the white supremacist bastions of southern Africa. African American intellectuals stood prepared to offer trenchant criticisms of US claims to offer anti-colonial solidarity and a viable model of governance. Acclaimed writer James Baldwin gave voice to similar sentiments during his sporadic residencies in Turkey. The story of Baldwin, as expatriate interpreter of his native land, is developed by Begüm Adalet's chapter. It is, in considerable part, a retrospective story—and as much about Baldwin's views of Robert Kennedy as of those toward his late elder brother. Baldwin had met RFK in 1963 and found the attorney general's reassurances patronizing.

Adalet's chapter bifurcates between Baldwin's own distinctive response to the Kennedys, and the only partially congruent views of Turkey's government and broader society. Baldwin was unlikely to share the Ismet Inönü government's outrage over the 1963 withdrawal of Jupiter missiles, nor does it appear that he embraced Ankara's outlook toward the Cyprus dispute. He explored similarities between Turks, whom he viewed as pawns in the Cold War, and African Americans—but he appears to have been reticent in his appraisal of Turkey's own nettlesome ethnic politics. The most tantalizing area of overlap appears to have been his criticisms of US foreign policy, particularly the Vietnam War, which were held by Turkey's increasingly restive student movement. Most famously, student radicals set Ambassador Robert W. Komer's car ablaze, on January 6, 1969—an incendiary rebuke to one of the original architects of Kennedy's program of Third World outreach. But, then again, engagement and other Kennedy-era initiatives had their own detractors.

Around one-third of these chapters depict a US relationship with an ally during the Kennedy years. These stories are never simple accounts of admiration. Alliances are often fraught affairs, and the Kennedy years were a difficult period for a specific subset of US allies. Allies across the Global South were unsettled by Kennedy's pursuit of rapprochement with nonaligned states, much as his removal of the Jupiter missiles alienated Turkey. Pakistani President Ayub Khan complained of US policy, in a January 1963 interview, "The line between friends and those that have not been friends is now getting obliterated."[9] Other governments, which had hitherto come to expect unambiguous US support in exchange for their Cold War loyalty, felt similarly.

It is clear, for example, that Mohammed Reza Shah Pahlavi—Garakani's ruler—felt none of the admiration or affinity for Kennedy described by others above. His biographer, Abbas Milani, describes the Kennedy years—which witnessed sustained US pressure on the Tehran government to reform—as the shah's most trying period in power since the 1953 coup. News of Kennedy's assassination prompted him to draft, in an apparent act of catharsis, an irate letter to President Johnson enumerating the various mistakes his predecessor had made.[10] One doubts he would have much approved of Garakani's gift—and the hierarchy that it implied.

Mexico sought not reassurance, but autonomy. As depicted by Vanni Pettinà, the government of President Adolfo López Mateos prepared carefully for Kennedy's summer 1962 visit, which has received comparatively little scholarly attention. López Mateos sought US aid, without the appearance of subordination, to reconcile the Alliance for Progress with the legacy of the Mexican Revolution. For his part, Kennedy—sensing his counterpart's need to demonstrate independence—made a point of saluting the Mexican Revolution, while embarking upon an ambitious tour of the capital city. The chasm in appearances between Kennedy's warm embrace of Mexico and his tense, private conversations with its host government is striking.[11]

Felipe Pereira Loureiro's chapter—by far the most quantitatively based in the collection—probes Kennedy's general but apparently ill-defined appeal in Brazil. Loureiro intriguingly suggests that the Kennedy image floated freely of Brazilian esteem for the United States, or the declining state of the bilateral relationship. Targeted initiatives such as the Alliance for Progress (AFP) and the expanding US public diplomacy campaign in Latin America had very little effect. Similarly suggestive is the tactical decision, on the part of the South Korean opposition press, to avoid direct attacks on Kennedy's person, while it sought to publicize conflicts between GIs and their civilian hosts: better to harness the "cultural capital" of the Kennedy image, and to claim a shared liberal ideology, while seeking to conclude a more equitable Status of Forces Agreement. The Kennedy image held no such utility, however, to the conservative Moroccan opposition described by Stenner. Indeed, it would seem, given the regime's limited toleration of an independent press, that criticisms of Kennedy could function as indirect challenges to the king. As in Iran, Mexico, and South Korea, the rhetoric of the US president could be echoed, adapted, or rebutted for local purposes.

The widespread enthusiasm for Kennedy in South Vietnam both speaks to the suppleness of his appeal and elucidates the irony and tragedy of his final confrontation, over autumn 1963, with President Ngo Dinh Diem. Other than West Germany, no other country could have been more receptive to his famous inaugural pledge to "support any friend" and "bear any burden" in pursuit of Cold War victory. Kennedy could embody multiple agendas to a beleaguered South Vietnamese audience: a staunch ally against the National Liberation Front and its northern patrons; or an earnest voice for reform and democracy in Saigon. Popular familiarity with the United States or Kennedy, as in the case of Brazil, was not extensive, and the construction of the Kennedys as glamorous and dynamic appears to have been as effective in South Vietnam as it was anywhere else.

The theme of aid or gift giving recurs throughout the chapters. In addition to the individual offerings made by Garakani, Pazos, and innumerable others, the chapters touch upon the implications (and complications) of US foreign assistance programs, and on the sometimes-solicited advice proffered by Americans in the Third World. The ambiguity of gift giving, as described by Cyrus Schayegh, is ever-present. Mexico sought AFP funds—but on its own terms, without compromising on its relationship with Cuba or symbolically abandoning the heritage of its own revolution. Seeking to consolidate their embryonic relationship, the Kennedys and Parks traded a child's cowboy outfit for a traditional Korean *hanbok*. Park's son apparently took to the former; it is not clear that the latter was ever donned. Kennedy's 1963 gift to Ireland—a visit that conferred valuable prestige upon the small state and proved a boon for local tourism—entailed tacit Irish acceptance of both US foreign policy and Washington's silence on the Northern Ireland question. In his chapter on India, Siegel notes recurring Indian suspicions that US aid would inevitably come with strings attached.

Even so, these chapters highlight the potential geopolitical and popular impact of foreign aid. Moskowitz's chapter offers compelling evidence of the wide-reaching effects of US assistance programs in Kenya. The 1960 airlift of hundreds of Kenyan and other eastern and central African college students to the United States had an outsized impact on the Kennedy image within the colony. So, too, did Kennedy's approval of Food for Peace famine relief aid to Kenya in 1961. In gratitude—and perhaps in the hope of further attention—Kenyans sent their own gifts, including a carved chess set and a silk zebra-pattern scarf.

Moskowitz also calls attention to a related, overlapping facet of Kennedy's outreach to Kenyans: his hospitality. She notes his numerous, well-received meetings with the Kenyan students—who were by no means the sole objects of this treatment. Philip Muehlenbeck's chapter, based upon his extensive research on Kennedy's African policy, reveals the broader patterns of Kennedy's interpersonal outreach. Kennedy clearly believed that time with African visitors was time well spent, and his practice of bringing guests to the upstairs residential area of the White House, and introducing them to his wife and children, appears to have been particularly effective. Hospitality is perhaps the most universally recognized form of generosity, and its individual acts, ingrained by millennia of human tradition, render it especially difficult to counterfeit.

Close examination of the Kennedy means of interpersonal engagement here is vital, as Kennedy's generally successful head-of-state diplomacy is too often reduced to a consequence of his innate charisma. The concept of charisma is helpful, but by itself insufficient. Kennedy's charm and the loyalty he inspired in friends and staff are well known, but it is best not to underestimate his foreign counterparts—often themselves practitioners of charismatic politics. Stray reminiscences by Kennedy and aides remind us of his own insecurities, the toll exacted by crises, and his own capacity for intense self-criticism.[12] One would do well—at all times—to recall also his brother Robert's reminder that "at least one half of the days he spent on this earth were days of intense physical pain."[13] Charisma, such as Kennedy employed it, was amplified and channeled by a well-honed method of interpersonal engagement. The outcomes of his meetings and correspondence testify to method, discipline, interest, demeanor, and a strong support staff.

In meetings, Kennedy often effectively ceded the floor to his guests—a further gesture of hospitality. Memoranda of conversation repeatedly depict Kennedy acting as a kind of interviewer—perhaps harnessing skills he developed during his brief stint as a journalist after his wartime naval service. Frequently, he employed the question, itself, as a means of conveying his own views.

Kennedy's questions themselves may be divided into three groupings. The first and least remarkable were questions on matters of mutual concern: pertaining to foreign aid, bilateral relations, and regional policy. Yet the conversation often ranged more widely. Senegalese President Leopold Senghor's discussion of postcolonial identity led Kennedy to inquire about the concept of negritude.[14] Kenyan labor leader Thomas Mboya was struck by Kennedy's interest in African trade unions.[15] The president inquired after the origins of regional conflicts, the nature of domestic politics, and the local impact of the Cold War. Finally, he often asked his guests for advice: in dealing with regional problems, in implementing aid programs, and toward the broader strengthening of relations.

Here, Kennedy made effective use of a dedicated support staff. As Muehlenbeck and Moskowitz note, Assistant Secretary of State G. Mennen Williams was particularly effective in preparing useful, digestible memoranda in advance of visits by prominent Africans.[16] Energetic White House staffer Robert W. Komer served a similar purpose in preparing the president for conversations with Middle Eastern and South Asian leaders, often with bracing candor. A September 1961 memorandum on the question of Moroccan bases termed King Hassan a "vain" and "jealous" young man—by way of urging Kennedy to play to the monarch's ego.[17] Outgoing presidential letters were subject to an exacting process of drafting and revision, to ensure that they emerged in Kennedy's voice.[18] The president, finally, was a tireless consumer of embassy and intelligence reporting, fed to him by a highly responsive National Security Council staff.

Consequently, guests were quite often impressed by Kennedy's range of knowledge and depth of interest. Nigeria's Prime Minister Abubakar Balewa recalled in 1964, "He appeared to me to be more informed on current events in the world than any other person."[19] Particularly revealing is Indonesian President Sukarno's exclamation after a spirited debate with Kennedy in April 1961, "The Americans have a very well-informed president. He is charming and was very gracious to me. I feel that he can be ruthlessly practical when the situation calls for it."[20]

Kennedy kept to his own views—and he found Sukarno's particularly disagreeable—but he avoided the appearance of dogmatism. Professions of fallibility served to insulate him from the appearance of arrogance, so, too, did his lamentations about the limits of US power. In his conversations and correspondence, he often invoked a principle of reciprocity. "We both lead countries that are not easily governed," he wrote to Nehru in January 1962, after India took the Portuguese-ruled territory of Goa.

> I should not willingly do anything to make your problems more difficult—shall hope, when something bears on Indian public opinion, to consider this closely, and to be informed if I am ever indifferent. Similarly, I think it is reasonable that American public opinion should be a subject of concern to you.[21]

Carefully cultivated, through meetings and correspondence, interpersonal currency could be utilized at moments of crisis: to persuasive purposes, or to add a complementary carrot to a rhetorical stick.

JFK, thus, approached international politics, particularly outreach toward nonaligned states, as interpersonal challenges. His own charisma mattered less than his realization, in Komer's words, that he was "dealing with a large group of charismatic personalities" who lacked the benefit of a long-established "firmly structured constitutional system."[22]

Mboya offered perhaps the best description of the institutionalization of Kennedy's personal approach:

> I think what struck one very, very strongly was the relations at personal levels. I think there was something in the Kennedy Administration which was so personal that everything became identified with his own personality and his own personal relations with people. His keen personal interest was immediately conveyed to the heads of state who met him and this almost created, as it were, not just better diplomatic relations but personal relationships between Africa and America.[23]

To be sure, the Kennedy appeal was not omnidirectional. As seen above, it did not sway Baldwin, anxious allies, or other critics. Muehlenbeck also notes the anxiety and antipathy felt by the racist South African government, and its imperialist counterpart in Lisbon. The latter was one of only a few governments that declined to send condolences after the assassination.

Even the reactions of Cold War antagonists can be revealing. Matthew D. Johnson's study of China's response to the Kennedy phenomenon is especially illuminating. He demonstrates clearly that Mao's government perceived, in the Kennedy presidency, a more ominous, devious adversary. The expansion of US cultural diplomacy and development assistance programs in Third World battlegrounds such as Ghana unnerved the PRC—even as it likely overrated Washington's gains. The subsequent restructuring of the PRC's foreign ministry, intensification of cultural diplomacy, and expansion of foreign language instruction offered a kind of backhanded compliment to the Kennedy program. So, too, does Mao's perception of Kennedy add significantly to our understanding of his increasingly public denunciations of Nikita Khrushchev. Alongside Kennedy's apparent policy of promoting the "peaceful evolution" of the communist bloc, peaceful coexistence could only have struck the Chinese leader as inexplicable knavery or abject betrayal.

At first blush, the North Vietnamese reading of Kennedy appears largely similar to that of its northern ally. Hanoi's media outlets, like their Chinese counterparts, touched upon Kennedy's wealth and conveyed some anxiety about the effectiveness of his message. Kennedy's visible policy choices—he continually deepened the US commitment to Saigon—could scarcely have led to him receiving a favorable reading in Hanoi. Yet Lillie and Nguyen's chapter notes a startling, if retrospective, exception from North Vietnam's denunciations. Interviewed by John F. Kennedy Jr., General Vo Nguyen Giap expressed regret at the assassination, musing that events might have unfolded differently in Southeast Asia, had JFK survived. Was it hospitality toward a Kennedy or evidence of the ever-expanding reach of the late president's appeal?

This chapter will not venture onto the speculative territory of how Kennedy's Vietnam policy might have evolved, if given another few years. Yet some speculation is evoked by Myra Ann Houser's fascinating study of the South African Lawyers' Committee for Civil Rights Under Law. John F. Kennedy's South Africa policy—while serving to unnerve Pretoria—fell short of providing outright confrontation. The changing stances of his two brothers, Robert and Edward, suggest a possible arc for their elder brother's own position toward the white redoubts. Houser suggests a deep linkage between the youngest brother's December 1960 African travels and the subsequent choices of his elder siblings. The Kennedy men placed great stock in personal fact-finding tours. John and Robert Kennedy's postwar travels in Europe and Asia proved deeply formative to their views on the Cold War and decolonization. So, too, may it have been with Edward Kennedy—whose interest in South Africa proved lifelong.

On a final related note, these chapters suggest further consideration of another individual who advanced the Kennedy image around the world: Jacqueline Bouvier Kennedy. Siegel and Kunkel both note the whirlwind success of Mrs. Kennedy's 1962 Indian tour (and, in the latter case, the apparent fondness Nehru felt toward her). Her televised tour of the White House proved a great hit throughout the Global South—surely the most far-reaching act of hospitality ventured by a Kennedy during those years. Diederich notes the First Lady's idealization in the South Korean press, as well as the parallels drawn between her and Park's wife, Yuk Young-soo, which further helped the Seoul government legitimate itself after the 1961 coup. Her hairstyle found a following in Mexico even before she and her husband boarded their flight back. It also appears to have attained some popularity in South Vietnam. A charismatic spouse and adorable children completed the Kennedy image—and depictions of their grief in autumn 1963 would help it to remain indelible ever after.

For a brief span of time, Kennedy—his message amplified by family and subordinates, its receipt facilitated by political, cultural, and technological change—captivated the world. His appeal was by no means universal, yet it was remarkably widespread, and the imprint it left remains visible today. Not all were so moved, and it is indeed possible that his wave had crested by the time of his death, that it might have visibly receded had he been afforded the chance to serve out a second term. At the very least, recent experience suggests that lofty rhetoric creates problems of rising expectations, all the more so when the audience is global.

Figure 16.1 "The Bullet Is Stronger than the Ballot."

Mboya was, himself, assassinated on July 5, 1969, mere weeks before his thirty-ninth birthday. While the gunman was apprehended, tried, and executed, the killing remains a traumatic and ill-explained event in Kenyan history—much like the two Kennedy assassinations. Cartoonist Kenneth Mahood made this linkage explicit. In a July 8 cartoon, he depicted Mboya's tombstone alongside those of Martin Luther King Jr., Robert F. Kennedy, John F. Kennedy, and Abraham Lincoln. In the foreground, dwarfing the respective memorials, stands an ominous statue of a revolver (Figure 16.1).[24]

As the voice of both a rising generation and of the aspirations of decolonized peoples in Africa and elsewhere, Mboya's thoughts about Kennedy bear particular relevance. Warm, but not uncritical, they suggest why JFK's image has endured, and offer an evocative note upon which to close this volume.

From the point of view of the younger generation, President Kennedy offered so much excitement and hope in the future. They saw in him a young man who understood the modern world and the problems of the younger generation—the problems of younger people who were trying to handle all the intricate questions of the scientific and modern world. They saw in him a very enlightened outlook, full of youthful hope for the future. This is a difficult thing to say in so many words, but it's something that struck one, something that one began to hope for. Even though he did not say very much or do very much, there was always this feeling that at least there was someone talking the same language with all of us.[25]

Notes

1 Anders Stephanson, "Senator John F. Kennedy: Anti-Imperialism and Utopian Deficit," *JAS* 48, no. 1 (2014): 3.
2 Barry Blitt, "Bad Reception," *New Yorker*, February 1, 2016, cover.
3 Michael Hogan, *The Afterlife of John Fitzgerald Kennedy: A Biography* (New York: Cambridge University Press, 2017), 219.
4 Larry Sabato, *The Kennedy Half-Century: The Presidency, Assassination, and Lasting Legacy of John F. Kennedy* (New York: Bloomsbury, 2013), 420.
5 See also Hogan, *Afterlife*, 129–31.
6 George Frost Kennan, *Memoirs: 1925-1950* (Boston: Little Brown, 1967), 295.
7 See also Jason Parker, *Hearts, Minds, Voices: U.S. Cold War Public Diplomacy and the Formation of the Third World* (New York: Oxford University Press, 2016).
8 David Engerman, *The Price of Aid: The Economic Cold War in India* (Cambridge: Harvard University Press, 2018).
9 Robert Rakove, *Kennedy, Johnson, and the Nonaligned World* (New York: Cambridge University Press, 2012), 165.
10 Abbas Milani, *The Shah* (New York: Palgrave Macmillan, 2011), 233, 304–5.
11 See also Renata Keller, *Mexico's Cold War: Cuba, the United States, and the Legacy of the Mexican Revolution* (Cambridge: Cambridge University Press, 2015), 134–37.
12 Kennedy was famously frustrated with his June 1961 meeting with Nikita Khrushchev in Vienna, and with Jawaharlal Nehru's visit to Washington the following November. State Department officer Arva Floyd recalled a "nervous" Kennedy receiving Sukarno

and Keita in September 1961, following the Belgrade Conference. See Association for Diplomatic Studies and Training, Oral History Interview, Arva C. Floyd, March 20, 2000, 26.
13 James Giglio, *The Presidency of John F. Kennedy* (Lawrence: University Press of Kansas, 2006), 7.
14 Memorandum of Conversation, Kennedy and Senghor, November 3, 1961, *FRUS*, 1961–1963, vol. 21, doc. 630.
15 Thomas Mboya, Oral History Interview, March 10, 1965, 6, John F. Kennedy Presidential Library, Boston (JFKL).
16 See also Thomas Noer, "*Soapy*": *A Biography of G. Mennen Williams* (Ann Arbor: University of Michigan Press, 2005), 231–32.
17 Memorandum, Komer to Kennedy, September 25, 1961, NSAM 34, Memorandum on Moroccan Bases (JFKNSF-329-009), National Security Action Memoranda, Meetings and Memoranda, National Security Files, JFKL.
18 Komer, Fifth Oral History Interview, December 22, 1969, 66–67, JFKL.
19 Abubakar Tafawa Balewa, Oral History Interview, May 7, 1964, 2, JFKL.
20 Rakove, *Kennedy*, 84.
21 Kennedy to Nehru, January 18, 1962, *FRUS*, 1961–1963, vol. 19, doc. 198.
22 Komer, First Oral History Interview, June 18, 1964, 2, JFKL.
23 Mboya, Oral History Interview, 6.
24 Mary Dudziak, *Exporting American Dreams: Thurgood Marshall's African Journey* (New York: Oxford University Press, 2008), 152–54.
25 Mboya, Oral History Interview, 7.

Contributors

Begüm Adalet is Assistant Professor of Government at Cornell University and the author of *Hotels and Highways: The Construction of Modernization Theory in Cold War Turkey* (2018).

Inga Kim Diederich is a PhD candidate at the Department of History, University of California, San Diego.

Myra Ann Houser is Assistant Professor of History at Ouachita Baptist University. Her works include "Whose Atlantic?: South Africa, Namibia, Central America, and OPSAAL in the 1980s," *History in Africa* (2019).

Matthew D. Johnson is an independent consultant and associate fellow of the Global Diplomatic Forum. He is a co-founder and director of the PRC History Group (prchistory.org).

David P. Kilroy is Professor in the Department of History and Political Science, Nova Southeastern University. His works include *For Race and Country: The Life and Career of Colonel Charles Young* (2003).

Sam Klug is a PhD student at the Department of History, Harvard University. His dissertation is titled, "Making the Internal Colony: Black Internationalism, Development, and the Politics of Colonial Comparison in the United States, 1940–1975."

Sönke Kunkel is Professor of North American History at Freie Universität Berlin. His publications include *Empire of Pictures: Global Media and the 1960s Remaking of American Foreign Policy* (Paperback, 2018).

Aaron Lillie is a PhD candidate at the Department of History, University of Washington-Seattle.

Felipe Loureiro is Associate Professor at the Institute of International Relations, University of São Paulo (IRI-USP). His works include *Empresários, Trabalhadores e Grupos de Interesse: A Política Econômica nos Governos Jânio Quadros e João Goulart* (2017).

Kara Moskowitz is Assistant Professor in the Department of History at the University of Missouri-St. Louis. Her works includes *Seeing Like a Citizen: Decolonization, Development, and the Making of Kenya, 1945–80* (2019).

Philip E. Muehlenbeck is Professorial Lecturer at George Washington University. His works include *Betting on the Africans: John F. Kennedy's Courting of African Nationalist Leaders* (2012).

Diu-Huong Nguyen is Visiting Assistant Professor at the Department of History, Haverford College. Her writings include "Hue Prepared for a Holiday, Then the War Came," *New York Times*, February 2, 2018.

Vanni Pettinà is Associate Professor of Latin American International History at El Colegio de México, Mexico City. He is the author of *Historia mínima de la Guerra Fría en América Latina* (2019).

Robert B. Rakove is Lecturer in International Relations at Stanford University. He is the author of *Kennedy, Johnson, and the Nonaligned World* (2012).

Cyrus Schayegh is Professor of international history at the Graduate Institute for International and Development Studies, Geneva, and the author of *The Middle East and the Making of the Modern World* (2017).

Benjamin Siegel is Assistant Professor of history at Boston University and the author of *Hungry Nation: Food, Famine, and the Making of Modern India* (2018).

David Stenner is Assistant Professor in the Department of History at Christopher Newport University. His works include *Globalizing Morocco: Transnational Activism and the Postcolonial State* (2019).

Bibliography

Baldwin, James. *Collected Essays*, edited by Toni Morrison. New York: The Library of America, 1998.
Bodroghkozy, Aniko. "The BBC and the Black Weekend: Broadcasting the Kennedy Assassination and the Birth of Global Television News." *The Sixties*, 9, no. 2 (2016): 242–60.
Bradley, Mark. "Decolonization, the Global South, and the Cold War, 1919–1962." In *The Cambridge History of the Cold War*, edited by Melvyn Leffler and Odd Arne Westad, 464–85. Cambridge: Cambridge University Press, 2010.
Bui, Diem. *In the Jaws of History*. Boston: Houghton Mifflin, 1987.
Clymer, Adam. *Edward M. Kennedy: A Biography*. New York: William Morrow, 1999.
Connelly, Matthew, Robert J. McMahon, Katherine A. S. Sibley, Thomas Borstelmann, Nathan Citino, and Kristin Hoganson. "SHAFR in the World." *Passport*, 42, no. 2 (2011): 4–16.
Costigliola, Frank. "US Foreign Policy from Kennedy to Johnson." In *The Cambridge History of the Cold War*, edited by Melvyn Leffler and Odd Arne Westad, 112–33. Cambridge: Cambridge University Press, 2010.
Daum, Andreas. *Kennedy in Berlin*. Cambridge: Cambridge University Press, 2008.
Dinkel, Jürgen. *The Non-Aligned Movement: Genesis, Organization and Politics (1927–1992)*. Leiden: Brill, 2019.
Elliott, Duong Van Mai. *The Sacred Willow: Four Generations in a Life of a Vietnamese Family*. New York: Oxford University Press, 1999.
Ellis, Sylvia. "The Historical Significance of President Kennedy's Visit to Ireland in June 1963." *Irish Studies Review*, 16, no. 2 (2008): 113–30.
Giglio, James. *The Presidency of John F. Kennedy*. Lawrence: University Press of Kansas, 2006.
Giglio, James. "Writing Kennedy." In *A Companion to John F. Kennedy*, edited by Marc Selverstone, 7–30. Chichester: Wiley Blackwell, 2014.
Gillingham, Paul and T. Smith Benjamin, eds. *Dictablanda: Politics, Work, and Culture in Mexico, 1938–1968*. Durham: Duke University Press, 2014.
Gilman, Nils. *Mandarins of the Future: Modernization Theory in Cold War America*. Baltimore: The Johns Hopkins University Press, 2003.
Go, Julian. *Patterns of Empire*. Cambridge: Cambridge University Press, 2011.
Haefele, Mark. "Kennedy, the USIA, and World Public Opinion." *DH*, 25 (2001): 63–84.
Hellmann, John. *The Kennedy Obsession: The American Myth of JFK*. New York: Columbia University Press, 1997.
Hogan, Michael. *The Afterlife of John F. Kennedy: A Biography*. Cambridge: Cambridge University Press, 2018.
Immerwahr, Daniel. *Thinking Small: The United States and the Lure of Community Development*. Cambridge: Harvard University Press, 2015.
Joseph, Gilbert. "What We Now Know and Should Know: Bringing Latin America More Meaningfully into Cold War Studies." In *In from the Cold: Latin America's New*

Encounter with the Cold War, edited by Gilbert Joseph and Daniela Spenser, 3–46. Durham: Duke University Press, 2008.

Keller, Renata. *Mexico's Cold War: Cuba, the United States, and the Legacy of the Mexican Revolution*. New York: Cambridge University Press, 2015.

Kim, Byung-Kook, and Ezra Vogel, eds. *The Park Chung Hee Era: The Transformation of South Korea*. Cambridge: Harvard University Press, 2011.

Kim, Charles R. *Youth for Nation: Culture and Protest in Cold War South Korea*. Honolulu: University of Hawai'i Press, 2017.

Klein, Christina. *Cold War Orientalism: Asia in the Middlebrow Imagination, 1945–1961*. Berkeley: University of California Press, 2003.

Kochavi, Noam. *A Conflict Perpetuated: China Policy during the Kennedy Years*. Westport: Praeger, 2002.

Kramer, Paul. "Power and Connection: Imperial Histories of the United States in the World." *AHR*, 116, no. 5 (2011): 1348–91.

Latham, Michael E. *Modernization as Ideology: American Social Science and "Nation Building" in the Kennedy Era*. Chapel Hill: University of North Carolina Press, 2000.

Loureiro, Felipe. "The Alliance For or Against Progress? US-Brazilian Financial Relations in the Early 1960s." *JLAS*, 46, no. 2 (2014): 323–51.

Lubin, David. *Shooting Kennedy: JFK and the Culture of Images*. Berkeley: University of California Press, 2003.

Mahoney, Richard D. *JFK: Ordeal in Africa*. New York: Oxford University Press, 1983.

McGarr, Paul M. *The Cold War in South Asia: Britain, the United States and the Indian Subcontinent, 1945–1965*. Cambridge: Cambridge University Press, 2013.

McMahon, Robert. *The Cold War on the Periphery: The United States, India, and Pakistan*. New York: Columbia University Press, 1994.

McMahon, Robert. "The Republic as Empire." In *Perspectives on Modern America*, edited by Harvard Sitkoff, 80–100. New York: Oxford University Press, 2001.

Merrill, Dennis. *Bread and the Ballot: The United States and India's Economic Development, 1947–1963*. Chapel Hill: University of North Carolina Press, 1990.

Monjib, Maâti. *La monarchie marocaine et la lutte pour le pouvoir*. Paris: L'Harmattan, 1992.

Muehlenbeck, Philip E. *Betting on the Africans: John F. Kennedy's Courting of African Nationalist Leaders*. Oxford: Oxford University Press, 2012.

Munro, John. *The Anticolonial Front: The African American Freedom Struggle and Global Decolonization, 1945–1960*. Cambridge: Cambridge University Press, 2017.

Nhan Dan [*The People Daily*]. Hanoi, 1960s.

Niu, Jun. "1962: The Eve of the Left Turn in China's Foreign Policy." *The Cold War International History Project Working Paper Series*, 48 (2005): 1–36.

Ojeda, Mario. *Alcances y límites de la política exterior de México*. México: El Colegio de México, Centro de Estudios Internacionales, 2001.

O'Sullivan, Kevin. *Ireland, Africa and the End of Empire: Small State Identity and the Cold War, 1955–1975*. Manchester: University of Manchester Press, 2012.

Parker, Jason. *Hearts, Minds, Voices: U.S. Cold War Public Diplomacy and the Formation of the Third World*. New York: Oxford University Press, 2016.

Pereira, Anthony. "The US Role in the 1964 Coup in Brazil: A Reassessment." *Bulletin of Latin American Research*, 37, no. 1 (2018): 5–17.

Rabe, Stephen. *John F. Kennedy: World Leader*. Washington: Potomac, 2010.

Rakove, Robert B. *Kennedy, Johnson, and the Nonaligned World*. New York: Cambridge University Press, 2014.

Rasberry, Vaughn. "JFK and the Global Anticolonial Movement." In *Cambridge Companion to John F. Kennedy*, edited by Andrew Hoberek, 118–33. Cambridge: Cambridge University Press, 2015.

Schlesinger, Arthur M. Jr. *A Thousand Days: John F. Kennedy in the White House*. Boston: Houghton Mifflin, 1965.

Shachtman, Tom. *Airlift to America: How Barack Obama, Sr., John F. Kennedy, Tom Mboya, and 800 East African Students Changed their World and Ours*. New York: St. Martin's Press, 2009.

Shuman, Amanda. "Friendship is Solidarity: the Chinese Ping-Pong Team Visits Africa in 1962." In *Sport and Diplomacy: Games within Games*, edited by J. Simon Rofe, 110–29. Manchester: University of Manchester Press, 2018.

Singh, Nikhil. *Black is a Country: Race and the Unfinished Struggle for Democracy*. Cambridge: Harvard University Press, 2004.

Stenner, David. *Globalizing Morocco: Transnational Activism and the Postcolonial State*. Stanford: Stanford University Press, 2019.

Stephanson, Anders. "Senator John F. Kennedy: Anti-Imperialism and Utopian Deficit." *JAS*, 48, no. 1 (2014): 1–24.

Stoler, Ann, and Frederick Cooper. "Between Metropole and Colony." In *Tensions of Empire*, edited by Ann Stoler and Frederick Cooper, 1–56. Berkeley: University of California Press, 1997.

Taffet, Jeffrey. *Foreign Aid as Foreign Policy: The Alliance for Progress in Latin America*. New York: Routledge, 2007.

Tonra, Ben. *Global Citizen and European Republic: Irish Foreign Policy in Transition*. Manchester: University of Manchester Press, 2012.

Tye, Larry. *Bobby Kennedy: The Making of a Liberal Icon*. New York: Random House, 2016.

Westad, Odd Arne. *The Global Cold War*. Cambridge: Cambridge University Press, 2005.

White, Mark. *Kennedy: A Cultural History of an American Icon*. London: Bloomsbury, 2013.

Young, Cynthia. *Soul Power: Culture, Radicalism, and the Making of a U.S. Third World Left*. Durham: Duke University Press, 2006.

Zaborowska, Magdalena. *James Baldwin's Turkish Decade: Erotics of Exile*. Durham: Duke University Press, 2009.

Index

16th Street Baptist Church 57
20th Congress of the Communist Party of the Soviet Union 153

Abram, Morris 254, 256
Adenauer, Konrad 6, 102, 120, 266
aesthetics
  French 5
Africa 34–47, 48–63, 250–63
  and Ireland 85–7, 90, 92, 96
  media in 101–4
  nationalism in 24, 34, 35–7, 39, 42–4, 49, 50, 117, 267
  and the People's Republic of China 151, 153, 160, 162–3
  and Portuguese colonialism 119
  and sense of historical agency 109
  students from, in White House 101
  United States Information Agency in 104
  and US civil rights 36–7, 50, 56–8, 110–11, 121–2
African Americans 11, 19–21, 24–9, 57, 58, 121, 155, 157–8, 239, 242, 244, 267. *See also* Black freedom movement; Black Power movement
African American Students Foundation 53–5
African National Congress 250, 255
Afro-American Association 28
age, Kennedy's 6
Ahidjo, Amadou 37, 41
Ahmad, Muhammad. *See* Stanford, Max
aid. *See also* development
  Baldwin on 235
  as gift 142–3
  postcolonial reactions to US 111
  US economic 19, 51, 70, 105, 107, 108, 125, 160, 228
Aiken, Frank 91

Airlift from Kenya to the United States 53–5
Alam, Asadollah 135
Algeria 1, 24–5, 27, 29, 39, 117–18, 120, 123, 143, 163, 258, 266
  Kennedy's 1957 speech on 86, 88, 116
Alliance for Progress 2, 64–83, 89, 105–8, 118, 121, 138, 169–82, 268
Alulu, Ainea 57
American Bar Association 254
American Committee on Africa 252
American Revolution 20, 27
American Society of African Culture 19, 26, 27
Angola 40
Ankara 138, 237, 238, 267
anti-colonialism 20, 23, 25
anti-communism 37, 65, 87, 94, 117–18, 120, 142–3, 153, 187–8, 206, 208–9, 212
anti-imperialism 94, 206, 240, 244
apartheid 4, 37, 119, 122, 240, 250–63
April Revolution (in South Korea) 185, 195
Apter, David 25
Arbour Hill cemetery 88, 94
Asia
  in Bandung 23
  colonized people in 26
  communism in 8, 207, 227
  Chinese presence in 151–3, 160, 162–4
  decolonization in 50, 85, 86
  East 135, 138
  Henry Reuss' tour across 225
  India and 230
  Ireland as ally of 87, 90
  John F. Kennedy's journey across 1, 205
  media in 101, 103–4, 106
  nuclear arms in 221

South   26, 51, 221–34, 270
Southeast   23, 157, 203, 206, 271
    students from   101
    United States domination in   206
    United States Information Agency
        in   107
    views in, about Kennedy   100, 108,
        109, 117, 122
Asian and Asians. *See* Asia
assassination of John F. Kennedy   4, 5,
    37, 38–42, 49, 56, 57, 58, 124–5,
    155, 191, 196, 207, 210, 213, 214,
    221, 230, 231, 237, 250, 252, 267,
    271, 273
Attwood, William   42, 49, 57
Australia   138
Austria   137, 138, 141
Ayub Khan, Mohammed   267
Azikiwe, Nnamdi   36, 39

Bahia   137
Baldwin, James   235–49, 267, 271
Balewa, Abubakar   40, 270
Ball, George   96
Banda, Hastings   36
Bandung Conference   23
Barcelona   138
Belafonte, Harry   53
Belfast   93
Belgium   34, 43
Belgrade Conference   119, 255
Ben Bella, Ahmed   6, 39, 118, 251
Berger, Samuel   189, 196
Berlin   120, 137, 138, 139, 246 n.28
    Kennedy's visit to   5, 86, 94, 109
    Wall   121
Black Americans. *See* African Americans
Black freedom movement   26–9
Black Panther Party   28–9
Black Power movement   26, 28–9
Blitt, Barry   264
Borstelmann, Thomas   2, 6, 11
Bose, Subhas Chandra   92
Boston   90, 140, 208, 221, 259
Botha, Pik   259
Bourguiba, Habib   35
Bowles, Chester   221, 225, 226
Bo Yibo   153
Brain trust   186

Brazil   3, 4, 64–83, 108, 137, 138, 268
Bretton Woods Institutions   50
British Broadcast Company   4, 52, 205,
    212
Buddhism   204, 213
Bui Diem   211
Burns, James Macgregor   185
Bush, George H. W.   34
Buthelezi, Mangosuthu   259
Buu Y   212

Cambodia   163
Cameroon   37, 41
Canada   22, 138, 233 n.52
Cao Dai   202
Capitol Hill   88, 255
Carlson, Joel   253–4, 256
Carmichael, Stokely   29
Carter, Jimmy   42
Cassam, Annar   34–5
Castro, Fidel   6, 36, 64, 74, 118, 119
    and cultural diplomacy   163
Catholicism
    and Brazil   65, 71, 72, 78
    and Iran   137
    and Ireland   89, 93, 94, 266
    and Kenya   57
    and Mexico   172, 178
    and Vietnam   202, 204, 206, 210, 212,
        213, 214
Cayton, Horace   24
Center for International Studies
    (MIT)   26
Central African Republic   37, 39
Central Intelligence Agency   116, 156,
    172, 235, 240, 255
Chang, Chun-ha   193–4, 196
Chang, Myŏn   186
charisma   269
Chiang Kai-shek   151, 163
Chicago   25, 90
Chile   68, 73, 138, 163
    ambassador to Mexico   172, 174, 176,
        179
China. *See* People's Republic of China, the
Chittagong Armory Raid   92
Chou en-lai   7, 119
Christmas   130
Churchill, Winston   87, 231 n.4

cinema 4, 101, 102, 105, 110, 121, 159, 160, 163, 191
civil rights 25, 26, 27, 28, 36–7, 39, 44, 50, 56, 57, 58, 103, 110–11, 121–2, 158, 236, 238, 239, 241, 243, 251, 252, 256, 257, 261, 267
  See also Black freedom movement; Southern Africa Project of the Lawyers Committee for Civil Rights Under Law
Clarke, John Henrik 27
Clinton, Bill 34
Cold War
  globalized by decolonization 2
  historiography of 2
  and India 225
  Ireland in the 87, 88, 91, 94
  and Latin America 64, 68
  liberalism during the 20
  "peaceful evolution" as US strategy in 152
  and South Korea 183–4, 186, 188, 193
  and Turkey 267
  and US civil rights 26, 28, 57–8, 111
  and US policies vis-à-vis decolonization and postcolonial countries 21, 24, 25, 34, 40, 41, 48–9, 57–8, 105, 108, 111, 119–21, 142, 251, 258, 270
  and US strategy vis-à-vis the People's Republic of China 152, 156, 157, 160, 271
  and Vietnam 206, 207, 209, 268
Collins, Michael 92
Cologne 137
Colombia 73, 100, 101, 103, 107, 109, 137, 138, 139
Colonialism
  definition of 20, 21, 23–5, 27–9, 31 n.21
  internal 19, 21, 26–9, 33 n.61
  and racism 21, 24–6, 27–9
  settler 24, 28
Communism
  in Africa 37
  in Asia 8
  in the Global South 86, 108, 110, 162
  in India 101, 223, 225, 227, 229
  in Latin America 65, 66, 74, 109, 121
  and Mexico 171, 174
  in the People's Republic of China 143–68
  and repression of Catholicism 89
  and South Korea 186, 187
  in the United States 28
  and/versus United States 9, 25, 118, 119, 120, 143, 152, 153, 157, 188, 271
  in Vietnam 3, 4, 201–16
Communist Party of the United States of America (CPUSA) 27, 28
Confederación de Trabajadores de México (CTM) 169
Congo 42, 85, 90, 91, 93, 95, 96, 118, 119, 123, 157, 163, 258, 266
Congress Party (India) 101, 224, 231
Connelly, Matthew 2
Cooper, Frederick 8
Cork 85
Costa Rica 138, 139
Côte d'Ivoire. See Ivory Coast
Cousins, Norman 8
Cruse, Harold 19, 20, 21, 27–8
  and internal colonialism 27–8
Cuba 28, 79, 94, 105, 119, 121, 208, 212, 268
  Bay of Pigs invasion 37, 69, 110, 118
  missile crisis 65, 73, 74, 94, 119, 121, 230, 237
  revolution 170, 171
cultural diplomacy. See diplomacy
cynicism
  lack of 5
Cyprus 237, 246 n.18, 267

Dacko, David 37, 39
Daily Good Neighbor, The 170, 175, 176, 178
decolonization
  African 19, 21, 24, 49, 50, 58, 183
  Algerian 105
  and black freedom movement 26–9
  and development 51
  and diplomacy 111
  heroes of 6
  historiography of 2

and increased South-South interstate
relations   10
and Ireland   85–99
meaning of   31 n.21
peak coinciding with Kennedy's presidency and Kennedy   134, 206, 265, 266, 272
and sense of agency   109
war and   201, 203
Deen, Kabiru   56
De Gaulle, Charles   6, 24, 120, 157
De Lattre de Tassigny, Jean   205–6
democracy
anti-colonialism linked to   187
and India   223
and Ireland   87, 89, 90
and Kennedy   108, 109, 124, 186
and South Africa   260
and South Korea   183, 185–7, 193, 196
United States and   5, 22–3, 26, 28, 57, 187, 203, 241
and United States and Latin America   65, 72
demonstrations
in Brazil   65
in South Korea   183, 193–5
in Turkey   237
in the United States   110
Deng Xiaoping   153
Desai, Morarji   231
De Valera, Éamon   86, 87–8, 89–90, 92, 93, 96
development. *See also* aid
Brazilian   67
Indian   221–34
Iranian   136
Irish   87, 89
Mexican   170, 172, 173, 175, 179
South Korean   188, 192, 196
Soviet foreign   62
US foreign   19, 22, 42, 48–52, 65, 105, 124, 134, 143, 193, 271
US foreign versus Chinese foreign   152
diplomacy
alliance building through   188–9
gift exchange as a form of   189–91
international   121

Kennedy's personal   44, 49, 53, 269
Moroccan   126
people-to-people   142
travel for   188–9
US cultural and Chinese   151–68
US cultural and public   152, 159, 160, 161, 163, 235, 240, 241, 268, 271
US in South Asia   120
US *via-à-vis* French Algeria   123
Disneyland   35–6
domestic colonialism. *See* colonialism, internal
Dominican Republic   137, 139
Drake, St. Clair   24
Dublin   86, 88, 91, 93, 96, 266
Dulles, Allen W.   145, 156, 157
Dulles, John Foster   20, 152–3, 156
Duong Van Mai, Elliot   201, 211–13
Duong Van Minh   213

East African Standard   52, 54, 57
Easter Rising   87
Ecuador   73, 138
Eden, Anthony   6
Egypt   4, 6, 40, 118, 156. *See also* Nasser, Gamal Abdel
Eisenhower, Dwight D.   5, 6, 20, 34–5, 43, 52, 55, 116, 125, 134, 142, 154, 155, 208, 209, 254
Eldoret, Kenya   57
elections
Kennedy's as president   4, 92, 93, 101, 116–18, 140–1, 155, 184–5, 190, 195, 207, 208, 211, 221, 225, 226
Kenyan in 1961   55
Korean democratic   186, 188
South African in 1994   260
El Paso   138
El Salvador   138
embroidery   130–2
Emerson, Rupert   23–5
From Empire to Nation   24, 25
emotions   5–6, 10, 11, 36, 85, 95, 100–14, 178, 192, 256
Engerman, David   266
England   88, 203. *See also* United Kingdom
Episcopal Society for Cultural and Racial Unity   25

Ethiopia 39, 41, 255, 258
Eurasia 9
Europe
  Eastern 21, 88, 154, 260
  Empires of and imperialism 1, 5, 9, 10, 19, 25, 118, 205
  fascism in 26
  John and Robert Kennedy's travels in 272
  nationalists in 23
  and the People's Republic of China 164
  press of and readers in 51, 52, 241
  and the United States 49, 88, 120, 121, 157
  Western 90–2, 135, 138
European and Europeans. *See* Europe
European Economic Community 9, 85, 89, 90, 92
Excelsior, El 171, 178

famine relief. *See* food aid
Farley, Hugh D. 184
Farley, Vince 36, 41, 44
Fassi, 'Allal al- 119
Federal Bureau of Investigation 235, 239–42, 244, 247 n.29, 248 n.50
Federal Republic of Germany. *See* Germany
federalism 20–3
  of the early United States 22
Fianna Fáil 87, 91
film. *See* cinema
First Lady. *See* Kennedy, Jacqueline Bouvier
first new nation
  idea of United States as 19–23, 26, 27, 29
food aid 55–6
Food for Peace 55, 105, 269
Ford Foundation 197 n.7, 229
foreign aid. *See* aid
France
  aesthetics in White House 5
  and aid to India 233 n.52
  colonial rule by 122, 201, 202, 205, 206, 211, 212
  gifts from 138
  Kennedy on 116, 205, 206
  liberty and 27
  and Marshall aid 143
  news sources from 212
  as postimperial polity 9
  settlers from 120
  universities in 117
  and US foreign policy in Africa 52
Fredericks, J. Wayne 55
Freedom from Hunger campaign 55
French (language) 117, 131, 162, 212
French, the. *See* France
Freund, Richard 48

Gabon 39
Galbraith, John Kenneth 265–6, 267
  addresses on Indian economic policy 228–9
  appointment as Ambassador to India 226–7
  initial work in and study of India 224–5
Galway 85
Gandhi, Mahatma 41, 130, 136, 137, 221
Ganges 5
Garakani, Fakhri 10, 130–48, 264
Gaza 85
gender
  domesticity in relation to 189–91
  femininity and 189–92
  masculinity and 186, 189–92
  political performance of 184, 189–92
  and polling 68–9, 79
  "wholesome modernization" and 190–1
generation 7
Geneva Accords of 1954 202, 208
Gerig, Benjamin 22
Germany 9, 162, 202. *See also* Berlin; Cologne; Wiesbaden
  defeat in World War II 9
  East 162
  West 50, 120, 138, 139, 233 n.52, 268
Ghana 26, 34–5, 38–9, 41–2, 91, 159, 271
gift-giving 130–48, 268–9
globalization 9
Go, Julian 8
Goa 270
Goldberg, Arthur 254

Gordon, Lincoln 67, 225
Goulart, João 65–7, 70, 75, 78
Great Britain. *See* United Kingdom
Greece 138, 238
Green Belt Movement 54
Guatemala 138
Guevara, Che 6
Guinea 10, 35–6, 38, 40, 160, 163, 236
Guomindang 202

Hammarskjold, Dag 40, 42
Hanoi 202, 204, 208, 271
Harriman, Averell 42
Harrington, Donald 253–4
Harvard University 224
Hassan II 6, 115, 116, 122, 123, 124, 125, 126, 266, 270
historians. *See* historiography
historiography 1–3, 8–11, 30 n.5, 38, 49–50, 59 n.7, 59 n.10, 60 n.15, 80 n.17, 85, 101, 102, 111, 125, 135, 163, 203–5, 222–3, 230, 264
Hizb al-Istiqlal 115, 116, 117, 125
Hoa Hao 202
Hoang Quoc Viet 208
Ho Chi Minh 14 n.38, 201, 203
Holy Family Cathedral, Nairobi 57
Honduras 265
Hoover, J. Edgar 4, 239, 241–2, 247 n.30
hospitality 269–70
Houphouët-Boigny, Félix 38
Houser, George 252
Hoveyda, Amir Abbas 135
Huang Hua 160
Hue 202, 210, 212, 213
human rights 155
Hungary 153. *See also* Europe, East

idealism 8
India 221–34, 265, 266, 269, 270
  delegation to Dublin in 1947 96
  economic development in 221–34
  inspiration for Morocco 115
  and Iran 130
  Jacqueline Kennedy's tour in 222, 229, 230, 272
  nationalism 92
  opinions on Kennedy 108, 109
  and the People's Republic of China 151, 161, 163
  press 52, 101–4
  United States Information Agency in 104, 108
Indonesia 115, 119, 162, 270
Ingles, Brian 85
Inönü, Ismet 237–8, 267
International Bank for Reconstruction and Development 50, 171
International Commission of Jurists 254
internationalism 23, 25, 26, 50, 184, 186, 188, 194
International Monetary Fund 50
Iran 4, 6, 10, 104, 130–48, 264, 267, 268
  See also Mohammad Reza Shah Pahlavi
  1953 coup d'Etat in 132, 136
Ireland 85–96, 266, 269
  anti-colonial nationalism and 88, 89, 92, 93, 94, 95, 96
  Catholicism and 93, 94
  Dáil 87, 94
  Department of External Affairs 85, 93, 96
  home rule 92
  Kennedy visit to 5, 85–96
  neutrality and 87, 94
  Northern 93–4
  Oireachtas and 85, 90
  partition and 88, 93, 94
  Programme for Economic Expansion 85, 89
  War of Independence of 87
Irish Press 92
Irish Times 91, 94, 95
Isaacs, Harold 26–7
Israel 138, 236
Italy 137, 138, 139. *See also* Naples; Rome; San Remo; Sicily
Ivory Coast 38, 40–1, 264. *See also* Houphouët-Boigny, Félix

Jackson, Jesse 259
Japan 9, 138, 154, 162, 188, 201, 243
jazz 159
Jesus Christ 130
Jim Crow 157
Johannesburg Bar Association 252

John XXIII, Pope   130, 133
John F. Kennedy Presidential
    Library   137
Johnson, Lyndon B.   41–3, 155, 252,
    267–8
  visit to India   227–8
journalists   160
Jupiter missiles   267

Kaiser, Philip   36
Kamonya, Gladys   49
Kaunda, Kenneth   43
Kayibanda, Gregoire   37
Keita, Mobito   37
Keita, Modibo   119
Kennan, George   265
Kennedy, Edward M.   250–2, 257–61,
    271–2
Kennedy, Ethel   253, 259–60
Kennedy, Jacqueline Bouvier
  1962 White House tour film by   4,
    104, 272
  gifts to and by   38, 56, 137, 141
  interpretation of President Kennedy
    by   111
  motherly advice by   141
  popularity and views by postcolonial
    media and publics of   5, 10, 103,
    104, 109, 189–92, 121, 229–30, 272
  and stage craft and symbolic
    politics   5, 141, 272
  visits abroad by   5, 103, 109, 121, 169,
    177, 222, 229
Kennedy, John Fitzgerald, Jr.   266, 271
Kennedy, Robert F.   205, 213, 238–40,
    246 n.24, 250, 252–4, 257–60, 267,
    269, 271–2, 273
Kennedy Foundation   54–5
Kenya   10, 36, 39–42, 118, 265, 266, 269,
    270, 271, 273. *See also* Kenyatta,
    Jomo
  National Archives   58
  National Assembly   57
Kenyatta, Jomo   57
Kheel, Theodore   54
Khrushchev, Nikita   6, 36, 120, 153, 154,
    266, 271
Kiano, Julius   53
Kim, Charles R.   190

Kim, Dae-Jung   192
King, Martin Luther, Jr.   26, 42, 236, 252,
    257, 273
Komer, Robert W.   267, 270
Korea. *See* South Korea
Korean War   184

languages   139, 142, 152, 161, 162, 257,
    264
Laos   29, 157, 158, 162, 163
Laski, Harold   23
Latin America. *See also* Alliance for
    Progress; Brazil; Mexico
  Brazil in   64–82
  Britain in   9
  gifts to Kennedy   135, 138
  Mexico in   169–82
  the People's Republic of China
    and   153, 162, 163
  polls in and opinions by about
    Kennedy   64–82, 100–11, 169–82,
    221, 268
  in postcolonial media's reporting on
    Kennedy   119, 121, 153
  US hegemony in   64
  views of Jacqueline Kennedy   10,
    100–11, 169
  at the White House   5
Latin American and Latin Americans. *See*
    Latin America
Lawyers' Committee for Civil Rights
    under Law   251–2, 254, 256–7
  liberal democracy and   26
League of Nations   86, 91
Lemass, Seán   85, 89, 90, 92, 93–5, 96
Lewis, John   261
Libapu, Jairo Murunga   57
Liberal internationalism   23, 184, 186,
    188, 192, 194, 196
liberalism   20, 26, 86, 119, 124, 183, 184,
    186, 191–4, 196, 223–5, 226, 228,
    237, 251, 255, 268
Liberia   37, 39
Limerick   88
Lincoln, Abraham   6, 37, 41, 122, 130,
    273
Lipset, Seymour Martin   20, 21–3
  The First New Nation   21–3
literature, on. *See* historiography

Liu Shaoqi   151, 154
London   9, 86, 91, 179, 241
London School of Economics   23
Look magazine   93
López Mateos, Adolfo   169, 170, 171, 172, 175, 177, 179, 268
Louw, Eric   37
Lowenstein, Allard   253
Lufthansa   132
Lumumba, Patrice   6, 27, 41, 43, 123, 251, 265
Luthuli, Albert   253
lynchings   193–4, 236

Maathai, Wangari   54
MacBride, Seán   92
Macdonald, Donald   184
MacDonald, Malcolm   57
Machakos, Kenya   54
Madrid   241
Mahalanobis, P. C.   222, 224
Mahoney, William   38
Mahood, Kenneth   273
Mali   37, 42, 119, 163
Mandela, Nelson   250–1, 255, 260
Mandela, Winnie   250, 258–60
Mao Zedong   151, 152, 153, 154, 155, 271
Marshall, Thurgood, Jr.   260–1
Marshall Plan   121, 143
Massachusetts   88
mass media. *See* media
Mau Mau State of Emergency   51
Mauritania   37, 41
Mauss, Marcel   134
Mbayah, Mungai   54
Mboya, Thomas   36, 39–40, 52, 53–5, 57, 58, 270, 271
   assassination of   273
media   4, 5, 49–52, 134, 140–1. *See also* newspapers; radio; television
   cartoons in   192–5
   censorship of   185, 188
   editorials in   185–7, 190–1, 193–4
   government outlets   188
   mass   101, 102, 109, 152, 157, 163, 164, 265, 266
   opposition outlets   192–5
   photography in   188–9, 194

Meredith, James   122
Mexican Revolution   170, 173, 174, 175, 176, 178, 179
Mexico   1, 137, 138, 169–82, 268, 272
   See also Partido Revolucionario Institucional
Mexico City   169, 172, 173, 174, 177
Middle East   9, 115, 205, 270
modernity   8, 173–4, 188–90
modernization theory   19–33, 49, 52–3, 58, 64, 79, 89–90, 107, 175, 190, 224. *See also* social sciences
   and African American thought   27
   and "first new nation" idea   19–23
Mohammed V, King   115, 125
Mohammad Reza Shah Pahlavi   130, 267–8
Montero, Frank   53, 55
Morocco   39, 266, 268, 270. *See also* Hassan II; Mohammed V
   Union nationale des forces populaires in   125
Mosaddeq, Mohammad   132, 136
Moscow   9
   Film Festival   159
movies. *See* cinema
Muehlenbeck, Philip E.   53
Munge, Joseph Dugere   52
Murrow, Edward R.   266
Myrdal, Gunnar   230

Nairobi   39, 53, 56, 57
Namibia   255–7, 259
Naples   138
Nasser, Gamal Abdel   6, 35, 39, 118, 156
nationalism
   in Africa   34–7, 39, 40, 42, 43, 44, 49, 50, 267
   anti- and postcolonial   23–4, 86, 92, 265
   black (American)   27–8, 267
   economic   91
   European   23
   in India   92, 231
   in Ireland   86, 87, 88, 89, 93, 94, 95
   in Mexico   171, 178
   in Morocco   115, 116, 117, 123, 266
   in the People's Republic of China   202
   in South Africa   259

in South Korea   187, 188, 189, 190
in Turkey   240
in Vietnam   201, 209
National Liberation Front (Viet Cong)   206–7, 210, 213
National Union of South African Students   252
Negro Digest   25
Nehru, Jawaharlal   119, 136, 224, 225, 227, 229, 230, 270, 272
Nepal   154, 163
Netherlands, The   138
New Deal   185
New Frontier   7, 20, 25, 65, 141, 156, 160, 184–6, 189
New Imperial History   2, 8
New Leader, The   27
New Left   28
newspapers. *See also* media
  across postcolonial world   100–14, 266
  Brazilian   68
  Chinese   153
  Indian   101
  Kenyan   49, 51, 52, 266
  Mexican   169, 170, 174, 178
  Moroccan   116, 117, 126, 266
  picture of Kennedy in   41
  South Korean   185, 194
  Tanzania   103
  Turkish   236, 240
  from the United States in Europe   241
  United States Information Agency and   78
  Vietnamese   203, 204, 205, 207
Newton, Huey P.   28
New World of Negro Americans, The   26–7
New York   19, 27, 35, 40, 50, 90, 115, 123, 159, 236, 244, 255, 259
New York Journal-American   87
Ngala, Ronald   55, 56, 57
Ngo Dinh Diem   202, 208–14, 268
Ngo Dinh Nhu   213
Ngo Kha   212
Ngo Vinh Long   203
Nguyen Van Thieu   211
Nguyen Xuan Bao   210
Nhan Dan   204, 205, 207, 208, 209

Niemba   95
Niger   41, 265
Nigeria   36, 39, 101, 110, 111, 138, 241, 270
Nixon, Richard M.   7, 34, 38, 43, 65, 99 n.56, 117, 155, 214, 225
Njenga, Father   57
Nkrumah, Kwame   6, 34–6, 38–40, 42, 91–2, 229, 251
Nobel Prize   54
Nogueira, Franco   38
Non-aligned Movement   119, 120, 125, 223, 229, 251, 252, 255, 267, 270
North Atlantic Treaty Organization   50, 86, 94, 121
Nowruz   135
Nujoma, Sam   255
Nyasaland   36
Nyerere, Julius   34, 42, 229, 251, 253

Obama, Barack   34, 58
O'Brien, Conor Cruise   91
Omwando, Zebedeo   10, 48, 50, 264–5
O'Neill, Terence   94
Ould Daddah, Moktar   37

Packenham, Robert   142
Paine, Thomas   19
Pakistan   104, 109, 138, 163, 223, 230, 267
Palestine   118
Pan-Africanism   27, 35, 250, 257
Panama Canal Zone   155
Pan-Americanism   103, 138, 139
Paraguay   138, 139
Paris   26, 115, 141, 227, 236, 241
  the Kennedys' visit to   5, 103, 120–1, 229
Park Chung Hee   266, 269
  American tour taken by   183, 188–9
  anti-communism and   187
  assassination of   192
  domestic opposition to   183, 188, 192–3, 195
  Junta led by   186–8
  military government of   186–9, 193–5
  Park Ji-man, son of   189–90
  public image   184, 188
Parsons, Talcott   22

Partido Revolucionario Institucional (PRI)   169, 171, 178
Paterson Belcher, Stephen   41
Patron-client relationship   10, 48–50, 53–4, 56, 58, 59 n.12, 132, 140, 186, 210
Pazos, Armando   100
Pazos, Carlos   264
Peace Corps   8, 48, 56, 160, 225, 235, 237, 240–1, 244, 247 n.43
peaceful evolution   152, 154, 155, 164
People's Republic of China, the   37–8, 64, 110, 118, 151–68, 168, 208, 223, 271
   External Cultural Association   163
   External Cultural Liaison Committee   161
   Ministry of Education   162
   Ministry of Foreign Relations   159, 161
people-to-people diplomacy   142
Peru   138, 139, 264, 265
Philadelphia   90
Pillsbury, Philip, Jr.   42
Pittsburgh Courier   24, 26
PL-480. *See* Food for Peace
Planning Commission (India)   222, 224, 231
pluralism   20, 21–3, 24
Poitier, Sidney   53
Poland   89, 138, 153, 162, 259. *See also* Europe, East
political science   22, 23
populism   22, 185, 193, 196, 237
Porter, William   39
Portugal   37–8, 40, 43, 96, 119, 270, 271
postcolonial
   agency and self-determination   2, 4, 9, 10, 49, 102, 111, 187, 222, 265
   and aid and development   48, 53, 58, 268, 271
   circulations and relations across   4, 10, 265
   emotions   5–6, 10, 58
   gifts by and in   5, 130–48, 268
   heterogeneous   3
   Ireland and / as a model for   85, 86, 89, 95
   and Kennedy   1–6, 11, 20, 35, 49, 52–3, 65, 102–4, 109, 111, 116, 118–20, 123, 125, 126, 134, 143, 155, 183–7, 235, 266, 267
   liberal internationalism tied to   186
   media   3, 4, 5, 101–4, 109, 111, 134, 266
   in modernization theory   53
   and the People's Republic of China   151, 152, 155
   project   265
   and the Soviet Union   21, 24, 64, 89, 120
   state authoritarianism   5, 58
   and the US empire as a joint analytical field   8–11
   and the US federal system as a model   20
   and the US first new nation discourse   20
   and US views and policies   8, 10, 11, 20, 21, 22, 24, 53, 89, 118–19, 125, 134, 143, 164, 183–7, 268
   and Western postimperial entities   9
postcolonialism. *See* postcolonial
postcolonial people. *See* postcolonial
Potsdam Conference   87
Prasad, Rajendra   225
Presbyterian missionaries (US)   131, 132
press. *See* media; newspapers
Princeton University   133
Profiles in Courage   141
propaganda   51, 68, 70, 71, 115, 152–4, 159–60, 162, 164, 170, 205, 207, 241
prostitution   193–4
Punta del Este, Conference in   65, 171

Qajars   135
Quadros, Jânio   66, 70, 75, 78

race   6, 134
racism   21, 22, 24–6, 27–9, 39, 41, 56, 122, 207, 235–6, 240–4, 267
radio   4, 39, 49, 51, 52, 58, 68, 78, 101, 104, 105, 106, 107, 109, 134, 203, 204, 205, 266
Rasht   131, 132, 142
   Presbyterian Girl School in   132
Ray, Satyajit   225
Reagan, Ronald   34, 99 n.56, 260
Redding, J. Saunders   19, 20, 27

Republic of Korea. *See* South Korea
Revolutionary Action Movement   28
Pahlavi, Reza Shah   130
Rhee, Syngman   185, 195, 266
Rhodesia   24, 37, 254, 258
   Northern   118
Rift Valley   52, 55, 57
Roberto, Holden   40
Robinson, Jackie   53
Rockefeller Foundation   197 n.7
Rome   86, 138, 139, 241
Roosevelt, Franklin   6, 185–6, 211, 238, 265
Roosevelt, Theodore   34, 186
Rosenthal, Abraham Michael   187
Rostow, Walt   64, 184, 224–6
Royal Navy   87
Rusk, Dean   38, 85, 133, 172, 189, 225, 226, 227
Rwanda   37

Sabato, Larry   264
Saigon   204, 205, 208, 213
Saitoti, George   54
Salazar, Antonio   96
San Remo   138
Santiago de Chile   163
Saunders, Harold   133, 142
Scheinman, William   53
Schlesinger, Arthur, Jr.   1
Scholarship. *See* historiography
Seale, Bobby   28
Second World War   87, 122
segregation   39, 110, 111, 116, 121, 122, 124, 243, 252, 259
Selassie, Haile   39
Senegal   36, 110, 236, 270
Senghor, Lépold Sédar   36, 270
Shannon Airport   94
Sharpeville Massacre   24
Shastri, Lal Bahadur   231
Shriver, Sargent   41, 54
Sicily   137
Sierra Leone   236
Sihanouk, Norodom   6
Sinn Féin   87
Sino-Indian War   163
Sino-Soviet split   151, 163
Smitmans López, Juan   169, 172, 179

Snow, Edgar   154
social sciences   20, 21, 26, 29. *See also* modernization theory; political science; sociology; World Congress of Sociology
Société Africaine de Culture   26
Sociology   8. *See also* social sciences
Somalia   254
South Africa   24, 37, 43, 119, 250–61, 271–2
South African Lawyers' Committee for Civil Rights under Law   271
South Korea   138, 266, 268, 269, 272
   See also Korean War
   authoritarian regimes in   183, 185, 187–8, 193
   economic development in   184–5, 188, 196
   First Republic of   185
   political corruption in   184
   postwar poverty of   184, 193
   Second Republic of   185, 188, 193, 195
   sovereignty of   188, 193
   Supreme Council for National Reconstruction (SCNR)   184
   US development policies for   184–5
   US military presence in   184, 193–5
South-South relations. *See* postcolonial
Soviet News Agency (TASS)   207, 209
Soviet Union. *See also* Khrushchev, Nikita; Moscow
   ambassador to Mexico   179
   antagonist of and compared to the United States   5, 9, 10, 25, 73, 119, 120, 157, 159–60, 202, 226, 238
   at Bandung   23
   and Eastern Europe   21, 23, 25, 88, 154
   economic assistance to postcolonial countries   64, 67, 226
   and India   226
   and Ireland   91
   James Baldwin in   236
   and the People's Republic of China   151, 153, 154, 157, 159–60, 163
   postcolonial views of   74, 79, 120
   and Turkey   237, 238

and the United Nations   255
and US policy *vis-à-vis* postcolonial
    countries   20, 21, 23, 25, 67, 73, 88
Spain   137, 138. *See also* Barcelona;
    Madrid
sport   103, 163
Stanford, Max   28
Stephanson, Anders   264
Stevenson, Adlai   43, 226, 254
Stoler, Ann   8
Stone, I. F.   209
students   2, 8, 48, 53, 54, 57, 58, 89, 101,
    109, 110, 111, 121, 161, 162, 169,
    185, 193, 194, 195, 201, 210, 224,
    236, 237, 238, 240, 243, 253, 260,
    267, 269. *See also* universities
Studies on the Left   28
Sudan   36
Sukarno   6, 119, 270
Switzerland   137, 138, 236

Taiwan   137, 138, 141, 151, 154, 155, 160,
    163
Tambo, Oliver 255, 259
Tanai, Philomon   55
Tanganiyka   52, 56, 138
Tanzania. *See* Tanganiyka
teachers   160, 162, 169, 240, 252
Tehran   130–3, 140
television   4, 40, 95, 101, 105, 110, 134,
    241, 266
Third World. *See* postcolonial
Tibet   151, 154, 160
Time magazine   90
Togo   137, 139
Touré, Sékou   10, 35–6, 38, 40, 42
Townsend, Kathleen Kennedy   259
translation   4
Trinh Cong Son   212
Trinh Tuc   210–11
Truman, Harry S.   155, 237, 238
Tshombe, Moise   42
Tubman, William   37
Tum Kaptulus, Frederick Kemboi
    arap   57
Tunisia   35, 39
Turkey   3, 137, 138, 235–49, 267. *See also*
    Ankara; Inönü, Ismet
Tutu, Desmond   258–60

Ugly American, The   8
Unidad Independencia   175, 176, 177
Union of the Soviet Socialist Republics.
    See Soviet Union
United Democratic Front   250
United Kingdom   8, 9, 34, 50, 87, 233
    n.52, 87, 156, 160. *See also* England;
    London; Royal Navy
Commonwealth and   91, 96
Empire of   11, 87, 91, 92, 93, 95
United Nations   21, 27, 29, 35, 40–1, 43,
    48, 50, 86, 87, 90, 91, 92, 93, 95, 96,
    154, 160. *See also* Hammarskjold,
    Dag
Declaration on the Granting of
    Independence to Colonial
    Countries and Peoples   23
General Assembly   21, 35, 55, 85, 90,
    91, 95, 122
Operation in the Congo   95
Security Council   119
United States. *See also* postcolonial
Agency for International
    Development   52
Civil Rights movement   50, 56–8
Congress   43, 88, 105, 111, 124, 142,
    205, 209, 223, 266–7, 255, 260, 266
Consulate in Nairobi   56–7
democratic ideals of   183, 186–7
Democratic National Convention of
    1960   7
Forces Korea   184, 192–5
Foreign Operations
    Administration   51
House Committee on Foreign
    Affairs   88
House Subcommittee on Africa   53
imperialism by   9, 193, 196
imperial-postcolonial field   8–11
Information Agency   4, 5, 51, 104–8,
    134, 221, 235, 241, 243, 248 n.55,
    266
international empire   9, 134
military bases and forces abroad of   9,
    122, 123, 124, 125, 184, 193–5
National Security Council   96, 133
national security doctrine   9
Operations Mission   184
Senate   88

Senate Foreign Relations Subcommittee on African Affairs   19
State Department   53, 88, 89, 90, 92, 93
Technical Cooperation Mission   226
United States Agricultural Trade Development and Assistance Act. *See* Food for Peace
United States Information Service. *See* United States Information Agency
United States-Republic of Korea alliance   183-4, 188, 193
United States-Republic of Korea Status of Forces Agreement   183, 193-6
Universal, El   173, 174, 176
Universities   48, 106, 110, 117, 121, 122, 160, 161, 162, 212, 223, 224, 225, 228, 229, 237, 240, 253
USSR. *See* Soviet Union

Venezuela   64, 73, 107, 109, 138
Vienna summit   120, 121
Viet Minh   201, 202, 205, 206, 209, 211-12
Vietnam   151, 158. *See also* Hanoi; Ho Chi Minh; National Liberation Front; Saigon; Viet Minh
  Army of the Republic of   209
  Associated State of   209
  Democratic Republic of   202, 207, 209, 213-14, 271
  Republic of   205-7, 210-11, 213, 268, 272
  War   42, 235, 237, 242, 246 n.28, 265, 266, 267, 268, 271
Voice of America   52, 104, 106, 205, 207, 212
Vo Nguyen Giap   214, 271

Wallace, George   122
Ward, Barbara   38
War on Poverty   29
Warsaw Pact   120. *See also* Europe, East
West Africa   40, 43-4
Westernization   160
West Germany. *See* Germany
Wexford   87, 93
White House   130, 141, 183, 188-9, 191
  mail room   133
  redesign   5
  televised tour by Jacqueline Kennedy   4, 5, 104, 272
  visits to the   5, 35, 43, 100, 101, 118, 119, 121, 125, 183, 188, 189, 191, 201, 269
Wiesbaden   139
Williams, G. Mennen   25, 36, 42-3, 270
Williamson, Francis T.   23, 29
Wilson, Woodrow   6, 186
Wine, James   40
Wofford, Harris   42
Wolff, J. A. H.   55
World Bank   50
World Congress of Sociology   22
World War Two. *See* Second World War

X, Malcolm   28

Yi Seungman. *See* Syngman Ree
Young, T. Cuyler   133, 142
Yudin, Pavel   153
Yuk Young-Soo   189-92, 272

Zahedi, Fazlollah   135
Zambia   43, 259
Zarembka, Dave   56
Zhou Enlai   151, 152, 156, 163